BRITISH DIPLOMACY
IN CHINA

1880–1885

BRITISH DIPLOMACY IN CHINA

1880 TO 1885

BY

E. V. G. KIERNAN

WITH A NEW FOREWORD
BY THE AUTHOR

1970

OCTAGON BOOKS

New York

First published 1939

New material copyright © 1970 by E. V. G. Kiernan

Reprinted 1970
by permission of the Cambridge University Press

OCTAGON BOOKS

A DIVISION OF FARRAR, STRAUS & GIROUX, INC.

19 Union Square West

New York, N. Y. 10003

LIBRARY OF CONGRESS CATALOG CARD NUMBER: 78-75999

Printed in U.S.A. by

NOBLE OFFSET PRINTERS, INC.

NEW YORK 3, N. Y.

IN MEMORY
OF MY MOTHER

CONTENTS

FOREWORD TO THE OCTAGON EDITION

A historian taking up again and re-reading for the first time a book he wrote thirty-odd years ago can scarcely help seeing it, and its writer, as themselves by now part of history, and being disturbed by a kind of double vision. He must feel too something of the trepidation of a diver exploring a sunken vessel which may or may not contain some rescuable cargo, if only the treasure of a few sea-worn coins from a forgotten mint. This little book grew, between 1934 and 1938, out of a Fellowship thesis I was writing at my Cambridge college; my first essay at deciphering the past for myself, set going as much by interest in politics as in history. Those were years of excitements and alarms in Europe, and beyond, where Italy was conquering Ethiopia, Indian nationalism was struggling against repression, China was undergoing both civil war and Japanese invasion. Cambridge, or the junior part of it, was a scene of political excitement too, which a pair of young American authors have well recaptured lately.[1] There were flocks of Indian, Chinese, African students with whom could be discussed what was going on in their countries. The grandfather of one Chinese student[2] had been among the first Chinese sent to study in England, where he was a class-fellow of the late Marquis Ito, and subsequently became a factotum of the Li Hung-chang who bulks so large in this book. Another friend, who had grown up in Japan and lived to write about its history and to be Canadian ambassador at Tokyo, taught me the art of eating with chopsticks.[3]

Watching the behavior of empires and empire-builders, I came to be much engrossed by the question of how much of it, and of the general conduct of Western nations in the world, had been dictated by economic forces and motives. China was suggested to me[4] as a field where this question might be scrutinised; the period 1880 to 1885 suggested itself as the most recent for which the archives of the Foreign Office and other British departments were then open. In this rather fortuitous way the work

came to be started; as it went on, interspersed with study of the
present, and student politics, I acquired a stronger and stronger
sense of history and politics being two sides of the same coin. In
1938 I found myself on a ship bound for India in the midst of
the Munich crisis, and reached Bombay with a typescript of the
book, then about to be published, which roused grave suspicions
in the British official whose duty was to intercept seditious literature. It came out just before the War broke out, and partly on
that account, and no doubt from its own shortcomings, attracted
little notice.

In a foreword to a new edition of an early work of his own
G. P. Gooch (who was one of my Fellowship examiners) regretted its "crudities of youthful style and opinion." As to style,
I must confess in this book a flavour of the romantic that will
not be to the taste of more staid and sober readers. It was the
overflow of a young man's curiosity about a world still strange
to him; a curiosity not quite extinct, since to my regret I have
never yet seen China, or any more of the Great Wall than the
brick in Dr. Johnson's house in Gough Square. I can understand why a French critic complained of a too obtrusively sar-
castic note in some of the narrative sections. Why I so often,
and so parochially, wrote 'we,' when I meant Britain or the
British government, I cannot now pretend to understand. As to
my opinions about the world, they have not altered in substance,
though they have changed in many particulars and both history
and politics seem harder to unravel as years go by, instead of
simpler. Diplomatic and economic history are, as I believed then
(p. ix), the same thing in two languages. The two may diverge
more than the metaphor suggests, with other media separating
them by one or more removes. Economic forces operate more
chaotically than political calculations, and unfold over longer
spans of time; there is a duality not overcome in the book between its narrative detail of six years and its commentary on
social and economic matters belonging to a wider, sometimes a
far wider, perspective. But there is no way of writing history
free from many pitfalls, practical and philosophical.

In its small way the book was a pioneer attempt at bringing

two fields of history together, and on the diplomatic level was an early effort to chart in detail one phase of modern China's relations with the outer world. Since then other tracts of the 19th century have been filled in.[5] The years I chose still appear to me significant, if not in every respect so full of meaning as I convinced myself. In the Far East there were wars and rumours of war; the world stood on the threshold of the age of Imperialism, while China stood close to the end of the brief decades when it could be expected to succeed, as Japan was doing, in modernising itself from above without a total upheaval from below; an impossibility that it was not too hard to recognize in 1938.

Because the book had more than one theme, a good deal of matter belonging to each had to be left out. I have since written short studies of some of the border areas where foreign encroachment was being felt, like Kashgharia just before the Chinese reconquest, and Tibet, British attempts to enter which from India were affected by the annexation of Burma at the end of 1885: China's authority over Tibet, and its vaguer suzerainty over Burma, were both admitted.[6] Nearly all British diplomacy in Asia was complicated by Indian considerations. In one part of a recent book I have tried to go more fully into the psychology of the relationships that were developing between the races confronting one another during the 19th century in the Far East.[7] This subject runs into that of Chinese emigration. Chinese had been going abroad for centuries, but were now, under the spur of over-population and of the needs of many colonial areas for cheap labour, doing so in large numbers.[8]

Of many vexatious topics agitating China's foreign relations in the 1880s, one that often recurs in this book is of course opium. I may not sufficiently have conveyed how much Anglo-Chinese relations were bedevilled by this trade, vital still for Britain because still vital to the finances of India. How chronically it came up at Peking one can only realise by going into a mass of negotiation too arid for any reader to bear. Missionary activity was another stumbling-block, ominous of the fact that the Boxer outbreak in 1900 was to start with attacks on missionaries and their converts. They were usually well-meaning but frequently unwise; their unwisdom was strikingly exhibited in one case that fatigued Sir Thomas Wade at Peking for a long time, when a schoolhouse built by the Church Mission Society on a hillock, the Wu Shih Shan, inside the walls of Fuchow, was destroyed in 1879 by rioters who alleged that it gave offence to a highly respected dragon residing there.[9] This was one of those subterranean creatures always in the way of foreigners who wanted the use of land—emanations of the Chinese popular mind and faithful enough reflections of it in their dislike of the foreign devil and their helplessness to repel him. Chinese authorities, for their part, less credulous of mythical beasts, must often have recalled how strangely Christian teaching had mingled with native superstition in the ideas of the Taiping rebellion.[10] A similar crossing of ideas was to go into the mixed pagan and Christian cults that sprang up in Africa, marking there too a first, elemental stage of mass protest.

It would have been impossible for me to keep up with all the new writings of these thirty years that touch at one point or another the diverse topics of this book.[11] Many of them are in Chinese, others in Japanese, and only available to me at second hand. Diplomatic affairs in themselves I have come to regard as a recreation, or antiquarian hobby; my interest in social and political structures has grown steadily—those of different Asian regions by comparison with each other, those of Asia by comparison with Europe. Of new books that have illuminated State and society in modern China it would be difficult not to refer first and foremost to the great synthesizing work of Dermigny,[12] which ranges so vastly far beyond its stated theme. One of its many explorations that are relevant to the later 19th century concerns the dynastic cycle, which it traces to basically demographic and fiscal causes.[13] New crops like maize, brought into China from America by Europeans, helped in the Ch'ing period to raise population to unprecedented and dangerous levels. It was straining at the bounds of the old China, like the Yellow River at the dykes that kept it flowing above the level of the plain. This dual phenomenon of a cycle of population and of dynasties would seem to confront us more forcibly in China than anywhere else. A point of crisis was being approached, but one that could not find the same simple solution as its predecessors—civil war or invasion, or both, thinning population (mainly by their after-effects of famine and epidemic) and bringing a new dynasty to preside over a rejuvenated government. Population was now too far swollen to be adequately thinned even by bloodshed on the scale of the Taiping rebellion; and on the other hand, thanks in some measure to new firearms acquired from the West, the dominant groups were able to suppress all the revolts, huge as these were, of the century.

In my tentative sketch of the Chinese State I was influenced by ideas about water-control as its prime function; ideas developed by Wittfogel and others into a 'hydraulic theory' of the Asiatic State, which has on the whole failed to gain acceptance. There is some inconsistency in my sketch between the notion of the State as a very exiguous outgrowth from society, and that of an economy depending essentially on water-control by the government, which must have produced a far more powerful State machine. It must also have produced a corps of well-trained hydraulic engineers in official service, of whose existence one never seems to hear. When the British began large-scale irrigation in India they sent a man to pick up ideas not in China but in Lombardy. I feel dubious about the statement cited on p. 232 that private works were nearly everywhere trivial compared with State works, and think it likelier that—as we find in old Ceylon, or south India—only a few great works were really the responsibility of government (whose outlay, less than 4,000,000 taels (p. 233) seems derisory), while lesser ones belonged to the sphere of the district or village. Of course the latter would often depend on the former, and would decay with them. Yet, puzzlingly, decay of canals and dykes is not one of the things that struck travellers when they began to explore the interior. Nor would extensive neglect of them be consistent with the rapid growth of population. Ceylon and south India may again suggest by analogy that the great works requiring lavish mobilisation of skill and labour were few, and were mostly carried out in earlier epochs; once constructed, they could survive with routine local maintenance for very long periods, however little fresh technological progress the country might make. If this is a correct view of Chinese history it may offer some sidelight on its salient feature, brilliant early achievement followed by ages of decline into diminishing originality, and the parallel decline of a bureaucracy once relatively active and vigorous—capable for instance of organizing a system of conscription for frontier defence —into the archaic, convention-ridden mandarinate of Ch'ing days.

One of a good many Chinese enigmas that crop up in Lord Macartney's journal of his embassy of 1793-4,[14] and were still being canvassed a hundred years later, was the status of the Manchus, descendants of the seventeenth-century conquerors. Two issues are involved, which I ought to have distinguished more clearly: how strong a hold Manchus had on the administration, and how far the ruling family was resented by its Chinese subjects as still foreign. On the second issue, what I wrote (pp. 224-5) appears to me not unreasonable, though it must be said that several authorities, including the late Dr. Purcell in his remarkable book on the origins of the Boxer rebellion,[15] have given considerable weight to the foreignness of the dynasty. Current Chinese writings can be quoted on their side; but current Chinese Marxism is much mixed up with Chinese nationalism, and it is often not easy to say where one ends and the other begins. Grumbling at 'foreign' rulers, at a time when anti-foreign feeling was rampant, could be a vent for miscellaneous discontents, like the Jacobite sentiment that lingered in eighteenth-century England. Bewildered by an unfamiliar age, China was as ready as Japan to look back in search of good old days; but whereas Japan had a nearly forgotten emperor to set up against a discredited Shogun, the Ming dynasty was more completely beyond recall than the Stuart. In 1900 Boxer rebels could be got to shout for the Ch'ing instead of against them. China always had the same utilitarian attitude to its sovereigns as to its idols, regaled with incense when they gave satisfaction and beaten when they did not.

As a ruling people the Manchus resembled in some ways the Muslim conquerors of India, but while these gave up their Turkish language and kept their religion, the Manchus had done the opposite. Both came to be a blend of class, and race. Professor Owen Lattimore has pointed out to me lately that Manchu notables accepted Chinese daughters-in-law, though not sons-in-law; also that they were often given fraudulently easy passage through the examinations. They had lost all semblance of a military aristocracy, which by European expectation would have been their natural rôle, and which the Muslims in India never lost. Instead they pushed into the civil service, where the number of Manchus in high positions, including provincial governorships, was increasing in the late 19th century.[16] No doubt a bad Manchu's unpopularity might rebound against the Court. Foreign relations, that new sphere of business, touched them closely. Professor Banno of Tokyo has found that Manchu officials, though a minority of those engaged in the peace negotiations of 1860, took the main decisions, and were more realistic than the blindly xenophobic Chinese;[17] and imperial princes took a leading part—so far as any leading was done—in the Tsungli Yamen or foreign office then set up. Service there was far from attractive to any official who could get anything better. But when so many qualified men were competing for a limited number of government posts, Chinese aspirants must often have felt a grudge against Manchu rivals. This might go with a sentiment, patriotic even if ignorant, that Manchu 'realism' in giving way to foreign requisitions was cowardice, or treason. Together the two feelings may on occasion have prompted clamour for a strong foreign policy, intended to expose to public censure those who failed to provide it. The denunciation of Chung Hou in 1880 (see Chap. III) may have been of this kind; the envoy whose death was so loudly demanded in Peking was a wealthy Manchu of the Bordered Yellow Banner.[18] What is obvious is that Chinese officialdom had no need to be timid of criticising a Manchu dignitary; and a Prince Kung in the Tsungli Yamen was as much at the mercy of palace intrigue or public disfavour as anyone else.

Complexities of Ch'ing dynastic law aided Tzu Hsi to usurp and hold on to power. But the fact of China being for so long in the hands of a monstrous regiment of women and eunuchs (much as tsarist Russia at the end was run by a dull emperor's consort and a Rasputin) is striking, and calls for explanation. Chinese history at large has been described as a contest between official intelligentsia and palace eunuchs.[19] All defects of a society and its political regime tend to concentrate themselves at the top, where the problem of how to crystallise the amorphous weight of a ruling class into a viable administrative cadre is most intractable, and has produced all over the world the most freakish experiments. None the less, in Tzu Hsi's time it should, on the face of things, have been a simple matter for the bureaucracy to turn out the palace parasites and take control, in the name of some boy-ruler or other. Manchu-Chinese frictions may have helped to prevent concerted action. But the bureaucracy as a whole depended too heavily on pretence and mystification, for its credit with the masses, to be able to expose the palace, central shrine of all the mysteries of State, to the public gaze. Most of its members were too deeply hypnotised by the past to act; those capable of initiative were incapable of combining and trusting one another in any novel course. Li Hung-chang, the most powerful of them, had a following of creatures and hangers-on, but he had no party.

Above all, this was a professional corporation sinking into moral crisis, more profound than ever before because it was faced with problems insoluble by any of the old statecraft, not to be banished by any of the old incantations. Corrupt and inefficient as it was, Tzu Hsi's reign must have suited the mandarinate collectively well enough. She feathered her own nest, and let others do the same. In one of the most fascinating works of recent years on China, Mrs. M. C. Wright showed how a Confucian programme of 'moral rearmament,' put forward by the austere zealot Tseng Kuo-fan after the crushing of the Taipings, failed to produce any genuine restoration of morality in official conduct or health in the body politic.[20] Unemployed intellectuals had always been numerous, as an eighteenth-century novel translated not long ago, *The Scholars,* graphically illustrates,[21] and competition was worsening. Foreign contact, dealings over trade and concessions, could be another demoralising influence, with the *comprador* class in the ports as go-betweens for Chinese officials and foreign businessmen. Sale of offices helped to lower standards; it brought new blood into the administration, but not healthy blood.

Mandarins were growing more unpopular, yet the *literati,* the general body of educated men they belonged to, seemed to Westerners to retain their high prestige all through the century, and to be looked up to by the people as their natural leaders. This paradox is symptomatic of a China uneasily stranded between two epochs, its commoners alternately looking up to and rebelling against their social superiors. It has come to be recognized that the mandarinate was far less of a democratic career open to talents, and more a distinct privileged order, than often used to be supposed.[22] The same must be said of the wider category of the educated, whose nucleus it was. Neither the older term *literati* nor the newer one, *gentry,* that has been coming into fashion as a label for this social stratum, is really adequate. Besides the men of true classical learning who enjoyed popular respect as custodians of Chinese tradition, it contained a miscellany of others who acquired a species of gentility by earning or buying the lower degrees or academic titles, and with them sundry legal privileges as well as social status. There are close resemblances between it and the *hidalguía* of old Spain when this came to be diluted by wholesale distribution of the rank of minor nobility, with the cherished right to be addressed as *Don* and exemptions from a series of public burdens.

In Spain the theoretical basis of the claim was blood, in China brain. But in any such case there must be an affiliation with some solid interest, some definite estate of the realm, founded on property; and in both these cases the affiliation was, at bottom, with property in land. Traders, any individuals with money, could get themselves inducted into the *Quality,* to borrow an expression current in England no more than a hundred years ago; but the great preponderance of property and influence was, as in old

Europe, in land. The mandarinate can only be viewed realistically as a professional body by and large recruited from or related to a class of landowners, who were, whatever dynasty sat on the throne, the ruling class of China. To shut one's eyes to this is to fall back into the illusion of Europeans of the eighteenth-century Enlightenment who admired China as an enlightened empire ruled by scholars and philosophers. Intellectuals may staff departments of State, but they cannot constitute a ruling class, such as no society above the primitive has ever been without. For lack of recognition of this, discussion of the 'gentry' has at times been abstract and unreal. A European may wonder whether it has not oftenest been academic in America, that fortunate land where landlords are as unknown as dragons, and where there has been a certain reluctance to think of history in vulgar Old World terms of classes and class conflict, and less impropriety in finding fault with native mandarins than with millionaires. How much, nevertheless, everyone interested in the Far East owes by now to American or American-sponsored scholarship, scarcely needs to be said.

My attempt at a rough analysis of Chinese society partook of the over-confidence of youth, and necessarily depended for the most part on contemporary Western description. This was incoherent, often contradictory; but it still remains indispensable, as for so much of modern Indian history, because while those countries wrote a great deal about themselves they were not self-conscious, self-critical enough to think much about themselves. It was a society disintegrating, but too big and old and close-knit to evolve quickly. One index of morbidity was the proliferation of secret societies, some of which helped to prepare the rebellions: forms of voluntary association enabling individuals torn from the old natural bonds to come together in search of fresh ties. There must always have been surplus hands seeking work, but they were now so many as to be an invitation to the trading class to seek profit along new lines, by transmuting the merchant capital of the old economy into industrial capital. Writers in communist China have surmised that a modern-style industry, a 'national' capitalism distinct from the *comprador* bourgeoisie, was indeed taking shape, and would have gained ground if it had not been suffocated by foreign interference. I must confess to scepticism here, and to thinking that in this respect China was closer to India than to Japan.[23] Its monied men had always had, and still had, easier ways of making money, and more congenial ways of spending it, than investment in industrial production, even if the old culture and style of life were now losing some of their appeal. My former estimate (p. 239) even of the part played by merchant capital in linking the provinces together and giving old China its homogeneity was, I am sure, an overestimate, as one critic observed.

More obscure still are the agrarian relations of old China, that vast labyrinth of human life that has ceased to exist. Most of what I wrote about it seems to me now to have been not wildly far from the mark. I must hasten to add that Purcell's survey, largely based on similar materials, was the work of a far better qualified student with later research to draw on. It occupies the first part of his work on the Boxers. I ventured to object to it that its picture of a society "very different from anything that Europe ever knew"[24] made too little room for the landlord class, ubiquitous in one guise or other over the whole of old Asia and Europe.[25] In China it was disguised by the fact that there was nothing like serfdom, and that most landlords were quite small men, with every gradation of wealth between them and the peasants from whose ranks their families were always emerging, only to fall back again after a few or more generations. Naturally this composition of the landed class affected the peculiar organization of the Chinese State. Besides the average landowner being, as an individual, quite a small man, ownership lacked the aura of aristocracy, because from early days land in China had been a market commodity instead of a feudal attribute as in Europe or a royal assignment as in India. This goes far to account for the superior prestige of the *literati,* the most highly cultured fringe of the landed class, which set an example of ostentatious respect towards it because its prestige redounded to the advantage of all conservative interests.

If it is necessary to insist on the presence of this landed inter-

est in relation to the mandarinate, it is still more so in relation
to the peasantry. Two very discordant images seem to emerge
from descriptions of the Chinese countryside a century ago: one
of a land of social harmony, civilized living-together, the other
of a mutinous mass kept down by brutal domination. Both
images must be accepted as part of the truth. When things ran
normally, all was, at any rate on the surface, harmony and sweet
reason; when social tensions grew critical, as they were always
doing in one region or another, there was rapid relapse into
brutality, rule by terror, massacre of rebels by tens of thousands:
all the ferocity of class war, with no modern institutions, real
law-courts for example, to serve as buffers between the two sides.
From Confucian civilization to Hobbesian state of nature was
only one step. Under the thin surface of official ritual lay an
underworld of primitive superstition and passion. Oudendyk, the
Dutch diplomat who came to China in 1894 and got to know it
well, remarks that this peaceful-looking country's favourite novels
and dramas abounded quite as much as those of other lands in
battle and bloodshed and deeds of violence, and when the old
régime crumbled away the instincts of a thousand years ago
revived "as if by magic."[26]

Landlords cannot have been so idle and functionless as I
depicted them (p. 234) if they did in fact have a good deal to
do with local water-control (which a dominant class always
wants to be arranged first and foremost for its own benefit). And
the tendency towards the end of the Ch'ing epoch was for landlords to take more local authority into their own hands, to
become a governing as well as a ruling class. A number of
writers have laid stress on the very important fact that the
Taiping rebellion and its suppression brought about a big shift
of power from the central government, whose feebleness stood
revealed, to the provinces, where the militias that finally restored
'order' were mercenary bands set on foot and paid by the landlords along with merchants and the abler provincial officials.
Wakeman's book[27] gives a splendid picture of the same development in southern China, while the old walls shook under the
impact of the foreign battering-ram. Some observers, both at the

time and since, have seen China less as a unified empire than as a congeries, a loose federation, of provinces; the decentralising tendency now went further. Meanwhile the structure of rural society grew more 'feudal,' as the balance of power between richer and poorer was, like that between the capital and the regions, upset.

Landlord-raised militias were ancestors of the warlord-armies that sprouted after the revolution of 1911, and of the Kuomintang army that grew out of them in the last days of old China when its fundamental antagonism of landlord and peasant became most nakedly visible. Their presence, and their ability to quell local revolt with only the rudiments of modern military equipment added to old-style weapons, supplies much of the reason for the failure of the government to modernise its armed forces. Peasant rebel, far more than foreigner, was the enemy instinctively feared by the rulers of China, and the means of holding this enemy in check were being found. An efficient national army, still more a navy, would be a luxury, the money for which would be far better embezzled. It would otherwise be incomprehensible that a régime faced all through the century with mass revolt did not show eager impatience to embrace foreign military methods, as a miraculous means of salvation.

China's size, and the absence until recently of any powerful neighbour, had unfitted it for the art of diplomacy as well as the science of war. Here too it was slower to learn than Japan. The Tsungli Yamen shared with the other departments a 'conciliar' or 'collegiate' character, which as in old European countries like Spain or Sweden were not ministries, but boards or committees, responsible collectively to the throne, so that individual responsibility was frittered away. We have from Professor Banno a very full account, from original sources, of its origin in 1861 and its early complexion;[28] this changed little, and many of the participants whom he discusses were to the fore in Chinese foreign policy in later years too. Among the diplomats they were dealing with in the early 'eighties I cannot shake off a fondness for Sir Thomas Wade, coloured by his later sojourn at Cambridge, where some interesting papers and notebooks from his active days are preserved in the Library.[29]

In the archives of the Foreign Ministry at Paris I have come on much of interest about the Far East in that epoch; for instance, about the efforts made by France's representatives to bring Japan into the Tonking war as an ally against China. Later history invests with a special meaning everything connected with the conquest of Tonking, that province with long memories of social revolt against the government of the Annamite kingdom —itself with age-long memories of armed struggles for independence—, which has become known to our world as North Vietnam, and in twenty years of war has displayed all the hardness, the capacity to undergo ordeals of blood and iron, that the old Far East concealed beneath its ornate civilization.[30] With China, Japan, Korea,[31] it has revealed too a national character, a sense of corporate identity, that the Far East shared with Europe, and that only awaited enforced contact with the West to assume modern form.

Since 1938 the Far East has undergone immense transformation. Chu Teh, the future builder of China's Red Army, was born in 1886.[32] When he was fifty, and I was beginning to think about China, there were said to be rustics still unaware that they no longer had an emperor, just as some in India were reported not to have heard of the death of Queen Victoria. Since then the last of the Ch'ing has returned to a throne in Manchuria, and from there again as a humble gardener's assistant in Peking, and Queen Victoria's statues all over India have been relegated to dusty cellars. China's revolution and India's independence, with many other things I was looking forward to and many I was not, were greatly accelerated by the second World War. Japan's navy, which had sent—as I wrote—all its challengers to the bottom of the sea, joined them there; and under American occupation Japan experienced a limited agrarian and political reform. America thus for the second time gave Japan a forcible push forward. China characteristically rejected interference and went its own way. Having failed to build a modern army or industry on Western models, as Japan did, it set out to build an army and economy on a model of its own, far more uncompromisingly new. Even Marxism, born in London, had to be reborn in Peking.

No nation, or even individual, can be completely changed so quickly, and commentators have noted sundry lingerings of old habit. Some of the old-fashioned decrees of censure on high officials quoted here (e.g. on p. 35) recall similar accents of denunciation in the 'cultural revolution.' More gravely, on the world's longest frontier relations thought to be opening a new chapter when China joined Russia in the communist camp have drifted back into an old groove. There is a melancholy resemblance between the Kulja crisis of 1880 and the border clashes of 1969. More melancholy still is the resemblance between the Tonking war of 1882-84 and the Vietnam war not yet in sight of a finish in 1969. Writing a preface in 1938 I thought of China as almost the greatest of human problems; writing another now, after China's gigantic strides forward, I might say the same of the problem of China and America. As a result of the World War, America has succeeded to the place formerly held in eastern Asia by Europe, an inheritance on which angels might have feared to enter. So far the result must be said to corroborate the words of the indignant American of 1882: "There is and can be no affinity between the people of the U.S. and China."[33] Many of his countrymen repeat his declaration today, many Chinese echo them. When so much else in the Far East has altered, it may not be altogether beyond the bounds of hope that this too may change.

E. V. G. KIERNAN

Edinburgh,
September 25, 1969

NOTES

1. P. Stansky and W. Abrahams, *Journey to the Frontier* (London, 1966).
2. Kenneth Lo, who still lives in this country. He was well known at Cambridge as a tennis-player, and is now known everywhere as a writer on Chinese cookery. His grandfather, despite long association with Li Hung-chang, did not leave any large fortune. A recent work on Li is S. Spector, *Li Hung-chang and the Huai Army* (Seattle, 1964).
3. Herbert Norman.
4. The late Prof. H. V. Temperley.
5. See e.g. D. Bonner-Smith and E. W. R. Lumby (eds.), *The Second China War 1856-1860* (Navy Records Soc., 1954); S. T. Wang, *The Margary Affair and the Chefoo Agreement* (O.U.P., 1940). Of works on other European Powers may be mentioned H. Stoecker, *Deutschland und China im 19 Jahrhundert* (Berlin, 1958); Chaps. X and XI concern Korea and Tonking in the period of my book.
6. 'Kashghar and the Politics of Central Asia, 1868-1878,' in *Cambridge Hist. J.*, Vol. XI (1955); 'India, China and Tibet: 1885-86,' in *J. of Greater India Soc.*, Vol. XIV (1955); 'India, China and Sikkim: 1886-1890,' in *Indian Hist. Qu.*, Vol. XXXI (1955).
7. *The Lords of Human Kind. European attitudes towards the outside world in the Imperial Age* (London, 1969). See also R. Dawson, *The Chinese Chameleon. An analysis of European conceptions of Chinese civilization* (O.U.P., 1967); and G. Woodcock, *The British in the Far East* (London, 1969). G. B. Endacott, *A History of Hong Kong* (O.U.P., 1958), also throws light on Anglo-Chinese relations.
8. On one aspect of this, besides the older work by P. C. Campbell, *Chinese Coolie Emigration to Countries within the British Empire* (London, 1923), there is a good study by W. Stewart, *Chinese Bondage in Peru* (Durham, N. Carol., 1951).
9. Papers in F.O.17.854. (I might have made it more clear that such a reference stands for Foreign Office achives in the Public Record Office, London, Class 17 (China), Volume 854.
10. A good deal has been written in these years about the Taiping rebellion, from which an insight into the realities of old China can be gained. Two works, to mention no more, are: J. C. Cheng, *Chinese Sources for the Taiping Rebellion 1850-1864* (Hong Kong, 1963); and J. S. Gregory, *Great Britain and the Taipings* (London, 1969).

11. Useful bibliographies will be found in J. K. Fairbank, E. O. Reischauer and A. M. Craig, *East Asia, the Modern Transformation* (1960; London, 1965); A. Feuerwerker and S. Cheng, *Chinese Communist Studies of Modern Chinese History* (Harvard, 1961); J. Chesneaux and J. Lust, *Introduction aux études d'histoire contemporaine de Chine 1898-1948* (Paris, 1964). An older bibliography that may be mentioned here is P. G. and O. F. von Möllendorff, *Manual of Chinese Bibliography* (Shanghai, 1876).

12. L. Dermigny, *La Chine et l'Occident. Le commerce à Canton au XVIIIe siècle, 1719-1833* (Paris, 1964). I may refer to my review of this work in *Eng.Hist.Rev.*, Vol. LXXXI (1966).

13. Dermigny, pp. 487-8.

14. An excellent recent edition of this is *An Embassy to China*, ed. J. L. Cranmer-Byng (London, 1962).

15. V. Purcell, *The Boxer Uprising. A Background Study* (Cambridge, 1963).

16. *Ib.*, pp. 11-12, 293.

17. Masataka Banno, *China and the West 1858-1861* (Harvard and London, 1961).

18. More properly, Ch'ung-hou (1826-93); see A. W. Hummel (ed.), *Eminent Chinese of the Ch'ing Period (1644-1912)* (Washington, 1943), Vol. 1, pp. 209-11.

19. Dermigny, *op. cit.*, p. 59; cf. pp. 301-2.

20. M. C. Wright, *The Last Stand of Chinese Conservatism. The T'ung Chih Restoration, 1862-1874* (Stanford, 1957). I attempted a review of this book in *Eng. Hist. Rev.*, Vol. LXXIV (1959).

21. Wu Ching-tzu, *The Scholars*, trans. Yang Hsien-yi and Gladys Yang (Peking, 1957).

22. On this whole subject see Ping-ti Ho, *The Ladder of Success in Imperial China. Aspects of Social Mobility, 1368-1911* (N.Y., 1962).

23. I have discussed some of the factors involved in an article, 'Marx and India,' in *The Socialist Register*, ed. R. Miliband and J. Saville (London, 1967). (On p. 240 of my book the term 'entrepreneur class' is unfortunate, because it suggests industrial instead of commercial capital.)

24. *Op. cit.*, p. 32.

25. See my review of the work in *Eng.Hist.Rev.*, (1964).

26. W. J. Oudendyk, *Ways and By-ways in Diplomacy* (London, 1939), pp. 337-8.

27. F. Wakeman, *Strangers at the Gate. Social Disorder in South China, 1839-1861* (U. of Calif., 1966).

28. I cannot refrain from expressing pleasure at Prof. Banno's mention (p. 343) of my "incisive analysis" of the Tsungli Yamen.

FOREWORD TO THE OCTAGON EDITION

Mrs. Wright, *op. cit.*, also has much to say about the early years
of the Yamen; Oudendyk, *op. cit.*, speaks of it later on from his
own experience. Some material on the setting up of Chinese missions abroad will be found in Ssu-yü Teng, *China's Response to
the West; a documentary survey 1839-1923* (Harvard, 1954).

29. A descendant of Wade, the late Mrs. C. A. Gordon, told me that
according to family report this author of our system of Chinese
romanization was tone-deaf. On some other Englishmen in China
at the time of this book, including Hart and Lay, something will
be found in J. Spence, *The China Helpers. Western Advisers in
China 1620-1960* (London, 1969).

30. Chaps. 7 and 8 of J. Chesneaux, *Contribution à l'histoire de la
nation vietnamienne* (Paris, ?1955), relate to the period of the
conquest.

31. A small symptom of how things have changed is that in 1938 it
seemed more natural to write 'Corea' than 'Korea.' A bibliography
of the country will be found in the new edition of H. B. Hulbert,
History of Korea (1905), by C. N. Weems (2 vols., London,
1962). Korea figures in the early chapters of Jerome Ch'en,
Yuan Shih-k'ai 1859-1916 (London, 1961). See also G. D.
Tyagai, *Krest'yanskoe vosstanie v Koree 1893-1895 g.g.* (Moscow,
1953).

32. See a biography by Agnes Smedley, *The Great Road* (N.Y., 1956).

33. Commodore Schufeldt. See p. 278; this sentence is from a version
of his statement that he sent to the local press, of which too Wade
sent a copy. A good recent background work is Akira Iriye, *Across
the Pacific: the Inner History of American-East Asian Relations*
(N.Y., 1967).

[I wrote Chinese names as I found them in my documents, and ought to
have taken more care to standardize them. Tso Tsung-tang, in particular,
should be Tso Tsung-t'ang.]

INTRODUCTION

ALL abstraction falsifies, and collation of diplomatic documents is in itself an exceedingly abstract pursuit. Diplomatic history is one strand in a coherent movement of historical forces, and should be so treated by the student. The ambassador was also a man, a creation of a certain environment, and his policy was an expression of the entire system of relationships composing his country. What importance his policy had, again, is not to be reckoned by the reactions of a number of professional rivals, but by its consequences for the life of the two peoples concerned. History refuses to be algebraised; nothing can happen except through individual brains; but it is not gibberish; its grammar can be mastered, if only in part. Diplomacy and economics are two languages describing the same events. However hard it may be to translate from one into the other, it is an attempt that must be made. Nor, in making it, can the student's mind be empty of criticisms of the past, and of the present that has grown out of it. If it could, it would be empty indeed.

The subject of this essay is surrounded by a ring of related problems in Asiatic history: British policy in Turkestan in the last years of Yakoub Beg; the question of Thibet, which we tried to enter in 1885, and that of Burma, which we annexed in 1886; Anglo-French rivalry in Siam; above all, the part played by Japan, and her relations with England. In describing Chinese events it has been of assistance to me to have made some study of these also. They must, however, be reserved for separate treatment. For the same reasons of space I have omitted from discussion here the intricate negotiations leading up to the Opium Agreement of July 1885, and material relating to certain missionary and commercial cases. In covering so long a period as six years it is equally difficult to draw on the large Consular, Intelligence, and Press material; though the real story of Anglo-Chinese relations is perhaps contained in these local chronicles—tea-prices at Hankow, a crowd "irrupting" into the Consulate at Fuchow. I have used only English documents. It goes without saying that the work of Chinese scholars on their own documents will modify any narratives written in the light of —or rather in the obscurity of—Western archives.

The period in Chinese history between the Taiping Rebellion and the Sino-Japanese War is as a rule mapped hastily, as an unvariegated plain. It is true that it does not contain many of those familiar high points at which the narrator, like a traveller arriving before the Taj Mahal, pauses for a chapter in his best manner. Yet it has much interest. Examination of the early 'eighties modifies a great deal the assumption expressed by, for instance, Joseph, in his study of the activities of the Powers after 1895: "It is undoubtedly fair to say that none of these powers seriously contemplated any political ambitions with regard to China until 1894."[1] In the years surveyed below, China's dependencies were being hacked away, and her own provinces and her national existence itself survived a series of hairbreadth escapes. During the succeeding decade there was a lull. Europe was busy with Africa, French capital was making itself at home in Russia and was digesting Indo-China, Peking was protected by military credit won in the war of Tonking. The years between 1880 and 1885 anticipated many features of the scuffle of the late 'nineties; and some features of 1938. They are deserving of study apart from their being the last years for which full (British) documents are available.[2]

---

[1] *Foreign Diplomacy in China*, ch. II.
[2] "From 1880 onwards, the character of the Chinese problem is profoundly modified." (Sargent, *Anglo-Chinese Diplomacy and Commerce*, 229.)

Mankind has "lived dangerously" in the last century. It has uncovered demonic energies, and created for itself problems some of which appear insoluble.[1] That of China is now almost the greatest of them. About 1880, more clearly than at any other single date, the problem of China was in preparation.

[1] "The tremendous pressure of modern imperialism coupled with modern capitalistic enterprise was, in China as elsewhere on earth, a constant menace to peace." (Overlach, *Foreign Financial Control in China*, III.)

CHAPTER ONE

The Diplomats and their Problem

THE inquisitive Western tourist has poked his walking-stick into every nook of China; he has loitered through the grounds of the Temple of Heaven and scribbled his myriad names on its wooden pillars. What he has discovered in his travels, might admit of Sir Thomas Browne's "wide solution". The mind of China was for too many ages sunk into a kind of solipsism, scarcely aware of anything but its own existence, to be so easily penetrated. It was a self-contemplative land, beset by buzzing importunities. The peculiar fascination, indeed, of the China revealed, or half-revealed, by our translations of her unique literature, is in the completeness with which this province of space and time makes its "reality" out of its own surroundings, so that one can hardly imagine the entry of anything foreign. The charm of the Flowery Kingdom lies in its dreaming, through thirty centuries, in one mood, or one landscape of moods melting into one another with an incomparable harmony, as perfect as that of a Chinese painting on silk, or of the image called up in half a dozen phrases of a Chinese poem—clouds floating over the Gorges, the wild geese flying towards the South. Wherever the thick volumes of China's poetry are opened it is the same world, haunted always by the same voices, the same sentiments and familiarities, too poignant, too perfect, ever to be relinquished; a broad moon is climbing the autumn sky, peach-blossoms hang over antique gateways, cups of wine are warmed and books stand on the table to shorten solitary days; there are blue mountains and silken women, slow rivers with stone-arched bridges, the tears and dreams of separated friends, and in the distance the vaguer recesses of feeling that language cannot be forced to express. Chinese painting has the self-same quality of being

(1)

withdrawn from time. One is "Waiting to cross a River in Autumn", or "Ascending a Mountain in Kiang-nan" (the names are already pictures)—but the moment exists for itself, for no future, the tranquil figures on the bank will never change their posture, the boat on the other side will never move out into the current. It was a mood, a life, more than any other interpenetrated by the suavities of a poetic spirit so attuned to all about it that even grief was a delicate moonlight reflection of the sunshine of happiness, and it felt no search for other knowledge, other meanings, other realms "beyond the sunset". It was an existence of a palace garden, a world of subtle experiences deposited century by century, and which embodied the culture, the thoughts, of a nation; for there were no rival philosophies, and some flavour at least of it touched the whole people. In its lotus-laden atmosphere the infinite gropings of Indian mysticism dwindled to a somnolent repetition of gestures. The Chinese universe had been too long lived in to retain anything unknown or hostile. Nature did not stand aloof, nature and art grew into one another, permeating earth and sky. The painter's jagged rocks and hanging trees are intimate even when they are fantastic, the "Mist on the Stream" which steals out of pale silk in almost imperceptible ink washes conceals nothing alien from human ways. There was nothing left to learn—least of all from the cruder uses of peoples in the outer space which the sun of Peking did not warm. Invaders could massacre millions, they could change none. Their ambitions, and the sects and empires, the passions of arms and religions, of the West and the Middle East, whose echoes disturbed an interminable and exquisite reverie, were only tumults of an hour of drunkenness. Beyond China was nothing, as though the world-surrounding river of the ancients had flowed at the foot of the Great Wall.

Such was the soul, as it can be paid the imperfect tribute of a barbarian, of that antique and unparalleled civilisation.

It was rarely a Camoens came to China, exiled, like a poet of a Chinese Court, for love of a royal mistress. Westerners did not come in search of verses, and much of what they saw repelled them as sordid. Lord Charles Beresford spoke for nearly all when he referred to a Mr Little as "the pioneer of steam and civilisation in the Yangtze gorges".[1] One hopes that Mr Little would not really claim to have given their first baptism of civilisation to the Gorges that had inspired innumerable verses, and Hsia Kuei's great picture in which the old painter rendered so finely the waters of the rapids like animate things, dragon claws extended to guard the passage against the invader of a thousand years later. Every nation appears to have two selves or existences, the one ideal, the other gross, and the foreigner is usually baffled by them, noting them without the intimacy that would let him see their subtle connections, the adjustment of body and soul. China and Victorian England touched each other in few points (notably in philoprogenitiveness), not enough to create mutual understanding. International rivalry had begun its work of setting obstacles between the minds of peoples. The Chinese, like the Irish, were turned into derision; the Chinaman was impervious to pain, he could sleep upside down, and he was, in the time-honoured word, inscrutable— much as women, also from not being treated as equals, came to be seen as insoluble riddles. A great deal was made of the "Oriental mind", and Europeans in the Far East hypnotised themselves with the fiction. They had a laughable habit of noticing out there for the first time some obvious universal human trait, and hailing it as a discovery in Oriental psychology, an authentic piece of *Chinoiserie*. Numberless platitudes are offered us with the prefix: "Among the Chinese..."—and we learn that "It is usual among Oriental diplomats to ask more than they are prepared to take."[2]

Since the British and French invasion of 1860, there was a lull in the pressure on China until 1876. Merchants settled down to see what could be got out of the new treaties. Their Governments, grudgingly, announced a policy of receiving China into the *soi-disant* "comity" of nations. No one was satisfied. The traders sat grumbling in their counting-houses,

[1] *Break-up of China*, 317.
[2] From Indian Government documents on Burma, F.O. 17. 1059.

since the money they had to count was not sufficient to employ their time. The treaties, they said, were broken every day. China was only waiting for the foreigners to go away, and felt that in adding missionaries to traders Europe was adding insult to injury. Periodically there was an outbreak, a gunboat, and a fresh penalty imposed on the weaker side. At length, in 1875, a British agent entering S.W. China from Burma was murdered. The British Minister wrote a list of demands for freer commercial activity, brought up a fleet, and required their acceptance under threat of war. China signed the Chefu Convention (1876). England promised certain counter-concessions having to do with opium, which she did not carry out.

The British Minister's action was strangely out of tune with his character.[1] It is the economic depression in England, just then beginning and destined to form the background of British foreign policy for a decade, that in part explains his violence. In the cotton trade profits were sagging to cruelly low levels. Heavy industry was stagnant, unemployment rife, radicalism spreading. In shipping, a Conference had to be called in 1884 to devise means of checking cut-throat competition in Eastern waters. New countries were creating industries and competing with us at home and abroad; above all Germany. More and more of the world was being walled off inside hostile tariffs. Naturally, thoughts turned to China, a country without industries and prohibited by treaty from raising its tariff above a nominal figure. A Mr Martin, during discussion of a paper at the Institute of Bankers, talked of the dismal state of trade and conjectured that "a solution will be found in opening up large markets in unexplored countries", referring especially to China.[2]

England was easily ahead of all rivals in the China trade, and did not want to destroy the Empire if that could be helped. But other nations also were desperately in search of industrial markets; the slump affected all Europe. And some of them lacked England's vested interest in China's survival. Russia,

---

[1] For a criticism of it see Morse and McNair, *Far Eastern International Relations*, 335 ff.   [2] *Journal of the Institute of Bankers*, VI, 50.

who had in past years stolen immense areas of vaguely Chinese territory, had now pushed her way across Central Asia and was in contact with a real frontier. Between this pressure on the hinterland and the revived pressure along the coasts, China was very literally between the devil and the deep sea. Imperialism in its modern form was taking shape. Already railway schemes were bound up with a larger policy "which can only be described as in intention a policy of colonisation".[1] In the early 'eighties China's protective ring of dependencies was being broken through. Russia took part of Turkestan. England took Burma. Japan played the part of a snapper-up of unconsidered trifles. France took Tonking—and it was in Tonking that Colquhoun, the celebrated traveller, saw the *modern* Far Eastern problem emerging.[2] In excuse for some of the disrespect shown towards China, one may remark that in Asia it was next to impossible to leave one's own door without encountering vague Chinese claims of suzerainty. A Japanese writer quoted a Decree addressed by some dead Emperor of China to some dead King of Corea—"Now all lands both middle and foreign have become united in one vast empire, and so the whole earth has become as one family and all the peoples are my children"— and exclaimed "Away with such pretensions!"[3] A parallel might be drawn between the dissolution of the Holy Roman Empire into national units, and the breaking-up of the Chinese Empire. Japan had even in old days played the recalcitrant rôle of France in mediaeval Europe. But it was not dependencies *only* that were placed in danger.

The political situation in Europe was no less strained than the economic. In 1877 Russia invaded Turkey. In February 1878 Disraeli moved the fleet up to Constantinople, and there was almost war. In June the Concert of Europe assembled at Berlin and compelled the Tsar to relinquish what he had hoped to win. Thus Russian expansion was forced eastwards again, and Bismarck, having earned the Tsar's displeasure, had to put on a spurious friendliness and urge him to satisfy himself in

---

[1] Kent, *Railway Enterprise in China*, 93.
[2] *China in Transformation*, 320.　　　　　　　[3] F.O. 46. 248.

parts of Asia where he would fall foul of England, not of Germany. In distant fields, it often happened that forces in European politics operated inversely. The more darkly Bismarck felt the shadow of the Colossus across his eastern borders, the more eager he would be to lure St Petersburg into Chinese puzzles, with the additional and even more handsome prospect of an Anglo-Russian collision; which would make the Polish marches as safe as the Bavarian Alps, and open the way to as many colonies as Germany chose to acquire.

In fact, the traditional Eastern Question was now expanded into a whole series of Eastern Questions.[1] Each Russian advance in Central Asia was a fresh threat to India, and when the Russians reached China our interests there also were threatened. "England and Russia"—wrote a religious maniac of the day, at the dictation of angels and spirits—"are as summer and winter, light and darkness among the races of mankind. Russia, like winter, sweeps over the world but to destroy. England, like summer, traverses the earth but to bless."[2] At any rate, there was a political if not a moral antithesis. The Austrian Minister at Teheran wrote, in a despatch shown secretly to the British Ambassador at Vienna: "Il faut s'attendre à voir éclater prochainement un conflit armé entre la Russie et l'Angleterre à moins qu'un partage préalable n'absorbe, au profit de ces deux Puissances, tout ce qui reste encore de territoires indépendants en Asie Centrale....La solution du problème asiatique qui tient le monde en haleine depuis si longtemps approche à grands pas."[3]

Anglo-French hostility was a scarcely smaller blessing to the international arms industry, now making the world its own. France was seeking, all over Africa and Asia, compensation for Alsace-Lorraine; and wherever she came her rival was sure to be in the field already. "I am an Englishman; I think nothing profitable to be alien from me." Throughout our period,

---

[1] As Sir Rutherford Alcock, formerly British Minister at Peking, wrote in the *Fortnightly* of Jan. 1876.

[2] E. Maitland, *England and Islam* (1877).

[3] Egerton (Vienna), 688, 29.10.79, 17. 826.

tension between London and Paris over Egypt was a factor colouring their relations in all other spheres as well.

There was a curiously mixed decade, introducing modern Imperialism, when statesmen hoped to quieten European enmities by turning energies abroad; when they tried to *push* one another into colonising. Utopians soon learned that colonial activity reproduced and envenomed the old feuds of Europe, and 1882, when Bismarck was forced to set himself seriously to acquire an empire, heralded the end of the overture to Imperialism.

There is only space here to remark that China had a great share in determining the groupings of Powers that were to emerge. The following study will show Russia and France drifting together by force of common designs against China and against Britain's Asiatic interests, before ever they had a union of policy in Europe. Later, a French diplomat would write that the Dual Entente "a été ainsi comme forgée tout d'abord sur l'enclume de l'Asie".[1] And Germany's policy of acting as a general irritant is clearly apparent.[2] Whereas up to the Chefu Convention there had prevailed a theory of "solidarity" among Westerners against the Yellow Race, from that date solidarity dissolved into a quicksand of mutual intrigue.

It was a far cry from the well-upholstered comfort of a European Embassy to the diplomatic life of Peking. There, the rude virtues of the frontier were still in demand. Conditions of work, with no operas, no duchesses, no levees, scarcely merited the name of diplomacy at all. A diplomat tries to melt into the landscape of any capital where he may happen to be, as an Arctic fox turns its fur white in winter. But at Peking! He could not be expected to grow a pigtail. The invisibility of women lent in itself an unnatural something to the atmosphere. At Paris—in the diplomatic philosophy of the day—it was all a question of the Jews; at Berlin, of Bismarck; at St Petersburg,

[1] Gérard, *Ma Mission en Chine*, ii.

[2] Already in 1882 a German in the Far East wrote that the British Minister was "als Engländer selbstverständlich antideutsch". (R. von Möllendorf, *P. G. von Möllendorf: ein Lebensbild*, 91.)

of women—and so eastwards, but there they were all shut up. That might be reckoned fortunate in a way, because though a Minister's wife might always be open to influence, when he had twenty it would be cumbersome.

The local habitation of the Envoys matched the austerities of their task. Peking in those days was "the dreariest wilderness of dirt and dust" that could be imagined,[1] except that now and then one could escape to the Western Hills, sniff fresh air, and, if young enough, get up early to watch the sunrise in feminine company. Peking lay eighty miles inland from the familiar sea, eighty miles spun out to a hundred and fifty by the aimless windings of the Pei-ho as it rambled through the level dullness of Pechili. There was, in 1880, no hotel for foreigners. The British Legation was an old palace, or spacious bungalow, once bestowed by an Emperor on one of his thirty-seven sons, and now, fallen upon degenerate days, known as the Ta Ying Kuo Fu. A rent of 1500 taels was paid for it. A traveller called it "a most gorgeous palace", with its ample halls and acreage of courts.[2] Others, harder to please, commented rather on its inconveniences.[3]

Lodged here, an Envoy had to rely very much upon his own wits. Despatches were a matter of months in reaching him, and his own analyses of critical situations must have been less useful to the Secretary of State than to the latter-day student. During winter months, when the Pei-ho was frozen, despatches were carried by native courier to Shanghai. It was discovered at one time that the bags were being tampered with *en route*— perhaps by pilferers, perhaps (which made it risky to send recorders of cypher telegrams in these months) by spies. The Legation had to ask for stouter envelopes to withstand eight hundred miles in the saddle-bag.[4] It lends a gusto to the handling of these pages to fancy them swinging at the saddle of a slant-

[1] Mrs Gordon Cumming, *Wanderings in China*, ch. xxxvii.
[2] Fortune, *Journey to China and Japan*, 35; cp. Lord Redesdale, *Memories*, ii, 346.   [3] E.g. Miss Parkes' description: *Life of Parkes*, ii, 368-9.
[4] Grosvenor (Chargé), 82, 5.6.83, 17. 923. Cp. J. Bredon, *Sir Robert Hart*, 159.

eyed rider—a Chinese spy?—across the ice-bound plains of the North. Incidentally, our Minister once observed that cipher F was the only one he had, and that he had had it a good many years.[1] Considering how clever the Russians were at deciphering codes,[2] and that the telegraph passed through Russian territory, it may be conjectured that St Petersburg was often well-informed on our proceedings. The Russians, in those days before the Railway, had an elaborate relay system for official letters which linked Peking with St Petersburg in twenty-six days.[3]

A Legation junior of 1900, looking backward through the haze of the Boxer guns, descried a time in Peking when "picnics and dinners, races and excursions, were the order of the day, and politics and political situations were not burning"; when Ministers "wore Terai hats, very old clothes, and had an affable air".[4] These happy times were something of an illusion, a mirage. A British Minister died in 1885 from overwork and anxiety. Yet outwardly, at least, the Legations in our period pursued their way in decent harmony. Some worthy people at home seemed to expect them, besides secular duties, to set a moral example to the natives: the Society for the Propagation of the Gospel in Foreign Parts wrote to the Foreign Office concerning "performance of Divine Service at Peking".[5] We need not feel any misgivings but that under Sir Thomas Wade the Ta Ying Kuo Fu set an excellent example. The Legations were jealous of their dignity among the alien masses that surrounded them. There was correspondence in 1882 on the topic of the horses supplied to the escort of our Legation, the only one that still kept up this expensive precaution. Mongol ponies were suggested, but, wrote our Chargé in all seriousness, "I

---

[1] Wade 22, 24.5.81, 17. 857.
[2] For an incident illustrating this see Rennell Rodd, *Social and Diplomatic Memories*, ch. II; also Redesdale, *Memories*, II, 206. Wade received a new Cypher Q next year; Wade 49 Secret, 6.7.82, 17. 897.
[3] A. Reid, *Peking to Petersburg* (1898), ch. XIV.
[4] Putnam Weale, *Indiscreet Letters from Peking*, 4.
[5] F.O. to Wade 163 of 1880, 17. 828.

would observe that the impression created by a large man in full uniform on the back of a small and usually restive pony... would be the reverse of dignified."[1]

The avowed motto of the German Minister Herr von Brandt was, in his own words, "China's difficulty is every foreign nation's opportunity".[2] On the whole this maxim was acted on by all the Western Powers. American Commissioners who came in 1880 to negotiate a treaty checking Chinese immigration were helped by the then prevailing tension with Russia. In 1883 the Governor of Macao advised Lisbon that now, with China at odds with France, was the moment to press the question of Macao's sovereignty.[3] And the bad faith charged against the Chinese Government was by no means all on one side. But "Chinese obstinacy" was made an excuse for everything. Some took it as proof that the Chinese mind was not capacious of rational processes. Sir Edmund Hornby, Chief Justice at Shanghai and a good fellow in many ways, proclaimed foolishly: "The only way to nail an Oriental diplomatist—and what Oriental is not born with a diplomatic spoon in his mouth...is to put your views shortly and strongly into writing, and insist on getting an answer in writing....The Chinese...are absolutely without the logical faculty."[4] His conclusion was that no satisfaction could be hoped until "the next war gives us an opportunity to force an absolutely essential measure down their throats". It was a temptation to weary diplomats to sigh for a war, any war, as a blissful time when all wishes could be gratified without argument.

Japan up to the 'eighties provided the classic example of the "common front" attitude of a Diplomatic Body in a "backward" country. In China, traces of the same thing survived. Early in 1880 the French Chargé wrote, in reporting some joint démarche, "Il importait avant tout de ne pas rompre l'accord unanime qui est ici notre seule sauvegarde vis-à-vis du

---

[1] On the Legation Escort, see 17.918. They were thirsty souls, these guards. Messrs Bass shipped out eleven hogsheads for them in 1883.

[2] Wade 59 conf., 24.7.82, 17.897.

[3] Grosvenor 89 conf., 18.6.83, 17.923.   [4] *Autobiography*, 236.

Gouvernement chinois."[1] There were bound to be issues on which foreigners would have a corporate feeling. The three dominant issues of the sort were the Mixed Courts (for trying cases between natives and foreigners), inland taxation of foreign goods, and intercourse between native and foreign officials. A joint Note covering these points was sent in in November 1879.[2] The sentiment might be voiced, with spurious heartiness, even years later. "Whatever our rivalries and jealousies", wrote a British consul in 1900, "we Europeans, including even Russia, are all imbued with the one spirit of humanity, justice, and progress, summed up in the word 'Christian'; and this is none the less so though half of us may be atheists, freethinkers, and Jews."[3] But China was too large, the foreign interests engaged too heterogeneous, for corporate diplomacy to survive. In the issues of high policy that agitated our period, every diplomat's hand was against every other's. The Russians had opposed at the outset (in 1860) the idea of a China with a Foreign Office regularly dealing with Legations. It was always hard to get at their real thoughts, because the Russians deceived everybody habitually as a matter of taste and culture, regarding truth as something clumsy and rustic, owing too little to art, and tending to coarsen the faculties. Probably, however, they would really have preferred a continuance of China's old unintelligible diplomacy, with the Westerners staying on the coast and the Tsar having a free hand in the North. Tentative moves did appear towards a new decentralising of China's foreign policy. At Fuchow the authorities had a local Committee on foreign affairs. Such a return to the primitive dispersal of responsibility would have suited the book of several Powers. The policy of regular and centralised intercourse, of not abandoning the provinces to local haggling and unseen encroachment—this policy was predominantly a British one. It flowed from England's desire to keep the Empire intact; which flowed from England's commercial ascendancy.

[1] Cordier, *Relations de la Chine avec les Puissances Occidentales*, II, 194.
[2] See Bluebook, China, no. 3 of 1882.
[3] Parker, *China Past and Present*, 44.

Of this policy Sir Thomas Wade, if we except the incongruous episode of Chefu, was the embodiment. He was scarcely a professional diplomat in the ordinary sense; there was something patriarchal about him. He had become, in a long and varied career, a Chinese scholar whose attainments are remembered. He had a sense of the grandeur and antiquity of the Middle Kingdom.

> We do it wrong, being so majestical,
> To offer it the show of violence.

He had an even rarer goodwill towards the humble masses of its people. A fellow-countryman said of him with astonishment that he seemed to think it an honour to be saluted in the street by any Chinese acquaintance, even a coolie.[1] At the last of his countless interviews with the Foreign Ministry, Prince Kung with warm expressions of regard presented to him a seal inscribed "ping sheng neng yu chi chih yin"—"How often in life is it that one meets a man who can understand one's words?"[2] This writer of slightly sesquipedalian despatches was "one of the most instructive and delightful companions possible", besides being "conscientiousness itself".[3] He was a first-rate mimic and an excellent raconteur, with the wit as well as the learning of several literatures at his command.[4] We meet him almost at the close of his career, mellowed by time and preferment from a slight irascibility he had been reputed to possess in old days when juniors looked on him with awe.[5] In his thirteen years as Chargé or Minister he had only one real holiday. He hoped to end his service in some minor Legation in Europe; he did not obtain his innocent wish, and it would impair our picture to think of him pottering with a few papers at Lisbon or Copenhagen. He took instead a Chair at Cambridge,

[1] Hornby, *Autobiography*, 233.
[2] The Chinese were perturbed at Wade's recall. Memo. by Pauncefote (F.O.), 7.8.82, 17. 913.
[3] Foreign Office Sketches, in *Vanity Fair*, 1883.
[4] Redesdale, *Memories*, I, 330, 347. Wade's hospitality was a proverb in Peking. (Gill, *River of Golden Sand*, 9.)
[5] Satow, *Diplomat in Japan*, 20.

where he may have found a somnolent flavour in the air to remind him of his Celestial Empire.[1]

Wade was recalled in 1882; the Foreign Office was not satisfied with his exertions about opium. He left in charge his Secretary of Legation, Grosvenor. Grosvenor was a man of some ability and some experience, but one above all with no intention of showing over-indulgence to the Chinese. He regretted Wade's having withdrawn a certain Note—had it been pressed on the Chinese we should now "have them by the throat".[2] The Representatives, he remarked in a private letter, would have to "rub along" with the Chinese until the latter should go too far and "get a licking" from somebody or other that would teach them to be obliging for awhile.[3] In 1883 he wanted to send a naval force to punish summarily some villagers who had been plundering wrecked ships.[4] Fukien officials, he inclined to think, were the worst he had to deal with, though some others "run them pretty hard".[3] This tone of the hunting-field betokens a mentality far removed from Wade's.

When Wade's successor was appointed, Grosvenor hinted that he did not expect to find the Chinese overjoyed with the choice.[3] There is every reason to suppose that he was substantially understating the case. The announcement was received by Prince Kung (head of the Tsungli Yamen or Foreign Office) coolly—so coolly that London wrote to assure him the nomination was made in a friendly spirit. The newcomer himself would not have been surprised had the Chinese refused to receive him.[5]

Sir Harry Parkes, who went to China at the age of fifteen, was another of those men whose lives were drawn permanently by the East out of the intimate orbits of European existence—

[1] "Sir Thomas Wade was, perhaps (when at his best), the most dynamic Minister we ever had, not even excluding Sir Harry Parkes." (Parker, *China Past and Present*, 216.)

[2] Private to Currie (of the F.O.), 4.5.83, 17. 923.

[3] To Currie, 4.5.83, as above.

[4] Grosvenor 2, 4.1.83, 17. 919.   [5] *Life of Parkes*, 386.

diplomats who were not characterless pawns to be moved from any capital to any other. There the resemblance with Wade ends—although strangely, the two men were close friends.[1] Parkes was a man of hasty as well as resolute temper. He certainly deserved the encomium made on him by a King of Siam, of being "Circumspect and industrious for very advantageous service to his Gracious Sovereign and subsequent happiness of his countrymen".[2] Placed in a tutelary position towards the young Government of Japan, during his long service there he prolonged an attitude of parental strictness beyond its proper time. Transferred to Peking, he did not feel at home, and regretted having taken up the post. The first time he had seen Peking was as a prisoner in the war of 1860, facing torture and death. He now "laid great stress on the necessity of keeping on good terms with the Chinese",[3] but he was disappointed to find them no more easy to keep on good terms with (i.e. get his own way with) than when he had last seen them. His "system"—domination of the Far East by a Western bloc directed by England—was growing obsolete, now that "solidarity" was disappearing. He died in March 1885 after three days' illness.[4] It was at the height of an Anglo-Russian crisis, and the Foreign Office must have felt that he had chosen an unconscionable time for dying. He was the idol and champion of the merchants; Imperial policy really demanded study now of wider interests than theirs. It was in his grand statue looking over the Shanghai water-front that he received his reward, and in the glowing tributes paid to his memory by the Shanghai Press. The *Courier* reached the pinnacle with the sentence: "His death, like Gordon's, disproves the conviction of the latter that God will specially

[1] See a letter to the Foreign Secretary written by Wade on Parkes' death: 25.3.85, 17. 1001.

[2] "English correspondence of King Mongkut", *Siam Society Journal*, XXI.

[3] *Life of Parkes*, II, 373.

[4] He had been in bad shape for some time. O'Conor found him hard to work with and prone to jealousy (O'Conor to Sanderson, 23.3.85, Granville Papers, 97. 621), though in a less spontaneous letter seven years later he compared Parkes with Warren Hastings. (*Life of Parkes*, II, 417.)

protect his servants so long as there is work for them to do."[1] Whether or no his work so engaged the concern of Providence, Parkes no doubt found Heaven easier to enter than the Celestial Kingdom below: St Peter cannot have proved as troublesome as the Ministers of the Tsungli Yamen.

Parkes' death broke the line of succession. At the point of departure there was an effort to keep up the old tradition, which proves that the Foreign Office was not blind to the advantages of intimate knowledge of the ground. The Legation was offered to Sir Robert Hart, chief of the foreign-officered Customs Service which collected the Chinese Government's tariff revenue. O'Conor, left as Chargé by Parkes' death, applauded: Hart was an able diplomat, "and we want one here for the next ten years very much indeed".[2] Governor Bowen of Hongkong judged the choice a risky game of "double or quits"; we might get Hart's influence with the Chinese in the Legation and keep it in the Customs Service as well, or we might get neither.[3] Hart expressed himself "dazzled" by the offer, and went so far as to receive his Letters of Credit before declining; as he did in the end lest his fosterling, the Imperial Maritime Customs, should fall into wrong hands.[4] Had he accepted, foreign Powers would certainly have taken offence; they disliked his influence with the Chinese already, since it was used in England's favour; still, it is a pity for China that he declined. He was a man capable of entering astonishingly into Chinese feelings; even when he wrote under the guns of the Boxers.[5]

Among the *chers collègues*, America naturally contributed the oddity, in a Minister who had started life in China as a missionary. Grosvenor called him a "clever, unscrupulous and adventurous

[1] Extract with O'Conor 146, 4.4.85, 17. 979.
[2] O'Conor to Granville, 21.4.85, 97. 621.
[3] *Letters etc. of Bowen*, ed. Lane-Poole, II, 380.
[4] Hart to Salisbury, 26.8.85, 17. 983. He had thought of asking for a baronetcy; O'Conor tel. ciph., 16.4.85 Priv. and conf., 97. 621.
[5] See his *These from the Land of Sinim*; e.g. p. 55 (The Chinese) "are well-behaved, law-abiding, intelligent, economical, and industrious..they are punctiliously polite, they worship talent, and they believe in right so firmly that they scorn to think it requires to be supported or encouraged by might..."

man".[1] The Corps Diplomatique was not always a band of brothers. Herr von Brandt stands out with unenviable prominence. He succeeded Holleben in 1875, and next year was delivered of an ultimatum. He had been long in the Far East, and had imbibed a hatred and contempt for all Orientals which Wade, not ordinarily malicious, put down to his mediocre success in diplomacy.[2] A Potsdam barracks would have been a better place for him than a Legation; in fact he began in the army. He carried to extremes all Parkes' less amiable features. Like Dr Johnson with the Yankees, he thought that anything we allowed the Chinese short of hanging, they ought to be grateful for. He throve on the ill-governed violence licensed by a state with its way to make, to which no complications came amiss. One imagines him roaring like Sir Anthony Absolute; a great many things "put him in a frenzy directly". Wade disliked both man and policy, and, though he found Brandt usually clever enough, once at least described his tirades as "all but incoherent".[3] Sir Claude Macdonald, as Minister at Peking in the 'nineties, remarked that all the three Germans who were in turn his colleagues there believed that the sooner China was conquered and shared out the better.[4] Brandt believed the same, and it was not mere coincidence. After leaving China he acquired "the reputation of being the greatest authority in Germany on the Far East".[5] His diplomatic life had ended on a ludicrous note; he fell in love with the daughter of an American at Seoul, married her in defiance of the Kaiser's orders, and was retired.[6] During the Battle of Concessions he reappeared in China as the agent of German capitalists.

Considering the danger of the Customs Service falling into

---

[1] Grosvenor to Sanderson, 8.2.83, 97. 621. For details of other Representatives, see Cordier, *Relations etc.*
[2] Wade 118 Very conf., 25.7.80, 17. 832.
[3] Wade 107 Very conf., 16.7.80, 17. 832.
[4] Lord Newton, *Life of Lord Lansdowne*, 219.
[5] Baron von Rosen, *Forty Years of Diplomacy*, I, 94.
[6] W. J. Foster, *Practice of Diplomacy*, 128.

"bad" hands, the offer of the Legation to Hart shows that no obvious successor to Parkes was in sight. The new Powers appearing on the scene, now that China was ceasing to be the fabulous country of the Grand Cham, naturally could not draw on agents of large local experience. The generation of diplomats who came with a grimace, talked through interpreters, and departed with relief like a colonial Governor fleeing from his swamps, was on its way; with the result that a writer of 1904 could speak of the Peking Legations as "the places in the world least well informed as to all that concerns China".[1] As the world came to be levelled up, the said Legations moved in a contrary direction to the democratising tendencies in diplomacy elsewhere—they took on polish instead of growing more homespun. "Damns have had their day." But it is curious that England, with her opportunities, had taken no care to provide men qualified in point of knowledge to follow Alcock, Wade and Parkes. First choice fell on Sir John Walsham. He was the earliest Minister, it is said, to try the experiment of bringing the ordinary manners of European diplomacy to the Tsungli Yamen—and hence his failure.[2] (His failure was also due to some negligence on his own part.)[3] After O'Conor's term in the 'nineties, Curzon, then Under-Secretary, urged on Lord Salisbury with commendable enthusiasm that the next man ought to be chosen for first-rate ability, resolution of character, and knowledge of the Far East. Quite so, rejoined Lord Salisbury, only where did such a paragon exist?[4]

A remedy could have been found in the earlier intermixing, in fields like the Far East, of the diplomatic and consular services. In the China Consular Service we had a body of men necessarily stationed in the Far East once for all, and chafing at their want of scope for advancement. By giving them a more comprehensive training, the Foreign Office would have raised

[1] Ular, *Russo-Chinese Empire*.
[2] H. Norman, *Peoples and Politics of the Far East*, 302.
[3] Dugdale, *Maurice de Bunsen*, 100.
[4] Lord Ronaldshay, *Life of Lord Curzon*, 252.

their usefulness as consuls, and made sure of finding among the best of them candidates for the Legation.[1]

In 1880 we had fifteen consuls and three vice-consuls, together with first and second-class assistants and student interpreters. So far as respectability goes, there was a good level; whereas the American consulates (according to H.M. Consul Giles) were homes of unblushing corruption.[2] In earlier times it had not been infrequent for consuls to engage in trade on their own account. In 1883 we find the German vice-consul at Swatow, a man named Schaar, to be also a participant in the firm of Direks and Co., and involved in a quarrel with the Chinese arising out of the Company's affairs. In the English service the objectionable practice had been put down. Pay was good compared with rates elsewhere—none of the consuls drew less than £700, and Fuchow was worth £1300 and Shanghai £1500. It appears that pay was not high enough to answer expenses and discomforts. The Service sent in a Memorial in 1882 airing its grievances, in terms which show that it thought as poorly of its advantages as others did of its merits. The consuls complained that the better-paid places were having their salaries docked on falling vacant. "Promotion is now so slow that a Student-Interpreter may have

[1] The chief posts in the Legation were filled in 1880 thus: Minister, Wade; Secretary of Legation, Grosvenor; Second Secretary, none: Chinese Secretary, E. C. Baber; Assistant Chinese Secretary, W. C. Hillier. Among these Wade alone was, so to speak, truly autochthonous. Grosvenor had served in many capitals, spoke Chinese, came to China first in 1871. Baber had been in China since 1866. Hillier had already served on a mission to Yunnan. It cannot be said, then, that there was a dearth of local experience. In 1881 a Second Secretary, Maude, was added; he had come out only the year before. In 1884 Grosvenor was replaced by the Hon. H. G. Edwardes, who had been at Peking for three years in the 'seventies. England had in 1880 seven military or naval attachés, all stationed in Europe. In 1883 there sprang up a "Naval Attaché to the Maritime Courts" (apart from one to the "Maritime Courts of Europe"). This officer's duties never wafted him up the Pei-ho in our period. Considering how important for British policy was our estimate of China's armed forces, it was false economy to have no military or naval observer at Peking.

[2] "Present State of Affairs in China", *Fortnightly*, Sept. 1879.

to remain five or six years before getting his first step."[1] Pauncefote of the Foreign Office, who had spent years in the Far East, minuted: "I must say that I agree with the Memorialists. The Consular Service of China should be kept up to the highest point of efficiency, and if we go on 'scraping' salaries we shall make a great mistake." Money was certainly not wasted. In 1878 there was much discussion of methods for bringing "within the narrowest limits" the cost of the six new consulates being opened.[2] One method was to give the Ichang consul a house that a traveller described as "something between a barn, a stable, and a Chinese inn".[3] In 1880 economy of stationery was recommended by circular.[4] Wade wrote jubilantly that he had discovered he could get ale for the Escort at cheaper quotations from Messrs Bass than from his present purveyor in Shanghai.[5]

As regards ordinary business, there was rather an excess of red tape; once in our years there was grave insubordination on the part of a junior, who absented himself without leave;[6] there were one or two Nestors in the senior posts, and a certain disposition to carp. Sinclair of Fuchow apparently disguised his age in order to cling to his post. In 1882 he wrote peevishly to the Chargé d'Affaires about the obstructiveness of the local Viceroy, and allowed himself to criticise Wade for not having put a stop to it. Grosvenor came down on him tremendously for the breach of etiquette; Sinclair retorted querulously, and the Foreign Office unofficially censured both parties.[7] We hear that most consuls spoke Chinese poorly.[8] In spite of all this, the Service functioned adequately according to its own lights. Archives and accounts were kept in good order.[9] Trade reports were intelligent. Whenever there was friction between British and Chinese, the consuls were unsparing in their

[1] Copy with Wade 68, 5.8.82, 17. 898.
[2] F.O. 366. 343, "Supply of Funds to Consulates, 1871–1881".
[3] Percival, "Land of the Dragon", 152.
[4] F.O. 124 of 1880, 17. 828.   [5] 17. 918.   [6] 17. 827.
[7] Grosvenor 119, 29.10.82, 17. 899; Currie to Grosvenor, 30.12.82, 17. 894.   [8] Parker, *John Chinaman*, 186.   [9] Hornby, *Autobiography*, 213–14.

efforts; they were "zealous and hardworking servants of the Crown", as one of them declared.[1] The same is true of the Legation. Yet the mandarins themselves were not more abused by our traders than were the consuls and the Legation. Curzon, out in China in 1894, found all our merchants critical—excessively so, he thought. They told him they wanted to see "unfair" commercial pressure by foreign agents repelled.[2] A few years later, when Lord Charles Beresford was sent out by the British Chambers of Commerce, merchants at Chefu put into his hands a memorandum contrasting the zeal displayed by German agents with "the apathy displayed by most of our consuls in China". Graver still, he was told that "the system makes men narrow and pro-Chinese in their sympathies"; consuls began their career at an early age, with no previous business experience to attune them to the wishes of the merchants.[3] It was recognised that the Far East made special demands. Thus at the Royal Commission of 1890 Bryce, who thought that Government agents ought not to act as commercial travellers, excepted the Far East as a field where it would be legitimate to do as much for trade as foreign officials did. The essence of the matter was that, about the 'eighties, our merchant began to find himself faced with novel competition backed by novel diplomatic activity, and could not adjust himself. He called on his Government to show a more active, a more positive interest. "The Treaties", wrote the *Shanghai Mercury* (26 Sept. 1882), "with Sir Thomas Wade and the present School of British Consular Authorities to put a gloss on them, are like the utterances of the witches in *Macbeth*—

'That palter with us in a double sense...'"

Consuls seasoned with the salt waters of Manchester thought it no part of their duty to explain to the merchant his own business. Commerce would do better on its own feet. They

[1] Medhurst, *Foreigner in Far Cathay*, 51.

[2] Curzon, *Problems of the Far East.*

[3] Beresford, *Break-up of China*, chapter on British Consuls. Parker agrees that consuls lacked the businessman's sense of method and punctuality. (*China Past and Present*, 213.)

found some critics to support them. "The British Merchant in the Far East is the first to condemn his own Minister and to abuse his own Consul, and he is the very last to help himself." [1] At bottom, the trouble lay in the disharmony of ideas engendered by two economic epochs.

More help was called for not only against German and American rivals but against native business men whom traders with dwindling turnovers were apt to regard as getting above themselves. The *North China Herald* hoped editorially that the Foreign Secretary would realise "our interests required more attention than they have received from his Department". Formerly China "was so weak that we could do pretty well what we liked at the ports. The recent policy of the Tsungli Yamen would lead us to believe that a majority of its members have convinced themselves that the Empire is now powerful enough to resume its old arrogant ways." The "astute Chinese" must be kept in their place. [2] Ever since the Burlingame Mission in the 'sixties there had been a cleavage between the foreign communities in China and what they regarded as the newfangled—the misguided—policy of treating China as an equal. Addresses presented by the British and American colonies to Mr J. Ross Browne, recalled in 1869 by Washington for his recalcitrance towards the new policy, set forth this cleavage plainly. "We claim", said the merchants, "that China, as she stands, is low in civilisation as she is in wealth and power....We claim that the presence of foreigners is a protection and a blessing to the people....The withdrawal of pressure would be dangerous to native and foreign interests." [3] An incident of 1885 shows the kind of thing that might happen in this state of friction between Western officials and their nationals.

One day in June, the Mixed Court at Shanghai was trying a case. On the Bench, side by side, sat the Magistrate Huang, with Mr Consul Giles as Assessor. Their Worships did not see

[1] Hamilton, *Corea*, 144.
[2] Sent to the F.O. by the Editor, 19.5.83, 17. 1009.
[3] Published in the form of a pamphlet, 1869.

eye to eye over the case before them, and somehow—it is not plain what started it—an unseemly scuffle broke out on the Bench. It was reported at Peking that the Chinese Magistrate had dealt his comrade a blow. It was not the sort of stroke that would have felled an ox: the consul later emended his description of it to merely a "technical blow". One ridiculous Press account conjures up a scene of comedy; Mr Giles in "raising his hands to give force to his remarks" inadvertently knocked Huang's pen out of his fingers, and Huang "raising his hands to give force to *his* remarks" accidentally hit Mr Giles on the chest.

O'Conor, then Chargé d'Affaires, was not excited; he considered Giles to have shown "want of tact and conciliatory disposition" in his relations with the Magistrate, and when the Chinese dismissed Huang and requested O'Conor to withdraw his consul, he agreed after parley to do so. The Shanghai Settlements always included a No Compromise element. The fiery Editor of the *North China Daily News*, a friend of Giles, blackguarded O'Conor as an inexperienced young man, an easy victim of Chinese astuteness. O'Conor wrote privately to the Foreign Office that to be guided by the more obstreperous portion of Shanghai would in the long run prejudice our interests. The Foreign Office supported him, and gave Giles a caution.[1]

The Consular Service could still at the end of the century be described as starved, overworked and underpaid. Perhaps the best thing to be said about it in its classic days is that its peaceful, vegetative immobility gave it little of the restlessness that sometimes led local agents beyond the intentions of their chiefs. By long routine, consuls became as it were indistinguishable from the Chinese scenery.

[1] O'Conor 280, 11.6.85, and 353, 16.7.85, 17. 983; also other correspondence in this volume; and F.O. to O'Conor 220, 237, 249, 272, in 17. 976.

CHAPTER TWO

The Chinese Foreign Office

THE Middle Kingdom, like the Holy Roman Empire and many lesser polities, indulged the illusion that its limits included all sublunary things. To do without a Department of foreign affairs was, accordingly, in older and better days, an economy that could be well afforded. There *were* no foreign affairs: the idea would have sounded like *lèse-majesté*. No wonder the Westerners found China an "Unclubbable" nation.

Before 1860 the Dragon resembled other primitive or pre-historic beasts in having its sluggish intelligence dispersed through its system, instead of focused in one organ. The victors of 1860 insisted on China's setting up a Department for the centralised control of her foreign relations, hitherto the province of a branch of the Ministry of Rites. The result was the Tsungli Yamen. It was intended to be the mechanism whereby foreign wishes could be carried smoothly into effect. It turned out to be the hearth and home of obstruction to those wishes.

The Tsungli Yamen was domiciled in no splendid palace, but (like the British Foreign Office not so long before) in a mean dilapidated house that some foreigners were disposed to take as an insult. The moral sentiments placarding the walls failed to mollify them. It could at all events be said of it that it was in slightly better repair than the "broken-down, weather-stained, rotting structure" which housed the Board of War; and no more could be expected when the Han-lin Academy, the pride of the Empire, was sheltered in a shabby building like a set of stables.[1] We hear in early days of grooms and understrappers peering in through the windows during conferences; while that other Foreign Office, the Yamen of the

[1] W. A. P. Martin, *Hanlin Papers*, ch. 1.

powerful Tientsin Viceroy Li Hung-chang, was still a "bare, dirty, whitewashed" hall full of hangers-on of foreign representatives straining their ears for secrets.[1] The Tsungli Yamen was a place where Mandarins watched their beards grow longer, amidst the crafty and unchanging race of spiders. Here resided the statecraft of China. And here a long line of Ministers Plenipotentiary sat on hard dirty seats and were plied with pastries they did not want, fretted by pointless conversation, and generally sapped of their vitality. It was a Chinese revenge. Lord Salisbury used to keep a sharp wooden dagger to press against his leg, so as to stay awake during vacuous diplomatic interviews.[2] The device would have been serviceable at Peking. A Frenchman describes vivaciously his first reception in this "sorte de kiosque, d'aspect plus que modeste". "Le scène a plutôt le caractère d'un lunch que d'une réception solennelle."[3] Hornby, the choleric Judge, says that the members were "all old men and looked and behaved extremely like old women".[4] To what exasperation foreigners might be driven is shown by a violent letter from Osborn to Lay, after the pair had failed in 1864 to buy a navy for the Chinese Government. "These oily wretches"—"these contemptible devils"—are not the worst of the angry sailorman's expressions. "I am told it sent Wade home seriously shaken", he winds up; "I don't wonder at it."[5] One person at least was equal to the problem; a Legation interpreter (some Ministers left these tests of physical endurance chiefly to their interpreters). He wore the Chinese down at their own game by always discussing the sweets on the table for two whole hours before coming to business.[6]

In our period, twenty years after its foundation, the Tsungli Yamen still did not figure in the official list of establishments.[7]

[1] Hornby, *Autobiography*, 234; Norman, *Peoples and Politics of the Far East*, 202, 297.
[2] *Life of Lord Salisbury*, by Lady G. Cecil, III, 210.
[3] Quoted by Cordier, *Relations etc.* II, 142.
[4] *Autobiography*, 234–5. See also Brigham, *A Year in China*, 41 ff., and Sir R. Alcock in the *Fortnightly* of May, 1876.
[5] H. N. Lay, *Our Interests in China* (1864).
[6] *Life of Parkes*, II, 391.   [7] Wade 26 conf., 27.5.82, 17. 985.

It was designed to be a feather-bed for Westerners to beat to their hearts' content. The plan risked explosions of impatience, recourse to violent methods. But it was a natural plan, in harmony with the nature of a Government to whose habits routine was life and thought noxious. Perhaps also a Court which could not closely supervise its Departments, and some of whose servants had their price, was reluctant to give wide powers to a set of officials who might abuse them through either ignorance or corruption. How often foreign agents in Peking used bribes is hard to say. They were freely suspected of it. "Most Chinese officials of any utility are in the pay of Russia", wrote Colquhoun in 1898[1]—rather recklessly; he gave no evidence. By the end of the century, in any case, the mandarinate had degenerated a stage; if bribes had been accepted wholesale in our period we should have seen the foreigners gaining their way much more easily than they did. We hear fairly frequently of copies of Chinese documents being procured "indirectly", or transcribed "hastily", by our agents.[2] It has been said, with perhaps some exaggeration, that "Japan had the run of every secret document in China".[3] Ignatieff used to get his way at Constantinople by keeping a dossier of the misdemeanours of each Turkish Minister, and threatening him with exposure.[4] This sounds as if it might have worked well at Peking.

The Envoys, at any rate, who arrived to occupy the new Legations after 1861, found themselves dealing with a set of functionaries who smothered them with "united and rude declamation" when torn away from the topic of snuff and pastries;[5] Poloniuses, the soul of whose wit was certainly not brevity, and who talked singly or in chorus until the nodding visitor may have fancied himself lying in a trance, plunged

[1] *China in Transformation*, 227.   [2] E.g. Wade 8, 13.3.79, 17. 826.
[3] Pooley, preface to Hayashi's *Secret Memoirs*.
[4] Stead, *Truth about Russia*, 274. Salisbury once asked his Ambassador at Constantinople whether it was true he was the only one there who did not keep a Minister in his pay, and how much it would cost. (*Life*, III, 215).
[5] Parkes 61 Most conf., 22.12.83, 17. 927.

into the unthinkable antiquity of the strange Empire, with the ghosts of ancient statesmen droning in his ears amid crumbling ruins.

In some ways the Yamen showed signs about our period of fitting itself into the conventions of Western diplomacy. A practice had grown up of New Year calls being paid to the Legations by its chief members.[1] In 1884 Parkes persuaded them to attend a banquet in honour of Queen Victoria's birthday, and before the end of the year they had not only paid the same tribute to the Tsar and the Mikado, but had entertained all the Envoys to lunch in celebration of the Emperor's birthday.[2] One obstacle to the growth of a really civilised diplomatic life was that Chinese Ministers so often had to attend at the Palace at the unwholesome hour of 3 a.m., and could not easily join in evening functions, finding no doubt that at their age they needed their sleep. Peking was not likely to turn into an Eastern Paris so long as this essentially barbarous custom persisted. Those members who attended to affairs at all had to attend to a great many. An American, talking to a senior member of the Yamen who held other posts as well, found that his daily routine of work extended from 2 a.m. to 6 p.m. It finished him off soon afterwards.[3] Another difficulty was that as the Yamen grew in experience, it grew more cautious and close. When it was at its youngest and most forlorn, one could talk to it freely on any subject. By the 'eighties this was not easy, and conversation was always taken down by clerks in attendance.[4]

Every Foreign Office has to take account of opinion in one quarter or another. The Tsungli Yamen had to fear cold winds from three main quarters of the compass: the Court, "public opinion", and rival self-appointed practitioners. To trace all the workings of these forces in the shrouded silence of an Oriental Government, behind the ornate conventional façade of the *Peking Gazette*, is not possible, but from time to time there were revealing glimpses. "The Court" meant the moods of

[1] Wade 9, 15.1.80, 17. 829.   [2] Parkes 316, 10.12.84, 17. 953.
[3] Holcombe, *The Real Chinaman*, 92–3.   [4] Wade 14, 27.1.80, 17. 829.

the Dowager Empress and Regent Tzu Hsi, as they might be swayed by her own character or by the promptings of those about her in the recesses of the Forbidden City. She had no distinct foreign policy; though there was enough for O'Conor to write in 1885 that the Empress, "from all one hears, is a shrewd and clever woman".[1] "Public opinion" in the China of 1880 sounds anachronistic, but public opinion is everywhere an odd and complex thing. In China it had its leaders in the famous scholars who sat in the Hanlin Academy or on the Board of Censors, or read old books in the Metropolitan Libraries and emerged to meet their compeers and deplore the wretchedness of the times—more fortunate than their ancestors who had been threatened with death by a radical Emperor for the invidious habit of lamenting the good old days. The ruler, the Son of Heaven, might answer criticism with violence, heads might fall; but, though a Western eye might fail to detect the play of forces, in the long run their criticisms would not be ignored. It was not only office-holders and retired elders who counted. Peking was crowded with graduates awaiting office, more reckless and inexperienced even than their seniors.[2] The lettered class was closely linked with the powerful middle class of provincial gentry, and its views on foreign affairs were inconceivably out of date. Wu K'u-tu, a Censor who committed suicide in as fine a spirit as the noblest Roman of them all, advised the Throne to carry no further the wrangle about whether foreign Envoys should kneel at audience. Why should good behaviour be expected from beings whose treaties talked only of commerce and contained not a word on the cardinal virtues?[3] Men like Wu, who despite mandarin corruption were not rare, could be neither bought nor taught; only hanging could cure them. The idea that the way to reason with a mandarin was to hold out a piece of money in one hand and grip his pigtail with the other, as

[1] Private to Lord Granville, 31.3.85, Granville Papers, 97. 621.
[2] Gamble reckons that in 1921 there were five thousand official posts in Peking and 110,000 expectant officials: *Peking, a Social Survey*, 30.
[3] Bland and Blackhouse, *China under the Empress Dowager*, ch. VII.

some Russian phrased it, belongs to the world of fiction. The Yamen, in daily intercourse with the foreigners, could not emulate the lofty and uncompromising spirit of Wu; but neither could it disregard it; and to frame workday policy with the sonorous declamations of the schools in its ears was no easy task. Thirdly, the Yamen had no monopoly of foreign affairs. Negotiations might be taken out of its hands by statesmen who enjoyed the confidence of the Court or of the patriotic party, or with whom the foreigners felt they could deal advantageously. Weakened from the outset by the fact of its creation having been dictated by foreigners, the Yamen's prestige was further dimmed by the prominence of men outside it, notably the Viceroys Li Hung-chang and Tso Tsung-tang.

As may readily be imagined, the Tsungli Yamen was not eagerly sought by Chinese politicians. Quite apart from the fact that salaries were microscopic,[1] entry was a punishment rather than a promotion. In judging the hesitations and fumblings of its members, it is profitable to remember that the penalty of failure for them was not the temporary loss of salary that awaits unpopular Western Ministers, but disgrace, banishment, and in the last resort, for themselves and their families, the axe. Several of them were condemned to death during the Boxer Rising.

They were recruited in part from reactionaries who were brought in because they made themselves intolerable outside. We hear in our years of several intractable critics of Government policy being thus forced to enter, in the hope that experience of business would sober them a little. Thus Mao Chang-hai, who died in 1882, had been brought in because of his impossible objurgations against everything smelling of beyond the seas. The treatment rendered him in the long run slightly less disagreeable than he was at the start, but though a member for thirteen years he always remained, so far as the thrashing out of affairs was concerned, the merest cipher.[2] Such a procedure was not calculated to smooth the work of

[1] Headland, Court Life in China, 45.
[2] Wade 11, 15.4.82, 17. 895.

the Diplomatic Body, unwittingly employed as pedagogues for the taming of the most indocile characters in the capital. Sir Robert Hart thought highly of the method, and considered that several men who entered the Yamen very obstinate "turned round and behaved very sensibly afterwards".[1]

The peculiar character of the Yamen established itself gradually. Article V of the English Treaty of 1858 prescribed the rank befitting whoever should direct foreign affairs; and at first the rule was observed. The Yamen began with five members, the number growing to ten, and at one time these ten included every member of the Grand Council. After a while the assiduity of the Ministers began to fall persistently, and so, foreigners noted with disapproval, did their rank. In 1883, four of them were still members of the Grand Council— Prince Kung, the Grand Secretary Pao, the Assistant Grand Secretary Li Hung-tsao, and Ching-lien—but these rarely troubled to attend at the Yamen. An Envoy who called for an interview might find no one better worth seeing than a clerk, however urgent or momentous his business; for one thing, in the early 'eighties it does not seem that much progress had been made towards dividing the staff into departments according to the countries dealt with, as was done in the next decade.[2]

In March 1883 Wu Ting-fen was gazetted a member. He was Vice-Director of the Imperial Clan Court, and was, as other members had been, a promoted Yamen junior. This seems nothing against him; however, Grosvenor (then Chargé d'Affaires) pitched on the appointment as a grievance; he was filled with a general dissatisfaction. He maintained that no official of so subordinate a standing as Wu had ever been heard of in the Yamen before, and founded on the incident a long despatch that may be quoted with some fullness.

Since, wrote Grosvenor, the departure of Wang (no genius, but Sir Thomas Wade had called him "the real *Chef politique*

[1] *These from the Land of Sinim*, 21.
[2] The Tsungli Yamen "is considered not so much a separate organisation... as a species of Cabinet formed by the admission of members of other Departments of State". (Mayers, *Chinese Government*, 15.)

of the Yamen"[1]), it had been difficult to buttonhole anyone worth talking to. He had written to Pao, but the latter said he was too old to attend. Business now lay with Ch'en Lan-pin and Chou Chia-mei,

and it is almost ludicrous to watch the expression of anxiety on their faces whenever they have reason to fear that they will be called upon to accept the very slightest responsibility.

The reason for this state of affairs is, I think, to be found in the increasing Power and influence of the Grand Secretary Li at Tientsin. He does not even care to conceal the fact that he is virtually minister for Foreign Affairs in China. . . .He even lately told a gentleman, who repeated it to me, that the Throne had no intention of filling up the vacancies which had occurred in the Yamen. . . and that no member of the Grand Council would under any circumstances be nominated as they all hated the affairs of the Tsungli Yamen.

In practice China's foreign affairs, in so far as they concern the Tsungli Yamen and foreign Representatives, are conducted by a Secretary of the name of Chang, evidently a very able man, but one whose subordinate position makes it impossible for him to come to any decision on any subject.

As I have earlier reported to Your Lordship all questions of any magnitude are referred to the Grand Secretary Li at Tientsin and foreign representatives are being gradually drawn into the position which it was one of the objects of the Treaty of Tientsin to avoid. I here more especially refer to those references to a higher power which have always been the safeguard of a Chinese official when all other pretexts failed.

It is not always possible, and I do not believe it to be always politically wise, to go to Tientsin for the purpose of discussing questions with His Excellency Li, especially as that exalted functionary can always free himself from all responsibility by the fact that he has no *locus standi* for the conclusion of arrangements with foreign Representatives.

[1] Wade 54, 20.6.82, 17. 897. When Wang was removed in December 1882, Grosvenor wrote that he was regretted by all foreigners, and that interviews at the Yamen had since become the purest waste of time: 158, 18.12.82, 17. 900.

In a word the Tsungli Yamen, as at present constituted and managed, is little more than a branch office of the Grand Secretary Li's Yamen at Tientsin, and most of the foreign Representatives with whom I have spoken on the subject, deplore this state of affairs as much as I do.

The real remedy would be the appointment of the Grand Secretary Li to the post of Minister for Foreign Affairs of the Chinese Empire; but as far as my information goes, His Excellency would never of his own free will accept a post which would entail residence in Peking. In the provinces he is sovereign except in name; in the capital he would be neither more nor less than a Minister for Foreign Affairs. In addition Li is at present straining every nerve to increase China's naval and military resources, and a residence in the capital would naturally hamper his freedom of action on those heads.

Grosvenor ended by saying that, while he might remind the President, Prince Kung, that Article V of the treaty was scarcely being observed, probably the result would be to secure the attendance at the Yamen of one or two men of the stamp of Liu Shu, Chief of Police of Peking; and the only time Grosvenor had seen Liu Shu the latter displayed "the most profound indifference to as well as the most profound ignorance of the subjects discussed". In view of Kung's lofty rank, as uncle to the child Emperor, and his ill-health, *he* could not be pressed to attend.[1]

One can easily see how irritating it was for diplomatists never to know where decisions were being made, and to have their business bandied about from one shuffling grandee to another. It was convenient for Li to conceal himself in the prompter's box and influence events from there; but the situation made for an atmosphere of intrigue and mistrust. Wade's belief was that the Government hoped, by devolution of authority to Li, to induce the Legations to leave Peking and go back again to the Ports, whence their importunities would be less felt.[2]

A memorandum by Carles of the Consular Service supple-

[1] Grosvenor 41, 17.3.83, 17. 922.
[2] Memo. 31.5.83 on Grosvenor's despatch, 17. 923.

ments Grosvenor's despatch.[1] Carles traced part of the un-accommodating spirit that was being shown to the Regency. The Emperor being a minor, all officials were inclined towards excessive caution, fearing to grant concessions that might be seized on then or later by some Censor as a chance to haul himself into prominence by a high-flown attack. Memorials of that sort were the Chinese equivalent to an English politician's stumping the country on a popular issue. China, as she began to read foreign books, was angry at discovering how nearly some of the rights she had given away touched her dignity and independence. This induced a spirit of obstruction.

A Decree of September 1884, on the occasion of three Ministers being dismissed, confirms some of the criticisms of Grosvenor and Carles. Chou Chia-mei and Wu Ting-fen are censured by it as incapable—Kun Kang does not understand foreign matters—Chou Te-pin can never agree with his colleagues—Chang Yin-huan is always having to be repri-manded—Ch'en Lan-pin is senile—Wu Hsien's language is too truculent: Yu Ching-ming, for a wonder, is passed as sound.[2]

After the Chefu Convention, Li Hung-chang is said to have suggested the forming of an Institution for study of foreign affairs.[3] Chefu did lead to the sending of Chinese envoys abroad, an alternative way of broadening minds. Residence in foreign capitals was bound to give more realistic notions of world politics than a sedentary scholar could strain through the opaque medium of his ideographs. At the same time, through reports from envoys the Yamen began to acquire some grasp of current world events. Prince Kung, calling on Wade in January 1880, enquired about the progress of Britain's Afghan and South African wars. Eighteen years earlier, Wade re-flected, Kung had not known where Turkey was.[4] After a term of service abroad, a man was a natural candidate for a seat in the Yamen, and a few were entering in these years.

[1] With Grosvenor 33, 3.3.83, 17. 922.
[2] Copy with Parkes 178, 5.9.85, 27. 2712.
[3] Mrs Little, Li Hung-chang, 119.   [4] Wade 9, 15.1.80, 17. 829.

Mao Chang-hai's place was taken by Ch'en Lan-pin, who, rendered futile though Grosvenor found him by dread of responsibility, nevertheless as an ex-Envoy to Washington knew something of the world. A converse case is the appointment of Chang Yin-huan as Minister to the U.S. and Peru in 1885. He had had a few months in the Yamen in the previous year,[1] long enough to get into trouble, it appears from the above-quoted Decree. Progressive men were soon to be found in the youthful diplomatic service. Hsu Cheng-tsu, appointed to Tokio in 1884 after three years as Secretary of Legation at Washington, was a man of advanced ideas who deplored the paralysing weight of Chinese conservatism.[2] Liu, one of the first two Envoys to come to England, acquired a noticeable degree of "enlightenment" notwithstanding that, as became a functionary of the Imperial Banqueting Court, he left China an arch-reactionary[3] and with a habit of spitting which he indulged too freely on the ship.[4] It is amusing to speculate on the feelings of these mandarins, setting off from the Flowery Kingdom to remote places of which their only ideas were drawn from classical poems—laments of exiled courtiers, or princesses sent away to marry chieftains of remote deserts. One of them, poor fellow, died in London in 1884, far from his ancestral grave. No doubt Westerners expected them to be overwhelmed with admiration of all they saw abroad, and no doubt such was not always the result produced. "I am heartily tired of (the Americans)", wrote one of them from Washington in 1880: "their estimate of themselves soars beyond my appreciation".[5]

There were risks in sending abroad, out of range of the most Catonian Censor's eye, members of a venial bureaucracy. In November 1885 Li Feng-pao, Minister at Berlin, was cashiered as depraved and immoral. We know him to have been assiduously cultivated at Berlin, and the charge that he was led by bribes in the placing of orders is not an improbable one. It is

[1] O'Conor 372, 5.8.85, 17. 983.   [2] Parkes 297, 30.11.84, 17. 952.
[3] Wade 41, 17.2.80, 17. 830.
[4] Boulger, *Life of Sir Halliday Macartney*, 267 ff.   [5] *Ibid.* 311.

fair to add that corruption was not unknown in the Corps
Diplomatique at Peking either. Seward, U.S. Minister, was
accused as to his integrity in a previous post as Consul-General
at Shanghai. He was examined by a Committee of Congress;
the facts were hushed up, but he was asked to resign.[1]

The most distinguished of China's agents abroad was the
Marquis Tseng. He possessed of course as his right-hand man
Halliday Macartney, his father's old ally against the Taiping
rebels; a soldier to whom almost fell command of the Ever
Victorious Army, and a diplomatist of ability; faithful to
China, although at heart never so much Chinese as English.[2]
On Tseng's own capacity there were several opinions. Cordier
criticises him as excessively influenced by foreign advisers; with
too much French ink on his pen, for he attributes to this the war
in Tonking! At the end of 1885 Tseng was gazetted Junior
Vice-President of the Board of War, and the Legation Quarter
indulged sanguine hopes that his influence would be felt in a
progressive sense;[3] but his Yamen was soon as shabby as any
other, he shrank from meeting foreigners and even so he was
suspect to his countrymen.[4]

Returning to the Tsungli Yamen, we may run over the
other references to members that occur in our years. In
February 1883 Wade remarked that apart from Kung and one
man who was out of other place and in his dotage, the Grand
Secretary Pao was the only man who had been there since
1870; and Pao was now seventy-six years old and "had never
taken more than a show part in foreign affairs".[5] Shortly
before this, the already mentioned Wang Wen-shao was put
on trial for peculation, with Ching-lien to keep him company,
while another member was degraded for misconduct in the
Police Department.[6] In an abrupt Decree of 8 April 1884,

---

[1] Wade 134, 13.8.80, 17. 833; Thornton (Washington) 90, 95, 102 of
1880, 5. 1721.
[2] He was given a C.M.G. in 1881; and in 1884 was offered the 3rd Class
of the Double Dragon, but as a British subject had to decline. (See 17. 957.)
[3] Parkes 295, 29.11.84, 17. 952.   [4] Mrs Little, Li Hung-chang, 170.
[5] Wade, 8.2.82, 17. 1008.   [6] Grosvenor 131, 17.11.82, 17. 900.

cashiering Kung and three of his colleagues for their handling of the French war, Kung and Pao were treated least severely; they were let off with simple dismissal, the former on the score of ill-health, the latter of old age. The Grand Secretary Li Hung-tsao came in for a heavier stroke; he was described as "hampered by a want of ability and experience, with the result that he mismanages everything that he undertakes".[1] These words in no way exceeded the truth—Li Hung-tsao was one of those diplomats who realise that the fewer thoughts one cultivates the better one can succeed at hiding one's thoughts—but it would seem a confession of the justice of foreign complaints to publish such charges. Three members put in as stop-gaps that autumn were obscure and insignificant.[2]

Ill-health and duties elsewhere had latterly rendered Prince Kung's attendance at the Yamen infrequent. Among many dotards and obstructionists he stood out as its most dignified figure. Even before it existed—and it was he who made it—he had been in charge of "barbarian affairs". He was among the highest personages in China, by his rank and by having been a fellow-conspirator with the Empress Tzu Hsi in the *coup d'état* that opened to her forty years of power. Even he was not safe from the treacherous whirlpools of Court life; he had suffered dismissal before 1884. His name in the streets of Peking was "Head Clerk No. 6" (chief Minister and Sixth Prince), or "Foreign Devil No. 6" (i.e. pro-foreign).[3] One who crossed swords with him professionally wrote: "Prince Kung is a past master in the art of Oriental diplomacy. He studies the men pitted against him in any given contest even more carefully than the question at issue."[4] He was a genial figure, handsome though pock-marked, and ready to chaff an English attaché about his eyeglass.[5] He must have added a touch of colour as

[1] Copy with Parkes 80, 16.4.84, 17. 849.
[2] O'Conor 371, 1.8.84, 17. 983.
[3] Holcombe, *The Real Chinaman*, 215.
[4] *Ibid.* 22. It is said that native employees in the Legations kept the Yamen informed of their masters' characters. (Mrs Little, *Li Hung-chang*, 182.)
[5] Redesdale, *Memories*, II, 358-9.

well as of dignity to the Yamen, for we read that he habitually dressed in Imperial yellow, or else in purple silk under an otter-skin jacket, and had yellow tassels on his pipe.[1]

Prince Kung gave himself to repairing Buddhist temples until 1895, and his place as President was taken by the Pei-le Yi K'uang. The latter, a cadet of the Imperial House, owed his advancement to the Seventh Prince, the ferocious Ch'un, father of the Emperor; that Scorpion being at the moment in the ascendant. In November of the same year Yi K'uang was raised to the dignity of a Prince of the second order, with the title of his adoptive father, Ch'ing. He remained head of the Yamen for many years, and was at last brought back to Peking, after the Boxer defeat, through streets crowded with foreign soldiery. He was grandson by adoption of Ho Shen, and lived in part of that fabulous old extortioner's palace; he is described as notoriously corrupt.[2]

Western estimates of this remarkable institution varied greatly. Looking at it, we may think of the verses of Su Tung-p'o on a young child:

> I, through intelligence
> Having wrecked my whole life,
> Only hope the baby will prove
> Ignorant and stupid.
> Then he will crown a tranquil life
> By becoming a Cabinet Minister.[3]

Occasionally, as always happens with an opponent of whom little is known, it was credited with a vast cleverness. Many considered, like Curzon, that the Yamen mastered thoroughly at least the technique of playing off one Power against another.[4] It may also be allowed that the Ministers—"the wary old rogues", as a vivacious consul called them[5]—were not always dense at moments when they looked dense. It was an asset to

---

[1] Mrs Gordon Cumming, *Wanderings in China*, China, ch. xxxvi.
[2] Bland and Blackhouse, *Annals and Memoirs of the Court of Peking*, 365.
[3] Trans. by Waley.
[4] *Problems of the Far East*, ch. ix.   [5] Parker, *John Chinaman*, 172.

them that some of them were stupid while some only looked stupid, and the foreigner did not always know which was which. It remains that they were no cabal of supersubtle intriguers, but a set of old men with minds half submerged beneath the waters of the past. In 1884 they betrayed ignorance of the fact that there was an Anglo-Chinese Convention on Chusan.[1] They persisted in obstruction long after they ought to have been maturing more potent strategies. And Chirol, who interviewed them in 1896, says: "Their Excellencies talk glibly of the balance of power in Europe, but Austria still seems hopelessly mixed up in their minds with Holland."[2]

[1] Parkes 33 Most conf., 11.2.84, 17. 948.
[2] Chirol, *Far Eastern Question*, 55.

CHAPTER THREE

The Kashgar Crisis

AT the end of 1879 the Governor of Hongkong wrote to Sir Thomas Wade that, according to the best-informed people in the colony, "we may look forward with confidence to a prosperous and quiet 1880".[1] The best-informed people of Hongkong were to prove, as not unseldom happened, mistaken.

During 1876 and 1877 the army of General Tso was making its way through the north-western deserts towards the re-conquest of Chinese Turkestan, lost to the Empire by rebellion and the usurpation of Yakoub Beg. On 16 March 1878, the *Peking Gazette* was at last able to announce that Tso's operations were complete. The Emperor worshipped and burned incense in the temples of the Forbidden City; and a Decree conveyed to all loyal subjects the pleasing intelligence that four rebel leaders had been made an example of by being cut in pieces, and eleven hundred of the commonalty had suffered decapitation.[2]

These arrangements having been adjusted, the question which placed itself on the agenda of Far Eastern history was: Whether Russia was to hand over, or be allowed to retain, the Kulja province in western Sinkiang, occupied "temporarily" by her during the anarchy in which Chinese rule had foundered.

The circumstances resembled those after the Boxer Rebellion when the Russians were discovered in possession of Manchuria. The steady oozing of Russian soldiery across Asia was in pro-gress, and there seemed little reason to expect the release of any area once submerged. Kulja had large mineral and oil deposits, and could be made a rich producer of cotton. Its soil was

---

[1] Governor Hennessey to Wade, 16.12.79, with Col. Off. to F.O. 30.1.80, 17. 845.   [2] Frazer (Chargé, Peking) 57, 23.3.78, 17. 826.

fertile, and though Kaulbars estimated the population at only
150,000, in Chinese times it had supported more than double
that number.[1] Schuyler, an American explorer, thought it the
richest district that had been acquired by Russia in recent years.[2]
But Russia had blundered in without much thinking, and was
now uncertain what to do. According to the Chinese, St
Petersburg began by promising to evacuate, but later sent a
General Bogolavsky to Peking to persuade them that they
would be much better off without Kulja.[3] Russian administra-
tors, not knowing how long they were to remain, had not
undertaken any work of development—a fact which tells
against the idea that they had from the first a settled intention
of keeping what they had got.

What most concerned China was that the loss of this remote
outpost would weaken her frontier and open the way to fresh
Russian advances. General Tso impressed this on his Government in several Memorials, copies of which were "procured
indirectly" by a British consul. "Foreign nations", he said,
"have for a long time turned their eager attention towards
China....If we are strong, they are friendly enough; if weak,
they all entertain hostile demands; but what, it is needless to
dwell upon, is the very real danger threatening China, is
Russia's gradual encroachment, inch by inch and foot by foot,
on the frontier."[4] China had watched Russia with suspicion
for twenty years.[5] Muscovy, the rising state in which Defoe
had seen a future conqueror of China, was at last ready to fulfil
his prophecy. All over Chinese Turkestan everything was still
in disorder, and our Ambassador at St Petersburg thought it
likely that some of the disorder was being fomented by Russia,[6]
who evidently meant to keep a free hand.

Behind and overshadowing the Russo-Chinese issue lay the
deep hostility of Russia and England. When China had first

[1] Schuyler, *Turkestan*, II, 197.   [2] *Ibid.* II, 198.
[3] Cordier, *Relations etc.*, 174-5.
[4] Copy with Frazer 105, 22.6.78, 17. 826.   [5] Wade 5, 5.1.80, 17. 829.
[6] Lord A. Loftus 17, 15.1.79, referring to an expedition into Kashgaria in
that month by Hakim Khan, a pretender to the throne.

sent her troops towards Kashgar, Sir R. Alcock had written that Russia and England would no more be able to remain passive spectators than could Austria and Russia in the Herzegovina.[1] The Indian Government was keeping a close eye on Turkestan.[2] In and out of Central Asia itself, Anglo-Russian enmity was a familiar fact. The Khan of Khiva, in January 1880, put himself in touch with our Ambassador at Constantinople, to know if we would help rid him of his enforced treaty with the Tsar. The Ambassador was informed from London that we could not see our way to helping the Khan just now.[3] It was far from impossible that the Anglo-Russian war everyone expected might be started by events in Kashgar. A Captain of the Royal Engineers, travelling in Western China, had to give up his plans of visiting the North West for fear of war breaking out and his services being required.[4] It was rumoured that the forces moving up in support of China's claims on Kulja were accompanied by British officers.[5]

In January 1879 a Chinese Envoy, Chung Hou, was sent to St Petersburg to secure a settlement. He had been to Paris in 1871 to apologise for the Tientsin massacre; this, among mandarins, was sufficient to invest him with a mastery of foreign affairs. Sir Harry Parkes, who had met him, thought him at all events politer than the ordinary run of mandarins, but Lady Parkes heard that his amiability had suffered with the years.[6] His main defects, according to Wells Williams, were "an unusually Boeotian temperament" combined with an inspissated ignorance of the case at issue.[7]

Some delay was caused on Chung's advent by uncertainty as to whether he ought to be treated as an Ambassador or merely

[1] "Relations of Western Powers with the East", *Fortnightly*, Jan. 1876.

[2] A Mr Ney Elias was sent on a mission of inspection early in 1880; and Hervey, Officer on Special Duty at Ladakh, mentions having sent a native agent to Kashgar. (Report with Indian Govt. 143, 19.12.79, 65. 109.)

[3] F.O. to I.O. 1106 Secret, 1.1.80, and 1153 Secret, 9.1.80; F.O. to Layard (Constantinople) 68 Secret, 28.1.80; 65. 1097.

[4] Gill, *River of Golden Sand*, 145.

[5] Mrs Little, *Li Hung-chang*, 131.   [6] *Life of Parkes*, II, 265.

[7] Wells Williams, *The Middle Kingdom*, II, 731.

as an Envoy Extraordinary and Minister Plenipotentiary.[1] But he had no reason to complain of his reception. The initial hitch smoothed out of the way, he found himself most flatteringly welcomed.[2] In April he told a member of the British Embassy that Russia consented to retrocede Kulja, and only commercial questions remained.[3] It is quite likely that the Russians duped him. An Oriental diplomat, in their view, does not know what truth means; there is, therefore, no point in telling it him. In September Chung finished his negotiations and went to Livadia in the South, where the Court lay, to sign a treaty. At the beginning of October Sir Thomas Wade at Peking congratulated the Tsungli Yamen on an arrangement having been effected. He detected in his hearers an ominous lack of enthusiasm.[4] On 11 October Chung left St Petersburg for Marseilles and home.

Of the Treaty of Livadia Cordier writes: "Il faut que' Tch'oung Héou ait été frappé d'aliénation mentale pour avoir signé un traité pareil."[5] What leaked out of the terms was received by the public at Peking with a furious outburst of resentment. Seizing its cue with panic-stricken promptness, the Yamen at once advised the Throne against accepting the treaty.[6] Chung landed at Hongkong and was welcomed by Governor Hennessey. The latter was reprimanded for giving him a salute of guns;[7] but Chung had worse things ahead. No sooner was he back in China than he was arrested and deprived of his rank, formally on the charge of having returned home without authorisation. Clearly the real charge against him was to have left a strategically important part of the disputed region in the

[1] Lord A. Loftus 40, 28.1.79, 17. 826.
[2] Kalnoky, Austrian Ambassador at St Petersburg, was impressed by "the caressing nature of the reception which the Chinese Embassy had met with in high quarters in Petersburgh". (Egerton (Vienna), 2.10.79, 17. 826; cp. Plunkett (Chargé, St Petersburg) 516, 10.10.79, 17. 826.)
[3] Dufferin (St Petersburg) 128, 19.4.79, 17. 826.
[4] Wade tel., 2.10.79, 17. 826.
[5] *Op. cit.* 191.
[6] Wade 24, 8.2.80, 17. 830.
[7] Correspondence on the Governor's mistake of etiquette in 17. 845.

hands of Russia. Tso was his most violent assailant;[1] he was naturally piqued at the thought of any of his laborious conquests being relinquished.

Sir Thomas Wade was taken aback. He was from the outset, it may be remarked, pessimistic about China's ability to enforce her claims—but then he had originally doubted China's ability to re-enter Turkestan at all. Western observers of the crisis suffered from two defects of vision. They did not comprehend the importance China attached to her distant land frontier, and her sense of the dangers it was exposed to, because they thought too much about the sea and the coast. Secondly, they failed to perceive in public feeling a genuine concern for China's integrity, the earliest ardour of a national sentiment in the Western sense, not a mere "obstinacy" of unworldly scholars. Wade interviewed the Yamen on 14 January, and warned the Ministers that, if their minds were made up to repudiation of the treaty, they must prepare for war. "They did not disguise their apprehensions." Wade derived the impression that they—like the luckless Khan of Khiva—would be glad of a defensive alliance with England.[2]

Tso's astonishing successes had riveted attention in England, and it was plain, wrote the *Quarterly Review*, that Chinese claims would be enforced at all hazards.[3] England was immediately and urgently desirous of averting war. Having most of the trade of China, she would lose most by the fighting. China, it was felt, was bound to lose in the long run, and then a wholesale Russian advance might ensue, and Russian dominance at Peking. To avert such consequences and the ruin of our influence we should have to enter the war ourselves, and not even a ghost of the European Concert of 1878 could be resurrected to confront the Tsar in the Far East. Already we were fighting in Afghanistan, and relations with Russia were sufficiently strained. When Lord Dufferin, our Ambassador, waited on Prince Gortchakoff with the compliments of the New Year, "His Highness seemed a good deal displeased and

[1] Wade 8, 14.1.80, 17. 829. [2] Wade 7, 14.1.80, 17. 829.
[3] April 1880.

agitated...and asked why it was we were so terribly suspicious of the Russian Government."[1]

As might be expected, Wade found the Russian Chargé d'Affaires in a state of high excitement over Chung Hou's disgrace. Koyander was proclaiming it a trick on China's part to get out of the Treaty, and insisting that here was an occasion for all the foreign Powers to stand shoulder to shoulder: if any of them selfishly encouraged China to "feel her own strength", she would end by expelling them all. This last had been a theme enlarged on by the Russian Legation in all the twenty years of its existence. "I have been satisfied for years", Wade commented, "that (Russia's) desire here is the non-emancipation of China from her barbarism."[2] England wanted the Chinese at least awake enough to buy goods. Russia wanted them torpid enough to be easily overpowered. At present, Koyander maintained—as did all who picked a quarrel with China at any time—that China's resistance was part of a general anti-foreign movement. In March the Russian consul at Shanghai suggested a joint naval demonstration.[3]

Wade was also testing his German colleague. Partly out of jealousy of England, Herr von Brandt had always co-operated closely with his Russian colleagues, with whom he was personally intimate. He was now saying that Chung Hou's fall would stimulate the war party at St Petersburg, and not troubling to affect much regret.[4] Thereafter he played the part of Sir Lucius O'Trigger, assuring the Tsar that there was snug lying in China. Germany, making due deductions from Brandt's tirades, wanted to see trouble in the Far East; first, because it would create arms orders (an agent of Krupps came out in the spring and did lucrative business); secondly, because it would give Germany—a newcomer—the chance of a foothold there; thirdly, for reasons of European politics. Bismarck would be glad to apply a Chinese leech to the Tsar, to bleed him into lassitude. The mandarins could not be too obstinate.

Li Hung-chang, the statesman who represented Reason in

[1] Dufferin 20, 14.1.80, 65. 1097. [2] Wade 14, 27.1.80, 17. 829.
[3] Dufferin 135, 16.3.80, 65. 1097. [4] Wade 14.

the Chinese Government tableau, was alarmed. He had just
bought some gunboats in England, and he ordered more. The
situation was complicated for him by the aggressive attitude of
Japan, over the Lewchew Islands dispute. He told Hart that
Japan was being egged on by Russia, and that China was facing
war with both. Hart believed that the war party in Japan was
likely soon to get the upper hand.[1]

With matters in this posture, Wade on 28 January surveyed
them in an exhaustive despatch. The time had come, he wrote,
when we must consider the advisability of assisting China to
organise her defences, if not of making an alliance with her,
supposing she requested this. Japanese and Russian designs
went so far as to threaten China's independence altogether, and
in view of our trade of fifty millions "it would be worth any
effort that we could make to prevent this Empire being broken
up". "Personally, I should advocate helping them (the Chinese),
guarantees or no guarantees....But this policy would not find
many supporters amongst Englishmen supposed to be ac-
quainted with China, out here or at home." It would certainly
involve risks. "There is not one of the larger Treaty powers
whose representative does not grudge us more or less our pre-
ponderant share in the trade with China. The magnitude of our
commercial interests is constantly mistaken for an equal measure
of political influence, which we no more possess than any
other barbarian state." Thus a British alliance with China
might launch such an invasion as would produce "the im-
poverishment of China for years to come, if not her complete
annihilation". Wade ended by asking for instructions on the
following points. If Japan blockaded the Yangtze, was he to
protest, resist, or acquiesce? Might he encourage China to hope
that British officers would be allowed to serve her in war against
Russia? What was he to say if China requested an alliance?[2]

Attention was given to the second of these questions, which
Wade brought up not for the first time. The War Office,
India Office and Admiralty were being kept closely in touch
with the crisis—though when the War Office asked for news

[1] Wade 14.   [2] Wade 15, 28.1.80, 17. 829.

about Kulja, Lord Tenterden (Under-Secretary at the Foreign
Office) minuted: "The War Office is rather leaky and it is not
desirable to send our Conf.dl papers about too freely."[1] Lord
Salisbury, as Foreign Secretary, had previously expressed his
belief in the utility of English officers entering Chinese service;
it gave them experience, and it was important "to have a
greater hold on the Chinese maritime power, whatever it
might be, than that of any other nation". Pauncefote, Assistant
Under-Secretary, considered that the risk of a breach of
neutrality outweighed the danger to be expected from China's
engaging German or American officers instead of British;[2] but
the War Office and Admiralty were confidentially advised
that they should not discourage officers from entering Chinese
service: such recruits would have to be struck off Her Majesty's
rolls in case of China being at war, but they might be reinstated
afterwards.[3] As to Wade's other questions, it is astonishing to
find how little notice was taken of them. They arrived shortly
before the fall of the Conservative Ministry, and Salisbury
minuted: "Stand over", not wishing to anticipate his successor,
Lord Granville. On 1 May the latter minuted: "This despatch
should now be considered", but his consideration did not go
far. There was an exchange of views among the permanent
officials. Tenterden scribbled to Pauncefote: "I should think
the best way to treat this Despatch which deals with hypo-
thetical questions as to what shd be done in case of war by
Russia and Japan on China would be to let it drop. What do
you say?" Pauncefote rejoined that Wade's questions could
not be answered now. He ought to be told to cable at once if
Russia or Japan blockaded the Ports. Belligerents were entitled
to blockade.

But the prospect of our enormous trade with China being suddenly
stopped by a Japanese blockade is so appalling that it has several
times occurred to me that it might be desirable to anticipate this
particular contingency by confidential consultation with France and

[1] Papers embodying these exchanges of views are in 17. 845.
[2] Memoranda on Wade 15.
[3] F.O. (to W.O. and Admiralty), 12.2.80 conf., 17. 845.

Germany and the U.S. and to ascertain their views on the question whether the Extraterritorial rights of foreign nations in Chinese ports, and the tremendous commercial interests at stake, would not justify them, morally at all events, in uniting to resist the exercise of this belligerent right at those Ports. On the whole however I am disposed to think that it would be wiser to wait till the pinch is felt—when public clamour may force the Govts. interested to adopt that view.[1]

It is always of interest to note Foreign Office references to public opinion, or "public clamour". It is instructive, one might add, to find English officials—usually engaged in asserting rights of blockade against recalcitrant neutrals—discerning moral grounds for denying those rights. The minute shows the high importance attached to our China trade. It also reveals a startling lack of preparedness on the part of the Foreign Office for the emergency it was warned might be near.

The hapless Chung Hou had been consigned to the Board of Punishments; it was declared that degradation alone was not enough to answer his case.[2] Prince Kung was a relation of Chung by marriage, but could not protect him; and some Ministers of the Yamen did not realise how perilous was the road they were treading. One of them, Wang, when the English Minister asked him if a rupture with Russia was at hand, exclaimed foolishly: "Rupture with a power with whom we have been two centuries at peace—impossible!" Wade urged on him that the Treaty should not be rejected with levity.[3] While they talked, Russia's Pacific squadron was being strengthened, and Wade was instructed to find out what he could of its movements.[4]

On 21 January the Board of Punishments represented that criticism of the Treaty was beyond its unaided perspicacity, and a High Committee was convened to examine it and Chung

[1] Memoranda on Wade 15. Cp. a letter of Parkes in 1885: "But if they (the Japanese) engage in war with China they would have to give a reason for it, and whether we shall let our large interests suffer for their rash fancies is a question." (*Life of Parkes*, II, 220 ff.)   [2] Wade 16, 29.1.80, 17. 829.
[3] Wade 18, 30.1.80, 17.829.   [4] F.O. to Wade 14, 29.1.80, 17. 827.

Hou's conduct.[1] His accusers for the most part knew as little of foreign affairs as of astronomy, and some of them were fastening on the case to make themselves a reputation; though the belief that the Chinese had no sense of patriotism and were indifferent to their country's fate is a fiction. Were not these scholars, vying with one another in classically-turned memorials on the dishonour of abandoning any inch of soil once owned by the Middle Kingdom, inspired by patriotism in its most authentic form?—even if they were the strangest war party ever seen, and their heads were filled with long dead bow-and-arrow campaigns, and they saw in fancy the armies of Holy Russia as another raid of nomads....[2] Li Hung-chang told Hillier of the British Legation later that the two Empresses themselves could not withstand the clamour for Chung's condemnation.[3] The Diplomatic Body met to discuss the situation; probably most of them agreed to some extent with Patenôtre, the French Chargé, who in a despatch to Paris described the outcry against Chung as "une sorte de manifestation du parti anti-Européen".[4] Von Brandt said that a protest from them would only make things worse for Chung. Patenôtre was at first inclined to concur, but Wade and Seward, the American, said they *must* protest because of public feeling at home. In the end four separate Notes were sent in. That of Seward was long and plainspoken, and described Chung's arrest as an "extraordinary proceeding". Wade pointed out to the Chinese Government how much its international relations would suffer if states to which it sent Envoys should see those Envoys dismissed and disgraced at a moment's notice. The Yamen was deaf to all appeals. It trusted to luck, and consoled itself with the thought that it was Li who would have to conduct the war.[5] Li, with more practical experience of war than the

[1] Wade 24, 8.2.80, 17. 830.
[2] Travelling in the interior in 1895, an Englishwoman was astonished to find the people crushed and stunned by the disastrous peace terms with Japan. (Mrs Little, *Li Hung-chang*, 246.)
[3] Wade 68, 19.5.80, 17. 831.   [4] Cordier, *Relations etc.* II, 193.
[5] Wade 24 and 25, 9.2.80, 17. 831; and Cordier, *Relations etc.* II, 193.

inmates of the Yamen, was far less at his ease. Tso, for his part, came out with another of his die-hard Memorials. He asserted that agitators with Russian passports were stirring up disaffection inside the country.[1] Koyander, still in his state of excitement, refused to make the usual (Chinese) New Year's call on the Yamen.[2]

Two despatches from Wade in mid-February give useful information about how the Chinese Government's mind was being made up for it. He happened to meet a Mr Martin, an American teacher in touch with members of the Yamen, and asked if he thought the latter were at all influenced by their notions of what was taking place in Europe. The native Press, Wade remarks, "now produces a vast amount of political matter, to which ten years ago, the government would have been utterly indifferent". Martin doubted if the Ministers were much actuated by reports of Russo-German tension in Europe, but they were counting on *English* help in case of a breach.[3] Wade also put on paper, in mentioning rumours that the Empress Tzu Hsi herself was swayed by the appeals of some of the fiery memorial-writers, the significant fact that the "patriotic" party were all *Chinese*, the Manchu councillors being in favour of peace but lacking ability as compared with their Chinese opponents, "who are all simply distinguished men of letters, but with no knowledge of foreign affairs, nor a notion of what war means. There is, unfortunately for the Dynasty, no doubt as to the deterioration of the Manchu, both in vigour and capacity."[4]

Wade visited Koyander to see if any means could be devised for healing the breach. Koyander put on a gloomy face, but Wade gathered the impression that this exterior concealed pleasurable anticipations of war. "He believes firmly that the Chinese will make no further way towards improvement, as we understand the word in our own interest, without another chastisement."[5] Brandt was now saying that Russia, by taking

[1] Copy with Wade 26, 10.2.80, 17. 830.
[2] Wade 33, 13.2.80, 17. 830.   [3] Wade 34, 14.2.80, 17. 830.
[4] Wade 38, 16.2.80, 17. 830.   [5] Wade 39, 16.2.80, 17. 830.

care of Kulja, had laid the Chinese under an ill-repaid obligation. Seward sympathised with the Chinese, but had been convinced by Russian assertions that the people of Kulja preferred to remain under the Tsar.[1]

Koyander—whom Wade judged an intelligent man—perhaps exaggerated his warlike sentiments in order to frighten Wade into frightening the Chinese into submission. There are three possibilities as to the policy of his superiors. Russia may have for a time intended war. Or she may have simply proposed to blackmail China. Or she may have been as destitute of a policy as the Foreign Office in London. The weight of indications seems to favour the third hypothesis. The language used by Giers, the acting Foreign Minister, was noticeably vague. He appeared reluctant to lay down definite terms. Russia had not recovered from the Turkish campaign (had it not been for that business she might have been tempted to play an even more officious part in the reconquest of Kashgaria); operations in the Far East would be difficult, Russian strategists regarded China as an unknown quantity, and they were not confident that she could be knocked down with a feather. Slight initial reverses would be damaging to prestige in Asia. Our Military Attaché at St Petersburg thought the Russian concentrations in Central Asia quite inadequate if China should prove to be in earnest.[2] It is not unlikely that the naval reinforcements were made with an eye mainly to what England might do. Giers may well have had enough insight to realise with what pleasure Bismarck would watch him gambling in the Far East. The Nihilist campaign was at its height, the Tsar virtually a prisoner. To drown the revolutionary movement with drums would be a familiar Tsarist manœuvre, but it had just been tried and had made the mischief worse. There was, indeed, a war party in Russia with which the idea of retroceding Ili was very unpopular; partly military, partly commercial. Commercial interest in Eastern Asia was neither absent

[1] Wade 40, 17.2.80, 17. 830.
[2] Dufferin 335, 12.8.80, 65. 1081. Cordier, who visited Russia in 1880, thought the same.

nor silent. During February the "Society of the Volunteer Fleet" despatched several of its ships on a Pacific tour.[1] It was collecting big boats, meant for transport of tea but capable of carrying troops. In the same month the "Society for Promotion of Russian Trade and Industry to China, Japan and East Siberia", in co-operation with the Ministers of Imperial Domain and the Interior, was sending out a M. Shalkovsky to investigate the decrease in sales of Russian manufactures in China, the competition met with in the tea trade, and so forth.[2]

The crisis continued to develope. On 23 February Wade cabled: "...Our squadron should certainly be reinforced. I do not think war certain but the Chinese are much alarmed and the danger from panic is great."[3] On 1 March the Chinese Government began work on a dry dock at Taku for repair of gunboats.[4] Two days later Chung Hou was sentenced to death.

The stir that Chung's degradation had created among foreigners was redoubled. All had reasons for making an outcry, either to dissuade the Chinese from running into war, or to add fuel to Russia's indignation, or to correct China's notion that she could get rid of obligations as easily as ambassadors. Besides, we can suppose the Corps Diplomatique to have felt some sympathy for a member of its profession suffering so undiplomatic a fate. Chung was to be beheaded after the autumn Assizes. Wade was at once instructed to try and save him. His efforts were encouraged by the Queen, who had received Chung during his former European mission.[5]

Thus, one year exactly since his brilliant reception at the Tsar's Court, the unhappy Chung lay awaiting the executioner's axe. He was timid of disposition, precisely the man to have been flattered or bullied by the Russians, and it was taken for granted

---

[1] Dufferin 62, 10.2.80, 65. 1078.   [2] Dufferin 62.

[3] Wade tel., 23.2.80, cypher, 17. 830.

[4] Wade 43, 1.3.80, 17. 830. A little later the Chinese Legation tried unsuccessfully to buy from England two ironclads recently acquired from Turkey. (Memo. by Pauncefote, 19.5.80, Granville Papers, 97. 621.)

[5] Minute on Wade's tel., 9.3.80, and letter from Ponsonby approving form of protest; 17. 830. The Queen sent a personal telegram to the Empress.

that the Yamen had been too slack to give him definite instructions. In April Wade again telegraphed to request more
protection for his nationals. Chinese troops were being moved
towards the frontier.[1] At this juncture other Powers began to
scent opportunity. Portugal talked more loudly about that
long-worried bone of contention, the sovereignty of Macao.
Italian interest in China now for the first time emerged into
daylight, although the first signal was nothing more unpleasant
than the visit of a Royal Prince.[2] Wade went down to Tientsin
to see his Admiral, Coote. The Chinese were sensibly shelving
their Japanese quarrel, but their fears of Russia were hourly
increasing and the foreign settlements in danger from mob
panic.[3] While at Tientsin Wade took the opportunity of
sounding Li Hung-chang. The "Bismarck of China" was in no
amiable temper; his nerves were evidently feeling the strain.
Chung Hou excepted, he stood to lose more than anyone in
the Empire, since he was sure to be blamed if things went
wrong. He received Hillier, of the Legation, brusquely, asking
unpleasaant questions—including the perennial one of why we
did not ratify the parts favourable to China of the Chefu
Convention. Wade called in person; Li was usually friendly
to him, and in this exigency, he thought, would be glad of a
discussion. But the Viceroy was as ungracious with him as with
Hillier. Wade was realist enough to guess that the Chinese suspected him of angling for a recompense for his good offices;
and at their interview he noticed the unnecessary presence of
two interpreters: he was convinced that they were spies set
upon Li by the Yamen, with a leading spirit of which, Shen
Kuei-fen, Li was on bad terms.[4]

Accordingly, Wade was not deterred from visiting Li a
second time. The Englishman begged urgently to be shown the
exact terms of the Treaty of Livadia. Li showed him a copy in
confidence, and he jotted down a hurried précis. Of eighteen
articles, China objected to eleven. The essential Russian gains
were: Five million roubles indemnity, opening of trade routes

[1] Wade 58 (Extender), 17.4.80, 17. 830.　　[2] Wade 66, 16.5.80, 17. 831.
[3] Wade 67, 19.5.80, 17. 831.　　[4] Wade 68, 19.5.80, 17. 831.

to Hankow, frontier "rectification" in Ili and Kashgaria, Russian consulates in certain places not open to trade. Li explained that he had been for temporising, Tso for violence, and Tso had carried the majority, the "purely academical" politicians. Li's arrogance was gone. He shared the apprehensions current over Russian reinforcements and Portuguese intrigues; we now hear of Spain too contemplating a little burglary. China's enemies were gathering round:

The little dogs and all,
Tray, Blanche, and Sweetheart, see, they bark at me.

Li was, then, "eager for the suggestion of any way of safety". Wade pressed home the warning that if China would not yield and could not resist, there would be many Powers eager to advance real or imaginary claims. Collective mediation, he continued, would be the best thing; but, knowing as he did that "in the opinion of many nothing was more desirable than the humiliation of China", he "could not undertake to reckon upon the equally cordial consent of all or even of most of the Treaty Powers". If China desired English mediation to persuade Russia to receive a new Envoy, Chung Hou must first be released.[1]

As a result of the talk Wade cabled his Government that it was essential negotiations should be kept open at St Petersburg: if Russia transferred them to Peking pressure on China would be greater, and the interference of other claimants would put her in a most serious position.[2] Wade also addressed an unofficial Note to Prince Kung, emphasising China's "extreme danger" and suggesting mediation.[3]

A few days later—the English Minister was still at Tientsin—Li called on him in no cheerful frame of mind with Peking's answer to the Note. The Yamen had caught at Wade's suggestion, but wanted Li to bear the responsibility, the odium, of memorialising the Throne upon it. Wade rejoined that Kung was the man who ought to undertake the duty. His

[1] Wade 69, 19.5.80, 17. 831.   [2] Wade tel., 24.5.80, 17. 831.
[3] Wade 74, 26.5.80, 17. 831.

motive was that he foresaw Chung's fate lying ready for the bold man who should recommend compromise, and he desired that Li, the life and soul of the cause of progress, should not be sacrificed. Li's language betrayed "how completely he mistrusted the Tsungli-Yamen's will or power for good. Its power, because of its lack of energy; and its lack of energy, because of its abject cowardice." He had told Hillier that forty Memorials demanded Chung's death, and ordinarily no one could live under such a pressure: five Memorials were enough to secure a man's dismissal, fifteen or twenty his death. Shen of the Yamen had procured Chung's appointment for the St Petersburg mission, and now he was so terrified at his nominee's disgrace that he had to take to his bed—the strain had "made an old man of him". Even Prince Kung could be accused of taking bribes.[1] Chinese policies must have been a good deal affected by the fact that there were always swarms of men waiting for office and factions inside the bureaucracy eager to dislodge each other in order to bring in their own supporters.

Wade's misgivings were deepened by another conference very soon after, when the Viceroy informed him that he had several times offered his resignation, which had hitherto been refused. "This last", Wade wrote home sadly with visions before him of years to be passed in argument with impossible senilities, "is news to me, and in my judgement very bad news. For if the Grand Secretary (Li) is despairing of his utility in the public service, the Empire stands a fair chance of being ruined between inaction and reaction. He is the chief of a small band of public men by whom, if by anyone, the Empire will be brought to adopt the reforms in its home and foreign policy that are indispensable to its independence."[2]

With another despatch Wade sent home a copy from the *Shanghai Courier* of one of the Memorials against Chung; that of Chang Chih-t'ung of the Han-lin Academy, "the ablest pen of the Empire". It is of interest because, as Wade said, the literati, "often ridiculed for their transparent selfishness", *were* nevertheless powerful. Chang expressed a deep concern at

[1] Wade 74.   [2] Wade 75, 26.5.80, 17. 831.

seeing "how troubles and difficulties daily accumulate, by the Europeans usurping our power, by the Japanese earnestly endeavouring to annex parts of our territory, and by the Russians who are stirring up mischief". Too sanguinely, he maintained that England and France would never allow a port like Tientsin to be bombarded. As to fighting, all would be well if the generals understood that they would meet with condign punishment in case of failure. Wade called the Memorial "a sadly bombastic and puerile state paper". It was not quite that. Chang's salient point was that to admit Russian overland trade on Russian terms would mean the eventual loss of Shansi and Kansu. His phraseology—"nothing more will be kept secret, everything will be known", the identification of "secrecy" and "sound government"—may sound childish, but it was a good argument all the same.[1]

The exertions of Li and Wade, now working cordially together, raised no rapid crops in the sterile soil of the Chinese Government's mind—"this wretched government", as Wade in his anxious impatience called it. He drew a little comfort from hearing that Chung had been saved from *instant* execution by no less than the Seventh Prince, Ch'un, father of the Emperor and the highest-placed subject in China, despite the fact that the Seventh Prince was a reactionary of reactionaries, and "reputed an intemperate savage, vicious and truculent".[2] There was marked division in the Grand Council, according to Li, on the proposal of mediation. Three members approved, one was neutral, one—probably Li Hung-tsao—was hostile. Wade asked his fellow-schemer if there was a prospect of China being induced by the crisis to put in hand reforms. Li Hung-chang shook his head.[3]

We now have some light on the attitude of another Power, France. A new French Minister, Bourée, arrived on 1 June at

[1] Copy with Wade 76, 26.5.80, 17. 831.
[2] Wade 77 and 78, 28.5.80, 17. 831. Ch'un's reputation seems partly undeserved; see Wade to Granville, priv. and conf., no. 2 of 22.12.83, 17. 943; and Balfour, *Leaves from my Chinese Scrapbook*, 50.
[3] Wade 80, 1.6.80, 17. 831.

Tientsin, and, as foreign Envoys always did on arrival, hastened to call on Li. Wade was naturally eager to meet him, and seized the earliest opportunity for a long talk. He was later to describe the Frenchman as "a somewhat audacious and not over discreet diplomatist";[1] at present he was much relieved to find him convinced that a Russo-Chinese war would be a disaster. Bourée had lately visited Russia, and considered her in far too bad a way to go to war.[2] It might be expected, seeing how soon afterwards France's ambition of an empire in the Far East began to disturb the air, that she would welcome a conflict likely to rob China of any power of resistance. Bourée, who plainly desired no such thing, had lately been head of the Oriental Department at the Quai d'Orsay, and it is natural to assume that he reflected official opinion. France in 1880 was only ten years away from Sedan. She could not afford to antagonise Russia by opposing her over Kashgaria; but she would not encourage Russia to attack China, for that would be playing into Bismarck's hands. France wanted the Tsar strong and determined, but in the Baltic, not the Yellow Sea. Bourée soon let it be known what was in his mind. As a Frenchman, he could say things to the Russians that they would not listen to from an Englishman.[3]

On 2 June Li visited Wade and begged him to stay on at Tientsin. He told the British Minister, under his breath, that there were hints of a reaction at Court. Prince Ch'un, worked on by the Grand Secretary Pao Yun, who had been worked on by Prince Kung—it showed how devious had to be the manipulations of those charged with China's foreign affairs—was bringing the all-powerful Second Empress to recognise the danger of shocking foreign opinion. This was agreeable hearing for Wade, but he reflected uncomfortably that if his and Li's efforts leaked out and raised a storm, Chung might be murdered in prison and the deed passed off as suicide. He was worried, too, lest Russia might consider it necessary to her dignity to make, instead of perhaps receiving, the declaration of war. Koyander was proclaiming that Chinese military

[1] Wade to Granville, priv. and conf., no. 1 of 22.12.83, 17. 943.
[2] Wade 81 and 82, 1.6.80, 17. 831.   [3] Wade 91, 29.6.80, 17. 831.

preparations justified those made by his own Government.[1] It was believed by observers on the spot that Russia would blockade Tientsin.[2] Our warships were being replaced with more powerful ones.[3]

On 27 June Wade was able to telegraph that the Yamen had shown him confidentially the draft of a Decree postponing Chung's execution. It was not satisfactory, "but the difficulties of this Government with the literary party are really very great". Bourée was promising to try and get his Government to join in mediation.[4] The Chinese Legation in London politely told the Foreign Office that Chung had been reprieved out of deference to the Queen's feelings, but Russia must not be told this.[5]

Before the end of June Wade returned to Peking, where in repeated interviews with the Yamen he strove to keep the Ministers' eyes open to the perils surrounding them. They had presented a Memorial, but the Empress was ill and Li Hung-tsao inflexible.[6] Wade urged with all the vehemence of which he was capable that they should not face Russia uncompromisingly, but should cede Kulja and give the indemnity demanded, "adding, what I have also repeated *ad nauseam*, in one crisis or another for the last twenty years", that China's true policy was to gain a breathing-space to organise her defences.[7] Wade, we see, was prepared for large concessions to Russia, in spite of British preoccupations in Central Asia, and, so grave was his anxiety, without instructions from home.

On 1 July Wade sent his gravest message hitherto. "Yamen hears...Russia is collecting large force in Siberia, and that Portugal will take part in the south. Situation is undoubtedly

[1] Wade 83, 2.6.80, and tel., 2.6.80, 17. 831.
[2] Wade tel., 11.6.80, 17. 831.
[3] Admiralty to F.O., 5.6.80, 17. 846. A minute on this says that the French and German ambassadors had asked whether we were strengthening our squadron in the Far East. This was also asked in the House of Commons.
[4] Wade tel., 27.6.80, 17. 831.
[5] Memo. by Lord Tenterden, 3.7.80, 17. 846.
[6] Wade 88, 28.6.80, 17. 831.
[7] Wade 91, 29.6.80, 17. 831.

serious. China is quite unprepared either to fight, or to say what she will yield." [1]

On 7 July the Decree of Grace reprieving Chung was circulated to the Corps Diplomatique. [2] China, however, was "making immense preparations for defence, though without much system". The Russian consul at Hankow began buying boats fit for landing troops. [3] Li now thought war inevitable, and was taking his measures in earnest. Wade doubted whether even Li's specially trained troops would stand against the Russians. In case of war he expected Russia would land troops between the Pei-ho and Newchwang, advance simultaneously from Vladivostok, and take Peking in no time. He had had occasion to work out similar plans himself before the Chefu Convention was signed. [4]

Wade was near giving up hope. When he interviewed the Yamen at the end of the first week of July, he was inclined to wash his hands of it and its fate. He made suggestions as to the line which a new Chinese Envoy might be instructed to take up at St Petersburg. [5] It will be seen that, however pessimistic about the situation, he was working in pretty close co-operation with the Chinese Government.

[1] Wade tel., 1.7.80, 17. 831.   [2] Wade tel., 7.7.80, 17. 831.
[3] Wade tel., 9.7.80, 17. 831.   [4] Wade 98, 9.7.80, 17. 831.
[5] Wade 90A, 8.7.80, 17. 831.

CHAPTER FOUR

Tseng's Mission to St Petersburg

I N June the Marquis Tseng at London acknowledged in a couplet of self-depreciatory verse[1] his commission to act as Chung Hou's successor. It was not a task that many men would have cared to receive. If he was firm in St Petersburg it meant war. If he was not firm there was every likelihood of his following his predecessor towards the block.[2] Chinese diplomats, sent abroad on impossible errands, resembled the mediaeval alchemist gaoled on bread and water and ordered to manufacture gold. In Russia Tseng was not credited with much skill, according to Koyander, who said Tseng was in the bad books of the Tsar for a speech he had once made at Hongkong.[3] However, he had with him his English Secretary of Legation, Halliday Macartney; and Li was corresponding steadily with him, an auspicious fact (except that Shen Kuei-fen was plying him with entirely opposite orders).[4] There were signs that Wade's adjurations were having some effect on the Yamen: Tseng called at the Foreign Office, before leaving London, to say that Sir Thomas was now looked upon at Peking as a friend to be consulted.[5] The Foreign Office realised how much would hang on Tseng's mission. Giers was saying that the time might be at hand when he would have to discuss intervention in China with England, whose commercial interests, he admitted, would

---

[1] Martin, *Hanlin Papers*, 387.
[2] There was nothing very exceptional in Chung's fate. Nine years later Sir Edwin Arnold crossed the Pacific in company with some suave and composed mandarins who were returning from a failure at Washington, and whose heads were rumoured to be in imminent danger. (Arnold, *Seas and Lands*, ch. x.)
[3] Wade 39, 16.2.80, 17. 830.   [4] Cordier, *Relations etc.* II, 219.
[5] F.O. (to Wade) 86 conf., 2.6.80, 17. 827.

have to be reckoned with;[1] although Koyander's instructions, so the French Chargé at St Petersburg was told, were that Russia would stand on the defensive and hear what Tseng had to say.[2] Lord Granville warned Tseng against the risks of war, and said Chung must be set at liberty; the Marquis said he would forward the advice to Peking.[3] But Macartney wrote a letter to the Press containing a warning to Russia not to count upon peace-at-any-price sentiment on China's side.[4] On 13 July Tseng appointed Chen Yuan-chi Chargé d'Affaires, and set off for St Petersburg.

His reception there was a good deal less expansive and cordial than that of his forerunner. Giers at their first meeting expressed strong displeasure at the non-ratification of the Treaty. He began, from his own account to Dufferin, by asking poor Tseng bluntly what he had come for, and "set forth in very energetic language his dissatisfaction with the general conduct of the Chinese Government".[5] Tseng answered in terms of vague import. In conversation with Dufferin, Giers took the line that Kulja in itself was not of value: what was crucial was the occurrence of Chinese outrages on Russian subjects.[6] This sounds disingenuous; and to talk of "Russian subjects"— mongrels from anywhere in Asia—was a perennial topic that a Minister might dilate on at any time when momentarily at a loss what to say. Dufferin did what he could for Tseng by telling Giers that England would use all her efforts to keep Russia and China friends. "For this announcement"—in the circumstances scarcely less than a veiled threat—"M. de Giers expressed himself duly grateful."[7]

Meanwhile rumours multiplied of Chinese troops crossing the border.[8] Dufferin's reports frequently mentioned the sending of fresh Russian warships to the Far East, and his Naval Attaché was busy finding out what he could about them. In

---

[1] Dufferin 235, 65. 1076.   [2] Cordier, *Relations etc.* II, 208.
[3] F.O. to Wade 105B, conf., 5.7.80, 17. 828.
[4] Boulger, *Life of Macartney*, 337.   [5] Dufferin 323, 6.8.80, 65. 1081.
[6] F.O. to Wade 127, 6.8.80, 17. 828.   [7] Dufferin 279, 29.6.80, 65. 1080.
[8] Dufferin 160, 6.4.80, 65. 1079; 257, 16.6.80, 65. 1080.

June a Ukase had contracted the authority of the Commander-in-Chief in the Pacific to simply naval affairs, which, wrote Dufferin, "at the present moment are considered to be of paramount importance".[1] More haste was shown than method. San Francisco was chosen as the base of supplies for naval operations, and a young man was sent off thither to take charge, in a great hurry but with no instructions whatever.[2]

Tseng begged for an audience with the Tsar; he was kept waiting for it, and Giers was very fierce about a "monstrous communication" he believed Tseng to have had from Peking, to the effect that Chung Hou was only being reprieved for so long as China should be satisfied with Russia's behaviour.[3] Tseng rightly judged it discreeter not to call on Dufferin, but was in touch with him through Macartney.[4]

To return to China. Wade was taking care not to let his colleagues know what had passed between him and Li at Tientsin.[5] He was aware that not all of them would approve. Brandt was his usual self: "To his colleagues he avows his desire to see China at war with no matter what power." He was deriding the Japanese, telling them what face they would lose if they yielded to China over the Lewchew Islands. Deveria, a French Legation interpreter, believed Japan and Russia had an agreement for common action from which the former would prefer to be free.[6] Brandt took a more open step in incitement of Russia. He let it be known that if fighting broke out he would allow no foreign-officered warship to interfere with German shipping, even carrying contraband.[7] It may be Brandt was bringing the idea simply out of his own head. He declared that he had taken the same line in Japan in 1874 when a Sino-Japanese war was in prospect, and had not even troubled to report his language to Berlin! He breakfasted with Wade on 13 July, and was keen on a joint arrangement

[1] Dufferin 265, 21.6.80, 65. 1080.
[2] Baron von Rosen, *Forty Years of Diplomacy*, I, 45.
[3] Dufferin 322, 2.8.80, 65. 1081.   [4] Dufferin 323, 6.8.80, 65. 1081.
[5] Wade 102, 10.7.80, 17. 831.   [6] Wade 103, 10.7.80, 17. 831.
[7] Wade tel., 14.7.80, 17. 832.

among the foreign admirals. As he was leaving he scandalised his host by remarking, "apropos of nothing, but with some emphasis...that he would tell the Chinese that he did not care a——for them".[1] Doubtless with a view to goading Russia on, he put it about that Chang Chih-t'ung's Memorial employed terms that made the Tsar a vassal of the Dragon Throne; and he let slip no chance of arguing that things were bound to get worse until someone brought China to her senses. He added, sincerely, he would rather see anyone else do the work than Germany. "The truth is", Wade wrote, "that Monsieur von Brandt and I approach the Russo-Chinese question in general as the advocates of entirely different policies."[2] When you are in Peking, was the German motto, do as the Russians do; and Wade cabled on 22 July: "I suspect him (Brandt) of an intention to annex something if Russia begins annexation."[3] As Bülow told the Reichstag when he took Kiaochow, the devil takes the hindmost and Germany would take care not to be the hindmost. In 1880 we are at the opening of Germany's colonial period, and Bismarck could not afford to be particular as to where he made his pile. Brandt's character, for the rest, only exaggerated the tendency of all foreign diplomacy in China, to render every difficulty of the Chinese Government an occasion for demands that might bring it down in anarchy.

On 21 July Wade telegraphed that the Yamen had given him a long memorandum, defending its whole case. This document, of which another copy was given to Bourée, was the most competent piece of work yet accomplished by the Yamen.[4] It asserted the importance of Ili as a key point on the frontier, and said that Chung Hou, when leaving, was ordered to be very cautious and report his every step: he first reported that Russia would give way, then that she wanted to keep

[1] Wade 107 Very conf., 16.7.80, 17. 832.
[2] Wade 108 conf., 19.7.80, 17. 832.
[3] Wade tel., 22.7.80, 17. 832. Cordier (*Relations etc.* II, 27) thinks that in the *Anna* incident in 1875 Brandt was aiming to acquire a naval station.
[4] Wade tel., 21.7.80, 17. 832. Cordier prints the memo. in full (*Relations etc.* II, 172 ff., 184 ff.).

certain territory, and then, despite notice that China could not agree, that he had already made terms.

Mediation was next discussed by the Corps Diplomatique, at which Koyander took offence; no one, he affirmed, could understand the dispute, except the two parties.[1] Wade telegraphed: "The great danger I apprehend if peace cannot be made, is more annexations on the vast Siberian frontier. That is the cradle of the ruling family, and loss of that territory may upset the dynasty, which there is nothing ready to replace."[2] Three days later Wade surveyed the ground in one of his encyclopaedic despatches. The severest difficulty he laboured under, he complained, was the "complete ineptitude" of the Chinese Government. There were only two men in the Yamen of any perceptible intelligence, Wang and Kung; and Kung, having already been twice disgraced, had to be cautious how he offended ruling opinion. "The chief power in the state I imagine must be the . . . Prince of Ch'un . . . who is credited with every vice." "His sentence is for open war." (It is pleasant to find Wade Miltonising under stress of emotion.) There was no love lost between Ch'un and Li Hung-chang. It was the latter who would have to bear the responsibility of war, and he was already contemplating fatalistically his certain failure and downfall. His own policy, Wade went on, was being guided by sympathy with China, and by British interests. Bourée made no affectation of sympathy. "Fresh from his own Foreign Office", he was convinced that the root of all evil lay in "the sinister influence of Germany in Europe". (A slightly melodramatic, but not meaningless, phrase.) Brandt would do his utmost to prevent peace, but the quarrel had in any case been growing for years. Russia's present conduct had a strong resemblance to previous actions of hers; the Treaty of 1858 which Mouraviev "wrested from an imbecile Governor", and which it was "an abuse of language to call a Treaty", and the immense concessions extorted by Ignatiev in the midst of China's misfortunes in 1860. He (Wade) was now satisfied that the Chinese were justified in denouncing Chung. "Whether

[1] Wade tel., 22.7.80, 17. 832.   [2] Wade tel., 22.7.80, 17. 832.

Chung Hou was cajoled or terrified [i.e. in Russia] I cannot ascertain. *He is too rich to have been bribed.*" Koyander, while denying that Russia meditated aggression, was inconsistently boasting that before long Russian troops would stand at the gates of Peking. War would make the loss of Manchuria certain, the end of the dynasty almost so. That would not disadvantage Russia, while Germany would probably step in eagerly and pocket some of the proceeds. If China were saddled with a large indemnity it could only be secured on the Customs, and foreign trade would suffer. As to Brandt, his latest aphorism was that "the Chinese would become insupportable once they were civilised".[1]

The Foreign Office was coming to share Wade's view that, policy apart, the Chinese had a case to state. When the Yamen's memorandum was received, Pauncefote minuted ungrammatically: "It is a clear and interesting statement and if true Chung Hou behaved very badly and the concessions exacted from him by Russia most grasping and excessive. . . .If the statement is true I wonder the Chinese don't give it the widest publicity." Dufferin should be instructed not to advise Tseng to ratify the Livadia Treaty.[2] This last is only a mild approach to what was being said in Russia, that foreign intrigue was inducing China not to carry out the treaty.[3]

The prospect of a blockade was coming nearer. In June Mr Fowler, M.P., had written to the Parliamentary Under-Secretary Sir Charles Dilke that there was much uneasiness in the City as to what Her Majesty's Government would do if the Russians blockaded Shanghai. Dilke persuaded him not to raise the matter in the House.[4] Hertslet, the Foreign Office Librarian, produced a memorandum on the blockade of Canton in 1857.[5] The Law Officers were asked whether extra-territoriality modified Russia's rights of blockade—if not, we might have to try and reach "some amicable understanding".[6] They

---

[1] Wade 118 Very conf., 25.7.80, 17. 832.   [2] Memo. 9.8.80, 17. 832.
[3] See e.g. Press extracts with Dufferin 138, 65. 1079.
[4] Fowler, 21.5.80, and minute, 17. 846.
[5] 15.7.80, 17. 846.   [6] 31.7.80, 17. 846.

considered it impossible to dispute the right of blockade, so that such an understanding would be desirable; but "The Cabinet", Lord Granville noted, "do not see their way to move in this."[1] Pauncefote, however, though "with great diffidence", repeated his opinion that Russia could not expect the Powers to submit tamely to a blockade, which would be to England especially a "very severe blow". We could neither evacuate all our nationals nor leave them at the mercy of the mob. He referred to the "solidarity" that had always been respected by the Powers in China, and argued that we were entitled to remonstrate and might well initiate joint mediation.[2]

On 9 August Wade wrote that war was imminent, while an authority on China at home was writing: "It is hardly possible to hope that war can be averted."[3] Admiral Coote had asked Struve, the Russian Minister in Japan, why the Russian fleet was assembling. Struve replied, making no bones about it— to settle with China. Brandt would do his utmost to keep China from accepting terms until Russia was ready to attack. A reliable French source of information said that while in Tientsin lately he had discussed with his Consul-General "what part of China would be suitable for immigration". Russia apparently was in one of the militant phases of her wavering policy. Wade detected hints of a new tactic: an armed demonstration and the setting up of a new Emperor under foreign influence.[4] This puppet would be Li Hung-chang, and the idea was being freely canvassed in the Press of the Ports and eagerly repeated by Li's enemies in the native Press.[5] "Chinese Gordon", paying an erratic visit to China at this juncture, found his old comrade-in-arms being instigated to rebel—probably by Brandt. He advised the Yamen to keep peace, or, if they must

---

[1] Law Officers to F.O. 11.8.80, and minute, 17. 847.
[2] Memo. 14.8.80, 17. 847.
[3] Boulger, in *Quarterly Review*, Aug. 1880.
[4] Wade 125 conf., 9.8.80, 17. 832.
[5] Boulger, *Life of Gordon*, 314. Boulger adds an absurd statement, that Brandt's orders were "to support the Peace Party in every way", and that Wade joined him in inviting Li to rebel!

fight, to remove the capital from Peking; and departed, leaving behind him a swarm of rumours.

During autumn the contest underwent rapid fluctuations. On 13 August Chung was unexpectedly liberated, in response, the Yamen told Bourée, to a telegraphic request from Tseng.[1] Brandt kept up his outcry for a collective naval gesture, at Chefu. Wade divined that Brandt's purpose was to leave the rest of the sea open for Russia; and he directed his Admiral to hold aloof. The Lewchew situation was turning out not to have been so far tranquillised as he had hoped. When Hillier went to the Yamen to sniff out what Brandt had been saying there, Shen told him that unwonted activity was noticeable in Japanese quarters.[2]

Some Ministers of the Yamen paid a visit to the British Legation, and observed that the minor claims on Russia's list were nearing settlement. Wade enquired sceptically what they would do if a Russian commissioner was suddenly heard to be on his way to Peking, ultimatum in pocket. The Ministers, their spirits dashed, said it would depend. Wade broke in that he saw they were resolved to frivol away time; they ought to make haste and settle all outstanding grievances of foreign Powers and especially those of Russia, and pay the required indemnity with a loan raised abroad on the security of concessions, mines, railways: for if ready cash were wanting the Russians might occupy, as security, frontier districts which could then be given up for lost.[3]

Russia in fact was about to bring forward new issues. Three Kurghiz Russian subjects, it was asserted, had had their ears treated by Chinese officials like those of Captain Jenkins.[4] Obviously Russia was gaining time to think. Chinese feeling seemed to harden. On 22 August Wade reported that changes in the Grand Council were imminent, and Li, compromised by the rumours about him, was in danger.[5] A Decree had just censured some members of the Council and ordered their trial.[6]

[1] Cordier, *Relations etc.* II, 217.   [2] Wade 140 conf., 22.8.80, 17. 833.
[3] Wade 140.   [4] Wade 142, 22.8.80, 17. 833.
[5] Wade 143, 22.8.80, 17. 833.   [6] Cordier, *Relations etc.* II, 219.

The notion was spreading in the Legations that women and children ought to be sent away. It may have emanated from Russian circles, which would be delighted to see the Legations withdrawn from Peking. Wade resisted any such ideas.[1]

A St Petersburg telegram of 24 August announced that Tseng had been received by the Tsar (who gave him a rub or two during the interview), so that negotiations could now go forward.[2] But Dufferin learned from Tseng that Giers was ambiguous and hard to understand; and a special agent, a M. Butsoff, was to be sent to Peking to conduct discussions there. The news about Butsoff alarmed Wade. On 10 September he, together with Bourée, wrestled with the Yamen to do anything, even ratify Livadia, before the Russian plenipotentiary could arrive. The Foreign Office thought this counsel precipitate; its nerves were not affected by the crisis like those of the man on the spot. Pauncefote minuted: "I was certainly startled by this announcement": Wade ought not to recommend unconditional surrender; Bourée undoubtedly must be aiming under cover of friendly advice to China, to promote a Russian triumph.[3] This was true up to a point.

On the day of Wade's struggle with the Yamen, the French Admiral arrived from Japan and said the Russian fleet had orders to be ready on the 15th. Brandt abruptly changed his tone in a pro-Chinese direction,[4] an odd but momentary shifting of his erratic violence. He speedily reiterated his orthodox doctrine that the Chinese stand against Russia was part of a vast anti-foreign movement.[5]

In the last week of September, the Chinese having agreed under pressure to furnish Tseng with full powers, the Tsar recalled Butsoff. The Russian paper *Golos* found something incomprehensible in China's sudden concession: "something

---

[1] Wade 147, 23.8.80, 17. 833.

[2] Plunkett (Chargé, St Petersburg) 402, 16.9.80, 65. 1081; and tel., 24.8.80, 17. 828.

[3] Wade tel., 10.9.80, and minutes, 17. 833. Boulger thinks the threat of transferring negotiations to Peking was only a bluff. (*Life of Macartney*, 343.)

[4] Wade tel., 10.9.80, 17. 833.   [5] Wade tel., 29.9.80, 17. 833.

mysterious" must have happened at Peking.[1] On 25 September the *Novoe Vremya*—called by Curzon the *ballon d'essai* of the Russian General Staff—threw out a presage of swinging indemnities by declaring military preparations to have cost 12 million roubles, and adding with crocodile tears that the entire salt tax, the harshest of peasant burdens, was needed to furnish that amount.[2] Tseng was anxious to be friendly, but the Bear's growls were still unintelligible, and he was waiting for Giers to talk plainly.[3] Plunkett—Chargé for Dufferin from September—came to the conclusion that Russia was no less anxious for peace than China, so that the latter might well simply leave Kulja under protest in Russian hands and let the question lapse. The Foreign Office, in passing information on to Wade, warned him that Tseng did not want what he told us bandied about. "It might be dangerous for him. The example of his predecessor evidently preoccupies him."[4]

Near the end of October, frightened by a hint that Butsoff might after all have to be sent to Peking, Tseng offered Kulja. He now declared he had given absolutely all he could, and begged the offices of England and other Powers to dissuade Russia from being too hard upon him.[5] Plunkett, running the risk of Russia's taking offence, appealed to Jomini of the Foreign Office not to put such pressure on China as would imperil the Dynasty. Jomini said there was no wish to do this, but affected an indifference towards Kulja as Russia's compensation.[6] If he really meant he did not desire a collapse of the Chinese Government, it must be that Russia felt her military strength at the moment unequal to the double task of beating China and securing the best share of the spoils. The Congress of Berlin was still green in her memory.

At the beginning of November Tseng felt his chances improved: Jomini agreed to put down his demands in black and

---

[1] Extract with Plunkett 420, 24.11.80, 65. 1082.
[2] Plunkett 423, 23.9.80, 65. 1082.
[3] F.O. to Wade tel., 18.10.80, 17. 828.   [4] F.O. tel., 19.10.80, 17. 828.
[5] F.O. to Wade tel., 27.10.80, and 1.11.80, 17. 828.
[6] F.O. to Wade tel., 1.11.80, 17. 828.

white.[1] Hitherto the Russian negotiators had been seeing what they could squeeze out of their victims, and declining to fix their price. Plunkett, whose reports were being read carefully at the Foreign Office (though the Queen seemed chiefly concerned at his blunder in spelling "Tsarevitch" instead of "Cesarewitch"[2])—Plunkett furnished on 10 November the Russian terms, divulged to him by Tseng: Livadia to be ratified but with a Protocol adding modifications. Tseng had offered all Kulja, but the Russians talked of returning part of it and appeared keenest on getting an indemnity to cover their military costs.[3] It shows how hard up they were; another reason for wanting to avoid a campaign. None the less, the response was unsatisfactory. Peking obstinately would not let Tseng agree to the word "indemnity", would allow Russia only one consul, and so on. Macartney was impatient, and thought a breach still to be feared unless friendly pressure were put on China. War, indeed, was still on the cards. A St Petersburg report stated that the Russian Government was trying to buy some British vessels for the convoy of 8000 troops to its Pacific ports.[4] Plunkett exhorted Tseng to show a conciliatory spirit, urging that China could not hope to defeat her adversary. Tseng defended his Government half-heartedly. He admitted he agreed with Plunkett—"War was now indeed probable, and, if so, defeat in the end for China was certain; but what could he do?"[5]

On 16 December Wade replied to an enquiry from the Foreign Office that the Yamen had during the past two months avoided the topic of Kashgar. Koyander declared that interference by any third party would make things worse, and the Chinese seemed afraid to talk.[6] A week later, however, Wade cabled: "I think peace more probable than I have yet thought

[1] F.O. to Wade tel., 3.11.80, 17. 828.
[2] Note from Windsor to Tenterden, 65. 1083.
[3] Plunkett 527A, Very conf., 10.11.80, 65. 1083.
[4] F.O. to Wade tel., 1.12.80, 17. 828.
[5] Plunkett 602 Very conf., 14.12.80, 65. 1083.
[6] Wade tel., 16.12.80, 17. 833.

it."[1] At St Petersburg there was a definite though somewhat obscure change; Macartney wrote to a friend that the devil was turning out not quite so black as he was painted.[2] On 3 January the Foreign Office, considering the Russian terms not excessive and their rejection by China equal to a declaration of war, told Wade to advise acceptance.[3] On the 14th a long telegram from Wade indicated how much the situation had changed:

With reference to my telegram no. 5 of last month, chargé d'affaires of Russia is become much more moderate as regards China, also more communicative. He believes there was a serious crisis at St Petersburg between 5th and 15th December after which the situation improved. He declared that annexation in the East would be fatal to Russia....French Minister has shown me a despatch of October last in which French chargé d'affaires at St Petersburg reports Russian Govt. much disquieted by sale of German rifles to China. China has at any rate contract for one hundred thousand German rifles, of which one fifth have been delivered. Fear of rupture with Russia is disappearing fast, but rumour of misunderstanding with Japan gains ground fast. Russia desires this. I suspect because she has designs on Corea. German Minister desires it because he believes trouble between China and Japan of advantage.[4]

Thus while Brandt was denouncing the Chinese Empire as a barrier to progress, his countrymen were busy selling China 100,000 rifles to employ against Russia. It was the same policy of egging on both sides that Germany adopted a year or two later in the Franco-Chinese war and is pursuing again in 1938. Armaments early became an important item in German sales in the Far East, and could be assisted by the fomenting of war scares. The 100,000 rifles, we may surmise, were eagerly brought to Koyander's notice by his French colleague.

At the time he sent the above telegram Wade still thought our naval strength ought to be raised. On the Foreign Office's

[1] Wade tel., 23.12.80, 17. 833.
[2] *Life of Macartney*, 349.
[3] F.O. to Wade 1, 3.1.81, 17. 833.
[4] Wade 5 tel. cyph. conf., 14.1.81, 17. 859.

enquiring why, he answered by cable: "I did not mean there was immediate danger. The position was this. Russia with large fleet doing nothing expected to attack Corea; Japanese affair further from settlement than ever....If China be drawn into trouble there will be serious insurrection."[1] But on 2 February he spoke of peace as nearly certain.[2] A few days later Dufferin telegraphed that a new treaty had been signed. By May the Russian Pacific fleet was known to be dispersing,[3] and on the 15th the treaty was confirmed at Peking. Tseng and Macartney returned to London "like conquerors from a triumph".[4]

In June Wade learned the terms concluded. Seventeen modifying articles were added to the old Treaty, regulating overland trade. In this commercial sphere Russia retained her advantages, and she was to have consulates at Suchou and Turfan at least. On the territorial question, which concerned China most nearly, Russia kept only the westernmost strip of Ili, the rest was retroceded; in return the indemnity was raised from five to nine million roubles.[5] These were the open terms. But the agreement set afloat many rumours. "When," Wade wrote a couple of years later, "much to the surprise of most people, and to the disappointment of all who desire for China a chronic state of trouble, the misunderstanding between China and Russia was brought to an end, it was very currently reported that Russia had obtained some concession not made public".[6]

So far as the published terms went, Gardner of the Consular

---

[1] Wade tel., 27.2.81, 17. 833.   [2] Wade 4, 2.2.81, 17. 857.
[3] F.O. to Wade 40, 5.5.81, 17. 856.   [4] *Life of Macartney.*
[5] Wade 32 conf., 22.6.81, 17. 856.

[6] Wade (in England) to F.O., 8.2.83, 17. 1008. He suspected that the secret concession related to telegraphs. On 20.2.83 he wrote: "My belief grows stronger that Russia came to an understanding with China in 1881 anent telegraphs." (*Ibid.*) Others thought it was a railway concession. A French text of the treaty was provided by the Chinese Legation in 1881; another was published in the *Journal de Pétersbourg.* Hertslet pointed out that the two differed somewhat. (Memo. 21.11.81, 17. 869.) The latter text appears in the Bluebook, China no. 1 of 1882.

Service, who was doing volunteer work at the Foreign Office on maps of Central Asia, observed that China gained a good deal by the new treaty, especially considering that the Tsar's holding Kulja during the war against Yakoub Beg had been of "enormous advantage" to her. "Except that the Treaty leaves Russia free to advance in other directions, I do not see that we are much interested in the matter."[1] Russia's new trading facilities caused some uneasiness in England.[2] Pauncefote observed that Russia could make what treaties she liked, "though it is a departure from the entente among European Governments in regard to China and Japan", but counter-concessions might be claimed from China.[3] The Law Officers found the question difficult: we ought not to admit in principle that China's neighbours could get lower tariffs on their land trade than we had to pay on our sea-borne trade; but each case must be judged on its merits, and this was hardly a satisfactory one on which to make out a general argument.[4] We allowed the matter to drop because we believed that transport costs would cancel out Russia's tariff advantage.

The significance of the crisis was twofold. It developed the breakdown of "solidarity", begun by our own separate action at Chefu and based on the new and divergent ambitions of the Powers. Secondly, China had now defied a threat of war and stood ready to defend herself with modern guns and warships.

Brandt was right in saying that the prospects of lasting tranquillity on the Russo-Chinese frontiers were illusory. The two Empires were now finally and intimately neighbours, and henceforth Russian pressure would be unintermittent. A St Petersburg Press article underlined the lesson. There was no hope in the long run, it said, of avoiding war. "China is seized with the universal spirit of progress and is striving to assert her position among nations....There can be no doubt that Russia

[1] Three memos in 17. 869.
[2] See e.g. memorials by London and other Chambers of Commerce, in 17. 912.
[3] Memo. 2.3.82, and memo. by Hertslet, 19.1.82, 17. 912.
[4] Law Officers to F.O., 16.5.82, 17. 913.

since her collision with China enters a new phase of her political position in Asia." Four years later Russia was again accused of fostering disaffection in Kashgaria; and England, partly to set a watch on Muscovite doings, took occasion to ask facilities for Indian trade there.[1] Russian economic and political penetration of Kashgaria continued up to the Russo-Japanese war.

Perhaps the best epilogue to this survey of the ways of Europe to China in 1880 can be taken from a communication addressed by the Portuguese to the English Government in June 1882.[2]

"As regards questions concerning the countries of Eastern Asia, the nations of Europe and America have maintained an unalterable good understanding in order to be able to lend their mutual aid in the effort to make the principles of the laws of peoples, and the legitimate interests of commerce and civilisation, to prevail."

[1] F.O. tel. 56 Secret, 17.3.85, 17. 975. Li told both the Legation and the Yamen he approved our request. (O'Conor 425, 12.10.85, enclosing a letter from him to the Viceroy of India, 17. 985). It was in line with Li's policy of multiplying foreign interests in areas menaced with absorption by a particular Power.

[2] Note on Macao. Copy with F.O. to Peking 82, 15.6.82, 17. 893.

CHAPTER FIVE

Corea, to the Rebellion of 1882

MORE and more, during the long struggle of words for
the war-scoured oases of Turkestan, Corea was in the
minds and despatches of the diplomats.[1] Russia had
designs there which were to develop irregularly until finally
scotched by the Battle of Mukden. Instead of returning to
tranquillity after the Treaty of Ili, the Far East only found itself
confronted by new problems.

The legendary history of the "Land of Morning Calm"
began in 2333 B.C., when the son of Heaven's creator came down
upon a mountain to rule under the name of Tan Gun for a
thousand years. He may have chosen his kingdom from appreciation of the scenery, and his people have appreciated it
ever since. Corea is a country of landscape: among its mountains
and valleys the Coreans lived from century to century in a
seclusion so deep, even beside that of China, as to earn their
land the name of the "Hermit Kingdom". It was poor, backward, ill-governed, famine-ridden. Still, though nobles might
monopolise high office, in the villages there was a good deal of
self-government;[2] and the people were rich in leisure if in
nothing else; they appeared to travellers from the active West
to do nothing except smoke and sleep.[3] Resigned to low
material standards, the Coreans evolved an outlook that had its
compensations in love of nature, of poetry, and of the arts
of social intercourse. Scholars of a district would meet and
"lament how short life was to play with the muse. The big

[1] And of unofficial observers; see Grundry, *China and her Neighbours*, 213,
and Ross, *History of Corea*, 307.

[2] W. R. Carles, *Life in Corea*, 153, 263.

[3] Cavendish, *Korea and the Sacred White Mountain*, 84; Brigham, *A Year
in China*, 82.

world was a kind of house, they said, where we lived but temporarily, dreaming a little romance, dreaming a little adventure, but we were soon sped on our way in order to make room for the other guests...." Life was a long unbroken sensation "lasting thousands of years, in which the same experiences, the same thoughts, the same life came unceasingly, like the constantly reappearing flowers of Spring".[1] Whatever the state of affairs, it would be hard at any rate to show that it has been improved by Corea's loss of independence.[2]

The Government was, indeed, as worthless as it could be made out. Its grand vice lay in the hordes of useless hangers-on who made every official a burden to his district. The army was the most preposterous of all the ragged regiments of the East: its muskets lacked triggers, and were tied together with string.[3]

Already before 1880 this fantastic kingdom, dozing with the monastery bells of the Diamond Mountains in its ears, felt its sleep disturbed by rude sounds from abroad. At the time of the Restoration in Japan the ancient claim of the Mikados to suzerainty was renewed, and refused. From then on there was a party in Japan straining at the leash to begin an attack. Other Powers soon began taking an interest. So early as 1874 Parkes, then Minister at Yedo, wrote to his friend Consul Robertson in China: "I hope Korea may not pass into (Russian) hands some fine day."[4] A British diplomat at Paris wrote to Lord Tenterden in 1876: "it is a mistake to go on feeling our way on the outskirts of Corea", especially with France watching and emulating our every move; if we meant to go on, we must make up our minds to use force.[5] Adventurous travellers were trying to get into the country. A Japanese smuggled himself in in 1875, disguised in native mourning clothes, and was disgusted by the stinking food and houses he encountered.[6] There

[1] Younghill Kang, *The Grass Roof* (autobiography).
[2] For a careful study of Japanese economic exploitation of Corea, see Hoon K. Lee, *Land Utilisation and Rural Economy in Korea.*
[3] Curzon, *Problems of the Far East*, ch. v.   [4] *Life of Parkes*, II, 194.
[5] Adams, 5.5.76, Tenterden Papers, F.O. 363. 1.
[6] *Transactions of the Asiatic Society of Japan*, XI.

was a tendency, soon disappointed, to imagine that Corea held a vast potential trade.[1]

Corea in the 'seventies was ruled by the Tai Wen Kun, once a ruined nobleman who was said to have forced the previous King on his deathbed to declare his son successor, and now Regent. He understudied, so to speak, the father of the Chinese Emperor, Prince Ch'un. His hatred of missionaries brought down an unsuccessful attack by France. The United States also failed in an armed attempt to open Corea. But in 1876 Corea had to make her first modern treaty, with Japan.

In the autumn of 1879, the Japanese Chargé at Seoul, Hanabusa, who had been negotiating for satisfaction of grievances, secured the opening to his country's trade of two fresh ports. The inclination of his Government at the moment was to hope that other Powers would establish relations with Corea, trusting that this would push open the door for advantages that Japan might be able to corner, and that it would forestall any sudden Corean coup meditated by Russia. In October the Foreign Minister Inouye informed the British Minister at Yedo that "Russia had made attempts to get possession of the port of Yinsan, and would certainly renew those attempts in the event of complications"; and on that account Japan would be relieved to see Corea fortified by regular relations with Western states.[2] Inouye was aware that his hearer would not be indifferent. The year before, Satow of our Yedo Legation had visited Corea, and was suspected of wanting to get a treaty.[3] Wade lost no opportunity of repeating to the Tsungli Yamen "that the persistent exclusiveness of the small states dependent on China...was a source of danger both to China and to themselves".[4]

China's attitude, like Japan's, was wavering and ambiguous. It was usually admitted that Corea was her dependency. The

[1] Morrison, "Notes of a Trip to Corea", in *Journal of the China branch of the R.A.S.* xviii (1883), 141 ff.
[2] Parkes (Yedo) 174, 10.10.79, and 190 conf., 27.10.79, 46. 248.
[3] Treat, *Diplomatic Relations between the U.S. and Japan*, 75.
[4] Wade 91, 29.6.80, 17. 831.

precise nature of the relation, however, was indefinite in the extreme. On this the whole strategy of Chinese diplomats hinged. According to the prevailing wind, they would assure importunate foreigners either that Corea was virtually autonomous and would listen to no advice from Peking, or that Corea belonged to them body and soul.[1] There was as a matter of fact room to conjecture that Corean exclusiveness had its roots in Seoul, not in Peking.[2]

Thus, when in June 1880 Sir Thomas Wade, having heard that a Japanese colonel was suspiciously busy surveying east of the Wall, conveyed to the Yamen for the hundredth time his advice to open Corea, Tung Hsun replied blandly that "the Coreans were too obstinate to listen to reason". Wade was disgusted. He, personally, expected little from Corea in the way of trade; his standpoint was that the loss of Corea would be politically serious for China, and the only way to avert it was to allow several Powers such a vested interest in the country that no one of them would be able to annex it. He also feared that the Americans, who wanted a treaty with Corea, might turn for help to the designing Russians, with whom they were already too much inclined to fraternise.[3]

In the summer of 1880 an English official visited Corea and made authentic observations. He composed a full account,[4] which still retains freshness and interest, and it may be permissible to abandon the Legation Quarter for a short time to follow him along the beautiful though treacherous coasts of Corea, whose rocks had seen the end of many a ship and many a mariner far from home.

Mr Spence, of the Consular Service, had received while in Italy an invitation to accompany the Crown Prince, the Duke of Genoa, on a Far Eastern cruise. The Duke had been welcomed

---

[1] Rockhill of the U.S. Legation at Peking set himself to examine the relationship (*Journal of the American Oriental Society*, VIII); he examined all possible documents and data, and ended by confessing definition impossible. Cp. translation of a Corean text in *Journal of the China branch of the R.A.S.* XVIII, 883, 25 ff.   [2] Ross, *History of Corea*, 290.
[3] Wade 91.   [4] Sent with Wade 5, 18.2.81, 17. 857; published.

by the Mikado in the winter of 1879, and had added to that pagan monarch's collection of foreign decorations the Most Christian Order of the Annunciata.[1] Spence joined his ship, the *Vettor Pisani*, at Kobe on 26 July, and two days later they began their Corean cruise from—it has a prophetic sound—Shimonoseki.

The Duke took pains to let everyone know that his visit was one of curiosity pure and simple. Spence did not take His Highness too literally, and warned him, as did other seasoned observers, that it was useless to think of getting into touch with any Corean officials through the Japanese, as the latter desired to monopolise the country. The Prince wrote to the Prefect at Fusan, their first call, though he could find no better pretext than the obligation of thanking the Corean Government for kindness shown to an Italian sailor shipwrecked on the coast some years before. The Prefect returned a reply through the Japanese consul to the effect that there was no need of thanks; as to the Prince's letter, he was forbidden by law to read it. The consul said that, unfortunately, the Prefect was just now far away. Spence, who had his wits about him, was amused to see the Prefect in the Japanese settlement, spending the day with the consul.[2]

They made their way along the as yet imperfectly charted coasts, gathering geographical data as they went. Here and there they diverted themselves by rowing ashore to converse with the natives. The latter were invariably friendly,[3] despite Japanese warnings, and there would be long though silent talks, each side scrawling Chinese characters on the sand. Once some fisherfolk were brought aboard, into Spence's cabin. A dialogue

[1] Kennedy (Chargé, Yedo) 204, 12.12.79, 46. 248.

[2] Treat (*Diplomatic Relations etc.* 125) seems not to admit that the Japanese had changed their minds away from the idea of welcoming Westerners into Corea, and refers to Japanese help given to the American envoy Schufeldt. But this was from desire to enlist his goodwill in the Lewchew dispute. See *Life of Parkes*, II, 205.

[3] Another explorer was warned off by officials, but a native told him that the people all wanted acquaintance with the foreigners. (Review of Oppert, "The Forbidden Land", *Chambers' Journal*, 18 Sept. 1880.)

took place, and was written down. It is a scene that appeals to the imagination, this fumbling eager contact of two worlds in a little stifling cabin tossing off a remote jungle-clothed coast. It is regrettable to have to add that Spence was annoyed by their dirtiness, and their wanting to feel his hair.

The Coreans could not be got to talk of their Government, and insisted there were no officials in those parts—"We never make a disturbance." All efforts to get hold of an official were of no avail, until finally one day there came off shore in a pair of junks a Prefect, an affable greybeard, with his tag-rag retinue. He was received with *empressement*, and conducted below. A picturesque scene ensued that fixed itself on the Englishman's memory—silent question and answer between himself, translating for the Prince's aide Count Candiani, and the old functionary with his secretaries sitting round him on the floor in a ring writing busily, while his disreputable followers pilfered whatever they could lay hands on, and the Prince watched with amusement. The Prefect was most unwilling to receive a despatch for the capital, but under pressure he with many misgivings accepted one. It harped once more on the shipwrecked sailor, who would have been flattered had he known the solicitude felt about him by the Crown Prince of Italy; touched on the Laws of Humanity; and, coming to the point, said that a treaty with Italy would be exceptionally advantageous to Corea. Candiani, to test the old man's grasp of foreign affairs, threw out a remark that China and Russia seemed about to go to war. The shot did not go home very effectively, and presently the visitors all poured off over the side into their junks, banging instruments and trying to eat all that had been pressed upon them, including a cake of soap Spence would have been glad to make them use properly. The guns gave them a salute, after they had been warned not to take fright, and they disappeared from the ship and from history.

Spence's narrative was "read with much interest" at the Foreign Office, where some modicum of thought was being expended on Corea. Satow was getting further information out of a young Corean, in the light of which it seemed that force would be necessary to open Corea. Kennedy, now Chargé d'Affaires at Yedo, thought it would be unwise to use force: Corea had been arming lately. In January these opinions were under discussion in London. Parkes, who was in England, was for risking an attempt, since he believed in the theory of a Russian menace to Corea.[1] Wade was instructed by telegram to sound the Chinese Government on whether it would lend us its aid in getting a treaty.[2] He had just cabled home: "It is generally thought that Russia will seize something in Corea in Spring."[3] In fact, he anticipated the Foreign Office's instructions. The Chinese Government's torpor was at last dispelled, and it was itself urging Corea to open her ports. Wade knew that for a single Power, especially England, to meddle in Corea, would simply precipitate the threatened Russian attack; so he asked the Tsungli Yamen to announce that Corea was open to treaty relations. The Yamen "very warmly" approved.[4] Li Hung-chang, who as Viceroy of Pechili had charge of Corean affairs, had already begged England to make a treaty with Corea,[5] so there seemed no obstacle.

None the less, developments were not forthcoming very rapidly. The Yamen, tractable enough in the spring when Admiral Lessolsky was concentrating his ships with the rumoured intention of seizing Port Lazarev,[6] abated its enthusiasm as soon as it felt the Russian crisis safely over. So did some English observers. Kennedy wrote privately in June: "My interest in that wretched country has subsided since the departure of the Russian Fleet",[7] though he heard a little later from a French missionary that the "wretched country" was

[1] Kennedy 131 Very conf., 27.7.80, with memo. by Satow and F.O. minutes, 46. 271.
[2] F.O. to Wade 7 (Extender), 20.1.81, 17. 856.
[3] Wade tel. 3, 7.1.81, 17. 859.   [4] Wade tel. 10, 9.2.81, 17. 859.
[5] Wade 17 conf., 12.5.82, 17. 895. In the autumn of 1878 Li wrote to a Corean dignitary—drawing an apt parallel from the history of the T'ang Dynasty—that Russia, having made peace with Turkey, would soon turn eastwards. (Copy with Kennedy 131 Very conf., 27.7.81, 46. 271.)
[6] Kennedy 30 conf., 24.3.81, 46. 271.
[7] Kennedy to Tenterden, 3.6.81, Tenterden Papers, 363. 1.

full of minerals.[1] The War Office asked for information about "the Corea" for its Intelligence Department. The Foreign Office said it had none.[2]

It was the United States that took the lead, with Commodore Schufeldt as pioneer. He was sent out in some secrecy, the U.S. Legation at Peking not being notified, and was furnished with full powers in January 1882.[3] The Admiralty soon had its eye on him, and ordered our Admiral on the China Station (now Willes) to watch what he was doing and, if possible, imitate him in securing a treaty. In May news was heard that an American squadron was assembling, apparently meaning to negotiate with a display of force.[4] The Russians, Wade noted, were suspicious of Willes, and he heard from the French, who were allowed to go over Russian warships, that many officers on the latter were disappointed at the Kashgar trouble having blown over without their getting at least Port Lazarev.[5] This doubtless renewed Wade's uneasiness; and the Yamen had reason to resume its progressive attitude of the previous spring. It bestowed paternal advice on Seoul. Its fear of Russian and Japanese intentions, wrote Wade, "which may be described as chronic, has I doubt not been stimulated by the proceedings of the French in Tonquin".[6] Besides, Commodore Schufeldt was bitterly offended, having been tricked, he considered, by Chinese offers to give him a naval post already filled. It was necessary to do something to soothe him.

By the middle of May, when he received instructions from the Foreign Office to exert himself against any interference with American wishes, Wade was able to report that Li, Schufeldt and Holcombe, the American Chargé, practically had the thing thrashed out among them already. Holcombe found that he could always keep the Chinese in hand by hinting that if they did not give him what he wanted he would have recourse to

---

[1] Kennedy to Tenterden, 28.9.81, *ibid.*
[2] F.O. to War Office, 19.3.81, 17. 870.
[3] Sears, *History of American Foreign Relations*, 380–1.
[4] Admiralty to F.O., 23.5.82, 17. 913; Wade 16, 12.5.82, 17. 895.
[5] Wade 17 conf., 12.5.82, 17. 895.   [6] Wade 18 conf., 12.5.82, 17. 895.

the Japanese. Wade saw the agreed terms in advance. Corea's dependence on China was not to be questioned; in this China drew her compensation. Schufeldt has been credited with defeating Li's desire for explicit recognition of China's suzerainty,[1] but the mere fact of his negotiating at Tientsin recognised it in actuality. There were several points in the treaty we did not like, the worst thing being the American promise not to trade in opium.[2] Allusions to opium, conveying the innuendo that India's export to the Far East was not quite wholesome refreshment, were always felt sensitively by Englishmen. Li told Wade, who was at Tientsin keeping in touch with the business, that he would insist on an article enforcing Chinese sovereignty in any treaty that might be made with Corea. China's prestige was suffering by the nibbling away of her tributary states—he mentioned Siam, Annam, Lewchew, and made "a slight allusion to the possible absorption of Birma by ourselves".[3]

Schufeldt went to Corea accompanied by some Chinese gunboats, and signed what most considered a bungled treaty. Whatever its details, Corean conservatives were outraged; one, named Ni Man-sun, put on mourning clothes, presented a petition to the King, and with seven hundred followers sat for seven days outside the Palace.[4] Rumours were put about, possibly from interested quarters, that Admiral Willes meant to follow Schufeldt to Corea with a fleet in order to secure a treaty. Wade took care to dispel any such fear from Li's mind.[5] He found Li a prey to anxiety over the responsibility he was committing himself to in helping England to a Corean treaty.[6] Because of this uneasy state of mind, as well as from filial piety, when his mother died at this juncture his petitions for leave to retire and mourn her were remarkably impassioned; though they only resulted in his being granted 100 days instead of the

---

[1] Sears, *History, etc.* 381–2. For text of the treaty see *British and Foreign State Papers*, LXXIII.
[2] Wade 19 conf., 12.5.82, 17. 895.   [3] Wade 20 conf., 12.5.82, 17. 895.
[4] Griffis, *Corea the Hermit Nation*, 431.
[5] Wade 22 conf., 17.5.82, 17. 895.   [6] Wade 23 conf., 23.5.82, 17. 895.

ritual twenty-seven months.[1] Wade was more sanguine; he, after all, stood in no danger of suddenly finding himself disgraced by a paragraph in the *Peking Gazette*.[2] He was furnished with a letter for Willes to put into the hands of Ma, Chinese Commissioner at Seoul, and the Admiral set off.

The French now entered the stage. Bourée wanted to imitate us. Wade had no objection; the more Powers stationed agents at Seoul, the more secure from Russian warships Corea's harbours would be. He tried to obtain for the French a letter of recommendation to Ma similar to the one provided for Willes. The Chinese put no very genial face on the matter. They alleged as an obstacle the connection between the French Government and the Roman missionaries, who were anathema in Corea. The Americans had sagaciously agreed to pocket their religious zeal and say nothing about missionaries. The *Missions Étrangères*, whose field embraced Corea, could be counted on for indiscretion; their members were all Frenchmen; no one short of the Pope could restrain them. Wade warned the Chinese that many a Frenchman who cared less than nothing for religion would be ready to see his Government take strong action in favour of the missionaries if he felt that the honour of France was being slighted.[3] But French aggression in Tonking was embittering Peking, and was aggravated by suspicions of undeclared designs in Corea also. French policy as regards Corea may have been meant partly to create a diversion and keep eyes away from Indo-China. It may have aimed directly at annexation in Corea. It almost certainly took Russia's peculiar interests into account and intended to put France in a position where she could be of use to Russia. Wade's object meanwhile was to smooth the way so as to lessen the risk of complications. France, if she saw others getting treaties while she was excluded, might launch an attack; and then the rest of the Powers, now loftily condemning French aggressiveness in Tonking, would not hesitate to join in and pick China's pocket.

[1] His petition is printed in Douglas, *Li Hung-chang*, 188–9.
[2] Wade 28, 27.5.82, 17. 895.
[3] Wade 31 conf., 2.6.82, 17. 895.

Russia would then inevitably obtain ice-free naval bases from whence to confront the fleet based on Hongkong, and no acquisition on our part could compensate for that.

Hughes, our Shanghai consul, contributed a bulletin at the end of May; Schufeldt had talked with him when passing through. The Commodore said he had found the Coreans "very anxious to sign a treaty", and that the Japanese agent at Seoul was dismayed at his having acted without Japanese sponsors. Hughes further mentioned that a German Commodore was leaving for Corea next Thursday.[1] The procession was thickening.

At the beginning of July Wade had a long report from Maude, who had gone with the Admiral as interpreter. When the report reached the Foreign Office Lord Granville marked it "amusing". Upon the Admiral and his faithful squire reaching Seoul, they were pleased to find the Tao-tai Ma very willing to help them; but when Willes requested an audience with the King, Ma said that would be difficult, as the Government was "une espèce de féodalité" (Ma had served a spell at Paris) and the King was almost alone in his family in favouring foreign relations. Besides the terms granted America, Willes wanted leave for English warships to visit Corean waters and survey the coasts; but Spence, who was expected, failed to turn up, and they did not trust themselves to alter the American phrasing for fear of losing the meaning.[2] During an interview a Corean Under-Secretary of State fell asleep and had to be kicked awake by an interpreter.[3] Willes got a treaty that might, he confessed, be thought somewhat bald; but he felt the main thing was to get a footing.[4]

During July the Germans also got a treaty, identical with ours. There was by now therefore a certain amount of vested interest in Corea, and with this bone to stick in Russia's throat if she tried to swallow the country both Wade and Li could sleep easier. One of our men, Aston, met the Japanese Resident

[1] Hughes 29.5.82, with Wade 33 conf., 3.6.82, 17. 896.
[2] For text see British and Foreign State Papers, 1883.
[3] Wade 51, 6.7.82, 17. 897.   [4] See his report, 9.6.82, 17. 915.

Hanabusa, who was taking philosophically the failure of his monopolistic plans and even remarked that, since Corea's dependence on China was beyond dispute, there was no reason why it should not be recognised in treaties.[1] As to trading prospects, the Germans were disappointed with what they saw.[2] Wade's own opinion was that the trade would have to be in the hands of Chinese factors; "but this, I take leave to say, is not... against the interests of the Western producer. The Western trader has heavy expenses to pay and a fortune to make. The Chinese factor's expenses are comparatively light, and his notions of fortune-making not extravagant."[3]

Harmony was rudely broken in upon. In July the faction of the Tai Wen Kun broke into insurrection and attacked Japanese in Seoul. The Queen had to make an escape, while a lady who impersonated her lost her life. She was an energetic woman, heiress of the powerful Min clan, and strove to keep the weak King independent of his father.[4] Twelve years later she was to be murdered with Japanese complicity.

News of the outbreak arrived at Peking about the first day of August. China acted with startling vigour and rapidity.[5] Within three weeks, three thousand Chinese troops and a squadron of warships were on the coasts of Corea. A few weeks more and the insurrection was crushed, not without some fighting. Most of the prisoners were summarily executed. Ma, just back from a mission to India, was given discretionary powers to arrest the Tai Wen Kun. He invited that statesman to dinner, put him into a sedan chair, and sent him a captive to Tientsin.

On 25 August Wade, who had been summoned home to confer on the opium question, had his farewell interview with the Yamen. Corea formed the staple of conversation, naturally. The Ministers were much perturbed, despite their bold action, as to what line Japan would take, and what England would

[1] Aston, 5.7.82, 17. 915.　　[2] Wade 63, 28.7.82, 17. 897.
[3] Wade 67, 3.8.82, 17. 897.
[4] See W. F. Sands, *Undiplomatic Memories*, 63.
[5] Grosvenor (Chargé, Peking) 85, 12.9.82, 17. 897.

think. Wade pointed out that Japan would of course be angry; her Government wanted to refurbish, in Corea, prestige lost in various failures abroad, and had already been sufficiently offended by recent infringements of her monopoly. Wade's advice to the Yamen—the last he was ever to bestow on it— was that, having once sent in troops, China should restore order vigorously, as delay would encourage the Japanese to take the law into their own hands, and other parties would not fail to egg them on.[1] The crisis caused the issue of a Decree hinting to Li Hung-chang that he ought to terminate his mourning.[2] But at the end of August a settlement was signed between Corea and Japan. It contained much that Wang of the Yamen described complacently as "empty words"; but it gave Japan 500,000 dollars indemnity, and 50,000 to the families of Japanese citizens who had lost their lives; and the limits within which the Japanese were free to travel were extended to 100 *li* from the Ports.[3]

Thus far, the Anglo-Chinese Corean policy, as it may be called, had worked out to the satisfaction of both its promoters. Corean envoys sent to Peking after the outbreak was suppressed gave the British Legation an assurance that Corea fully intended to abide by her treaties.[4] China for her part had publicly asserted her authority. Two Decrees inserted in the *Gazette* after the insurrection bore witness to her determination to retain absolute control.[5] Grosvenor feared that her success would further stimulate her arrogance.[6] But sanguine Westerners congratulated themselves that "the very last *Terra Incognita* among the nations of the earth has, at last, succumbed to the inevitable and irresistible march of human progress".[7]

[1] Wade 1 and 2 Separate, 25.8.82, 17. 898.
[2] Wade 3 Separate, 25.8.82, 17. 898.
[3] Grosvenor 84, 12.9.82, 17. 898. Text in *B.F.S.P.* LXXIV.
[4] Grosvenor 94, 25.9.82, 17. 898.
[5] Copies with Grosvenor 96, 30.9.82, 17. 898.   [6] Grosvenor 85.
[7] *Korea*, pamphlet by Frazar, Corean Consul-General at New York, 1894.

CHAPTER SIX

Tonking, to September 1883

ETWEEN 1882 and 1884, the northern frontier crisis
was repeated, with variations, from the south.
In the great peninsula where the Hindu and Chinese
civilisations shade into each other, France had long been busy
trying to compensate herself for the loss of India. By various
methods of fraud and violence, her power was gradually extending itself in the sun-drowsed, jungle-hidden seclusion of Cam-
bodia and Annam. There, where the tropical heat seemed to melt
everything into a languid indistinctness, ambitions grew with
a tropical luxuriance and found no fixed limits. The idea once
formed, of taking over as it were the family ancestors with the
estate—of assuming the time-blurred pretensions of the antique
capitals occupied—gorgeous vistas opened, for each of the
somnolent kingdoms of Indo-China had once been an imperial
mistress, and the ghosts of many vanished realms haunted this
world of ruins.[1] Thus, by an imitation of the Chambres de
Réunion of Louis XIV, Frenchmen made their way farther and
farther, as though pushing a path merely through so much
yielding vegetation. The rice country was rich; among the hills
minerals lay hidden;[2] and beyond—here was half the seduction—
stretched South China and all the unsounded, thrilling promises
of its commerce.[3] Partly the advance was the unordered work

[1] There was still a woman in Annam, descended from the ancient Cham
rulers who ruled before the name of Annam was known, saluted as Queen
by a few mountain villagers. (Norden, *Wanderer in Indo-China*, 76.)
[2] Mining experts of the French Government were at work from November
1881 to March 1882, and presented a rosy report. "These deposits", commented the *Journal of the Iron and Steel Institute*, "may prove to be of enormous
value for the supply of fuel to steamships in the far East." (Vol. II of 1883.)
[3] Tseng said to Granville in March 1884 "that the object of the French
was and had been from the origin the Chinese province of Yunnan". (F.O.
to Peking 60, 13.3.84, 17. 947.)

(86)

of officials and soldiers anxious to achieve some distinction in their exile and not remain buried out of mind, sunk amid their remote forests. Partly, increasingly, it came to be urged forward by the speculations and intrigues of men of finance in far away Paris, men to whom the bright-coloured sun-drenched lands of Indo-China were names, symbols of wealth, unsubstantial counters on a gaming-table.

Some of China's dependent states were connected with her by almost imaginary links: the Mandarin Road into Annam, before it became Route Coloniale No. 1, was something different. Cordier argues at length that China's suzerainty was, historically, a cobweb.[1] But a cobweb in Asia might be as strong and useful as a chain in Europe. The Annamese Royal House was a cadet branch of a Chinese imperial family. Officials were sent down from Peking as they might be to Hunan or Fukien. Annamese could serve as officials in China. Chinese traders were to a great extent in control of the economic life of the country. The frontier forts were jointly garrisoned. But the paramount feeling at Peking was that to have a Power as restless as France, and one friendly with Russia, installed on the southern frontiers, would subject them to the same pressure as the northern boundary had long known, and put in hazard the integrity of the empire. Vassal state or neutral zone, there must be a barrier between China's and France's possessions. It is worth remembering that England was ready to fight France in 1893 in order to enforce the same safeguard for her own empire in the same region.

The Treaty of 1874 with Annam was a milestone in French progress. It did not, however, satisfy the ambitions of the colonial party. "Les Annamites dans leur relations avec la Chine tenaient le traité de 1874 comme non avenu."[2] They continued to send tribute missions to Peking—in 1877, again in 1880.[3] The Chinese, for their part, when France announced that she had taken over the protectorate of Annam, were noncommittal.

---

[1] Cordier, *Relations etc.* II, 334 ff. [2] *Ibid.* II, 287.
[3] On these missions see C. B. Norman, *Tonkin*, 166, 173.

At the beginning of 1880 the Tsungli Yamen conveyed to the French Chargé d'Affaires, in a rather eccentric manner, that China's interest in Tonking was strong.[1] No reply was made. A new French Minister—Bourée—was coming out, and he was coming with "a plan drawn up in Paris": to occupy the Red River valley while China was engaged with Russia, and thus put a barrier between China and Annam.[2] In November Tseng wrote from St Petersburg to the French Foreign Minister to ask for reassurances as to Tonking, which he called a vassal of China. The Minister answered that, on the contrary, Tonking was a vassal of Annam, which was under French protection. Tseng's rejoinder was a strong one: China did not recognise the Treaty of 1874.[3]

The ground at issue was thus defined. Had the French been content to swallow Annam quietly and remain south of Hanoi, China might have kept equally quiet: once Tonking was put in question, Peking was compelled to make a stand. The French were mixing up two programmes; the stiffening of control over Annam, and the advance up the Red River through Tonking towards the trade of South China.

1882 was signalised by the French expedition to Hanoi, and the taking of the citadel by Rivière. A sum was voted in Paris for a flotilla to suppress piracy in Tonking. Really, wrote Halliday Macartney to Pauncefote, the money was for *starting* some piracy.[4] Tseng requested an interview with Lord Granville, to ask whether England assented to the Treaty of 1874; and Pauncefote pointed out that we had protested at the time and received reassurances from Paris that our interests in Annam would not be squeezed out.[5] Lord Lyons at Paris was instructed to find out what he could,[6] and our consul at Saigon was furnishing reports.[7] In May Tseng asked for the with-

[1] Cordier, *Relations etc.* II, 305-7.

[2] *Ibid.* II, 308.   [3] *Ibid.* II, 243, 316, 321.

[4] 3.1.82, 27. 2705; printed in *Life of Macartney*, 362.

[5] Memo. by Pauncefote, 25.2.82, 17. 912; cp. conf. memo. on French claim of jurisdiction over foreigners in Annam, 12.12.82, 17. 914.

[6] F.O. to Lyons 604, 26.5.82, 27. 2705.

[7] Tremlett, 7 Political, 25.11.82, 27. 2705.

drawal of French troops from Tonking, and the same language was used at Peking.[1] Wade, being at Tientsin, called on Li in a private capacity and discussed France's designs in Corea and Tonking. Li was "excited". He had once suggested that England should make a treaty with Annam in order to check the French,[2] but Wade did not think this feasible with the French so firmly established. He admitted that China was faced with the prospect of having "a very restless neighbour, whose declared object is to push a trade across the southern frontier".[3] A month later Tseng was expressing in London his fear that a French attack was in the offing, and China's determination not to recede.[4] The Press of the Far East was predicting a conquest of Tonking. Wade several times sounded his French colleague. Bourée assured the Yamen that France had no intention of destroying the autonomy of Annam; the Yamen took the statement for what it was worth, and remained "seriously irritated". Wade's personal view was that "There is nothing to be done": France could not be stopped. He advised the Chinese to avoid a collision. Germany's point of view was well defined; that was not difficult, as Brandt had only one motto, to fish in troubled waters and make sure that the waters were properly troubled. He had suddenly exchanged his tirades against all things Chinese for loud talk in support of the Chinese side[5]—after dinning incessantly into Bourée's ears that France ought to invade Tonking.[6]

The French pushed on with their task of bringing Liberty, Equality and Fraternity (as a Cochin China editor put it)[7] into

[1] Cordier, *Relations etc.* II, 353.

[2] At various times the French may have suspected that England might anticipate them in Tonking. Decazes, instructing a new Governor of Cochin China in 1877 that it would be too risky to embark on adventures in Tonking, added that France could not afford to see Tonking occupied by "une grande Puissance maritime hostile ou seulement rivale". (*Documents Diplomatiques Français*, Series 1, II, 202.)

[3] Wade 22 conf., 17.5.82, 17. 895.

[4] F.O. to Peking 76, 2.6.82, 17. 893.

[5] Wade 59 conf., 24.7.82, 17. 897.   [6] Cordier, *Relations etc.* II, 341.

[7] Reprinted in *Économiste Français*, 13.3.80.

the Red River valley; the Chinese with a deepening resolution to resist the said Trinity, continued to move their armies southward. A traveller in the south met a magistrate setting off to look into the conduct of certain unruly tribes—the French.[1] In November Bourée interviewed Li at Tientsin. Li insisted that the French must withdraw from positions they had lately been occupying. Bourée had cabled to Paris for powers to negotiate.[2] He had said at the Yamen, Tseng told the Foreign Office, that the Governor of Saigon was going further than any French Government would approve. Tseng was convinced it was a diplomatic manœuvre, and said "the French Government was so much influenced by speculators and others with schemes for their personal advantage in Tonquin that it was not safe to rely upon the Ministers having the strength and moral courage to carry out the good intentions by which they may possibly be animated....In view of the vital interests which China had in Tonquin they would feel themselves compelled in defence of those interests and in deference to public opinion, to resist at whatever cost, any attempt on the part of France either to annex Tonquin, or to establish a protectorate over it. ...War between China and France would be the inevitable result if the French Government persisted in the present policy of aggression in Annam." Tseng ended by making for the first time the suggestion that British intervention would be welcomed by China. Lord Granville replied that it might do harm as easily as good, but if a sound opening offered he would make use of it.[3] "I am afraid", scribbled a Foreign Office personage a few days later, apropos of the execution of a Chinese in Tonking, "that the Chinese Govt. mean to raise the question of their suzerainty over Annam."[4]

Both sides had used such warlike language that it is astonishing

[1] Colquhoun, Across Chryse, II, 201.

[2] Grosvenor (Chargé) 138 conf., 25.11.82, 17. 900.

[3] F.O. to Peking 169A, 4.12.82, 17. 894.

[4] 13.12.82, 17. 911. Papers on the case referred to in 17. 939. The French consul at Hongkong had given notice that "les Annamites n'ont aucun pouvoir pour traiter directement avec les nations étrangères." (6.7.82, with C.O. to F.O., 8.5.83, 17. 941.)

to find, in this same month of December, a compromise agreed upon at Tientsin. It was made between Li, who was throughout less warlike than Tseng, and Bourée, who was considerably less warlike than Paris. The day after Tseng's interview with Granville, Bourée was able to telegraph: "La guerre avec la Chine semblait inévitable; je crois maintenant que le danger est écarté; après une résistance opiniâtre, le Gouvernement consent à rappeler ses troupes du Tong-King."[1] A fortnight later he telegraphed the terms.[2] Yunnan was to be opened to trade: Tonking was to be "protected" by France, except for a frontier zone: France was to respect the autonomy of Annam.

Bourée had really got excellent terms; the South China trade was brought in sight, the autonomy of Annam was a metaphysical concept only. It is not certain that Peking would have accepted the terms; Li later said that they were examined by Ministers and rejected. On the other hand, later on in Paris Bourée showed Wade a telegram from Li indicating that Peking *would* have accepted the terms, and got Wade to write a statement that the Chinese text did convey that sense.[3] In any case, French recklessness ruined the chance of peace. In February 1883 Ferry became Premier, with Challemel-Lacour as his Foreign Minister, and Paris had now travelled far from Freycinet's dictum of January 1880 that whatever happened war with China should be avoided, because it would not be worth the candle.[4] The new men decided that Bourée's Convention could not be accepted, since it admitted China's right to interest herself in the status of Annam. To give point to their decision, they informed Bourée that he was to be recalled.[5] Much crestfallen at the *éclatant désaveu*, he replied:

[1] Cordier, *Relations etc.* II, 360.   [2] *Ibid.* 361.
[3] Wade to Granville priv. and conf., no. 1 of 22.11.83, 17. 943.
[4] Cordier, *Relations etc.* II, 308.
[5] Cordier (*ibid.* 364–6) believes that Bourée's fall was partly due to extraneous intrigues of French residents in Shanghai. Critics said that Bourée had been bluffed by Li into adopting his pacific views, with an abruptness for which his previous despatches left his chiefs unprepared. (*L'Affaire du Tonkin*, par un Diplomate, 20–21, 27.)

"Je doute que l'on ait pu peser à Paris toutes les conséquences de la décision que vous me notifiez."[1] He saw Li again in March, and the Viceroy "doubled his fists like a boxer" and said that if France would not recognise China's suzerainty "c'est comme cela qu'il faudra faire".[2] Next month a Decree was issued opening the Red River to trade. Since the French had asserted this to be their objective, the step was likely to take the wind out of their sails. Annam requested permission to station a consul at Hongkong.[3]

In the middle of April Grosvenor, our Chargé, had a most informing conversation with Bourée. The Frenchman, labouring under a sense of injury, talked with unprofessional lack of reserve. He asked what force would be needed to occupy Tonking. Twelve thousand men, answered the Englishman, and a fleet. Bourée broke out into a diatribe on his Government's folly. Paris, he said bitterly—just as Tseng had done—was in the hands of speculators, who had formed the Société des Mines de Tonquin and wanted to drive up the shares by means of the heartening effect on the Bourse of a military advance. "He added that with a Government in such Straits as that of France at the present moment, the threat of the loss of a few votes could drive the Government in any given direction. He said, moreover, that he was certain the French Government underrated the importance attached to the question by the Chinese Government and had no idea of the magnitude of the resistance they were likely to encounter in the event of the despatch of an Expedition." He ended with the first hint of an argument that was to grow steadily in prominence: that a military setback to France would strengthen China against all the other Powers as well.[4] It came to light just now that in January a Chinese embassy had gone to Hue to insist on the Annamese Emperor's denouncing the Treaty of 1874.[5]

[1] Cordier, *Relations etc.* II, 364.   [2] *Ibid.* 371.
[3] Hongkong Govt. to C.O. 58, 14.3.83, with C.O. to F.O., 8.5.83, 17. 941.   [4] Grosvenor 54 Most conf., 12.4.83, 17. 923.
[5] Cordier, *Relations etc.* II, 377–9.

On 30 April Tseng called on Lord Granville. Before doing so he visited the Russian Embassy to test the chances of Russia giving her good offices. The Russian Ambassador admitted that his Government regretted France's Tonkingese policy "as calculated, by engaging her forces in the Far East, to weaken her at home". But he recommended Tseng to appeal to Granville, because England had bigger interests at stake than Russia.[1] This is curious; if there was one Power whose interference would goad France into extremes, it was England. It may be he judged the French so deeply committed to their policy that by trying dissuasion Russia would merely sacrifice influence at Paris. It may be that fear of Germany in Europe was outweighed by the thought of France's attack perhaps providing opportunities for frontier rectification in the North.

On 19 May Rivière was killed in action.[2] His death opened a fresh phase. Supplies were voted, Harmand was appointed Commissioner in Tonking. In London an old General of the Second Empire pestered the Foreign Office; he detested Republics, and wanted to put himself at the head of a Chinese column.[3] Grosvenor went to Shanghai to have some teeth out, and "suffered from the greatest pain that a dentist knows how to inflict". He reported that Li, gazetted Commander-in-Chief for the southern provinces, regarded the appointment as a plot of his enemies to ruin him.[4] Grosvenor was preoccupied lest, if Li failed and suffered capital punishment, the reactionaries should take the bit between their teeth.[5] The Yamen admitted that Chinese troops were massing, even across the frontier.[6] At Tientsin, so far away, popular feeling was so intensely aroused that Grosvenor wanted a gunboat placed there for the winter, despite the Admiral's assertion that it would be bad both for the hull of his ship and the behaviour

[1] Wade (in England) to Currie, 1.5.83, 17. 923.
[2] For Rivière's mission and death, see Norman, *Tonkin*, 184–217.
[3] F.O. memo. 8.6.83, 27. 2705.
[4] Grosvenor to Currie, 17.5.83, 17. 923.
[5] Grosvenor 76 Most conf., 1.6.83, 17. 923.
[6] Grosvenor 66 Most conf., 29.5.83, 17. 923; cp. his 90, 18.6.83, and 94, 19.6.83, 17. 923.

of his crew. The Governor of Hongkong, Sir George Bowen, advised that our naval strength out there should not be inferior to that of France and Russia; also that the defences of Hongkong needed looking to—Vladivostok being only seven days' steaming away.[1]

Already in April there were rumoured collisions between French and Chinese troops. The Yamen cabled Tseng to protest at Paris; when he did so, he was told that the Yamen should apply to Bourée, who had full instructions; they applied to Bourée, and found that he had no instructions whatever.[2] Grosvenor later discovered that Bourée had read to the Yamen a telegram denying any hostile intentions on France's part, but that was Barmecide comfort with a French army actively at work.[3] Another French agent was appearing on the scene. M. Tricou, Minister in Japan, was ordered to China, to find out what preparations China was making while reassuring her that France did not desire a rupture.[4] He called at Hongkong on his way, and talked pacifically to the Governor.[5] At Shanghai he met Li, on his way to take up command in the South, and persuaded the unreluctant Viceroy to stop. Tricou stayed at Shanghai, making no other effort to enter on discussion with the Chinese, and advising Paris to go firmly ahead.[6] He laboured under the delusion that France had only to nod to secure an ally in Japan. "Je connaissais les dispositions du Gouvernment Japonais. Nous pouvons en tirer un très grand parti.... Vingt mille Japonais suffiraient pour mettre en déroute toute l'armée chinoise."[7] While at Shanghai, Li saw our Admiral, and in a talk "of a very cordial nature" offered to secure any terms we liked in Corea if we would make a commercial treaty with Annam.[8] Li returned to Tientsin early in

[1] Bowen 31.7.83, with C.O. to F.O., 14.9.83, 27. 2705.
[2] Grosvenor 76 Most conf., 1.6.83, 17. 923.
[3] Grosvenor 107, 16.7.83, 17. 923.
[4] Cordier, *Relations etc.* II, 394.
[5] Bowen, 30.5.83, encl. with C.O. to F.O., 14.7.83, 27. 2705.
[6] Cordier, *Relations etc.* II, 394, 397–8.
[7] Tel. 19.6.83, Cordier, *Relations etc.* II, 395.
[8] Admiral Willes 274, 30.5.83, with Admiralty to F.O., 25.7.83, 17. 941.

July, and told Consul Brenan that he and Tricou had been able to make "not the beginning of a beginning".[1] His plans appeared to be in accordance with a Chinese military programme drafted several years before—to stay on the defensive, wear down the enemy with skirmishes, and trust to his distance from home to exhaust him.[2] The French Ministry hinted broadly in the Chambers that "foreign intrigues" were to be blamed for the deadlock.[3]

At this point America, invited by China, offered mediation; France declined it. The American Minister was very keen on mediating, Grosvenor wrote, but made no headway.[4] At the beginning of July Tseng came back from Paris to England, and again requested Granville to mediate. Granville assured him that he was watching closely for an opportunity.[5]

On 17 July the Annamese monarch Tu Duc—"notre ennemi acharné", as Cordier calls him—died.[6] On 9 August the French Ambassador in London announced a blockade of the ports of Annam, on the strength of a prohibition of arms imports in the Treaty of 1874.[7] It was the first of a series of blockades which were to create more and more friction between France and England, and whose intention, it may well be, was to hit England's pocket until she put pressure on China to give in. Admiral Courbet attacked Hue, and Commissioner Harmand secured a new treaty giving France control of Annamite foreign relations and Customs, and the right to station Residents in Tonking. It was a pretty full bailiff's list of Annam's possessions. Lord Granville was consulting his Law Officers on the subject of the blockade.[8] An enquiry was addressed to the French Chargé d'Affaires, but his answer was not clear.[9] The Foreign Office decided that the best thing was simply to publish the fact

[1] Grosvenor 107, 16.7.83, 17. 923, enclosing letter from Consul Brenan.

[2] Memo. by Carles, with Grosvenor 33 conf., 3.3.83, 17. 922.

[3] L'Affaire du Tonkin, 47–8.   [4] Life of Parkes, II, 371.

[5] F.O. to Peking 102, 2.7.83, 17. 919.

[6] Cordier, Relations etc. II, 384.

[7] The Yamen was notified on 20 August, and made a temporising answer. Grosvenor tel. 16 ciph., 23.8.83, 17. 928.

[8] F.O. to L.O., 27.8.83, 17. 925.

[9] F.O. to French Chargé, 29.9.83, 27. 2705.

that import of arms into Annam was forbidden, without notifying a regular blockade.[1]

On 5 September *The Times* had an article prophesying that if there were war England would be drawn in. Apropos of this, Macartney called at the Foreign Office to explain China's position. The French, he told Currie, now had the treaty they wanted with Annam, and could afford to call a halt. But they were sending reinforcements into Tonking, and this meant war. The communication was sent to Plunkett, Chargé d'Affaires at Paris; he was to read it to the Foreign Minister, if the latter so desired.[2] On 8 September the French Ambassador called at Walmer Castle. M. Waddington told Lord Granville that he had pressed upon his Government the urgent need of settling both the Tonking and the Madagascar issues. He confessed that France had not so much schemed herself into Tonking as drifted there; she now wanted an arrangement, and her terms were: A neutral zone down to a line from 21° or 22° lat. to the Red River above Laokai; opening of the town of Manhao on the Red River; no insistence upon recognition by China of France's protectorate over Annam. He invited Lord Granville's approval. The latter was not to be drawn. He was anxious for peace, he said, but he could not sponsor a particular set of terms. Should he first sound the Marquis Tseng on France's behalf?[3]

On the 10th Challemel-Lacour accepted the offer, though expressing a belief that China was merely playing for time.[4] Granville immediately invited Tseng and Macartney to Walmer. Only Macartney came—on the 11th—Tseng being unwell. Macartney said that China had presented her terms in six articles. The chief points were: no annexations in Annam beyond the limits of 1867, no disturbance of Sino-Annamese

[1] Minutes with draft of F.O. to L.O., 14.11.83, 27. 2705. The L.O. advised in December that the claim based on the Treaty of 1874 should not be admitted (6.12.83, 27. 2706).

[2] F.O. to Plunkett 856A, Very conf., 5.9.83, 27. 2705; memo. by Currie, 97. 621.

[3] F.O. to Plunkett 872A, 8.9.83, 27. 2705. These French terms were embodied in a published memorandum of 15 September.

[4] F.O. to Plunkett 873A, Very conf., 11.9.83, 17. 920.

relations, opening of the Red River to all countries up to Sontay. An answer had not yet been returned. Granville said he had formerly declined to mediate, the time not being opportune, but now he might. Only the terms must be such as France could entertain. Macartney thought France might now be prepared to return to Bourée's position, but China had never accepted *his* terms. Granville warned him that China would be foolish to get herself into a war; France was bound to win. His visitor "spoke of the strength and violence of the war-party at Peking, whom the Empress and the Government had not strength to resist".[1]

Granville reported to Waddington what had passed. Waddington answered that Tseng had been told on 27 August his six proposals were inadmissible, since they reopened the question of Annam; and he begged Granville to press China, through his Minister at Peking, to be reasonable.[2] This was good enough for Granville to tell Tseng, when the latter came to Walmer on the 13th, that the French Government was now disposed to accept England's good offices. It was, he emphasised, not *mediation* he offered. He impressed on the Marquis that success depended on China's moderation. Tseng showed himself reluctant to step at all outside his fixed orders. He said China might go so far as to allow French garrisons in the towns opened to trade in the north of Annam. Granville observed that he found China's claims over Tonking a little shadowy. The Marquis replied that then there was the less reason for objecting to them.[3] Quite properly, for Granville's remark missed the point of the Chinese case, the danger of having France as an immediate neighbour. The same day another interview took place. The Foreign Secretary now pitched his warnings in a graver key. "Dawdling things out" was a favourite phrase with him, but by this time he felt called on to exert himself. If, he said, the French began fighting, they would be forced to go on to the end, and the collapse of the Dynasty and of the Empire itself would in that case not be an impossibility. Tseng declined

[1] F.O. to Parkes (Peking) 14 A, Very conf., 11.9.83, 17. 920.
[2] F.O. to Plunkett 882 A, Very conf., 13.9.83, 27. 2705. Cp. *L'Affaire du Tonkin*, 71–2.   [3] F.O. to Parkes 14 A, 13.9.83, 27. 2705.

to be frightened. He pointed out that a supine weakness in face of the enemy would be equally dangerous to the Dynasty. Personally, he observed, he would incur more blame by being conciliatory than by being too firm; though he did not let himself be swayed by the fact.[1]

The same day the Foreign Office cabled to its Peking Legation:"Ask Yamen what are real terms of arrangement with France as to Tonking, to which they could agree. Unless they are moderate it will be impossible for us to use our good offices."[2] Waddington was given the gist of what Tseng had said, and he telegraphed to Paris for the terms Tseng was waiting for. On the 14th he and Tseng were invited to Walmer together. Challemel-Lacour had sent the terms, but said they should not be communicated to China unless Her Majesty's Government were prepared to back them. Granville repeated that he could not commit himself to that, but he thought the proposals a basis of discussion. The two Envoys then, at his invitation, spent two hours together, and told him at the end that "useful light" had been thrown on the issue.[3]

While Tseng and Waddington argued above the white cliffs, Parkes, newly arrived from Japan to take over the Peking Legation, and talking Chinese very fast "with a very limited vocabulary and utter disregard of tones",[4] interviewed M. Tricou. Tricou's reports say that Parkes was sympathetic towards the French case.[5] Parkes' reports dwell rather on Tricou's fierceness. The Frenchman declared that the armed opposition France had been encountering was more Chinese than Annamese, and munitions as well as troops had been sent from China. Ferry had warned Tseng that this must stop, but it seemed a fleet might be necessary to enforce the order.[6] A few days later Tricou said he heard from Paris that M. Patenôtre

---

[1] F.O. to Parkes 14 C, 13.9.83, 17. 920.
[2] F.O. to Parkes tel. 20 ciph., 13.9.83, 17. 928.
[3] F.O. to Plunkett 882 B, Very conf., 14.9.83, 27. 2705.
[4] Parker, *John Chinaman.*
[5] See his two telegrams of 9.9.83, Cordier, *Relations etc.* II, 404.
[6] Parkes 5, 8.9.83, 17. 924.

was being sent as Minister. He confessed that the situation of the 4000 French troops in Tonking was growing critical; at least 10,000 more would be needed.[1]

On 16 September Tricou arrived in Tientsin from Shanghai. On the 18th he was amiably received by Li; on paying a short visit to Peking he was met with equal courtesy.[2] Sincerely or not, Li declared that Tseng was acting with clumsy obstinacy—a disavowal which Tseng repudiated.[3] It was Li, of course, not Tseng, who was billed in the oncoming drama for the classic rôle of Exterminator of Barbarians. On all sides clouds were gathering. On the 19th Waddington showed Granville, in confidence, the terms being offered in Paris—they were what he had talked of to Granville on the 8th—and asked for British influence to be used at Peking.[4] But at the end of the month, Parkes having conveyed Granville's message that he could only assist if China's terms were moderate, the Yamen declined to make any statement of policy, and declined also—with thanks—the British offer.[5] When they did disclose their hand, it was to insist that the recent Franco-Annamese Treaty must be torn up.[6] In Paris the Foreign Minister told the British Ambassador that "the last verbal proposals of the Marquis Tseng surpassed in absurdity all that it would be possible to conceive".[7]

Chinese strategy was unfolding itself. Cameron of The Evening Standard had been down to Tonking to see how the Black Flags—half patriots, half guerilla fighters, backed by the Chinese—could handle their guns. He now came to Canton to inspect the Chinese soldiery. Viceroy Chang demurred to his suggestion that fifteen thousand Chinese troops had crossed the border already, but added, with a sly complacency, that Chinese soldiers sympathised with Annam, and no doubt some had

[1] Parkes 10, 18.9.83, 17. 924.
[2] Cordier, *Relations etc.* II, 405–6.   [3] *Ibid.* II, 407–8.
[4] F.O. to Plunkett 906 conf., 19.9.83, 27. 2705.
[5] Parkes 17, 29.9.83, 17. 924.
[6] Parkes tel. 4 ciph., 28.9.83, and Grosvenor (Chargé) tel. 8 ciph., 28.11.83, 17. 928.
[7] Lyons tel. 59 ciph., 4.10.83, 27. 2705. The proposals were for a partition giving nearly all Tonking to China. (*L'Affaire du Tonkin*, 95.)

turned deserter and gone off to help her. "Yes", said Cameron, appreciating the Viceroy's joke, "stick to that word 'deserters'", and there was a laugh in the room. He next asked about a report that if Chinese troops came into action the French would attack Canton and impound the Customs. His Excellency pointed out comfortably that his Customs were mortgaged to a British bank; that would mean British help if they were threatened.[1] A letter from Mesny, a British adventurer who had gone south hoping for service against the French, added further information. Liu Erh, also known as Liu Yung-fu, a Black Flag chief who had long ravaged Tonking, had been invited to Yunnan and there given rank, a subsidy, and a park of artillery.[2] Oddly, the Black Flags, originally remnants of the Taiping armies that had pushed the Dynasty to the brink of ruin, were now the most forward of its defenders.

Pressure on the French was intensifying. Tricou read Parkes in confidence a telegram from Harmand, saying that if re-cruitment from China went on there would be no choice but to declare war and bombard the Chinese ports.[3] Henceforward the European residents were to live under constant danger from bombardment and riot.

The crowded diplomatic activity of this September ended with attempts at pacification breaking down, and open war in sight.

[1] Parkes 8 conf., 18.9.83, 17. 924.
[2] Copy with Parkes 12 conf., 29.9.83, 17. 924.
[3] Parkes 15 conf., 25.9.83, 17. 924.

CHAPTER SEVEN

Corea; the Second Treaty

SAFE on his throne again, or comparatively so, for a moment, the King of Corea wrote to his Chinese suzerain thanking him for his succour. His letter opened in terms that even the punctilio of Peking cannot have found fault with. "In humble meditation your servant reflects on the worthless manner in which he has discharged the duties of the post to which he was appointed by your Imperial Majesty...."[1]

As usual, the poor down-at-heel monarch was only exchanging one trouble for another. During the period surveyed above, political motives were uppermost in the treaty-making with Corea. These considerations did not disappear now. On 16 November 1882, the Foreign Office wrote to Grosvenor, having heard that a Russian was expected in Corea in search of a treaty, instructing him to collect all the intelligence he could concerning Russian activity.[2] Still, the Russian menace receded enough to let us reflect at more leisure on the mercantile aspect of our bargain; and when Admiral Willes' catch came to be examined, the feeling was that it would never do. Sir Robert Hart telegraphed: "New negotiations will effect nothing and will irritate: but ratify treaty opening door and rest will follow."[3] The Foreign Office thought otherwise. Annotations on its copy of the treaty show that the main

---

[1] Copy with Grosvenor 125, 8.11.82, 900.

[2] F.O. 155 conf., 16.11.82, 17. 894. Enomotto, Japanese Minister at Peking, told his American colleague at the end of 1882 that his Government was thinking of an international conference to neutralise Corea under guarantee. (Treat, *Diplomatic Relations etc.* 164.) Evidently Japan was suffering from another attack of nerves. The Foreign Office noted: "The Japanese Government are showing a very marked interest in the status of Corea." (To Wade, 20.11.82, 17. 897.)

[3] Telegram sent to the Foreign Office by Stuart Rendell, M.P.; 17. 940.

objections were to its lack of precision about tariffs, and its promise of abolishing extrality so soon as Corea should have reformed herself; this would embolden China and Japan in their cry for treaty revision.[1] In short, our treaty was "a very crude arrangement".[2] Perhaps, also, it was felt that the treaty had been made too much under Chinese auspices. Currie noted that a memorandum on Corea by Hertslet seemed to show that seven states had recognised China's suzerainty; this involved a danger that Russia might get hold of Corea by picking a quarrel at Peking. "Korea wd. probably be safer as an independent country having treaties with the European Powers and the United States." Granville was "inclined to agree".[3]

The Russians had tried to get a treaty with Corea regulating overland trade. The Chinese had informed them that the Coreans were unreasonable, and would not agree to overland trade with anyone. The Russian Legation was proportionately displeased to learn in December 1882 that Regulations had been drawn up, under the orders of Li Hung-chang, for land as well as sea trade between Corea and China.[4] Other Powers were not much better pleased at the news. Grosvenor said that China's action showed an arrogant intention of putting her own Corean trade on a better footing than anyone else's, and of denying the application to Corea of the most favoured nation clause. Currie minuted dogmatically at the Foreign Office that Corea was either independent, or not (a crude piece of Western logic): if she was, we claimed most favoured nation treatment; if not, our treaties with China applied equally to her. He proposed joining with Germany and securing a new treaty. Pauncefote agreed, suggesting also American participation. "It is clear that Li Hung-chang has been pulling the

[1] 17. 913.
[2] F.O. minute in 17. 914. The Chambers of Commerce of London, Shanghai, Hongkong and Yokohama were shown in confidence copies of correspondence relating to Corea, and consulted on the treaty (17. 915). They raised numerous objections; see 17. 940, and Grosvenor 147, 4.12.82, and minutes, in 17. 900. The India Office was also consulted; 17. 942.
[3] Memo. 8.1.83, and minute, 17. 915.
[4] Grosvenor 155 Most conf., 14.12.82, 17. 900; B.F.S.P. LXXV, 1334, 1339.

strings of all the negotiations between Corea and other Powers."
Jervoise remarked that China was obviously anxious to tighten
her hold on Corea, because everyone knew that if there were a
war between Russia and China there would be annexations by
the former in Corea.[1]

It was true and significant that China was showing signs of
waking up in the matter of her dependencies. To guard against
encroachments such as had taken place almost unperceived in
the vast northern borderlands, several administrative changes
were being made; and the resolve to assert control over Corea
was an integral part of the same new policy of "China for the
Chinese". The project of fostering trade with the vassal kingdom was not political only, it meant that Chinese trade intended
to skim some of the cream of its natural markets. Li, who drew
up the Regulations, was himself a business man and one of the
ablest in a nation of shopkeepers. He was said to be anxious to
"secure the monopoly of the Corean carrying trade to a
Chinese company"[2]—which can only have been his own
China Merchants' Steam Navigation Co. We have come to
one of the earliest concrete instances of the competition of an
awakened China, the dread which was constantly present to
the minds of Europeans in the Far East, and at times assumed
something of the quality of a nightmare.

It will be noticed that the Foreign Office at once formed a
plan of co-operating with other Powers, who were leading
commercial rivals of ours. Berlin was consulted, and agreed
that a new treaty was desirable.[3] Political considerations might
be in the background, but they survived; and there was no great
advantage to be had from scheming to get in ahead of Germany
and America. Having already treaties, they would at once
claim under the most favoured nation clause anything that was
gained. Commercial rivalry in the Far East was diverted by
this momentous clause away from competition for better
treaties than one's neighbours, into competition for particular,

[1] Grosvenor 147, 14.12.82, and minutes, 17. 900.
[2] Parkes 73, 31.12.83, 17. 927.
[3] F.O. to Board of Trade, Pressing, 9.10.83, 17. 942.

local concessions and privileges; except that on land frontiers special tariffs might be got—a powerful reason for annexing areas that marched with China.

In the same way as it had refused to ratify the Convention of Chefu, the Foreign Office felt no hesitation about declining to ratify the Corean treaty. The question of Corea's status was undoubtedly a *crux* in international relations. The Foreign Office had been puzzled in what terms the Queen ought to answer a letter received from the King of Corea.[1] The sense of the letter —that the signatory, while entirely dependent on the Chinese Emperor, was a fully independent sovereign—*was* confusing.

One of Parkes' first duties, when he was transferred in 1883 from Tokio to Peking, became, therefore, the drafting of suggestions for a better treaty with Corea. The Foreign Office emended his draft a little; the chief thing was that the sensitive Indian Government could not bear to see opium prohibited in the main body at least of a treaty. The United States appeared less dissatisfied with the old treaty as it stood; at any rate the Senate approved, during the spring of 1883, the appointment as Minister to Corea of General Lucius Foote. The General came out in May and ratified the treaty.[2] His first move was to get a Corean Mission sent to America, where it was cordially received. Germany was at this time more keenly interested than America in the Far East, and here was a chance of making herself felt. England was cordial: she needed German goodwill in Egypt, and it could be paid for cheaply at Seoul.

It was not until September that the Foreign Office's plans were ready. It then became known that Parkes himself was to be sent to Seoul, though he had only that month arrived from Japan.[3] His appointment signified that we did not intend to take No for an answer.

---

[1] F.O. to Wade, 20.11.82, 17. 894. The Foreign Office assumed that the King's letter had been dictated from Tientsin.

[2] Foote himself considered the treaty worthless. (*Life of Parkes*, II, 206.)

[3] Just before leaving Japan, Parkes interviewed Kim Ok Kun, the soon-to-be-famous Corean revolutionary. The latter prophesied rightly that there would be trouble before long over Corea. (Parkes 114 conf., 16.7.83, 46. 302.)

On 19 September Parkes wrote from Shanghai to his Admiral, asking for a ship to carry him to Corea and one for his advance representative.[1] On 21 September the Foreign Office cabled him to concert his tactics in every way with the German Plenipotentiary detailed to visit Corea.[2] On 5 October he was asked by cable if he could wait for this gentleman to catch him up, Berlin being "extremely anxious" for the two to act together.[3] Parkes composed a letter to the Corean Government, with an assurance that this fresh mission would fill them anew with a sense of England's esteem for their country. Possibly he felt that the fact did not quite jump to the eye, and needed pointing out. He entrusted his letter, together with one from the German Chargé Count Tattenbach, to Consul Aston, with orders to convey it ahead to Seoul and ask that Plenipotentiaries be nominated to confer with them on arrival. On 18 October Parkes sailed for Corea, timing himself to get there at the same time as his German colleague: Herr Zappe was coming from Japan, where he was Consul-General.[4]

On the way, H.M.S. "Sapphire", which bore Sir Harry and his fortunes, put in at Tientsin, and he had an interview with Li Hung-chang. As might be expected, it was not of the most cordial. Li took the line that it was disobliging of the English to seek a fresh treaty with Corea without first frankly and fully consulting him. It was certainly a pointed change of procedure. He asked what fault could be found with the old treaty. Sir Harry replied that with the tariff as it stood, remunerative trade would be out of the question. "His Excellency then observed that I had been long in Japan, and he feared that I wished to play the Japanese game and prevent the Coreans obtaining a proper revenue for their trade. The Japanese had deceived the Coreans; they had been trading with the latter for eight years, and had not yet paid them a farthing of duty." Parkes rejoined, it was true the Japanese had treated

[1] Copy with Parkes 13, 29.9.83, 17. 924.
[2] F.O. tel. 21 ciph., 21.9.83, 17. 928.
[3] F.O. tel. 25 ciph., 5.10.83, 17. 928.
[4] Parkes 28, 18.10.83, 17. 924.

Corea badly, but *his* country wanted nothing more than a fair tariff. "His Excellency then observed: I believe you want more than that; you want to expunge the opium clause from your treaty." Sir Harry denied it, and, a little irritated, said that Corea was likely to suffer more from importations of Chinese than of Indian opium. (A hint at the poppies supposed to flourish on Li's Anhui estates?) He continued, playing on his interlocutor's distrust of Japan, that his present aims would injure that country, by enabling England to supply direct to Corea the large quantities of British goods that at present passed through Japanese hands.[1]

Parkes reached Chemulpo on the 26th, at two in the afternoon. Owing to bad weather he found Herr Zappe there before him, a minor annoyance. There was some trouble over collecting baggage animals for the journey to the capital; and then Sir Harry's pony "refused to do more than crawl"; they got very wet, and Zappe exchanged *his* pony for a chair.[2] Parkes was satisfied with their reception at Seoul, which he found "most courteous and cordial".[3] Excellent lodgings had been prepared for them; a relief, since the squalor of Seoul had already struck consternation into Mrs Foote.[4]

There were merry dinners with Aston, Carles and Hillier, but Zappe, though a good colleague, was inclined to be despondent about the outcome of their adventure. Parkes cheered him with predictions of success: Zappe "asked me for my reasons, which I declined to give, as I had none".[2] Both felt their amour-propre at stake. After a preliminary round of visits, they spent four days in drafting their proposals, and a fifth day in having them read to the Corean Plenipotentiaries. Long discussion followed. Over details of the Treaty proper, agreement proved easy; trade regulations and the tariff were knottier points. However, in November our proposals were

---

[1] Parkes 37 conf., 3.11.83, 17. 926.
[2] Letter by Parkes, in his *Life*, II, 207 ff.   [3] Parkes 36, 1.11.83, 17. 926.
[4] Letter by Parkes, in his *Life*, II, 207 ff. For a description of Seoul in 1883, with streets littered with animal bones and other debris, see H. A. C. Bonar in *Transactions of the Asiatic Society of Japan*, XI.

accepted as a basis.[1] The Coreans complained of the tardiness of this renewal of communications, and of the absence of any replies from Queen Victoria and the Kaiser to the King's letters. The Envoys for their part complained that Corea had last year given new concessions to China, and since then to Japan. They contended that the present classification of goods and their duties, which had been inspired by Japan, unduly favoured Japanese goods; they proposed a different system of grading imports, with an average duty of $7\frac{1}{2}$ per cent, the level specified by the Hongkong Chamber of Commerce. The Coreans fought tenaciously. Parkes—who is accused of behaving in an overbearing manner[2]—had to compromise on small points in order to make sure of his main ones. He agreed to the exclusion of opium, the reference being decently concealed in the tariff schedule. Opium agitation at home was too strong to admit of opium being forced on a new country. The Coreans were anxious for reinsertion of the first treaty's provision, that extrality should be renounced when Corea had overhauled her laws. But Zappe had orders not to consent to this, and Parkes had to back him, although the Coreans at one time threatened to break off negotiations. Parkes detected a "certain foreign influence" in their tenacity. Business ended satisfactorily for the Envoys on the whole.[3]

The British Treaty had thirteen articles;[4] the important ones were:

1. Peace and friendship. If either Power should be in difficulty with a third, the other would use its good offices. (Twenty years later the Anglo-Japanese Alliance handed Corea over to the claws of Japan.)

4. Englishmen to be able to buy land and build factories at three ports. (The factory question was being much agitated in China.)

[1] Parkes 38, 7.11.83, 17. 926.
[2] R. von Möllendorf, *P. G. von Möllendorf : ein Lebensbild*, 61.
[3] Parkes 42, 6.12.83, 17. 926; review of treaty in his 70, 31.12.83, 17. 927.
[4] For text of the British and German treaties see *B.F.S.P.* LXXIV, 633 and 86.

5. Imports not to pay fresh duties inland. (This was to prevent our goods being harassed with internal tolls, our main grievance in China.)

8. Warships of each country to be free to visit "all the ports of the other". (Not much of a privilege for the Corean navy, but an appreciable one for the British.)

The Treaty was signed on 26 November. Next day Parkes and Zappe were received by the King. Sir Harry thought His Majesty a man of much civility and intelligence.[1] Perhaps his mind went back to that famous day in his career, long years ago, when he had first been received by the Mikado.[2] On the 29th he sailed, having met with no discourtesy during all his stay.[3]

As soon as he reached Tientsin on the way back he was begged by Li to see him. Li was anxious to know what sort of treaty had emerged, and Parkes showed it him in confidence. He did not say much about it, but he made remarks which revealed his fears of Russian encroachment and his determination to resist it. From what he said it also appeared that the French Minister had been prophesying trouble for China from the Anglo-German mission to Seoul. France could not be pleased to see her two main enemies arm in arm.[4]

Parkes told his Government that to appoint a Minister to Seoul, as America had done, would be unnecessary, were it not that Corea was anxious to have tokens of her independence in the shape of foreign envoys of rank. He asked that he himself should be given the post coincidently with Peking, a Consul-General residing on the spot. Currie was against this, Pauncefote supported Parkes, Granville supported Pauncefote.[5]

Corea designed a national flag for herself. But the Chinese commissioners at Seoul, who had, so far as appearances went, been little consulted by the Coreans during the making of the

---

[1] Parkes 39, 1.12.83, 17. 926.
[2] For that interview see Satow, *A Diplomat in Japan*, 358.
[3] Parkes 58, 17.12.83, 17. 927.   [4] Parkes 43, 7.12.83, 17. 926.
[5] Parkes 54 conf., 16.12.83, 17. 927. The arrangement was discontinued at Parkes' death.

Treaty, came out with a proclamation about Corean trade, over which they announced their complete authority. It contained the Manchesterian sentence: "The world has now become one family, and the various nations thereof trade with one another, exchanging each other's resources for their respective needs...."[1] China could sound very modern and sophisticated when lecturing her admiring little tributaries.

Some trouble might be feared to lurk in the Chinese attitude. Next March Parkes suffered from misgivings that the Treaty might not be ratified. Apart from rumours of the Japanese putting in their oar, Li attacked the Treaty in conversation with one of our consuls, and said the Coreans disliked it. It was whispered that the Tai Wen Kun might be allowed to return—an event prayed for by the reactionary opposition in Corea.[2]

In London the Chinese Minister asked for a copy of the Treaty, and regretted that it did not contain a recognition of China's suzerainty. The omission, he said, would expose Corea to Russian designs.[3]

But our uneasiness proved unnecessary. It may be conjectured that China's danger from France in Tonking, and need of English help, smoothed the way. In April Parkes sent Hillier to Corea to investigate, and was relieved to hear from him that the Treaty was confirmed.[4] On Hillier's return Li joked quite affably with him about the mysterious secrecy of his expedition.[5] The fall of Prince Kung, which occurred now, made Parkes hasten to get the ratifications exchanged, however, before anything else should happen.[6] He hurried to Corea and was well received: Ministers stood up while informing themselves as to the Queen's health; no difficulty was made about ratification. On 28 April he indited from our new Legation the first despatch of the Corean series.[7] The only untoward

[1] Parkes 73, 31.12.83, 17. 927.   [2] Parkes 66 conf., 31.3.84, 17. 949.
[3] Memo. by Pauncefote, 23.3.84, 17. 967.   [4] Parkes 78, 4.4.84, 17. 949.
[5] Hillier, from Tientsin, 9.5.84, with Parkes 96, 24.5.84, 27. 2708.
[6] Parkes tel. ciph., 16.4.84, 27. 2708.
[7] Parkes, Corea 1, 28.4.84, 17. 949.

circumstance was that changes had been made in the Government personnel, especially in the Foreign Board, in deference
to Chinese dislike of the Treaty.[1] On 2 May Parkes had an
audience with the King, and presented a belated letter from
Queen Victoria. (There had been much discussion at the
Foreign Office on the size and price of the silver box containing
the letter—Parkes had insisted on a silver box.[2]) A stickler for
forms, Sir Harry stipulated, and the Coreans agreed, that the
letter should be received with the same ceremonial as if it had
been from the Emperor of China.[3] The audience room, it is
true, was not imposing, being smaller than a big mandarin's in
China, with a coarse German carpet on the floor and inquisitive
eyes at the paper lattices.[4] That night the President of the
Foreign Board invited the English Mission to a banquet, at
which the Chinese Resident made a cordial speech.[3]

Banquets at Seoul were soon to acquire a sinister import.
But at present all was well. This same month an innovation was
announced that seemed an early tribute to foreign contact.
Corea was to have a postal system.[5]

As regards the possible competition of overland trade,
Parkes discussed it with the Germans, and then informed the
Coreans that if they gave Russia the same terms as China had
taken they must reduce their tariff on sea-borne goods accordingly.[6] It was often said that Russia had no trade, that her
designs were purely political; but our representatives did not
ignore her as a trade competitor in the Far East. The threat
was put in effect in the autumn, when Japan got the same tariff
as we had got without binding herself to pay the higher tonnage

[1] Parkes, Corea 19 conf., 20.6.84, 17. 951.
[2] Parkes, Treaty 2, 19.1.84, ext. tel., 17. 956, and F.O. minutes in 17. 954.
[3] Parkes, Corea 6, 2.5.84, 17. 949.   [4] Carles, *Life in Corea*, 66.
[5] Parkes, Corea 14, 31.5.84, 17. 949.
[6] The Board of Trade did not think the Chinese-Corean trade a serious
danger. (17. 969.) The Chinese regulations were, economically, an advance
on previous vexatious restrictions on frontier trade. It was reported that in
the month after the new system was started 3700 taels of revenue were
collected, more than the total annual revenue formerly. (Parkes, Corea 16,
4.6.84, with Copy of Regulations, 17. 951.)

dues provided for by our Treaty.[1] It was an instance of how a country tied by the most favoured nation clause was likely to see its autonomy nibbled away by competing foreigners.

Carles, installed at Chemulpo as vice-consul, quickly began to feel pessimistic about trade, when he saw even Japanese, the hardiest of merchants, collapsing.[2] He had already formed doubts about mining prospects; he toured northern Corea— hitherto quite unexplored—for six weeks, and strove to make head or tail of the jumble of contradictions with which his questions on trade were met.[3] During the autumn Aston undertook a trip to Songdo, fifty miles from the capital, and drew up a trading report which Parkes published at Shanghai.[4] Aston found the inhabitants uniformly civil; in the interior, their tempers had not been soured by Japanese methods of civilising them. He was soon busy with the issue of passports and other preliminaries of commerce, and with buying a house from a Corean nobleman who beat him up to twelve hundred dollars.[5] In London there was a great deal of fuss over getting out a new Order in Council for Corea.[6]

The Chinese garrison troops were building forts in and near Seoul, acting it is said on a secret understanding with the Queen's family.[7] During the summer an incident threw some light on China's relations with her vassal. There lived in the capital a Corean nobleman, I Pomsin, "of warm temper and advanced ideas"—Aston was struck by noticing on his table a translation of a work on international law. Two adjoining houses were occupied by a guild of Chinese merchants, who wished to secure his house to round off their premises. He refused their terms, and offered his house for sale to an agent of a British firm. The Chinese had I Pomsin arrested, gaoled, ill-treated, haled him before the Chinese Commissioner, and

---

[1] Parkes, Corea 33, 28.10.84, 17. 952.
[2] Carles, *Life in Corea*, 101.
[3] *Ibid.* 78, 109, 179. His reports were printed as Corea No. 2 of 1885.
[4] Printed as Corea No. 1 of 1885.
[5] Aston to Parkes, Accounts 1, 30.5.84, 17. 962.   [6] 17. 968, 969.
[7] G. T. Ladd, *In Korea with Marquis Ito*, 103-4.

forced him to sign a bond of sale.[1] Accounts of Chinese conduct vary. The Japanese Press dwelt on the misbehaviour of Chinese traders and soldiers.[2] But we also have a statement that the Chinese garrison was orderly and on excellent terms with the people, and that from a witness who otherwise draws a dismal picture of Corea.[3]

England's attitude towards two of her neighbours is revealed in her discrimination between two fresh missions that now set off to Corea. De Luca, Italian Minister at Peking, asked for our assistance, and was given it. Waeber, Russian consul at Tientsin, did not ask it, and did not receive it. When the latter arrived in Corea it was understood that he meant to shelve the frontier trade question and concentrate on getting what we had got;[4] but we soon hear of him warning the Coreans, in hectoring tones, that they had better not raise any difficulties about Russia's land trade. Aston, who suspected that Corea had secretly promised to give Russia what she wanted, warned Möllendorf, the Corean adviser, that it would be dangerous to give way.[5]

The unshackling of commerce between China and Corea led to an influx of Chinese merchants. To watch over them a Chinese official was appointed. Significantly, his rank was only that of an Expectant Taotai. A Chinese Viceroy was considered to rank equally with a King of Corea. The new official's duties consisted partly in seeing to it that Corea did not yield too quickly to foreign innovations, to the undermining of Chinese influence. He claimed diplomatic status, which the foreign Representatives, scenting his hostility, declined to admit.[6]

We leave Corea, after the signing of the Second Treaty, with time-bombs planted here and there, soon to explode.

[1] Parkes, Corea 28, 3.7.84, 17. 951, enclosing Aston 8, 23.6.84.
[2] E.g. extract with Parkes 81, 19.4.84, 17. 950.
[3] J. C. Hall, in *Transactions of the Asiatic Society of Japan*, xi.
[4] Parkes, Corea 18, 4.6.84, 17. 951.
[5] Parkes, Corea 24 conf., 3.7.84, 17. 951. An Italian treaty was signed on June 26 (*B.F.S.P.* lxxv, 308), a Russian treaty on 7 July (*ibid.* lxxv, 510).
[6] Parkes, Corea 33, 27.11.84, 17. 952.

CHAPTER EIGHT

Rioting at Canton

CONTEMPORARY experiences "among the natives"
were diverse. The cry of "foreign devil" was loud,
but a little tact often silenced it. A lady in Fukien in
1879 was besieged with invitations to visit cottages in the
villages she passed.[1] Another English lady wrote in 1881 that
she invariably met with "respect and studied kindness".[2] A
Frenchman of long residence found himself welcomed among
any crowd when he singled out and paid his respects to some
aged individual.[3] A couple of sportsmen up the Yangtze in
1887 found some Buddhist priests their surliest encounter,
and brought them round to an excessive affability by plying
them with punch.[4] But in the ports, where the intercourse of
races was summed up in the brutality of the drunken sailor
towards the helpless "rickshawman",[5] friction was endemic
and anti-foreign feeling universal. It was, probably, strongest of
all in Canton.

And of all Chinese cities, none inspired in Westerners a
stronger repulsion, a stronger sense of something alien and
inhuman. It was a huge cistern of life, always full, always
the same from century to century, constantly renewed by a
swirling current of existence. Kipling, visiting Canton,
jostled by myriads of Celestials, said to his companion: "It
would be quite right to wipe the city of Canton off the face of
the earth, and to exterminate all the people who ran away from
the shelling."[6]

[1] Mrs Gordon Cumming, *Wanderings in China.*
[2] Mrs Hughes, *Among the Sons of Han*, 75.
[3] E. Simon, *China*, 102 (Eng. ed.).
[4] Percival, *Land of the Dragon*, 44.
[5] Mrs Hughes, *Among the Sons of Han*, 287.
[6] Kipling, *From Sea to Sea.*

In 1883 there occurred severe rioting at Canton. It was a squalid episode in the meeting of two continents and epochs, but the story is worth recounting. It should be borne in mind that this was one of many such episodes; that when England had a grievance she was loudly indignant, and that when China had one she had usually to be silent. In 1875 a Chinese ship, the *Fusing*, was run down by an English captain who was sentenced by his Consul to pay damages and then allowed to abscond.[1] In 1880 an Englishman, Mesny, travelling in the interior after being refused a passport by Wade as a not too good character, got into a scuffle, killed one Chinese, and wounded five. Wade told his Government that China was not likely to press a complaint seriously.[2] China *could* not, because her international position was as usual insecure. It may have been a sequel to the affair when Wade was instructed to make it known that "for the future, British subjects possessing no official character will not be rescued at the expense of the State".[3] The rule was in accord with the excellent principle once laid down by Salisbury, when an adventurer appealed for help—"Buccaneers must expect to rough it".[4]

At Canton, China and Europe faced each other with mutual hostility across a canal which was the only line of separation between the foreign settlement and the seething life of the native town. The canal, or "Creek", was the home of a large water-population. It was in charge of a "Mandarin of the Creek" who was supposed to take his orders from the foreigners; but it had become "the rendezvous of the lowest and most dangerous classes of the Chinese population".[5] The Canton mob, the most vindictive in China, had long memories to nourish its resentment. A thousand years before, the Arab traders had often broken loose from their special quarter and pillaged the city. In 1635 there was a bombardment by British

---

[1] Wade urged payment of compensation; see his 49, 23.3.80, 17. 830. Papers on the case in pamphlet *England and China*, by "Justum", 1878.
[2] Wade 109, 19.7.80, 17. 832.
[3] Wade 38, 13.9.81, 17. 858.   [4] *Life of Lord Salisbury*, III, 217.
[5] Consul Hewlett to F.O. 7, 21.5.83, 17. 933.

guns. In this century the town had been entered and ruled by British soldiers. There were many in and about Canton who hated the Government, hated it above all because it was too impotent, or too treacherous, to drive the foreigner back into the ocean out of which, like a sea monster, he had come.

In 1883 French aggression in Tonking rendered the situation doubly dangerous, especially in the southern provinces that were not very far from Tonking. In March the Rev. G. John, touring in Hunan, where he had a brush or two with the natives, came upon some "ribald and lying placards". Deeply indignant, he sent copies of a pair of them to the Legation, which drew the Yamen's attention to them. The translations are not un-amusing at this distance of time, and derive a more sinister interest from their resemblance to the later Boxer placards. They call on all honest men to assist in extirpating the doctrines of the Christians, of whose rites a grotesque account is given, the fantastic refraction of a strange religion in the alien depths of the Chinese mind. The English come in for a special touch: "The despicable, rebellious and barbarous citizens of England, that kingdom situated in a remote part of the ocean, whose ruler is sometimes male, sometimes female, are of that nature half-human, half-brutal, classified in the Shan hai Ching under the denomination mean worms, and in the Han I under that of bull-headed creatures." Foreign ideas are polluting China; funds have now been collected for the purpose of exterminating them. Anyone who degrades himself by intercourse with the outlanders is to learn, by finding himself killed and his house burned, that the good old spirit has not yet died out in these parts. The indiscreet patriots responsible were not apprehended, but a local official was awarded a black mark for negligence.[1]

It was not by any means the only sign that the always smoking volcano of popular feeling was nearing another of its eruptions. Consul Alabaster was writing daily from Hankow in May about a panic there among the whites. His spelling gave way under stress of excitement—he wrote "realy" and "disperation".[2]

[1] Grosvenor 48, 29.3.83, 17. 922. [2] Consular Reports, Hankow, 17. 934.

Consul Hewlett—his destinies presided over by a watchful guardian angel—left Canton that summer for the quieter skies of England. While he was haggling with the Foreign Office for his wine allowance of 1s. 9d. a day for the voyage,[1] his successor was facing graver cares.

On 12 August, a tide-waiter of the Customs Service named Logan, formerly a police-sergeant in Hongkong, left his house for a stroll. He had a stick in his hand, and when he came to where some coolies were squatting in front of a tea-shop he pretended they were in his way and—so it was stated later in evidence—began hitting them, counting his blows out loud. One of the coolies objected; whereupon Logan flew into a rage, rushed to his house, and reappeared with two colleagues, a Russian and a Norwegian. He had a pistol now in his hand, and ran at the coolies; there was a tumult, and he began firing. A Chinese man and woman were wounded, and a boy shot dead.[2] The white men got away, but were placed under arrest by their consuls. Against Logan, wrote Acting-Consul Hance in his first report, the evidence was circumstantial, but "such that I cannot conceive anyone doubting his guilt". The affray let loose pandemonium. A Placard appeared, prophesying that the criminals would be certain to cheat the law; the citizenry must take justice into their own hands. The consuls joined in exhorting the Viceroy to preserve order. Hance summoned a gunboat from Hongkong.[3]

Things were bad enough, but they received a swift and dangerous complication. On 14 September Parkes, newly landed at Shanghai, received from Hance a telegram whose hurried jumble of words conveys the tension of an angry city more vividly than any formal narrative.

Portuguese watchman Steamer Hankow accused murdering Chinaman Steamer attacked left wharf Wharf burnt mob invaded Shameen burnt houses looted several three hours before Viceroy's troops arrived no foreigners' lives lost one received gunshot wound several Chinese looters killed Since

[1] 17. 933, Consular.
[2] Pamphlet, *Report of trial of James Henry Logan*, in 17. 942.
[3] Grosvenor 120, 5.9.83, 17. 924, with Consul's Report.

two o'clock order restored Logan safe Consulate not injured Viceroy's troops and gunboats guard Shameen intense excitement prevails in Canton two British and one French gunboat arrive protection now adequate.[1]

On 25 September a session of the Supreme Court for China was opened at Canton by Judge Sir R. T. Rennie. Logan's trial lasted six days. Judge Rennie was asked by a lawyer, who appeared for the Chinese Government, to issue a warrant for the arrest of Diaz, the Portuguese accused of murder, on the ground that the act had taken place on board a British ship. The Judge decided that he was not competent to issue one. Logan maintained an iron composure throughout the trial. He was found guilty of manslaughter, and sentenced to seven years in prison.[2] News of the verdict spread like lightning from the crowded court to the waiting town. The sentence was not one that could allay the fury of the populace. It was rumoured that a confederacy had sworn to murder foreigners if Logan escaped the noose.[3]

Hance wrote to the Viceroy, Chang, demanding an apology for the riot, and warning him of the extreme gravity of the case. Two other consuls, the French and the German, did the same. The American took an unsatisfactory line, out of that sympathy for downtrodden China that marked a good deal of early American diplomacy. Chang answered by showing reports from his military subordinates, painting the irresistible rage of the crowd and their own heroic exertions.[4] Torrential rain had probably done as much as they had to deter the mob. Chang said to the German Consul: "Le Gouvernement de votre noble pays et celui de l'Angleterre sont nos amis";[5] probably in expectation of German and English support over Tonking. With the latter struggle pressing he would regret China's being compromised by the rioting. One ought further

---

[1] Parkes 6, 14.9.83, 17. 924. Reports by naval officers with Admiralty to F.O. 27.10.83, 17. 942. Memo. on Diaz case 7.1.84, 17. 968.
[2] Report of Trial.
[3] Report from Hance with Parkes 19, 1.10.83, 17. 925.
[4] Correspondence with Parkes 23 conf., 16.10.83, 17. 925.
[5] Report of French Consul, with Parkes 25, 16.10.83, 17. 925.

to remember that these same crowds which attacked the foreigners were often a nuisance to their own authorities. It was the unemployed literati, not the officials, who on occasion stirred up anti-foreign crowds. The French consul telegraphed to his Minister: "Le Viceroi proteste violement contre la décision de la cour qu'il qualifie d'injuste et exprime la crainte que le peuple irrité n'obéisse plus aux autorités."[1] Hance reported that the Canton estuary forts were feeble and might easily be destroyed by our ships.[2]

Meanwhile Parkes arrived in Peking and took the matter fairly in hand; it was one suited to his robust temperament. He handed in person to the Yamen a stiff Note enforcing the doctrine that the Viceroy must not fancy himself released, by any sense of grievance, from his duty of keeping the populace within bounds. Kung sent a bitter answer: all the jury at Logan's trial were British subjects from the Shameen; unless Logan were subjected to a retrial it might be impossible to hold the mob in. Parkes retorted. Kung asked why the English authorities had not dealt with Diaz. Parkes said they had no power to try a Portuguese, but the man would be tried by his own authorities. A retrial of Logan would be contrary to British Law. The Judge had permitted a Chinese to sit on the Bench as an observer. Parkes told Hance, however, that he ought perhaps to have collected depositions in the Diaz case instead of at once handing the matter over to Portuguese justice, as this created an impression that we connived at Diaz's escape. He instructed Hance to collect claims for damages from the English residents who had suffered by the riots, adding that they should be told not to exaggerate.[3] Such claims were often grossly distended.

Hance was still engaged in angry correspondence with the Viceroy. Chang declared himself "perfectly astounded" at the verdict against Logan of "killing by error", which could not but exasperate the crowd and raise "a universal suspicion in their minds that the officers of the Supreme Court shield

[1] Copy with Parkes 26, 16.10.83, 17. 925.   [2] Parkes 26.
[3] Correspondence with Parkes 30, 18.10.83, 17. 925.

murderers, and that the lives of Chinese are cheap as common weeds". Hence professed himself shocked at such intemperate language. But, as he informed Parkes, at the time when Logan's sentence was announced a panic reigned among the Chinese authorities, who feared that the dreaded Secret Societies would not let this paroxysm of popular fury pass without using it to engineer a revolt. Chang's resolute tone was partly put on to satisfy his countrymen that he was not cringing to the foreigner. Some of his Notes to the consuls were appearing in the Press, probably communicated by himself. His subordinates presented him with a Memorial, recommending that the Chinese Government should "inform her Majesty's Minister in Peking distinctly of the adoption of the rule that in future cases when a Chinese subject shall have thus killed and wounded foreigners, Logan's case shall be followed as a precedent, and that, as in his case, no death sentence shall be passed". A scurrilous Placard came out addressed to "Chang, Jeopardiser of the Heir Apparent, President of the Board of Plunderers, and Dissipator-General", and denouncing the luckless Viceroy as an "incapable traitor" and "the hound of barbarians". The harassed scholar had nothing but trouble in sight whichever way he turned.[1]

British claims arising out of the riots reached 188,725 dollars and 35 cents, and in December, back from his Corean mission, Parkes warned Kung to pay up promptly without nonsense. While Parkes was away the Yamen had been trying what it could do to persuade his colleagues that England's misdeeds had caused all the trouble.[2] German claims totalled 80,000 dollars; French, 10,000 (later raised to 43,000); American, 10,000. All these were accepted; but three members of the Yamen called on Young, the American Minister—an unusual thing for them to do—and argued their case against the British claims, while Kung brought up the matter in the Grand Council.[3] An Opinion by an English lawyer, Francis of Hongkong, was being widely circulated in defence of the Chinese case. It pointed out how bitterly the Chinese felt it that foreigners

[1] Correspondence with Grosvenor 130, 29.10.83, 17. 925.
[2] Parkes 49, 13.12.83, 17. 926.   [3] Parkes 59, 21.12.83, 17. 927.

who injured natives often escaped punishment; only England of the Treaty Powers had set up Courts for dealing with offenders on the spot. Portugal had no treaties with China, therefore no extrality; therefore Diaz ought either to have been left to Chinese justice or treated as a British subject. Hance defended himself by saying that his consular gaol was unprotected and would have been attacked had he kept Diaz there.[1]

On 20 December Parkes went to the Yamen to dragoon it into docility. An astonishing scene ensued; one that must have made the very spiders gape in their dusty corners. Parkes began by insisting on payment—and one must remember his habitual violence of manner. The Chinese replied that they would not pay a farthing unless Diaz were punished and Logan better punished. They claimed compensation for the relatives of the dead boy, citing the Margary precedent. The irascible Parkes struck his hand on the table and was about to speak when Chang Ta-jen broke in, exclaiming that *they* could do that as well, and began to bang extravagantly on the table. The rest of the solemn greybeards joined in, shouting at the tops of their voices and assailing the English Minister with personal abuse and invective. Chang cried that Parkes had caused one war between the two countries and had now come back to be the cause of another. The Grand Secretary Li Hung-tsao was so swept away by "the vehemence of his passion", as to upset his teacup. Wu Ta-jen's reason, what there was of it, appeared to have deserted him. He turned "purple with passion", and asked Parkes why he did not draw a pistol and shoot him. Parkes, dazed by the unexpected turning of the worm, kept trying to make himself heard, but a fresh outburst of clamour drowned him—"multa volentem dicere"—every time. They threatened with expressions "violent and abusive", to report him to the Queen, and the interview came to an unseemly end.[2]

It is not obvious what construction ought to be put on this surprising demonstration. Parkes represented it as a comedy planned by the Ministers to fasten a personal quarrel on him

[1] Copy of Opinion, and Hance's reply, in 17. 927.
[2] Parkes 57 Most conf., 20.12.83, and 61 Most conf., 22.12.83, 17. 926.

and so escape the issue,[1] and indulged in some reflections on the
hollowness of Chinese courtesy. It is much more likely that
the outburst was a genuine expression of strong dislike towards
the British Minister personally, together with resentment at
the way China was being bullied at Canton. Parkes' reputation
of a man determined to keep the East in an inferior position,
was well known. He had no sooner reappeared in China than
he was thrusting on her conditions that were felt as a flagrant
injustice. On the other hand, the Chinese had nothing to gain
from a histrionic quarrel; it would not release them from the
Canton claims, and in this juncture, when they were anxious
for British help against France, it was the last thing they would
deliberately bring about. The Foreign Office took a similar
view. Currie minuted: "It is probable that Sir H. Parkes gave
them some provocation." Pauncefote thought the incident an
outbreak of animosity against Parkes personally, and added as
regards Canton: "In my opinion they have reason to complain
of the leniency of Logan's sentence. I have read the evidence
and I think he shd have had 20 years penal servitude and de-
portation."[2] The Law Officers also considered the sentence
inadequate; the crime was "a very bad case of manslaughter,
approaching as nearly as possible to murder".[3] O'Conor,
forwarding Logan's petition for remission, said that it would be
neither just nor prudent to grant it, for the crime had been
"manslaughter of the most deliberate kind".[4] Colonel Derby
at the Colonial Office, moreover, considered that Diaz ought
to have been dealt with by the British Court.[5] All these reflections only led the Foreign Office to offer a "voluntary gift"

---

[1] Lane Poole says that Chang Pei-lun was told off beforehand to irritate
Parkes into an indiscretion. (*Life of Parkes*, II, 387.)

[2] Minutes on Parkes 57. Pauncefote also thought it strange Logan was
not tried for wounding two people. (Minute on Parkes tel. 1 ciph., 3.1.84,
17. 954.)   [3] L.O. to F.O., 22.1.84, 17. 968.

[4] O'Conor 381, 13.8.85, 17. 893. Logan said the Crown Advocate told
him after the trial that the sentence was only meant to placate the Chinese,
and doubtless he would be let off after a year or so. Did Logan invent this?
Papers on Logan's appeal in C.O. 129. 224.

[5] C.O. to F.O., 29.1.84, giving Bowen's report on the Diaz case, 17. 968.

—not compensation—to the family of the murdered boy; five hundred dollars would be liberal, Parkes advised, the boy's father being a mere scavenger, but in view of the notoriety of the case it might be politic to give a thousand.[1] The Treasury, which in those days did not like paying out money, insisted on Judge Rennie being told that his sentence on Logan was too light; which was unofficially done.[2]

On 22 December the Foreign Office cabled to Parkes its approval of his line of action, and its regret at the Yamen's behaviour.[3] The Chinese were not long in deciding that they could not afford the luxury of standing their ground. On 23 December Parkes was informed from London that the Chinese Envoy meant to ask for cancellation of instructions he had received to lodge a complaint against Sir Harry.[4] On the 28th he and the Yamen made a reconciliation—on the surface. Wine and food were partaken of. Chen and Wu were sulky but civil.[5]

China's climbing down went further. She had so many enemies that she was always having to compromise with one in order to turn against the next. At the beginning of January the Yamen agreed to pay our claims on condition we compensated the family of Logan's victim and induced the Portuguese Government to let Diaz be tried at Hongkong: the Throne would then be advised not to demand Logan's retrial.[6] England however would not pay "compensation", and Portugal refused to remove Diaz's trial from Macao.[7] Meanwhile things simmered down at Canton to a "sullen antipathy".[7] Rumours got about that gunpowder was being stored in the French Cathedral in readiness to blow up the town. French and American missionaries were attacked in January a few miles away. Their chapels were assaulted in the midst of service, the clergy having to run

[1] Parkes 31, 5.2.84, 17. 948, answering F.O. 28, ext. tel. 5, 28.1.84, 17. 947.
[2] Treasury to F.O., 1.3.84, and minute, 17. 969.
[3] F.O. tel. 32 ciph., 22.12.83, 17. 928.
[4] F.O. tel. 35, 23.12.83, 17. 928; memo. by Pauncefote 21.12.83, 17. 943.
[5] Parkes tel., 28.12.83, 17. 927.   [6] Parkes 1, 3.1.84, 17. 948.
[7] Hance 42, 10.12.83, with Parkes 3, 14.1.84, 27. 2707.

for their lives. The Rev. W. White reached Canton still sore from the brickbats aimed at him; the Rev. B. C. Henry, betrayed into a pardonable exasperation, declared to his consul that "immediate and decisive action" was necessary, and that he ought to be sent back with an escort of soldiers.[1] At Amoy a "People's League" was offering 200 taels for any specimen of a foreign head. The houses sacked by the rioters in the Shameen still stood "roofless and deserted" to chill the spirits of visitors to Canton.[2]

In March Parkes informed the Yamen of the Portuguese attitude, and required that examination of the British claims should at once proceed; though no trial seemed to be starting at Macao.[3] He was only at the beginning of a long course of rolling the stone uphill and seeing it roll down again, and of annoyances which, he told a friend, "have really embittered my life".[4] A better example of the ordinary day-to-day toil of diplomacy at Peking could hardly be chosen. The Yamen gave orders for the Claims and the homicide to be examined concurrently. Parkes protested at this jumbling of issues, verbally and in writing. Kung responded with his same old "trivial arguments". Parkes had to suspend the "wearisome correspondence" till June, being away in Corea. Then he saw the Ministers and explained, once for all, he wanted to hear no more of Logan or of Diaz. They asked again, notwithstanding, for Logan's sentence to be stiffened. After sharp debate they agreed to have the claims inspected and the needier claimants paid at once. A few days later they sent yet another Note asking a larger payment to Logan's victims. Parkes retorted angrily that our claims must be as well treated as those of the other Powers, and that delay would "prove very costly to the Chinese Government". They wrote back, maddeningly, that Logan must be resentenced, and if Diaz were not severely punished they would appeal to Her Majesty's Government.

---

[1] Report by U.S. Consul at Canton, with Parkes 5 conf., 14.1.84, 17. 948.
[2] Bowen, *Letters*, II, 296 ff.   [3] Parkes, 53, 19.3.84, 17. 949.
[4] *Life of Parkes*, II, 388. The following correspondence is annexed to Parkes 333, 26.12.84, 27. 2719, which sums up the case.

He replied that Her Majesty's Government could satisfy neither the one wish nor the other. They made an "unscrupulous and untruthful attempt" to blame the delay on an imaginary refusal of his to accept arbitration.

It was by now well on in July, and Parkes sent down Wilkinson, Crown Advocate, to Canton as our Commissioner. Kung, a Chinese Commissioner, began work with him on the claims on 29 July. Their work was finished on 21 August.[1] They agreed on every case, and awarded a total of 136,500 dollars. Governor Bowen hoped it would be a lesson to the Chinese.[2] In London, Tseng begged the Foreign Office to suspend pressure for payment, in view of China's embarrassments in Tonking, and a grudging consent was given.[3] By this time a promise to pay had been made at Peking.[4] On 10 September Parkes invited payment.[5] The Yamen said it had given the necessary orders. A fortnight later he still had to send in one final reminder; he was justified in telling the Foreign Office that he had won success only by "incessant and laborious effort". On 4 November the money was at last handed over.[6] Eleven hundred dollars were then bestowed on Logan's victims.[7]

The case was finally closed by London in March 1885.[8]

[1] Correspondence with Parkes 334, 26.12.84, 27. 2719.
[2] Bowen 295, 24.8.84, 27. 2714.
[3] F.O. to Parkes 155, ext. tel. 18, 29.7.84, 17. 947.
[4] F.O. to Parkes 168, 15.8.84, 17. 947.   [5] Parkes 333.
[6] Parkes tel. 43, 6.11.84, 17. 954.   [7] Parkes 338, 27.12.84, 27. 2719.
[8] F.O. to Parkes 48, 3.3.85, 17. 975.

CHAPTER NINE

Tonking, to the Bombardment of Fuchow

IN October 1883 a fresh turn seemed to lend colour to Chinese hopes of a successful resistance to France. The French Admiral had to restrict his Annam blockade within narrow limits, finding his resources inadequate. Tricou, who was ill, was leaving Tientsin after fresh debates with Li that led to nothing.[1] The Vicomte de Semallé was left at Peking as Chargé d'Affaires, without either instructions or information.[2] Li was busy making Port Arthur, the harbour which within a few years has sheltered many flags and ambitions, a protected base for his fleet of gunboats.[3] "Enormous" purchases of arms were made, as much by local Viceroys as by the Central Government. Arms were being bought chiefly from Germany, as in 1880, and from the United States. Kung was at one with Li in desiring peace, but both were being swept away.

The Shen-pao (wrote Grosvenor at the end of October), a newspaper in the vernacular, of immense circulation in the Chinese Empire, contains, almost daily, some allusion to the impending hostilities between France and China. It appears to me that the present state of affairs is very grave. Should a war between the two countries be the result of the present state of feeling, the losses of British merchants engaged in the Far East will be enormous. The questions to which such a war would give rise will be of so complicated a nature as to require years for their adjustment, and they would probably be of such a nature as to embroil us in disputes with other Western Powers besides France.

France chose a wrong, ignorant man for Tricou's special mission.[4]

[1] Parkes tel. 17 ciph., 29.10.83, 17. 928.
[2] Cordier 410.   [3] Grosvenor 128, 29.10.83, 17. 925.
[4] Grosvenor 127 conf., 29.10.83, 17. 925.

This is a large change from the carefree levity with which in May Grosvenor had contemplated a French annexation of Tonking. In November the American Minister Young told him that Li had been ordered by Decree not to allow Chinese troops in Tonking to evacuate any posts whatever. The Germans and French refused to credit this, whereupon Grosvenor asked the Yamen if it were true. Chou Chia-mei, "who became excited at the mere mention of Tonquin", affirmed that there were Chinese troops at Bacnin and at Sontay. "It would almost seem", the British Chargé wrote home, now really alarmed, "as if a conflict between the armed forces of the two countries was unavoidable."[1] De Semallé had a talk with Tattenbach, the German Chargé, in which he lost his head and promised that France would lay in ruins the native quarters of all the Treaty Ports—each warship already had its orders which port to attack.[2] Tattenbach repeated the threat to Grosvenor, and that harassed diplomat passed it on to Admiral Willes;[3] he also extracted from the Yamen a semi-official undertaking that foreign residents would be protected in case of war, though its terms were found to be unsatisfactory.[4] Willes began distributing his ships so as to afford the greatest protection to British nationals.[5]

On 15 November Semallé called at the Yamen and announced that France would negotiate only at Paris.[6] Next day Kung sent him a statement that if France ignored the fact of Chinese suzerainty over Annam, responsibility for whatever followed would rest on her. Kung's Note was circulated to the Diplomatic Body.[7]

[1] Grosvenor 137 Most conf., 9.11.83, 17. 926; cp. his 134, 5.11.83, 17. 926.
[2] Grosvenor 140 Most conf., 12.11.83, 17. 926.
[3] Grosvenor tel. 20 ciph., 12.11.83, 17. 928. Willes had lately reported that fear of French bombardments was growing. (Willes 453, 5.10.83, with Admiralty to F.O. 10.11.83, 17. 942.)
[4] Copy with Grosvenor 143, 20.11.83, 17. 926. L'Affaire du Tonkin, 124–5.
[5] Letter from Willes with Parkes 51, 15.12.83, 17. 926.
[6] Cordier 412.
[7] Grosvenor 142, 19.11.83, 17. 926.

A few days earlier Count Münster, German Ambassador in London, had called at the Foreign Office to say that Bismarck viewed with "serious concern" the probable effect of hostilities on neutral trade. He and Granville agreed that full communication between Berlin and London was desirable.[1] Next day Waddington gave an important assurance that France would not act against Chinese ports unless molested by the Chinese fleet[2]—an assurance he repeated on 17 November and on 11 December.[3] Tseng told Lord Lyons in Paris that the Yamen had informed Semallé there were imperial troops around Bacnin and Sontay which would resist any attacks.[4] He gave Ferry the same warning in writing.[5] Lord Granville wrote to Waddington about this, going further than he had yet moved in the direction of intervention: he said that "every reason combined to make Her Majesty's Government anxious for a peaceful solution"; the issue ought to be submitted to the arbitration of some European Power or the U.S.A., though England would not formally recommend this unless invited.[6] Waddington said that Tseng was playing a double game, and had indirectly offered to evacuate Bacnin and Sontay and resume negotiations.[7]

Lord Ampthill at Berlin formed the impression, "notwithstanding Count Hatzfeldt's habitual reserve", that Germany would welcome a settlement by arbitration.[8] Ampthill may or may not have been correct. At any rate Germany was ready for naval co-operation with us to protect neutral residents in China,[9] and the United States also joined in. England initiated the arrangement, believing a crisis at hand.[10] In France great

---

[1] F.O. to Ampthill (Berlin) 405 conf., 12.11.83, 27. 2705.

[2] F.O. to Lyons 1091, 13.11.83, 27. 2705.

[3] F.O. memo. 17.11.83, 27. 2705, and F.O. to Lyons 1236, 11.12.83, 27. 2706.   [4] Lyons tel. 61 ciph., 17.11.83, 27. 2705.

[5] *Life of Macartney*, 365.

[6] F.O. to Lyons 1105 conf., 20.11.83, 27. 2705.

[7] F.O. to Lyons 1113 Most conf., 27. 2705.

[8] Ampthill 320 Secret, 24.11.83, 27. 2705.

[9] Ampthill 318 conf., 23.11.83, ext. tel. 27, 27. 2705.

[10] F.O. to Ampthill tel. 23; to West (Washington) tel. 21 ciph., 27. 2705.

uneasiness prevailed.[1] Tseng telegraphed to Peking, exaggeratedly, that the Powers had secretly concerted to prevent blockade or bombardment of Chinese Ports.[2] The Foreign Office was now inviting Italy, Russia, Portugal, Spain, Japan, and even Austria, to join in naval measures for protection of neutrals.[3] Russia was evasive,[4] but most of the others promptly agreed. Governor Bowen at Hongkong set himself to entertain the Admirals and their staffs so as to "keep them in good humour with England and with each other".[5] Ferry suspiciously asked what measures were being planned.[6]

Tseng sent Macartney over from Paris to tell the Foreign Office in confidence, in view of numerous rumours afloat in the Press concerning English mediation, how much China could really concede. She would renounce all claims along the Red River south of Sontay, but France must abandon the Delta north of the Red River. The Delta would be opened to all. The river would be a neutralised boundary. Macartney asked if England, Germany, America, Italy and Russia could not interpose collective good offices.[7]

On 7 December Granville wrote privately to Waddington that Tseng had made a communication to him. The Ambassador rose to the bait, and came next day to ask what terms had been proposed. Granville observed, it was no use his disclosing the terms, as they did not come up to what Ferry had defined as his minimum. Waddington said that if he saw them he could consider how near France could come to them. Granville rejoined that his visitor should first say how far he could go. The Ambassador came out of cover and declared that France was

[1] Lyons 814, 30.11.83, 27. 2705. [2] Cordier 417.
[3] F.O. to Admiralty, Secret and Very Pressing, 9.12.83, 27. 2706.
[4] Vlangali kept delaying Russia's answer, and then assented on condition activity was restricted to what was done at Alexandria in 1882; this, he explained, "meant nothing more than that the object of the concert would be purely humanitarian". (Papers in 27. 2706. Part of the correspondence is published in B.F.S.P. lxxv, 969 ff.)
[5] Bowen 73, 11.3.84, with C.O. to F.O. 24.4.84, 27. 2708.
[6] Lyons 846, 13.12.83, 27. 2706.
[7] F.O. to Parkes 107 Secret, 12.12.83, 17. 920.

ready to "come to an arrangement" about Bacnin, as it was north of the River. The Foreign Secretary then revealed China's terms. Waddington exclaimed at the proposed treatment of the Delta—it was already in French hands. But it was agreed that the merits of the case should not be discussed.[1] The Yamen, incidentally, when Parkes mentioned Tseng's terms, repudiated them.[2]

Tseng told Lord Lyons he believed France would be glad to escape her embarrassments by making concessions on the invitation of a third party. Lyons said he feared not, in view of the "patriotic" tone of the Chamber.[3] Wade, visiting Paris, found Tseng more disposed towards a settlement than he had been last summer, when he took a very warlike attitude in order to impress Wade, hoping that fears for her commerce would force England to intervene; a hope Wade had warned him was not likely to be gratified. Now, Tseng was declaring that the Li-Bourée agreement would certainly have been ratified by China.[4]

On 18 December a telegram was despatched to Parkes (on Granville's own suggestion): "Send briefly by telegraph any information you have on difficulty between France and China."[5] On the 19th Macartney called, very keen on knowing how ready was France to accept mediation, and how ready to offer it were the Powers. Unofficially and in strict confidence, he continued that China would make concessions if the Powers would collectively approach France with good offices; Tseng was thinking of asking for authority to request the Powers in this sense. What did Lord Granville think would be their response? Macartney came back from Paris on the 21st, and let Granville know that Tseng did mean to cable for authority to appeal to the Powers. He begged urgently to know the

[1] F.O. to Lyons 1198 Secret, 10.12.83, 27. 2706.
[2] Parkes tel. 14 ciph., 14.3.84, and minute, 27. 2708. The Foreign Office was surprised at his mentioning the subject to the Yamen, since he had been informed of it in a Secret despatch.
[3] Lyons 840 conf., 11.12.83, 27. 2706.
[4] Wade to Granville, priv. and conf., 22.12.83, no. 2, 17. 943.
[5] F.O. tel. 32 ciph., 18.12.83, 27. 928.

opinion of Her Majesty's Government. On the 24th he was informed privately that Her Majesty's Government did not think the Powers would see their way to embarking on mediation unless solicited by both parties.[1] By this time Parkes had answered the cabled enquiry by reporting a complete deadlock, with the French waiting for reinforcements and the Chinese waiting for them to come on.[2] News reached Peking on the 23rd that France was mobilising the 12th Army Corps, and had taken Sontay.[3] Troops were being rushed to Canton, whence the Viceroy telegraphed to his Government that the situation on the war front was "extremely critical". He was not discouraged: the Black Flags were doing well, and he used the proverbial saying "France is riding a tiger and cannot dismount".[4]

So the motley soldiery continued to pour down along the southward roads, with their sedan-borne officers and their gong-beaters and their ill-assorted guns. Their fighting, when they reached the dangerous jungles of Tonking, was a peculiar mixture of the heroic and the grotesque. They had huge ammunition dumps and supplies, only they could not shoot straight, and their shells, even when coaxed from the cannon's mouth, rarely exploded. But in hand-to-hand fighting it was very different. In those obscure vindictive struggles, white man and yellow man, almost for the first time, stood on the same ground. And "the sympathies of the inhabitants, at any rate of the northern part of Tonking, were entirely with the Chinese".[5] The French had to impress carriers by force, and behaved with a brutality that deepened popular hostility. China has been invaded eight times in the last century, but has not yet been given one exhibition of the "civilised warfare" for which the West is renowned.[6]

[1] F.O. to Lyons 1282 Secret, 24.12.83, 27. 2706; memos by Pauncefote of 20.12.83, and 21.12.83, 17. 943.   [2] Parkes 56 (recorder), 20.12.83, 17. 927.
[3] Parkes 64, 24.12.83, 17. 927.
[4] Tel. no. date, with Parkes 64, 24.12.83, 17. 927.
[5] J. G. Scott, "The Chinese Brave", in *Asiatic Quarterly*, 1886.
[6] W. S. Blunt, in Paris in 1891, went to a barber who had soldiered in Tonking, and who vented the most bloodthirsty sentiments. "En agissant avec des brutes, il faut être brutal. Si j'avais été nommé gouverneur pendant un mois seulement, j'aurais exterminé tout ce monde Tonquinois. Il faut les

Further complexities arose. About the beginning of 1884 a rumour was heard that France was trying to buy Macao from Portugal as a war base.[1] It was also being said that the French meant to make China responsible for their war expenses, and to occupy Formosa, Hainan and Chusan as guarantees.[2] Parkes requested a special report from his consul on Hainan.[3] Chusan was an important strategical point, commanding access to the Yangtze.[4] In the war of 1840 it was freely supposed that Chusan was "destined henceforward to be ranked amongst the Eastern possessions of the British Empire".[5] We retained by treaty certain pre-emptive rights, and now, with Hongkong opinion taking alarm, Parkes telegraphed to ask if it would be well to remind China of the Chusan Convention of 1846.[6] He was informed that the time was not yet ripe for the action he proposed.[7] Later in the year the Law Officers were consulted, and held that Article 54 of the Treaty of Tientsin maintained the Chusan Convention in force.[8] "Certainly", noted Paunce-fote, "the possession of Chusan by France would be a constant menace to us in China."[9] A further preoccupation was the

assommer, Monsieur...." He plied his trade, incongruously, in the Rue de la Paix. (Blunt, Diaries, 28.4.91.)

[1] Letter to Chairman of Eastern Extension Tel. Co. from an agent, 29.1.84, 17. 1010. In the summer of 1884 Lisbon denied reports of a Franco-Portuguese alliance against China. (Petre (Lisbon) 45, 13.7.84, 27. 2709.) In Feb. 1885 Bowen, who was friendly with the Governor, wrote that Macao was observing a proper neutrality. (Bowen 79, 16.2.85, 27. 2784.)

[2] Parkes 24 Most conf., 28.1.84, 17. 948. (Cp. Bowen 60, 26.2.84, 27. 2708.)   [3] Parkes 77, 8.4.84, 17. 949.

[4] Moule, Half a Century in China, 3.

[5] Ouchterlong, pamphlet on Chusan, 1841; cp. Martin, British Possessions, 167, and Wells Williams, The Middle Kingdom, II, 580.

[6] Parkes tel. ciph. Most conf., 19.1.84, 17. 954.

[7] F.O. to Parkes tel. 2 ciph., 21.1.84, 27. 2707.

[8] L.O. to F.O., 18.9.84, 17. 972.

[9] Memo. 23.8.84, 17. 971. The Colonial Office asked if Bowen could be told that the French had promised not to occupy Chusan. But the French, it was found when correspondence was examined, had promised no such thing. (Memo. 23.2.84, on C.O. to F.O. conf., 15.2.84, 17. 2707.) Bowen approved the Hongkong Chamber of Commerce's request that our rights in Chusan should be maintained, and the London Chamber of Commerce endorsed it. (Bowen 13, 16.1.84, with C.O. to F.O. conf. 10.3.84, 27. 2708.)

decision of the Canton Viceroy to block the Whampoa River. The British and American Ministers and the German Chargé protested to the Yamen. The Chinese were sulky. One, Chang, said to the American with animated gestures—"Here is the robber coming—coming—coming; we want to keep him out, we want to close the door, and you say no!"[1] The British and German Admirals considered China would be resorting to legitimate means of defence by blocking the river;[2] and Paunce-fote considered she was entirely in the right, and that we might get ourselves into a war with her by interfering.[3] Waddington was asked if France would renew her promise not to attack Ports without due warning and declaration of war. He promised to telegraph to Paris, and the same day read out an answer promising not to attack Ports unless China became aggressive, and then only after notification—which meant, Waddington explained, "after declaration of war".[4] Blocking measures at Canton were suspended.[5]

About this time, in reply to Mr Blowitz of *The Times*, who was advocating a simple division—Tonking to China, Annam to France—Macartney laid down categorically that China *must* have control of the Red River.[6] Tseng, calling at the Foreign Office, said he feared war was imminent. Granville warned him that war would be "onerous" to France, but "an immense danger" to China. Tseng requested him to declare in advance that he would stand neutral when war came. Granville answered that the request was a grave one, and he doubted whether his Government would consent so to tie its hands. He went on to ask what the Chinese would do if France took Bacnin. Tseng replied firmly: they "would attack the French in every possible way that was open to them". Granville warned him that that would be a most dangerous path.[7] At Peking they were waiting

[1] Parkes 7 conf., ext. tel. 3, and 12 20.1.84, 27. 2707.
[2] Parkes 14, 21.1.84, 17. 948.   [3] Minute 17.1.84, 27. 2709.
[4] F.O. to Lyons 59 and 59A, 18.1.84, 27. 2707.
[5] Parkes 20, ext. tel. 6, 26.1.84, 27. 2707.   [6] *Life of Macartney*, 366 ff.
[7] F.O. to Parkes 18.1.84, 27. 2707. Boulger (*Life of Macartney*, 370-1) is at pains to refute the French idea that Tseng was Gallophobe and not very anxious for peace.

in suspense to see whether Bacnin would be assaulted. Parkes hoped the French would have neither will nor strength to come on farther.[1] Since capturing Sontay on 17 December they had been inactive, and Chinese confidence was mounting.[2] Governor Bowen found 'the situation more and more perturbing, however. On 4 March the Kowloon commandant called on him agitatedly to say that an insurrection had been started some miles north by the Secret Societies, whose numerous adherents in the colony meant to revolt that very night. Precautions were taken, and the night passed quietly; but Bowen repeated his Cassandra cry that Hongkong was "practically defenceless" against foreign attack.

If four or five thousand soldiers of any foreign Power were landed at the back of this island, they could, of course, march into the town (a distance of only four miles) without effective opposition from our small garrison: they could then occupy our Arsenals and barracks, confiscate the large amounts of specie in the Banks: and seizing our few batteries, which are all open to the rear, turn the guns against our own ships in the harbour.[3]

Late on 13 March, a telegram reached Saigon announcing the capture of Bacnin.[4] The news reached Parkes next day simultaneously with the Foreign Office despatch containing Tseng's threat of war if Bacnin should fall. He hurried to the Yamen to ask if Tseng had used the threat by its authority. The Ministers said yes, but that they did not mean to fulfil the threat at present; their chief object was the protection of their own frontier.[5] They took their time to think over this and other reverses, wrote Parkes, and "instead of making them a *casus belli*, as foretold by the Marquis Tseng, the Chinese Government affect to regard them with indifference and will simply continue to act on the defensive". They admitted that

1 Parkes 23, 28.1.84, 27. 2707.   2 Parkes 35, 11.2.84, 27. 2707.
3 Bowen 71, 8.3.84, with C.O. to F.O. 29.4.84, 17. 969.
4 Consul Tremlett 2 Political, 14.3.84, 27. 2708.
5 Parkes tel. 15 ciph., 15.3.84, 27. 2708. Tseng himself did not know what to expect when Bacnin fell, and said it would depend on which party at Peking had the upper hand. (Memo. by Currie, 24.3.84, 17. 947.)

their reason for authorising Tseng to speak as he did was to get the British Government to declare neutrality, and so debar the French from making use of Hongkong.[1] Parkes took an opportunity to complain of a letter by Tseng in the *Deutsche Revue*, according to which England had she chosen could have stopped the French invasion with a word.[2] Tseng had not been seeing Granville much lately, the latter told Waddington when asked if Tseng were requesting good offices.[3]

The two countries hovered between peace and war. On 8 April the Chinese Government betrayed its nervous condition by a Decree which abruptly dismissed and disgraced Prince Kung himself and three of his colleagues of the Yamen and the Grand Council. The Grand Council was left with only one member, and it—or rather he—was ordered to consult, during the Emperor's minority, with the Seventh Prince. The Governors of Yunnan and Kwangsi were degraded. Two officers who had retreated in face of the enemy were to be decapitated in front of their troops. Tseng was to be replaced at Paris (not at London) by the anti-foreign Su King-ch'eng.[4] The prospect of an administration inspired by the Seventh Prince was one to alarm. The much-thinned Yamen, when interviewed, professed astonishment at the landslide, but naïvely stated that it had nothing to do with foreign affairs. That resolution had been duly toned up appeared when Ministers assured the American Secretary of Legation that China would not merely refuse to give any indemnity but would attempt to retake Bacnin and Sontay. Sir Robert Hart believed that Prince Ch'un had secured an ascendancy over the Empress; and that the French would make a descent on the Chinese coast.[5] Prophecies of such a raid seemed, indeed, about to be fulfilled. Waddington took occasion to say that rumours of a French occupation of

---

[1] Parkes 70, 2.4.84, 27. 2708.   [2] Parkes 72, 2.4.84, 17. 849.
[3] F.O. to Lyons 251, 19.3.84, 27. 2708. The Ambassador was afraid the Liberal Government was going to resign, and also nervous over its Egyptian policy. Detring, a creature of Li's, returned to China from Europe in March and repeated stories of intrigues by Macartney for the formation of a European bloc inspired by Germany. (Cordier 431.)
[4] Parkes 79, 15.4.84, 17. 849.   [5] Parkes 84 conf., 19.4.84, 17. 950.

Hainan were "utterly untrue".[1] And on 3 May he declared it would be a great mistake if further fighting were allowed— "The military operations are terminated".[2] But the Russian Minister at Peking expressed to his Government the belief that the Decree of 12 April on the loss of Bacnin and Sontay amounted to an official declaration of war.[3] Japan believed war to be at any rate near.[4]

Again, as at the time of the Bourée agreement, a peaceful conclusion was abruptly brought in sight. Detring, a Customs officer and confidant of Li, happened to be travelling in a French warship, and suggested to the Captain, Fournier, that he should hold discussions with Li, with whom he had some acquaintance.[5] Detring went to Tientsin and got Li to invite Fournier there. The latter cabled home urgently on 8 May for permission to treat, fearing, says Cordier, lest Parkes should try to keep the Tonking sore open because of the state of affairs in Egypt.[6] Powers to treat were sent him from Paris. Li meanwhile had also been obtaining authority.[7] The Yamen confessed on 28 April that he was to be allowed to negotiate, and Hart believed that the Empress was too sensible to want war.[8] On 9 May Li had a very long and frank talk with Hillier, disclosing much of what was in his mind. No doubt he felt that with Kung gone it was for him to step into the breach. When Hillier mentioned Kung's fall he "dropped his hands and made a gesture of regret"—"the Yamen was now composed of men who knew nothing about international questions". He declared that while China would *never* pay an indemnity she could not conduct an offensive campaign. If France sent out 50,000 men, China would be crushed. He begged Hillier to tell Parkes all this, and say he would like to see him.[9]

[1] F.O. to Lyons 314A, 10.4.84, 27. 2707.
[2] F.O. to Lyons 394, 3.5.84, 27. 2708.   [3] Cordier 427.
[4] Plunkett (Tokio) 63 conf., 26.4.84, 27. 2708.
[5] Mrs Little, *Li Hung-chang*, 139.   [6] Cordier 433.
[7] Maude (Peking) tel. ciph., 29.4.84, and 29.4.84 Separate (Extender), 27. 2708.
[8] *Life of Parkes*, II, 376.
[9] Hillier, 9.5.84, with Parkes 96, 24.5.84, 27. 2708.

Two days later the Li-Fournier Convention was signed. It gave France what Fournier had been told to get; China would evacuate Tonking, acquiesce in any Franco-Annamite treaty, and admit trade into Yunnan. France waived her indemnity "pour rendre hommage à la sagesse patriotique de Son Excellence Li Hung Tchang".[1]

Consul Davenport at Tientsin learned the terms at once, and Maude, who was in charge at Peking, cabled them home on the 12th.[2] The Foreign Office at once began to ponder the question of how British trade was likely to be affected.[3] In China, where popular feeling had been rising perilously, Parkes rejoiced in the lightening of tension.[4] He was to be speedily disabused. There had been a party at Peking averse to letting Li treat at all.[5] His report to the Throne was couched in very nervous language: he had worked at making peace "with fear and trembling, as one who drives a team of horses with reins of rotten rope". He made the best of his terms, affecting to consider that he had preserved China's suzerainty over Annam.[6] He is said to have got his first answer in a scathing letter from the Empress, upbraiding him with cowardice;[7] and the Censors rose as one man to denounce him.[8] He was reported to be in great despondency, shut up in his room and staring vacantly at the moon.[8] Feng Yu-lin, Military Commissioner at Canton, was one of those who attacked the Convention. The troops were firm; why such timidity? Unless the "French barbarians" were chastised, China's reputation would sink, and she would be

---

[1] Text in Cordier 435. An indemnity claim was brought up for bargaining purposes only. (L'Affaire du Tonkin, 159-61.)

[2] Maude tel. Separate, 12.5.84, 27. 2708.

[3] Minutes on above. The London Chamber of Commerce was disquieted by rumours that our Tonking trade was to be heavily discriminated against. (Letter to F.O. 16.6.84, 27. 2709.) The Law Officers were consulted.

[4] Parkes 98, 4.6.84, 17. 951.

[5] Maude Separate and conf., 13.5.84, 27. 2708.

[6] Copy with Parkes 114 conf., 11.7.84, 17. 951.

[7] Mrs Little, Li Hung-chang, 140.

[8] Copy of Memorial by Censors with Consul-General Hughes, 27.6.84, 27. 2709.

beset by fresh and voracious enemies. If Yunnan were opened
to the commerce of the French they would seize the province,
after effecting a "widespread propaganda of their depraved
religion in order to spread their wings". Frenchmen and
Catholic Missions in China ought to be extirpated.[1]

The half-expected breach opened up when telegrams reached
Paris on 26 June reporting that Chinese troops had attacked a
French column entering Langson.[2] What had happened was
that after signing the Convention Fournier had an interview
with Li as to details of the evacuation, and then, assuming Li
to have spoken more precisely than in fact he had, telegraphed to
General Millot to occupy Tonking up to the frontier after a
specified time-limit.[3] A Chinese commander, called on to
withdraw at the end of this time, said he was only waiting
for orders from home; by some blunder, fighting was renewed.[4]

Semallé lodged a complaint with the Yamen on 28 June.
The Chinese contended that the treaty contained no dates or
details of evacuation, and they produced the Chinese text.[5]
There was angry controversy over an extra group of clauses
said to have been signed by the Viceroy. Li's explanation to
the Yamen was that Fournier brought him three supple-
mentary clauses, number 2 being a time-limit for evacuation:
this he declined to sign.[6] Fournier offered to fight anyone who
doubted his word, and fought a duel. It is hard to imagine how
the divergence could be due to an accident. Either Fournier,
or his assistants, inserted the clause in an already signed paper,
or else he was tricked in some way by the Viceroy. Possibly
the latter, finding what opposition there was to his treaty,

[1] Copy with Parkes 109 Very conf., 3.7.84, 17. 951. At the end of 1884
the Hongkong Government unsuccessfully prosecuted native editors for
publishing something like an incitement to the massacre of French
residents.
[2] Lyons tel. 12, 26.6.84, 27. 2709.
[3] Cordier 441–3. Cf. *L'Affaire du Tonkin*, 167 ff.
[4] Cordier 450–1.
[5] Parkes 108, 3.7.84, 27. 2709.
[6] Cordier 458–60.

wanted to provoke a breach.[1] Semallé was struck by the genuine astonishment of the Yamen;[2] if there was a plot on China's side, they were not in it.

Tseng and Ferry exchanged protests. On 1 July Patenôtre, the new French Minister, landed at Shanghai. His previous post had been Stockholm, and our Minister there described him as amiable and moderate, a friend of Bourée who had only with reluctance stepped into Bourée's shoes.[3] Arrived in China, however, he showed a different temper. He cabled Ferry advising an ultimatum, on the ground that delay would benefit China.[4] On the 7th Ferry cabled back that he did not want to break off negotiations.[5] But on the 9th he told Lord Lyons that the Yamen was shuffling, and it would be necessary to make a peremptory demand for an indemnity, and perhaps occupy territory as security.[6] On the 10th Parkes learned that the Yamen was sending two of its members to join Li in treating with Patenôtre at Tientsin; and, as Patenôtre seemed to be staying at Shanghai, Sir Robert Hart was taken off from other duties and sent there to conciliate him.[7] Patenôtre told Hart that it was too late for talk,[8] and on the same day Semallé at Peking presented a Note—an "espèce d'ultimatum", he called it[9]—demanding a huge indemnity of 250,000,000 francs under threat of seizure of territory at the end of seven days. When Parkes cabled this news next day he added that China had already refused the indemnity and declared she would appeal to the Powers. "This looks I fear like war", wrote Pauncefote at the Foreign Office.[10]

Parkes saw the Yamen on the 15th and heard its views on the Langson affair.[11] On the 16th he sent Hillier to interview the

[1] In July a Shanghai paper had an article, inspired by the Chinese Government and purporting to come from an eyewitness, according to which Li refused to sign and Fournier left Tientsin hastily, pretending that Li *had* signed. (Parkes 134 conf., 31.7.84, 27. 2709.)

[2] Cordier 458.   [3] Rumbold 87 conf., 30.8.83, 27. 2705.
[4] Cordier 466.   [5] *Ibid.* 467.
[6] Lyons 408, 9.7.84, 27. 2709.   [7] Parkes 113, 10.7.84, 27. 2709.
[8] Cordier 468.   [9] Parkes 117, 16.7.84, 27. 2709.
[10] Parkes 115, ext. tel. 23, 14.7.84, 27. 2709, and minute.   [11] Parkes 117.

Ministers. They were still obdurate on the indemnity point. A Decree, however, ordered the withdrawal of troops from Tonking within a month. At the same time General Tso was put in command of the Peking Field Force, and the public lived in expectation of war. Li was again begging and being refused permission to resign and mourn his mother.[1] On the 17th Parkes, and on the 19th the rest of the Corps Diplomatique, received copies of the Yamen's correspondence over Langson, with a note to the effect that while China would do her best to protect foreigners France must be responsible for any harm that might befall them.[2] The seven days allowed by Semallé's Note were up, but China had asked and been granted an extension. She used it to make fresh overtures to Patenôtre, and to ask the United States Minister for mediation. Young cabled to Washington; he expected small results.[3] When Washington tendered good offices at Paris, Ferry insisted on China's accepting the principle of an indemnity as the first step.[4] Parkes addressed a note to the Yamen, with a warning that *China* would be held responsible for any injuries suffered by British nationals.[5]

Tseng Kuo-ch'uan, the Nanking Viceroy, arrived at Shanghai on 24 July with two thousand troops and full powers to treat with Patenôtre—symbolising China's readiness to accept either peace or war. Chinese officials, our Consul-General there reported, were emphatic that no indemnity would be paid under any circumstances.[6] French warships, Parkes telegraphed in response to an enquiry from home, were commanding Fuchow, Formosa, and other points.[7] On the 28th Hart sent a telegram from Shanghai expressing almost despair: Patenôtre would not behave reasonably "...possible ending, French Chinese

[1] Parkes 118, 17.7.84, 27. 2709.
[2] Parkes 119, 17.7.84, and 126, 24.7.84, 27. 2709. Part of the latter appears in *B.F.S.P.* lxxv, 974.   [3] Parkes 128, 24.7.84, 27. 2709.
[4] *L'Affaire du Tonkin*, 304 ff. Young is here accused of distorting his instructions, because he wanted to arbitrate, not mediate.
[5] Parkes 129, 24.7.84, 27. 2709; *B.F.S.P.* lxxv, 975.
[6] Hughes 45, 25.7.84, 27. 2709.
[7] Parkes tel. 26 ciph., 25.7.84, 27. 2709.

Empire".[1] On 2 August Patenôtre rejected an offer of 500,000 taels by way of compensation to the French soldiers injured at Langson, and informed China that France resumed her liberty of action.[2] Nearly all the Englishmen serving in the Chinese fleet resigned, in expectation of immediate war.[3]

Ferry promised Lord Lyons that he would try not to injure trade;[4] evidently he felt it necessary to lull British apprehensions. At Washington, Acting Secretary Davis told the French Minister Roustan that the United States was entitled by Treaty to exert good offices on China's behalf if the latter country suffered aggression. The two did not understand each other very clearly, our Minister found, as Mr Davis spoke little French and M. Roustan little English.[5] The American President wrote to the French President.[6] But on 5 August Hughes telegraphed: "French decline American Minister's mediation. Kelung will be taken immediately."[7]

The first act in France's new unrestricted warfare did, indeed, follow immediately. Three warships destroyed the forts of Kelung, the Formosan port. On 11 August contradictory telegrams from Hongkong and Amoy reported that the French had occupied Kelung and were demanding 80,000,000 francs as its ransom, and that a French landing party had been repulsed with loss. The latter news was correct.[8] Tseng called at the Foreign Office and asked England's assent to the proposition that the attack was an unjustifiable act; the Foreign Office cautiously said it had not learned enough to pronounce.[9] At Peking firmness was in the ascendant. France was obviously uncertain at every stage what to do next, and a Yamen Minister told Parkes that there had been so many ultimatums he had lost

[1] Forwarded to the F.O. by a China Customs officer; 27. 2709.
[2] Cordier 474.　　　　　　　　[3] Parkes 133, 31.7.84, 27. 2709.
[4] Lyons 452, 2.8.84, 27. 2710.
[5] West (Washington) 251 conf., 3.8.84, 27. 2710.
[6] Correspondence re American mediation with Parkes 141, 13.8.84, 27. 2710.　　　　　　　　[7] Hughes tel. ciph., 5.8.84, 27. 2710.
[8] C.O. to F.O. Pressing, 11.8.84, with message from Hongkong; Consul at Amoy 8, rec. tel. ciph., 11.8.84, 27. 2710.
[9] Memo. by Pauncefote 12.8.84, 27. 2711.

count of them. China moreover believed Anglo-French relations to be so strained that France would not dare to fight in the Far East.[1]

The Yamen seemed more elated by the measure of success enjoyed by the defenders of Kelung than Parkes thought warranted,[2] but he was more and more convinced that the French lacked any precise plan and were getting themselves into an impasse.[3] On the 18th the Yamen circulated a fresh note to the Diplomatic Body, restating its case at length and repeating that foreigners could apply to France for compensation if their property suffered;[4] while at Shanghai the consuls were furnished with photographic copies of the Li-Fournier Convention.[5] The rival negotiators were still at Shanghai, wrote Hughes, but no discussions were in train. Apparently Li had authorised a Spanish Secretary of Legation to mediate, but Patenôtre had told him the indemnity was the first essential. "Peace though not expected is universally desired by the business community", added Hughes. "Heavy losses in business are spoken of."[6] The French Chambers voted a new credit.

Semallé wound up his series of ultimatums with one on the 19th, demanding the indemnity within forty-eight hours. It was reduced to eighty millions, in view of the promise to evacuate Tonking. Parkes cabled that day: "Failing payment Admiral will act. Tsungli-Yamen state to me China will pay no indemnity."[7] He called at the Yamen to enquire whether its Circular of the 15th implied a state of war. The Ministers said it did not. He did not recommend payment of the indemnity, feeling such advice hopeless since Kelung.[8] Before

[1] Parkes 139, 8.8.84, 27. 2710.
[2] Parkes 166, 28.8.84, 27. 2711.
[3] Parkes 148, 15.8.84, 27. 2710.
[4] Parkes 149, 18.8.84, 27. 2710; 156, 21.8.84, 27. 2711.
[5] Hughes 50, 15.8.84, 27. 2710. Cp. Part 6 of War Office Intelligence survey of Operations in Tonking, 27. 2770.
[6] Hughes 51, 15.8.84, 27. 2710.
[7] Parkes tel. 29 ciph., 19.8.84, 27. 2711.
[8] Parkes 156, 21.8.84, 27. 2711.

the ultimatum expired Semallé was handed his passports.[1]
He rode out of Peking with his staff at 3.20 p.m. on the 21st.[2]
The Chinese Minister to Berlin, temporarily replacing Tseng
at Paris, was ordered by his Government from there back to
Germany.[3]

Rumours sprang into life again that France would seize
Chusan.[4] They were disturbing because, Pauncefote noted,
"It is very doubtful whether the Treaty of 1846 about Chusan
is still in force".[5] Ferry—still out to carry on war peacefully—
insisted that Semallé's withdrawal was not a full withdrawal
of representation, since Patenôtre was to stay at Shanghai.[6]
The Foreign Office, however, prepared a Proclamation of
Neutrality for the Law Officers to check—"A state of war is unhappily impending if not existing between France and China."[7]
On the 23rd the British Chargé questioned Ferry, and was told
that there was a "nuance" perceptible to French eyes between
the existing state of affairs and war; but that an attack on
Fuchow had been ordered. "It may be more than a question",
reflected the Foreign Office, "whether M. Ferry's 'nuances'
really exists (sic), as it is convenient to the French Govt. to
contend."[8] Governor Bowen, who on 17 July had written,
not for the first time, to ask instructions as to observance of
neutrality, cabled on 21 August: "Telegraph at once instructions."[9] The Law Officers were called on to solve the puzzle:
Were France and China at war?[10] On the 24th Macartney
called privately at Pauncefote's house to propose a "friendly

[1] Parkes 159, 22.8.84, 27. 2711, gives copies of the last exchanges between
Semallé and the Yamen. The rest of their correspondence was communicated
to the Diplomats a week later. (Parkes 168, 29.8.84, 27. 2711.)
[2] Parkes 160, 22.8.84, 27. 2711.
[3] Walsham (Paris) tel. 19 ciph., 21.8.84, 27. 2711.
[4] Parkes tel. 30 ciph., 21.8.84, 27. 2711.   [5] Minute on above.
[6] Walsham tel. 21 conf., 23.8.84, and 502, 24.8.84, 27. 2711.
[7] F.O. to L.O., 23.8.84, 27. 2711.
[8] Walsham 507, 24.8.84, and minute, 27. 2711.
[9] Bowen 261, 17.7.84, and tel., 21.8.84, enclosed with C.O. to F.O.
Immediate 25.8.84, 27. 2711.
[10] F.O. to L.O. Pressing, 27.8.84, 27. 2711.

understanding" between England and China. It was practically an invitation of alliance. Failing that, he asked that England should observe strict neutrality. A formal reply was written three days later: England would be strictly neutral.[1]

In short, as Consul Sinclair wrote from Fuchow, there was a state of affairs "which 'no feller can understand', if I may be pardoned for quoting Lord Dundreary".[2] A French squadron had come up the Min River; China like Africa was betrayed to the foreigners by her rivers. French and Chinese warships were lying cheek by jowl waiting to attack one another, and the Frenchmen hoisted flags to salute the Emperor's birthday! Sinclair's little joke was the last he was able to afford himself for some time. There had for some time been unrest at Fuchow under the French menace, though the authorities behaved calmly—unlike the old Dey of Algiers who, when exactly two centuries earlier the French attacked his town, blew the foreign residents one by one from the cannon's mouth. The stroke fell on 23 August. The French squadron carried out a bombardment that was virtually a massacre. Away at Shanghai a crowd sat for hours on the Bund to watch the telegraphic news from the doomed town; and it seemed to them that it was not the French who were the heroes.[3] Some of the Chinese guns were bravely fought, though Imperial Commissioner Chang fled to the hills as soon as the battle opened, to await a Decree commending his bravery.[4] Fire was kept up for hours after the land batteries were silenced. Native accounts said that three thousand lives were lost.[5] The French were evidently embarking on a policy of frightfulness. There was no French trade at Fuchow, so they had nothing to lose. A mob attacked the foreigners at the

[1] Memo. by Macartney, 24.8.84, and F.O. to Tseng, 27.8.84, 27. 2711.

[2] Sinclair, 18.8.84, with Parkes 163, 27.8.84, 27. 2711.

[3] Moule, *Half a Century in China*, 222.

[4] Parkes 200, 1.10.84, 27. 2713. Chang was denounced by forty officials at Peking, natives of Fukien. (Hughes 71, 29.10.84, 27. 2715.)

[5] For an eyewitness' description see Sergeant, *Empress Dowager of China*, 126. Cp. Morse and MacNair, *Far Eastern International Relations*, 352: "Only on the ground that an Asiatic nation has no rights which the European is bound to respect can the course of France be explained."

Anchorage, and terrorised those on Nantai Island. Poor Sinclair, despite his "well-known Chinese sympathies and long residence", had to make a nocturnal escape, disguised as a Celestial.[1]

Parkes wrote that the bombardment was "little less than treacherous", and that the French would not dare to attack Port Arthur like that.[2] With England possibly on the brink of intervention, it was a confession of military impotence and desperation.[3]

[1] Mrs Gordon Cumming, *Wanderings in China*, ch. VI.

[2] *Life of Parkes*, II, 379.

[3] Baron Rosen says that bombardment of the Ports by Russia, had it come to war in 1880, would have been "quite out of the question, as this would necessarily have embroiled us with all the other so-called Treaty Powers." (*Forty Years of Diplomacy*, I, 45.)

CHAPTER TEN

Tonking, to the end of 1884

TSENG immediately denounced the bombardment of Fuchow to Lord Granville as a piece of barbarism.[1] In Peking a Decree was issued, but not communicated to the Corps, which, Parkes cabled, "amounts to declaration of war".[2] City merchants suggested that Her Majesty's Government ought to seize the moment to bring about peace, China paying an indemnity—which she deserved, on general principles as it were, to do.[3] As Parkes wrote: "The position was very peculiar and embarrassing."[4] On the 27th the Yamen announced that China could not guarantee protection of foreigners. Parkes frightened them into retracting.[5] One of the Law Officers wrote to Currie that orders must be given for observance of neutrality. "It is quite clear that France and China are now at war."[6]

It was now that the French took the step of declaring Shanghai outside the sphere of hostilities;[7] a concession to neutral feeling badly needed in the circumstances. Excitement there was very great; the "Shanghai Volunteers" were out parading, to strike awe into the rabble, and as their armament consisted of two brass howitzers chiefly dangerous to themselves, it was felt they ought to be re-equipped.[8] The French Consul-General's Proclamation, that no real trouble existed, was described to Parkes by Young as "fantastic"; and "the whole

[1] Tseng to Granville, 27.8.84, 27. 2711.
[2] Parkes 31 (recorder), 27.8.84, 27. 2711.
[3] Johnstone to Currie, 28.8.84, 27. 2711.
[4] Parkes 169, 29.8.84, 27. 2711.   [5] Parkes 170, 29.8.84, 27. 2711.
[6] Sir H. James to Currie, 30.8.84, 27. 2711.
[7] Papers printed in B.F.S.P. lxxv, 979 ff.
[8] Report by Maj.-Gen. Sergeant, O.C. China and Straits, with Parkes 131, 31.7.84, 17. 951.

business", the American added, "is strange, eccentric and unsatisfactory".[1] Enomotto, the Japanese Minister, assured Parkes that "Japan had no idea of joining with France against China and had no reason whatever for doing so",[2] which may have been part of the truth, but was not the whole truth. The War Office wanted to know whether the defences of Hongkong ought to be strengthened. Granville—curiously—thought the colony in little danger of external attack, but perhaps in need of an Indian regiment to check internal disorder.[3] A Declaration of Neutrality was held ready; on 2 September the Straits and Hongkong were informed that it would not be issued until war was declared: in the meantime the Foreign Enlistment Act was to be enforced.[4] The Law Officers were satisfied that a state of war existed, but the Foreign Office after consulting the Colonial Office decided that it would be impolitic to take this for granted as yet.[5]

Developments in China showed how excitement was gathering there. It was feared that Russia was about to make demands on China.[6] On 3 September a Decree discharged three members of the already well-shuffled Yamen.[7] A British gunboat, the *Zephyr*, was fired on by the Kinpai Forts near Fuchow, and an officer was killed. A great deal of correspondence ensued. The Chinese said they mistook the *Zephyr* for a Frenchman. Parkes did not believe it, but we accepted a verbal and written apology from the Yamen, an apology from the Fukien Viceroy, an apology from Tseng in London, and £3600 for the officer's family.[8] There was other "melancholy evidence" from Fuchow that China either could not or would not protect foreigners.[9] The Canton Viceroy was feeling his way towards

[1] Parkes 172 conf., 3.9.84, 27. 2712.
[2] Parkes 171 conf., 2.9.84, 27. 2712.
[3] War Office to F.O. 1.9.84, and minute, 27. 2712.
[4] Tel., Secret, 27. 2712.
[5] L.O. to F.O., 5.9.84; F.O. to L.O. Immediate, 9.9.84, 27. 2712.
[6] Memo. by Currie of interview with Macartney, 1.9.84, 17. 972.
[7] Parkes 178, 5.9.84, 27. 2712.
[8] Correspondence in 27. 2712, 27. 2715, 27. 2717.
[9] Parkes 186, 19.9.84, 27. 2712.

a foreign loan—money *must* be found for the troops, wrote Hughes, or there would be anarchy.[1] Canton authorities also called on patriotic Chinese in the Straits to poison every Frenchman in sight. Parkes denounced this at Peking, and Tseng was made to get his Government to quash the order.[2] Rioting and strikes broke out at Hongkong, where a "Peace Preservation Act" was passed and 16,000 stand of arms confiscated. The Chinese there complained that labourers were being forced to work at refitting French ships.[3] The Viceroy of Yunnan and Kweichow was ordered (if a secret Memorial obtained by Parkes was authentic) to keep all his troops in Tonking in their positions.[4] Germany obtained an assurance that France would respect her interests; so England obtained a similar one.[5] The British Telegraph Company's Shanghai agent cabled that there was a prospect of China collapsing and Russia as well as France annexing provinces; while the Chairman, scenting a subsidy, admonished the Foreign Office that as our present telegraph line ran through French Indo-China, "we should be entirely in the hands of the French in case of political complications arising".[6]

The problem of whether war legally existed was insistent. The Law Officers were now not unanimous.[7] A French gunboat exasperated the problem on 26 September by searching two British steamers off Kelung.[8] Hughes was at once told to make enquiries from Patenôtre. The latter replied that France was *not* at war.[9] Admiral Dowell protested to the French, and

---

[1] Hughes 63, 26.9.84, 27. 2713.

[2] Parkes tel. 34, 26.9.84, tel. ciph. 36, 30.9.84, 27. 2713, and other correspondence in this volume.

[3] Correspondence in 27. 2715, 27. 2716, 27. 2717, 27. 2718.

[4] Parkes 195 conf., 30.9.84, 27. 2713.

[5] Papers in 27. 2712, 27. 2713. Two of them are printed in *B.F.S.P.* LXXV, 976.

[6] Pender (Chairman) to F.O., 30.9.84, and enclosures. It is curious that neither the Company nor the F.O. thought of this a year earlier when they were getting a concession through Siam and Cochin China.

[7] L.O. to F.O. 27.9.84, 27. 2713.

[8] Consul Frater (Tamsui) 16, 29.9.84, 27. 2713. Fuller reports in 27. 2714.

[9] Parkes 207, 8.10.84, 27. 2714; Hughes tel. ciph., 29.9.84, 27. 2713.

the Admiralty thought him right. So did the Foreign Office, which had the question brought up at Paris; Lloyds were raising an alarm.[1] Ferry explained that his Admiral had had orders just at the moment of the incident to blockade Tamsui. The Foreign Office found the explanation "very unsatisfactory".[2]

Military measures developed on both sides. The telegraph line, which formerly ended at Tungchow fourteen miles from the capital, was being brought up to Peking.[3] The Chinese wanted to block the river at Shanghai; there was an indignation meeting there, but Parkes considered the plan legitimate in view of the attack on Fuchow, which to his mind violated Waddington's assurance to Granville of 18 January.[4] At the beginning of October, Courbet attacked Kelung again, this time with success, but was driven off from Tamsui. Formosa, it was clear, was marked out as temporarily or permanently French prey, and Parkes had a special report drawn up on it which contained the phrase: "The natural resources of Formosa are capable of a development which is practically limited only by the demand for its products abroad."[5] Parkes circulated to his consuls a confidential memorandum by the Crown Advocate on the attitude British subjects ought to adopt as regards neutrality.[6] A bombardment of Tamsui was followed by a French landing and a serious repulse.

The position was bound to reawaken ideas of mediation among neutrals, though Parkes, for one, was ready to despair of any solution. "I don't see any turning in the long lane ahead of us", he wrote to a son-in-law.[7] The first step was taken by

---

[1] Dowell to Admiralty tel. ciph., 28.9.84; Admiralty to F.O. Immed., 29.9.84; F.O. to Parkes 206 ext. tel. 25, 1.10.84, F.O. to Walsham 831, 1.10.84, Lloyds to F.O., 1.10.84, Walsham 572, 2.10.84, 27. 2713; F.O. to Walsham 853, 6.10.84, 27. 2714.

[2] Walsham 595, 10.10.84, tel. ciph. 25, 11.10.84, 599, 11.10.84, and minutes, 27. 2714.   [3] Parkes 211, 9.10.84, 17. 952.

[4] Papers in 27. 2712, and Parkes 202, 1.10.84, with correspondence, 27. 2713.

[5] With Parkes 216, 13.10.84, 27. 2714; published as China, no. 3 of 1885. Parkes himself thought Formosa very valuable. Its open Ports had a trade of 7 or 8 million taels.

[6] Copy in 27. 2714.   [7] *Life of Parkes*, II, 414.

the United States. Secretary of State Freylinghuisen cabled to his Peking Minister on 13 September that he believed a Chinese overture to France through America on the basis of eighty million francs and the terms of the Li-Fournier Convention, would be considered. "While willing to give our good offices to serve China as requested we are not to be understood as proposing the foregoing settlement. We have further reason to believe that France would be willing to receive an equivalent substitute for the indemnity." Mr Young had a long interview with the Yamen, and urged that such an overture should be made. The members positively refused to think of making any concessions. At his request they put their refusal in writing. Young—with too much optimism, Parkes thought—went down to Tientsin to try and get Li to make proposals. He had a long interview with the Viceroy on the 26th, and found him if anything less ready for compromise than the Yamen. Li "declared emphatically that there could now be no alternative for China but war with France". Young suggested that China could not bear the cost of protracted hostilities. Why not, asked Li—China had ample means. As to indemnities, after Fuchow not a cent! "I would rather see the eighteen Provinces sink beneath the sea." [1] The heroic spirit of 1937 was being born in China.

Young's motives, Parkes wrote rather critically, "may have been laudable", but he had completely failed. Talks between the French and Chinese representatives at Berlin under the auspices of Count Hatzfeldt were equally fruitless.[2] The British Minister obtained from another source a vague memorandum containing the Chinese Government's terms. These were very stiff. France was to pay an indemnity for attacking Kelung and Fuchow; all Powers were to have equal status in Annam; the position of foreigners in China was to be "reconsidered".[3] The Foreign Office had received only telegraphic reports of the American failure when it took up again the task of mediation

[1] Parkes 223 conf., 14.10.84, 27. 2714, with correspondence; cp. his 194 conf., ext. tel. 37, 30.9.84, 27. 2713. Cp. also *L'Affaire du Tonkin,* 318 ff.   [2] *L'Affaire du Tonkin,* 314 ff.   [3] Parkes 223.

which it had not seriously prosecuted since the previous September. On 4 October Lord Granville reminded Waddington that his good offices were always at the disposal of the two parties. Unfortunately their dispositions to accept had never yet coincided. He had no wish to obtrude, but over-scrupulosity on his part would be blameworthy. On the one hand he did not want the Chinese market exhausted by long hostilities; while on the other hand "any triumphs for China would have serious consequences for Europeans generally". He had been much pressed lately "by persons of high standing, with a great knowledge of China", to get the combatants to accept American mediation. France, he gathered, did not desire this. Waddington was not encouraging. He answered that France could accept no one's mediation. Lord Granville contented himself with pointing out that as France was not at war she could not stop British shipping. "M. Waddington appeared to assent."[1]

On 11 October Waddington informed Granville that the French Government was grateful to him, but America had already tendered offers which were still *sub iudice*.[2] On the 20th he furnished a memorandum of France's terms, which apparently had been submitted to Li: Chinese evacuation of Tonking—ratification of the Convention—possession by France for some years of the mines and Customs of Tamsui and Kelung instead of an indemnity.[3] The Foreign Office at once instructed Parkes by cable to consult Sir Robert Hart and find whether China would accept mediation on this basis.[4] Before a reply could arrive Waddington called to say that America was ready to mediate on the basis of arbitration, but France could not accept that. To show its appreciation of England's good-will, the French Government would take an equivalent of an indemnity of forty millions. It was rather fear

---

[1] F.O. to Walsham 852, 4.10.84, 27. 2713.

[2] F.O. to Lyons 886 conf., 17.10.84, 27. 2715.

[3] Memo. in 27. 2715. These terms were sent to Patenôtre on 11 October and came to be known as "the October 11 programme". (*L'Affaire du Tonkin*, 164 ff.)

[4] F.O. to Parkes 227, ext. tel. 27 ciph., Secret, 21.10.84, 27. 2715.

of the threat of intervention implicit in our offer than gratitude. On the 22nd the Prime Minister, at Granville's request, called a Cabinet to consider this "important communication". At the end of it, Waddington was asked whether the mediating Power would be allowed to fix the term of occupation of Tamsui and Kelung.[1] Waddington said he thought so, but the point was referred to Paris, while Granville warned him that we should claim whatever trading privileges France might secure.[2]

On the 23rd Parkes telegraphed that Li did not dare deliver the French proposals to the Throne, and that he (Parkes) and Hart agreed it was no use offering mediation until China asked it.[3] Waddington was so informed at once.[4] Parkes' despatch of the 26th gives a fuller picture. He and Hart had previously heard nothing of the French proposals, but they had known Li, Detring and Ristehueber (French consul at Tientsin) to be conferring secretly under cover of darkness, until the conferences were broken off by news of the French repulse at Tamsui. When Hart got the French proposals from Detring he thought them moderate, though he "avowed that his sympathies in this dispute were wholly upon the side of the Chinese Government". Li had to devise surreptitious modes of getting the proposals laid before the Peking functionaries, and enlisted Hart's help. China wanted to avoid mediation if possible, since American efforts had not been impressive, Russia was known to have her own schemes, Germany was believed to desire the war to continue—and England the same, because she wanted to be rid of French opposition in Egypt. Parkes laboured to convince Hart that this was an injustice to British motives, using the plausible argument that if fighting went on France might occupy the whole of Formosa and then never abandon it. The Yamen, all this time, knew nothing of the Tientsin discussions—or so it told Parkes.[5]

[1] Granville to Waddington, 22.10.84, 27. 2715.
[2] F.O. to Lyons 902, 23.10.84, 27. 2715.
[3] Parkes tel. 40 Secret, 23.10.84, 27. 2715.
[4] Granville to Waddington, 23.10.84 conf., 27. 2715.
[5] Parkes 235 Secret, 26.10.84, 27. 2715.

In the meantime French belligerent claims were to the fore. Pauncefote considered that if they declared a blockade they were declaring war.[1] Ferry told Lyons that orders were out for establishment of a blockade, which could be done—as in Madagascar—without a state of war being called into existence.[2] We inserted notice of the blockade in the London *Gazette*, but were not prepared to let matters rest. Waddington explained in a private letter to Lord Granville that France did not intend to search vessels on the high seas, and objected to our using the word "neutrals": as there was no war there could be no neutrals.[3] A "pacific blockade", Pauncefote commented, was very doubtful in law; however, we could agree to a modified belligerent blockade, which would not be unjust to China if we gave her the same rights. What good blockading rights would be to China, is not evident. Granville consulted the Chancellor, Lord Selborne, who agreed.[4]

Accordingly, on 31 October the Foreign Office wrote to Waddington that definition was desirable. If France undertook to keep operations localised and to waive the rights of search and capture, England would not extend her observance of neutrality beyond the Foreign Enlistment Act.[5] Waddington answered that France would neither exercise full belligerent rights nor open a fresh phase of hostilities, but considered that a blockade *could* be established without war.[6] The Foreign Office rejoined that, whether or no a "pacific blockade" was conceivable, the actual one was certainly not pacific, and in England's opinion the two Powers were at war.[7] At this point, on Granville's suggestion, the correspondence was shown by the Foreign Office to the German Ambassador.[8] It was growing patent that the French were merely quibbling in order not to be cut off from use of British ports; and the Foreign Office on

[1] Memo. 15.10.84, 27. 2715.   [2] Lyons 612, 18.12.84, 27. 2715.
[3] 30.10.84, 27. 2715.   [4] Minutes on above.
[5] B.F.S.P. LXXVI, 424. In Sept. 1883, War Office Intelligence had discussed French coal supplies and the question of our selling coal to their ships. (27. 2705.)   [6] Ibid. LXXVI, 425.
[7] Ibid. LXXVI, 426.   [8] 27. 2717.

26 November rehearsed its views explicitly, asserting France to be at war *de facto* and *de jure*.[1] Tseng had written that China expected the Foreign Enlistment Act to be enforced all over the Empire. The Foreign Office assented.[2]

On 4 November Waddington told Granville that the French proposals were to be discussed next day in the Grand Council at Peking; also that America had now come round more to the French view, and offered to arbitrate on the indemnity instead of on the whole dispute. He left it to Granville whether he should associate himself with the American course. Granville thought it would not be judicious to embark on a joint mediation.[3] In fact, the French proposals had been laid before the Grand Council on 28 October. They reached the Seventh Prince, deviously, though he refused to see Detring. Each member of the Council was made to write out his opinion separately. Their opinions were diverse, but all seemed willing to accept a reasonable settlement. Hart and Detring recommended the Yamen to close with the French terms. "They advised the mediation of Austria rather than that of England, as the latter, like Germany, is supposed to be interested in the prolongation of French difficulties in China."[4] It is curious that within a year of this plain speaking Hart was made British Minister at Peking.

On 6 November the Yamen empowered Hart to inform the French that their terms were inadmissible.[5] On the 10th they informed Parkes that they were drawing up counter-proposals, which they would give him to forward to Lord Granville, for his transmission to the French Government if

[1] *B.F.S.P.* LXXVI, 429. Hertslet drew up a memo. on whether French and Chinese warships could coal at Hongkong. (27.11.84, 27. 2780.) Tseng had raised the question officially. We admitted that China could forbid foreign residents to sell contraband to France. (F.O. to Parkes 252, 14.11.84, 27. 2717.)

[2] *B.F.S.P.* LXXVI, 428, 430.

[3] F.O. to Parkes tel. 31 ciph., 4.11.84; to Lyons 942, 4.11.84, 27. 2716.

[4] Parkes 252 Secret, ext. tel. 42 Secret, 6.11.84; 263 Secret, 11.11.84; 27. 2716.

[5] Parkes tel. 44 Secret, 7.11.84; 253 Extender, Secret, 8.11.84, 27. 2716.

he should approve them.[1] Granville told Waddington that he
meant to transmit these counter-proposals when they arrived,
unless they proved actually "insulting". He confessed he was
not "extremely sanguine".[2] On the 13th Prince Yi K'uang,
Kung's successor at the head of the Yamen, and three other
Yamen Ministers called on Parkes to show him their eight
counter-proposals. They said they had already cabled them to
Tseng. A curious narrative in Boulger's *Life of Macartney*,
however, reveals that the proposals had their origin in an
exchange of letters between Macartney and a French journalist
in Paris (his name is suppressed) in touch with official circles.
Macartney made it clear to this correspondent that no indemnity
would be paid, and then, after mentioning his intention to
Granville, drafted eight articles, which Tseng cabled to Peking.[3]
Parkes discussed the terms with the Ministers for two hours.
Having cast his eye over the document, he said he did not think
it could stand a chance of being accepted. They promised to
submit his criticism to the Empress—after asking if Lord Granville would mind sending them a cable to say that the fourth
proposal was impossible: a very circumambulatory mode of
putting advice before the Throne.[4] On the 15th Tseng, under
instructions, wrote to Lord Granville that China would be
happy to receive his mediation;[5] and the Yamen formally
desired Parkes to transmit their eight heads. He telegraphed
them in full. The important points were no. 1, the Tientsin
Convention to be replaced by a fresh one; no. 4, Annam to pay
tribute to China, and France not to interfere in any way with
its government; no. 7, Kelung to be evacuated; no. 8, China in
return to waive her claim to an indemnity![6] No. 4 had been
recast, but Parkes could discern little difference. The Prince,
who came in from an interview with Young in which he

[1] Parkes tel. 45 Secret, 10.11.84; 262 Extender, Secret, 10.11.84, 27. 2716.
[2] F.O. to Lyons 963, 13.11.84, 27. 2717.
[3] *Life of Macartney*, 371–83. The terms were too stiff to have been drafted
by Macartney alone, however, and must have been based on instructions
from Peking.   [4] Parkes 271 Most conf., 14.11.84, 27. 2717.
[5] 27. 2717.   [6] Parkes tel. 46 ciph., 15.11.84, 27. 2717.

turned down some modified French proposals, struck Parkes as looking remarkably confident, as though he had reasons to believe France very eager indeed for peace.[1] Parkes found out from Young that the proposals he had been commissioned to sound China on were: Ratification of the Tientsin Convention, temporary occupation of Tamsui and Kelung, five million francs indemnity, Chinese evacuation of Tonking. The figure of five millions was so astoundingly low—France had begun by asking 250!—that Young had cabled to Washington for confirmation. What China objected to in these terms was the Formosan occupation.[2] French sources suggest that the five millions emanated from Washington and were rejected in Paris.[3]

The Foreign Office at once cabled back to Parkes that while ready to mediate it could see no point in transmitting *these* terms.[4] At the same time Granville told Waddington that China accepted British good offices, but that her terms—he declined to express an opinion on their merits—did not appear to him worth communicating.[5] Parkes repeated Granville's comment to the Yamen, who said they would none the less like their counter-proposals transmitted by way of initiating discussion.[6] A Foreign Office minute found some consolation in the mere fact of England's being employed as go-between: "This friendly intervention may grow into mediation or even quasi-arbitration."[7]

An unsigned memorandum marked "secret" and dated November 22, evidently emanating from Tseng, said that agreement was possible if the frontier were to be drawn westward from Langson and Annamese missions to Peking were allowed: "Otherwise we must fight and take our chance." When Waddington called for news he was shown this memo-

[1] Parkes 276 Most conf., 17.11.84, 27. 2717.
[2] Parkes 277 Most conf., 17.11.84, 27. 2717.
[3] *L'Affaire du Tonkin*, 320–1.
[4] F.O. to Parkes 255 ext. tel. 33, 17.11.84, 27. 2717.
[5] F.O. to Lyons 987, 17.11.84, and 988 conf. 17.11.84, 27. 2717.
[6] Parkes tel. 48 ciph. 21.11.84, 27. 2716, and 281 Extender 21.11.84, 27. 2717.
[7] Memo. 20.11.84, 27. 2717.

randum "confidentially and as a matter of gossip only."[1] On the 23rd Macartney furnished a draft treaty in eight articles; the essentials were a frontier on the line of Langson, speedy evacuation of Kelung, and recognition by China of any proper treaty between France and Annam.[2] Next day it was shown in confidence to Waddington. The Ambassador said he would rather not even forward it to Paris unless Lord Granville absolutely wished it; Granville agreed with him that it could not possibly be accepted.[3]

Things seemed at a standstill. "This is the fault of both France and China not having accepted *my* mediation", wrote a Mr Kleinwächter, apparently an imbecile, who was always explaining to Lord Granville how he ought to handle Far Eastern questions.[4] Patenôtre stayed at Shanghai, and had little better to do than bitterly contrast life in that town with life at Stockholm. "He is driven at times to ask himself what he is doing at his Post, since none of his suggestions are attended to..."[5] At Peking Prince Ch'ing (Prince Yi K'uang) was unable to see Parkes for some days, as preparations for Tzu Hsi's fiftieth birthday were in hand. When Parkes called at the Yamen on the 21st he pressed the Ministers to modify their proposals, but found them bolstered up by a sense of the feebleness of French activity in Formosa and Tonking.[6] Macartney returned on 1 December, when Pauncefote explained to him that though England was anxious to do all she could, there was no point in transmitting Tseng's draft, especially after Waddington's comment on it.[7] On the same day Waddington laid down as France's two fundamental conditions, the Tientsin provisions and occupation of Kelung until the treaty was fulfilled.[8] Granville passed on the information to Tseng.

[1] F.O. to Lyons 1004 conf., 22.11.84, 27. 2717. (*Two* memos are mentioned, but no other appears here.)   [2] Draft in 27. 2717.
[3] F.O. to Lyons 1005 conf., 25.11.84, 27. 2717.   [4] 27. 2717.
[5] Rumbold (Stockholm) 120 conf., 2.12.84, 27. 2718 (referring to a private letter from Patenôtre received by someone there).
[6] Parkes 290, 25.11.84, 27. 2718.
[7] F.O. to Parkes 274A, 1.12.84, 27. 2718.
[8] F.O. to Lyons 1043 conf., 1.12.84, 27. 2718.

The latter called on the 3rd, and traversed the French assertion that there was any authentic boundary between China and Annam, at variance with the frontier line he desired. Apart from that he admitted the objections to the Tientsin Convention to be mainly formal. Lord Granville put it to him that, if so, it was not right to let a war go on; and begged him to take time for consideration. The Marquis agreed to take twenty-four hours to think the question over.[1] Granville repeated the conversation to Waddington. "His Excellency observed 'It is with regret I have to state that this is war.'"[2] Tseng, after re-examining his instructions, felt that he could not comply with Waddington's two demands. Occupation of Kelung "would only be an indemnity in another and more objectionable form".[3]

The Ambassador was notified of the reply on the 6th. On the 10th, Granville gave an interview to Tseng, who repeated that he could concede no more, and did not believe his Government could. Did France, he enquired, consider negotiations closed? Certainly, replied the Foreign Secretary, adding that he could at present see no ending to a war which, "while onerous to France, might be most dangerous to China". Had his visitor reflected upon the possibility of internal disorder breaking out in his country? Tseng rejoined that patriotic feeling was all against concessions, especially among the governing classes.[4] Next day Ferry expressed regret that China had not accepted the generous terms offered her, and thanked Lord Granville for his tactful assistance. Granville replied with the hope that Her Majesty's Government would be able to resume its efforts at a future date.[5]

As it happened, that moment was not to be long delayed. A week later the Foreign Office heard, from "authoritative though not official" sources, that China was hesitantly in-

[1] F.O. to Parkes 277, 3.12.84, 27. 2718.
[2] F.O. to Lyons 1044A, 3.12.84, 27. 2718.
[3] Communicated by Macartney; memo. by Pauncefote 4.12.84, 27. 2718.
[4] F.O. to Parkes 285 conf., 10.12.84, 27. 2719 (copy also in 17. 947).
[5] F.O. to Lyons 1071 conf., 11.12.84, 27. 2719. The English mediation is traced fairly fully, but only for this period of Oct.—Dec. 1884, in L'Affaire du Tonkin, 323 ff., on the basis of the French published documents.

clining towards making further proposals. Ferry was approached indirectly, but said there was no hope of China making a reasonable offer, and if she did want to propose anything she should do so directly to France.[1] Perhaps Ferry felt that French dignity was being compromised by such long-drawn chaffering in an unfriendly capital. On the 24th Macartney called to say the Yamen approved the proposal of which Granville had heard, made by Hart and "a private gentleman in England"; it was that China should ratify Tientsin with the addition of an article prescribing missions from Annam to Peking and a frontier drawn south of Seong Shan.[2] Granville wrote privately to Waddington that the Chinese overture had now taken official form. Waddington wrote back on the 27th, saying he had consulted Ferry, and wishing His Lordship a Merry Christmas—"may the coming year see the settlement of all the outstanding questions between our two countries".[3]

On the 29th the Ambassador was forced to report that Ferry refused to reopen negotiations, but authorised him to keep informally in touch with Granville on Chinese affairs: he therefore asked to see the new Chinese suggestion.[4] Ferry, on seeing it, at once told Lord Lyons that it showed no great advance, and involved two inadmissible points: the frontier, and the assertion of Chinese suzerainty over Annam. France must now occupy Tonking up to the "real" frontier, and was preparing to do so.[5] The Foreign Office notified Parkes, telling him to keep in touch with Hart.[6] From now on Hart was to be more and more the main negotiator on the Chinese side, spending a fortune on telegrams to Paris,[7] and earning a Peacock Feather as his reward.

[1] F.O. to Lyons 1090 conf., 19.12.84; Lyons 721 A, 22.12.84, 27. 2719.

[2] Memo. by Pauncefote 24.12.84, 27. 2719.

[3] Granville to Waddington priv., 26.12.84; Waddington to Granville priv., 27.12.84, 27. 2719.

[4] Waddington to Granville priv., 29.12.84; F.O. to Lyons 1116A, conf., 29.12.84, 27. 2719.   [5] Lyons 735 conf., 30.12.84, 27.2719.

[6] F.O. to Parkes tel. 1, 1.1.85, 27. 2769.

[7] 80,000 taels, it is said. (H. Norman, *Peoples and Politics of the Far East*, 234). Cp. Juliet Bredon, *Sir Robert Hart*, 176. Tseng was less suitable because "personally obnoxious" to Ferry. (*Economist*, 11.4.85.)

When Parkes conveyed Ferry's reply to the Yamen, the Ministers declared they could go no further unless France also made concessions. Parkes enquired what concessions *they* had made. The Prince "observed that they had proposed to give up nearly the whole of Annam, inclusive of Tonking, to France, subject only to the observance of the tributary relations of that State to China". The Englishman said he thought France meant to declare war. A Grand Secretary "observed with grim humour that it would be interesting to see in what respect open hostilities on the part of the French would differ from those they had hitherto carried on against China".[1]

[1] Parkes tel. ciph., 3.1.85; 4 conf., 4.1.85, 27. 2769.

CHAPTER ELEVEN

Corea, 1885

THE equilibrium effected in Corea by the treaties of 1884 was only a temporary lull in the conflict of foreign rivalries. While English merchants tried what could be made out of Corean commerce, China was backing the inertia of the Conservatives at Seoul, Japan intrigued on the side of the soi-disant "Progressives" and Russia watched for an opening. Already in November 1882 Admiral Enomotto expressed strong dislike of China's Corean policy and prophesied that it would one day produce war. Li, at a dinner at Tientsin, invited officials of all foreign nations except Japan.[1] These portents were ominous. Meanwhile the hoped-for rejuvenation of the country was further off than ever.[2] Aston in the middle of November 1884 drew a gloomy picture of prevailing conditions. Political circles at the capital were uneasy. The Treasury was empty. Only a third of the taxes raised was reaching the Government. The crops had failed. The currency was depraved. There was no force capable of repressing disaffection. The pay of the militia was in arrears. The functions of the Council were being usurped by powerful families. Some Coreans sounded Aston as to whether England would lend support to a movement of reform by violence. Aston gave "a decided negative".[3] To other foreign interests, the suggestion was not so unwelcome.

On the night of 4 December occurred the celebrated Banquet given by the newly appointed Post-Master General, Kong Yong Sik; when six Councillors were assaulted by members of Kim Ok Kun's "Progressive" faction and hacked to death

[1] Grosvenor 142 conf., 24.11.82, 17. 900.
[2] Parkes, Corea 38, 12.12.84, 17. 953.
[3] Aston 46 conf., 15.11.84, with above.

before the eyes of the assembled foreign representatives. As in 1882, it was the Queen and her party who were the real object of attack. The conspirators made at once for the Palace, where they murdered other dignitaries. The capital was instantly filled with turmoil as the intrigues and animosities of the last months broke into eruption. In three days' anarchy three hundred lives were lost. "The Minister for Foreign Affairs, Kim Hong Jip, was almost the only Corean of note left alive." [1] Takezoye, the Japanese Minister, on the fatal night received a letter begging for protection, which purported to come from the King. The Coreans subsequently maintained that the letter was sent without the King's knowledge, by someone who had access to his seal.[2] The Japanese guards came into action, and were soon in conflict with the Chinese garrison, while an angry crowd attacked the Japanese Legation and killed thirty Japanese residents. After fierce fighting Takezoye had to retreat in the direction of Chemulpo. Kim Ok Kun escaped with him and went to Japan, never to return until his murdered body was brought home to be mutilated and quartered. Takezoye must at least have known, wrote Aston, that his guard was being used in the interest of a pro-Japanese faction, which at a recent public dinner he had declared his intention of supporting.[3] But the Case of the Seoul Murders would have fully taxed the acuteness of Mr Sherlock Holmes—in 1885 sitting in his rooms in London awaiting Watson and fame.

[1] Carles, *Life in Corea*, ch. XVIII. Carles had his details from eyewitnesses. See also *Life of Parkes*, II, 217–18; R. von Möllendorf, *P. G. von Möllendorf: ein Lebensbild*, 72 ff.

[2] Carles (Acting Cons.-Gen.) 30 conf. of 1885, with O'Conor 130 conf., 26.3.85, 17. 969.

[3] Parkes 6, 10.1.85, 17. 977. The dinner is described in R. von Möllendorf, *P. G. von Möllendorf: ein Lebensbild*, 71. Conceivably it was not Takezoye himself but some member of his staff who was guilty, for we are told that "He was an amiable scholar rather than a diplomat and had always maintained the most cordial personal relations with the King." But this statement comes from a highly partisan account written by a Mr Stevens, who, though an eyewitness, wrote twenty years later when in Japanese service. (Quoted in Ladd, *In Korea with Marquis Ito*, 205 ff.)

News of the outbreak was rushed to Port Arthur by a Chinese gunboat and thence cabled to Li at Tientsin. It reached Peking on the evening of 13 December. By that time the Japanese Government was said to have two ironclads and 700 men on their way to Corea.[1]

The affair at once focused diplomatic attention. Parkes' personal view was that Kim "certainly ought to be brought to the gallows", that Takezoye had showed himself "true to the old Japanese spirit of intrigue and murder", and that Tokio had no just pretext for war.[2] He did not tell the Chinese all this, however. He made haste to see the Yamen, and warned the Ministers not to antagonise Japan, lest she join forces with France. They said they would await the report of a Commissioner. Japan was doing the same—at least, Enomotto denied that troops were being sent.[3] On 18 December Plunkett at Tokio informed his Peking colleague that military preparations were being made, but Count Inouye, the Foreign Minister, was going in person to Corea to examine the problem. Parkes, enlarging his homily, pointed out to the Yamen that if Japan were provoked into joining France, Russia would welcome the opportunity for a little self-help. Japan probably did not intend a conquest of Corea "at this date", and should not be hindered from keeping some troops there to guard her Legation.[4]

Tokio now demanded that China should send a plenipotentiary to Corea qualified to settle the whole issue, hoping that Li himself would go;[5] but it was not likely that the great man's dignity would admit of such condescension. The day when he was to sail for Japan to sue for peace was still eleven years off. Enomotto called on the British and American Ministers asking them to support his Government's wish; neither agreed.[6] They did not want the status quo disturbed just now, when any changes might slide into a spate of "com-

[1] Parkes 321, 14.12.84, 17. 953.   [2] Life of Parkes, II, 220 ff.
[3] Parkes 327, 20.12.84, 17. 953.
[4] Parkes 328 Very conf., 28.12.84, 17. 953.
[5] Parkes 330, 22.12.84, and 332, 24.12.84, 17. 953.
[6] Parkes 339, 30.12.84, 17. 953.

pensatory" encroachments. China was unwilling to do anything that might lead to her suzerainty over Corea being called in question. Amid a confusion of conflicting reports it emerged that five Chinese warships and a detachment of troops were on their way. Learning of this attempt to repeat the policy of 1882, the Japanese Government stopped Inouye at Shimonoseki and then sent him on to Chemulpo with a thousand soldiers and three ships. It conjures up an extravagant fancy of the urbane Lord Granville posting off to Egypt to argue with the French with a thousand men at his back.

Parkes went to see the Yamen again, and Prince Ch'ing showed him a Proclamation by the King of Corea. It laid the entire blame on seditious politicians encouraged by Takezoye. The Prince asked if Parkes had heard anything of a secret Franco-Japanese understanding.[1] Parkes handed the question on to Plunkett. The latter telegraphed back at the New Year: "Cabinet seems to desire peace, but afraid of offending the war party." Enomotto read Parkes in confidence a telegram from Tokio to the effect that Japan, wanting peace, would "ignore or rather deny" China's sovereign claims if they came up, but otherwise would not debate them. China on her part did not want a fresh war while her troops were involved in Tonking. But she was determined not to be ousted from Corea. Her Commissioner's escort would bring up her strength at Seoul to 2000; and ships had been sent "of a more formidable type than any possessed by Japan".[2]

On 2 January Aston reported that Takezoye was back at Seoul with an escort. Government feeling was acid against him, and the King refused to see him. Foote, the American Minister, who had gone to Japan to attempt mediation, was also back. The Russian Representative was said to have expressed a strong wish, after receiving special instructions from Petersburg, that the quarrel should not lead to hostilities.[3] It is not obvious what train of reasoning this, if correct, reflected.

[1] Parkes 2, 3.1.85, 17. 977.
[2] Parkes 3 conf., 4.1.85, 17. 977.
[3] Aston, 2.1.85, with Parkes 30, 24.1.85, 17. 977.

At any rate, with the added complication of the Afghan crisis, Russian policy soon changed.

Möllendorf—a German in Corean employ—met Inouye at Chemulpo, but the Envoy was not to be put off. He made straight for Seoul, where he insisted on immediate audience. It was granted on 3 January, though feeling was so bitter that he insisted on bringing a guard with him to the Palace, and ten men into the King's presence.[1] On 9 January Corea promised to send a mission of apology to Tokio, and to pay 120,000 dollars.[2] It is a trifle grotesque to find Corea having to apologise to Japan for the results of a Japanese conspiracy. An apology, or a dozen, would not, it is true, burden the Corean peasantry, but a fresh indemnity would. Between Japan and China the issue still remained open. Fresh versions of the events of 4 December were coming in.[3] Takezoye and the Chinese Commanding Officer each said the other party fired first; and the Japanese were accused of committing atrocities on their retreat from Seoul.[4] Plunkett continued to report war preparations in Japan. Parkes was frankly puzzled. He had lived among the Japanese and treated them as a nation of fractious school-children so long, that he could not adjust his mind to the idea of their doing anything so mature as going to war. He advised Plunkett to warn the Japanese Government "that under pressure of the difficulty with France China was rapidly becoming a military nation, and that although she would be most unwilling to enter on a conflict with Japan, her present successful resistance to the demands of France would not dispose her to submit to intimidation by the former Power".[5] To the Foreign Office Parkes confessed: "I feel at present at a loss to understand the attitude taken by Japan in regard to the Corean question, but it is evident...that there is a party in that country who would wish to make it a cause of war with China."[6]

[1] Parkes 60, 7.2.85, 17. 978.
[2] Text of Convention in B.F.S.P. LXXVI, 574.
[3] Correspondence with Parkes 17, 17.1.85, 17. 977.
[4] Parkes 18, 17.1.85, 17. 977.   [5] Parkes 16 (Extender), 17.1.85, 17. 977.
[6] Parkes 23 Very conf., 17.1.85, 17. 977.

Parkes received from Aston copies of the acrimonious correspondence that had passed between the Coreans and Japanese; Corea had appealed to England, Germany and America for mediation under the Treaties,[1] but this was already superseded by the Convention, as Inouye had counted on its being. "It is melancholy", Parkes reflected with British sentiment, "to note the foul character of the conspiracy and the atrocious manner in which it was carried out, and it is greatly to be regretted that the Japanese Minister should have allowed himself to become so closely connected with the conspirators and their criminal proceedings."[2] The sentiment is well clothed, and applies to the greater part of Japanese diplomatic history; though Parkes might have remembered that he himself, when Japan was at a stage like that of Corea in 1885, had as a foreign Envoy lent his countenance to a faction inside the state.

The Chinese Commissioner who had been sent to investigate Corean affairs was named Wu, and he interviewed Inouye before the end of January. Enomotto put into Parkes' hands a Chinese abstract of their conversation written by Wu, and a telegraphed account by Inouye. According to the latter, Wu rudely intruded on a conference between the Coreans and Japanese, and Inouye refused to treat with him unless he received full powers from Peking.[3] By implication, the sovereignty of Corea was at stake; the question immediately at issue was that of the garrisons kept in the country by China and Japan. The Yamen betrayed no anxiety, but evidently both antagonists were as desirous of enlisting English sympathy as were the English of keeping a finger in the pie. Parkes was furnished with Takezoye's apologia, and Inouye's vindication of him.[4] Ch'ing professed himself unsatisfied, and said even Enomotto had admitted that Takezoye overstepped the limit.

[1] Copies with Parkes 27, 24.1.85, 17. 977. In his 29 Parkes reflected that the Coreans probably did not know what "mediation" meant. It later appeared that Corea had intended to ask mediation, as distinct from good offices, from England alone. (Parkes 73, 14.2.85, 17. 978.)
[2] Parkes 28, 24.1.85, 17. 977.
[3] Parkes 31 conf., 24.1.85, 17.977; cp. Ladd, *In Korea with Marquis Ito*, 210.
[4] Copies with Parkes 48, 31.1.85, 17. 978.

Ch'ing was also at pains to deny that the King of Corea would like the Chinese garrison removed. Parkes thought it necessary to exhort him again in favour of peace.[1]

Early in February Inouye offered to go to Tientsin to treat with Li, if the latter could not undertake a journey to Corea. Li was inclined "to represent himself as the absolute disposer of Corean affairs", and in moments like this the pedestal he put himself on became uncomfortable. Corea would have resisted had China seemed disposed to back her; but probably the Chinese realised that Inouye personally desired peace and would compromise if not offended. It was agreed as a preliminary that Takezoye should be withdrawn, a battalion and a half of Japanese troops being left in the country.[2] The King issued an Edict in terms of conventional self-reproach. "Alas for our shortcomings!" All his reign he had slaved at public affairs— "We have not taken off our clothes at night nor taken food till dusk"—yet everything was in disorder. He consigned the administration to his Ministers. A step towards constitutionalism, remarked observers from the land of Bishop Stubbs.[3]

In March Japan gained her way to the extent of inducing Li, with full powers, to undertake discussion with Ito, the Premier, who went to Tientsin for the purpose.[4] Ito came first to Peking with Count Saigo, to verify Li's powers before treating with him[5]—somewhat pointedly. Before his arrival Parkes renewed his appeals to the Yamen to be moderate. War would give Russia her chance, and already now the Afghan crisis was taking form. If Japan were to fight as France's ally, she would be removed, perhaps permanently, from our influence, and could not be *our* ally against Russia. Parkes admonished the Ministers, therefore, that they must expect Ito to demand the removal of the officer who had fired on the Japanese guards; adding frankly that Corea resented the misconduct of the Chinese garrison and could never make progress while dependent on an external military force. He felt certain, he con-

[1] Parkes 48, 31.1.85, 17. 978.   [2] Parkes 71, 14.2.85, 17. 978.
[3] Copy with Parkes 74, 14.2.85, 17. 978.
[4] Parkes 102, 15.3.85, 17. 979.   [5] Parkes 124, 23.3.85, 17. 979.

tinued, that Ito's mission meant more than appeared on the surface. "There was a strong feeling of hostility towards China amongst a majority, I might say, of the Japanese people, and however much the Government might be disposed to act with moderation they would find it difficult to run counter to popular opinion." If provoked by China, Japan "would be more than likely" to join France. He suggested their reminding Ito that the Western Powers also had to be taken account of in Corea. A discussion ensued on China's treatment of her vassal states. The Ministers said their policy was to avoid interfering with internal matters. Just so, replied Parkes: and the results were bad internal conditions, foreign interference, and the calling in question of China's claims. Prince Ch'ing admitted that Corea "was in a hopelessly wretched condition" as regards administration.[1] But the discussion illustrates the difficulty with which representatives of such different polities comprehended one another. The reason lay in the different structure of China and the Western states, which made the economic demands of the latter on their colonies, and consequently their political control, much more extensive. Advice, in short, that seemed to a European as self-evident as Euclid, was to China novel and embarrassing.

A Decree in the *Gazette*, at the time of Ito's arrival, announced the gratitude of the King of Corea for China's help in the fighting of December.[2] It was obviously likely to offend Ito, and revealed Parkes' failure to convince the Yamen, now when at the very end of his life he had belatedly convinced himself, that the Japanese menace was serious. He died on 22 March after three days' illness.

Ito, through Enomotto, proceeded to lay three requests before the Chinese Government; one, that he should be received in audience by the Empress; second, that negotiations should be held at Peking; third, that Li's powers should be formally confirmed. The first point was refused; also the second, on the reasonable ground that Li could not leave Tientsin. Even the

---

[1] Parkes 112 conf., 20.3.85, 17. 979.
[2] O'Conor 120, 21.3.85, 17. 979.

third point was only conceded under pressure.[1] To the regret
of O'Conor, now Chargé d'Affaires, no discussion passed
between Ito and the Yamen directly; and he took it on himself
to try and arrange an interview. The Chinese were not cordial;
they complained that Japan was using the Corean issue vexatiously in sending an unnecessary embassy, and that she alone
of foreign states was secretly rendering assistance to France,
when she ought to see that she had with China a common
interest in checking "the aggression from Russia with which
they were continually threatened". Their visitor was tenacious,
and a meeting between Count Ito and Prince Ch'ing took
place. It was conciliatory in tone.[2] On 31 March Ito left for
Tientsin.

Negotiations there did not go well at first. They turned
chiefly on details; neither side seemed anxious to embark on
discussion of first principles. Ito had no wish to push things too
far, but bellicose feeling in Japan was strong, and he could not
go home empty-handed. By the middle of April a compromise
was patched up; assisted, certainly, by the unexpected peace
between China and France, who at the end of March seemed
irrevocably committed to war. The settlement between them
disappointed the Japanese as much as it astonished them,[3] for
it greatly strengthened China's hands. It is in fact remarkable
that Li did not exploit this advantage further than he did:
Halliday Macartney, always a critic of Li's Corean policy,
fastened on the present agreement as a blunder Tseng would
not have made.[4] China and Japan both undertook to withdraw their troops. Each was to be able to send them back on
emergency, after giving notice to the other.[5] The flaw, so far
as Chinese interests went, was that Tokio was tacitly admitted
to an equal voice in Corea. Our Legation was concerned over
a more immediate point. A provision was made in the Con-

[1] O'Conor 135, 29.3.85, 17. 979.
[2] O'Conor 137 and 138 conf., 30.3.85, 17. 979.
[3] Plunkett 105 conf., 16.4.85, and 120, 27.4.85, 27. 2772.
[4] *Life of Macartney*, 457.
[5] O'Conor 153, 8.4.85, 17. 979; text in *B.F.S.P.* LXXVI, 297.

vention for the organising of a native force to keep order and protect foreigners, but the time allowed—four months—was meagre; and O'Conor thought he perceived that the Yamen rather hoped for a speedy recurrence of trouble that would enable them to send back their troops.[1] Lord Salisbury, who now returned to the Foreign Office, minuted that China and Japan ought to be warned of the dangers that would result from Russian officers getting control of a Corean force.

The Chinese seemed rather elated than relieved at having got out of the scrape. Their successes against France imbued them with a feeling of superiority to the Japanese. It is likely that in 1885, as distinct from 1882, China's Corean policy (apart from the Convention) was the work of the Yamen rather than of Li, whose prestige was dimmed by failure to meet impossible demands during the war. In May a decision was taken which convinced the English Minister that they were "deliberately courting a fresh revolution in Corea for their own ends".[2] The Tai Wen Kun, the King's exiled father, had always agitated for permission to return to his country. Now, the Censors were won over to his cause, and promises given him that he would soon be repatriated. O'Conor felt certain his return would lead to fresh disorders. With the peace with France China was rid of embarrassment in the south, and had numerous troops released for action. Brandt also was nervous about European interests in Corea, and at the Foreign Office a suggestion was made that action might be concerted with Germany.[3]

China's growing truculence coincided with an apparent tendency on Japan's part towards altering her policy and withdrawing for the present from active competition in Corea.[4] If she really meant to withdraw, the duty of keeping order would fall on the Chinese, who no doubt would welcome it. O'Conor in fact was pressing China in July to keep part of her

[1] O'Conor 166, 16.4.85, 27. 979; 183, 21.4.85, 27. 980; 190 conf., 25.4.85, 17. 980. [2] O'Conor 252 conf., 27.5.85, 17. 981.
[3] O'Conor 302, 17.6.85, 17. 982 and minutes. Salisbury noted: "No: better not move at present." [4] O'Conor 332, 2.7.85, 17. 982.

troops in the country.[1] He may have wanted to see some force in Corea ready to resist a Russian invasion.

So far as her own interests went, China had room for complacency; but the Anglo-Russian crisis, with Japan again trying to make up her mind to enter the imminent war, kept Chinese statesmen perturbed. In June Russia's designs on Port Lazarev were disquieting them, and the Corean Government was so weak and hard up that it might sell far-reaching concessions to one or other of the Powers besetting it.

In September a Decree announced definitely that the Tai Wen Kun was to return, at the same time re-emphasising China's claims over Corea.[2] During the same month the Chinese Telegraph Administration was learned to be constructing a line to Seoul, and contemplating another to Chemulpo—to the chagrin of the King, who foresaw that it would mean increased dependence for him.[3] The Tai Wen Kun landed from a Chinese warship on 23 October; decidedly in the character of an agent of the Power which had formerly kidnapped him, although his subsequent career was not to be marked by Quixotic loyalty to anyone. Many an old friend came down to the port to greet the hoary ruffian, and tears were affectingly mingled. Officially, his return was almost ignored. Aston called on him at Seoul and found him paler than in former times, but active and effusive, saying that life in China had changed all his ideas. On the way home Aston came on a significant sight—the naked mangled bodies of two men executed by order of the Queen for their share in the riots of July 1882;[4] riots believed to have been engineered by the Tai Wen Kun.

Along with the ex-Regent's return arose a corresponding threat of intervention from the Japanese side: it was rumoured in December that Kim Ok Kun had left Japan with an armed force, and that China would order in her troops.[5] O'Conor

[1] O'Conor 358, 18.7.85, 17. 983.   [2] O'Conor 403, 23.9.85, 17. 984.
[3] O'Conor, Corea 19, 29.9.85, 17. 984.
[4] Aston 109, 8.10.85, with O'Conor, Corea 22, 22.10.85, 17. 985.
[5] O'Conor 492, 16.12.85, 17. 986. Kim had the hotheaded sympathy of

made enquiries. The news was not true—yet. Li believed that
Kim was only waiting for a chance. Plunkett reported that
the exiled revolutionary was being watched by the Japanese
police, who, however, refused to comply with China's wishes
and arrest him.[1]

In short, so far from the Sino-Japanese Convention restoring
tranquillity to Corea, the state of affairs remained for months
as grave as ever. It improved only when tension among the
major Powers relaxed. On 22 December a telegram from Corea
declared that there was no immediate danger of disturbance.[2]

Liberals in Japan who saw in him a Kosciusko, as well as of officials who saw
in him a useful tool. The "Osaka affair" (when thirty-seven Radicals were
arrested on the point of going off to Corea with arms to assist liberty there in
the hope that it would stimulate liberty at home) occurred in 1885. Plunkett
secured a secret report on Kim. (Plunkett 73 Very conf., 2.3.85, 46. 328.)

[1] Communicated in O'Conor 497, 28.12.85, 17. 986.   [2] *Ibid.*

CHAPTER TWELVE

Tonking, to the Settlement

IN the last months of 1884 more and more was happening to strengthen the section of opinion in England which regretted the Franco-Chinese war, against the opposite tendency to welcome it. To begin with, China was becoming a dangerous place for all foreigners. There were formidable riots at Canton in 1883 and at Hankow and Wenchow in 1884; reports were coming in of inflammatory placards at Wuhu, unrest at and around Chinkiang, anti-Catholic outbreaks at Swatow.[1] Moreover, French agents in China were threatening a blockade of the Gulf of Pechili in the spring, for the purpose of cutting off rice from the capital. This, Parkes realised, would not cripple Peking, but it would cripple British trade in the north.[2] The effects of the Formosa blockade, re-established from 7 January, were described as "very serious to foreigners, but almost harmless to the Chinese".[3] Foreign vessels, Admiral Dowell explained, were pulled up by the French, whereas native junks slipped in and out as they pleased.[4] The Governor of Hongkong wrote that all traders there welcomed Britain's mediation, the hostilities being "disastrous to the interests of that great commerce, of which England enjoys by far the greatest share".[5] An Englishman in Chinese service, Captain Harvey—inventor of a Sea Torpedo—wrote to a friend at home: "If the contest with France continues trade will be ruined, the people will rise first against the foreigners, then against the mandarins, and there will be horrible doings.

[1] Parkes 248, 4.11.84, 27. 2716; 254 and 255, 6.11.84, 27. 2716; 260 and 261, 10.11.84, 27. 2716; 282 and 283, 24.11.84, 27. 2717; 287, 25.11.84, 27. 2717; 300, 301 and 302, 1.12.84, 27. 2718.

[2] Parkes 319, 13.12.84, 27. 2719.   [3] Parkes 343, 31.12.84, 27. 2719.

[4] Extract from letter to Sir C. Key, 27. 2769.

[5] Bowen 381, 17.11.84, 27. 2719.

Shanghai nearly ruined already. The Germans get all the war orders because they bribe the Mandarins so unblushingly."[1]

In the third place, the ill-defined neutrality formulated by England in November was increasingly difficult to keep up to everyone's satisfaction. We had to guard ourselves, the Foreign Office observed to Lord Lyons, "not only from Parliamentary attacks, but from very serious pecuniary claims".[2] There was a swelling chorus of Parliamentary criticism. Early in December two questions were put down on the revictualling of French ships at Hongkong. The Colonial Office telegraphed to Bowen, and found that the suggestion was correct.[3] A rule was laid down that coal should not be furnished—in the curious diction of the Colonial Office code—"to any blowpoint than biquintile necessary for moving to muckrake where no lections bismuth calflike no coal bignonia supplied to the same ship . . .": in other words, that warships should be allowed only enough coal to get them to their nearest national port.[4] The distinction was tenuous, and Tseng asked querulously what difference the Foreign Enlistment Act was making.[5] The French besieged the Foreign Office with a complaint of their own. They pointed out that there was no restriction on import of arms from Hongkong into China, and considered that as a counterweight we ought to relax Section 10 (on the coaling of ships, etc.) of the Foreign Enlistment Act. Before we could decide what to do, Waddington informed the Foreign Office that France intended to exercise full belligerent rights. England had stiffened her neutrality, he asserted, in a way that substantially altered the *modus vivendi* established in November.[6]

There were British ships picking up arms at Hamburg and taking them to Hongkong, as a dropped pocket-book which

[1] Précis communicated by Mr Norris; 27. 2769.

[2] F.O. to Lyons 8 Treaty, 28.1.85, 27. 2780; extract in 431.

[3] C.O. to F.O. 10.12.84, enclosing tel. from Hongkong, 27. 2719.

[4] C.O. to Hongkong tel. ciph., 20.1.85, C.O. 129. 224; decision by Law Officers 22.12.84, 27. 2780.

[5] Memo. by Pauncefote 30.12.84, 27. 2780.

[6] F.O. to L.O., 27.1.85, 27. 2780; L.O. to F.O., 28.1.85, 27. 2780; Waddington to F.O., 29.1.85, 27. 2780. (*B.F.S.P.* LXXVI, 432.)

found its way to the Home Office disclosed.[1] France brought up her complaint again, alleging that a German ship had just unloaded several 15-ton guns at Hongkong for the Chinese Army.[2] The Foreign Office reminded itself of a decision of 1870, that to prohibit trade in arms with belligerents would be both "impracticable and impolitic";[3] but the Colonial Office pressed for consideration of this "question of policy".[4] Waddington was informed that we might give way if France waived her right of search.[5] The Chancellor was nervous; we might find ourselves landed in another "Alabama award".[6] Bowen wrote that the idea of Hongkong being more useful to France than to China was an illusion; China was securing large quantities of munitions through the colony.[7] The Law Officers were invited to reconsider their opinion, and admitted that it was a question of policy rather than of law; adding that they had been influenced by what they gathered were the feelings of certain Cabinet Ministers they had met in Gladstone's room at the House of Commons.[8] The Chinese were threatening to cut off food supplies from Hongkong if the arms trade were stopped.[9] When hostilities ceased and the problem could be dropped, the Foreign Office heaved a sigh of relief.

While friction was thus engendered between France and England—worsened by a "very grave outrage" at Singapore in January when French officers fired on deserters in British waters[10]—China's arms continued to prosper. Parkes noted signs everywhere of a rising war spirit, and the Tsungli Yamen's tone was one of "contemptuous indifference" to the French.[11] The Governors of Yunnan and Kwangsi were sentenced to death for pusillanimity, and all officials who had ever recom-

[1] 27. 2782.   [2] Waddington, 4.2.85, 27. 2781.
[3] Memo. by Tenterden, 18.7.70, with above.
[4] C.O. to F.O. Conf. and immed., 10.2.85, 27. 2781.
[5] F.O. to Waddington, 6.3.85, 27. 2783. Also Waddington, 18.3.85, and memo. by Pauncefote 23.3.85, 27. 2784; L.O. to F.O., 18.2.85, 27. 2782, and 2.4.85, 27. 2785.
[6] Selborne, 8.4.85, 27. 2785.   [7] Bowen 97, 3.3.85, 27. 2785.
[8] F.O. to L.O., 9.4.85, and L.O. to F.O., 16.4.85, 27. 2785.
[9] Bowen conf., 17.3.85, 27. 2785.   [10] Papers in 27. 2770.
[11] Parkes 21, 17.1.85, and 43, 31.1.85, 27. 2769.

mended them, including five Viceroys, were censured.[1] In Formosa the French had accomplished little in three months— "an indifferent achievement for a force of the strength commanded by Admiral Courbet".[2] Consul Spence at Taiwan saw the French preying upon native fishing boats, and carrying off the crews to labour on their works.[3]

On 20 February the French Ambassador opened another controversy, the most serious of all those between France and England, by announcing that from the 26th rice would be treated as contraband of war.[4] The French, Pauncefote scribbled on hearing this, seemed "determined to disregard the principles and rules of internat¹. Law and to ignore the rights of neutrals".[5] The Colonial Office raised again the question of whether we ought not to declare neutrality.[6] Pauncefote explained the Foreign Office's attitude in an unusually frank minute.

We shd. be quite justified no doubt in issuing the usual Proclamation of Neutrality but it was thought desirable to wait a little in order to see to what extent the French would really give us trouble— and to hold the Proclamation as it were "in terrorem". We have one or two questions now pending with them [Egypt, Burma?] which render it desirable to avoid the extreme measure if possible for awhile—but I have no doubt that as soon as it can conveniently be done, the Proclamation shd. be issued in order to quiet the doubts which the present unusual situation creates.[7]

The hard-worked Law Officers were consulted about rice, and answered that France's action was "not warranted by the Law of Nations".[8] The French, feeling they had gone too far, restricted their rice blockade to ports north of Canton, but England refused to admit that rice could be contraband unless destined to immediate military purposes.[9] China begged Lord

[1] Parkes 45, 31.1.85, 27. 2769.   [2] Parkes 10, 10.1.85, 27. 2769.

[3] Parkes 39 Extender, 30.1.85, 17. 987. Later the French tried to win the goodwill of the Formosans. (Despatches from Spence with O'Conor 177, 20.4.85, 17. 980.)   [4] B.F.S.P. LXXVI, 435.

[5] Minute in 27. 2783.   [6] 27. 2781.

[7] Minute on C.O. to F.O. Conf. and Immed., 21.2.85, 27. 2782.

[8] L.O. to F.O. 24.2.85, 27. 2782.   [9] B.F.S.P. LXXVI, 436.

Granville to prevent the French from carrying out their intention;[1] Waddington called and also wrote on 10 March to argue his point of view.[2] Parkes wrote that British merchants, who had big rice commitments, would suffer most, and he heard that food riots at Fuchow were inevitable if rice were cut off.[3] The Foreign Office made enquiries both in Paris and in Berlin about reports that German shipping was being better treated than British.[4] Lord Chancellor Selborne expressed the gravest anxiety. England was dependent on food imports, and it was "*of most vital* importance" to her to resist the French pretension. If rice could be contraband, anything could. "Such a doctrine would make a clean sweep of all international law whatever on this subject."[5] The Foreign Office therefore gave Waddington a very carefully drafted Note, dated 4 April, embodying its views and refusing to submit to decisions of French Prize Courts if contraband were to be thus arbitrarily defined.[6] Lord Selborne had the last word; after peace returned he wrote that we had been shown, alarmingly, what might befall us if we went to war, and that we might have to denounce the Declaration of Paris.[7]

By the middle of February the French columns had got within striking distance of the Tonking-Yunnan frontier, though the Court was still bringing out Decrees filled with exaggerated successes.[8] "The war between France and China", lamented the *Economist*, "differs from all modern wars, in that there appears no reason why it should ever end."[9] Parkes was again anxious about Chusan, and cabled that the danger there would be all the more pressing if Japan joined in the war.[10]

[1] Parkes tel. 14 ciph., 28.2.85, 27. 2782.
[2] F.O. to Lyons 23 A Treaty, 10.3.85, 27. 2783; *B.F.S.P.* LXXVI, 438.
[3] Parkes 8 Treaty, 10.3.85, 27. 2783, and 118, 20.3.85, 27. 2784.
[4] F.O. to Scott (Berlin) 11 Treaty, 23.3.85; to Lyons 32 A Treaty, 23.3.85; 27. 2784. In reply to the Kiel Chamber of Commerce, Bismarck laid it down that the French action was a legitimate war measure. (Scott 13 Treaty, 11.4.85, 27. 2784.)   [5] Selborne to Granville, 30.3.85, 27. 2784.
[6] 27. 2785; *B.F.S.P.* LXXVI, 441.   [7] 24.4.85, 27. 2785.
[8] Parkes 76, 18.2.85, 27. 2770.   [9] 27.3.85.
[10] Parkes tel. 16 Secret, 1.3.85, 27. 2771.

Early in March the French were rumoured to have crossed the frontier and captured a post in Kwangsi.[1] Meanwhile informal exchanges were taking place once more. Macartney's mysterious Paris correspondent came over to London with a French official, and by 13 March the three of them had a draft treaty worked out. They showed it to Ferry, who sent it to Patenôtre, who presented it to the Yamen as a French production. Apparently the Chinese Legation in London did not know this, because Tseng cabled to Peking and was told that negotiations had already been put in hand.[2] These latter, the real peace discussions, were going on in Paris between Hart's agent Campbell and Billot of the Foreign Office. They were kept secret from everybody in China except Prince Ch'ing and one other minister, and London was not in touch with them from any quarter.[3] On 26 March O'Conor cabled that peace was almost settled;[4] he believed Ferry had shown this haste because eager to finish the matter off before the Elections.[5] On the 28th he was able to telegraph the chief terms: armistice, execution of the Tientsin Convention, *status quo* in Tonking pending definitive settlement.[6]

As usual all through the long controversy, a sudden upset followed. The Chinese army recaptured Langson, and the French Government fell. London expected France to declare war immediately, and was wondering how it could bring out a Declaration of Neutrality, since the Queen was abroad and a Privy Council had never been held outside England.[7] The

---

[1] Parkes tel. 18, 7.3.85, 27. 2771.

[2] Unless the negotiations by *Hart* were meant. This episode is described in *Life of Macartney*, 387–93, and in a minute by Currie of a talk with Macartney in 27. 2771.

[3] J. Bredon, *Sir Robert Hart*, 161 ff. For the negotiations, which turned mainly on phraseology and procedure, see *L'Affaire du Tonkin*, 338–76.

[4] O'Conor tel. ciph. 21 Secret and conf., 26.3.85, 27. 2771. (Blue Book, China, no. 1 of 1886, p. 7.)

[5] O'Conor 129 Secret and conf., 26.3.85, 27. 2771. (Blue Book, p. 7.)

[6] O'Conor tel. 22 Secret and conf., 28.3.85, 27. 2771.

[7] Currie to Sir H. James 31.3.85, 27. 2771; Selborne to Granville 2.4.85, 27. 2772.

French were reported to have seized the Pescadores and to intend sending their ships against North China.[1] The Tsungli Yamen was hard pressed by the war party.[2] Yet observers were once more mistaken. On 4 April, Preliminaries of Peace were signed in Paris. On the 7th O'Conor congratulated the Yamen.[3] On the 10th a Decree confirmed the Protocol, and commanded immediate withdrawal from Tonking.[4] O'Conor learned that the German Minister, under orders from Berlin, had tried in vain to avert peace.[5] On the 27th O'Conor telegraphed: "French negotiations begin immediately Tientsin. Strong feeling against peace in military and Mandarin class. Yamen pretty firm."[6]

British preoccupations at once took a fresh turn. O'Conor heard that the French were trying to secure a special commercial status; and he admonished the Yamen not to allow this.[7] At the end of April he cabled that the French were aiming at two things: a promise by China of applying to France when she should want railways built, and a frontier tariff one-third lower than that at the Ports. He suggested that we should ask as a counter-balance the opening to trade of the West River at Canton.[8] Currie talked to Sir Thomas Wade, who thought it "very undesirable" that there should be any mention of railways in France's treaty.[9] Hertslet believed that our Treaty of 1858 entitled us to share in any land frontier privileges, and O'Conor was so instructed.[10] He wrote that if the French obtained frontier stations with the status of Treaty Ports, as they desired, it would give their trade with South China "an immense impetus". He took for granted that the Foreign Office would wish him to protest if he saw France scheming for "a most objectionable monopoly" in railways; which was

[1] C.O. to F.O. Immed., 2.4.85, 27. 2772; O'Conor 156, 9.4.85, 27. 2772.
[2] O'Conor 142, 3.4.85, 27. 2772.   [3] O'Conor 155, 8.4.85, 27. 2772.
[4] O'Conor tel. 25 ciph. conf., 10.4.85, 27. 2772.
[5] O'Conor to Sanderson, 9.4.85, 97. 621.
[6] O'Conor tel. ciph. 30 conf., 27.4.85, 27. 2772.   [7] Blue Book, p. 11.
[8] O'Conor tel. ciph. 31 conf., 29.4.85, 27. 2772. (Blue Book, p. 9.)
[9] Minute by Currie on above.
[10] Memo. 1.5.85 with above; F.O. to O'Conor tel. ciph. 17, 5.5.85, and 18, 7.5.85; 116, 23.5.85; 27. 2772.

approved.[1] Macartney confided to the Foreign Office that France wanted an undertaking by China to continue any railway that might be run up to her frontier in Tonking. He believed that this would be refused;[2] and O'Conor cabled on 10 May that France's trade privileges were to be strictly limited. At that time the state of affairs continued very critical, "owing to the intervention of high personages against the conclusion of peace".[3] On the 21st O'Conor told the Yamen that he had waited hitherto, so as not to hinder the peace settlement, but would now be glad to hear some details. The Prince begged him to set his mind at ease: England would suffer no detriment. The Chargé d'Affaires replied that he hoped not, as otherwise he would have to claim redress.[4]

On 22 May Prince Ch'ing warmly praised to O'Conor the skill shown by Hart in the negotiations.[5] On the 24th the vexed formula about Annam was known to be settled.[6] On 11 June

[1] O'Conor 198, 29.4.85, and minute, 27. 2772.

[2] F.O. to O'Conor tel. 21 ciph., 11.5.85, 27. 2778. (Blue Book, p. 10.)

[3] O'Conor tel. 34 (Blue Book, p. 10) and 220 Extender, Very conf., 10.5.85, 27. 2772. For the discussions on the British side of the commercial effects of the peace, see 27. 2772, 2773, 2774; most of the papers are in Blue Book, China, no. 1 of 1886. During the debate in the French Chambers on the peace, Freycinet said that the most favoured nation clause did not apply to land frontiers. The Colonial Office brought up, not for the first time, the opinion of Bowen and the Hongkong Chamber of Commerce that now was the moment to secure the opening of S.W. China. The Board of Trade took a serious view of the new French facilities for entering S. China, and thought a lowered duty would be "even more inconsistent with our Treaties with China". Effects on Burma were discussed with the India Office. One of our consuls took refuge from the prospect of hostile tariffs in the French sphere, in the idea that "the French, belonging, as they do, to a civilised nation...whatever duties they may impose...will grant every facility of locomotion". No doubt if the wishes of British merchants were confined to locomotion pure and simple they could be gratified, but if they wanted something more lucrative it was likely to be different.

[4] O'Conor 237, 22.5.85, 27. 2772.

[5] O'Conor 248 conf., 26.5.85, 27. 2772. Hart meanwhile was being offered the British Legation; a rumour got out, and the French threatened to break off negotiations if it were true. (O'Conor tel. ciph., 2.5.85, 97. 621.)

[6] O'Conor 238 conf., ext. tel. 41, 25.5.85, 27. 2772.

Li and Patenôtre signed a treaty at Tientsin, whose text O'Conor was able to send on the 17th. It was, he thought, "politically less interesting" than the Tientsin Convention; also it seemed to give the French nearly everything they wanted.[1] Sun Yat-sen and the revolutionaries were one day to blame the Manchus for letting slip the prizes of war.[2] At present there were many who took the same line. Peng Yu-lin had a violent Memorial against the conclusion of peace. Commencing by saying he "lacked words to express his admiration" for the profundity of Imperial policy, he went on to say that China was making herself "contemptible" by wasting the huge preparations she had made for war. It was on all fours with the blunder of the Sung Dynasty in making peace with the Kin. China ought to line her coasts with ironclads and then put under "bit and bridle" those "malignant bandits" the French.[3] Chang Yin-huan, however, appointed Envoy to Washington this year, let drop the idea that had the French realised China's exhaustion and pushed on, there might have been a total collapse.[4] "China," the *Economist* had written in March, "though she is displaying much resolution, is also suffering. Her coasting trade is ruined.... Above all, the ruling group at Peking must now be aware that their hopes of dissensions among the foreigners are vain; that locally the tie of race is too strong for them, and that in Europe the Courts are not thinking very seriously of Chinese affairs."[5] Besides, the peace gave France no more than Li had offered at Tientsin; relatively it was a huge triumph for China, and was so regarded everywhere.

A curious and pathetic Memorial in the *Gazette* painted the sufferings of the Chinese armies in the torrid, poisonous climate of Tonking: whole battalions died, corpses had to be thrown in heaps into large holes; losses were between ten and twenty thousand; survivors heard the cries and moans of the ghosts over

[1] O'Conor 300, 17.6.85, 27. 2772.
[2] Sun Yat-sen, *The Three People's Principles*, Lecture 2.
[3] With O'Conor 274 conf., 9.6.85, 27. 2773.
[4] O'Conor 448 Secret, 2.11.85, 17. 985.
[5] 21.3.85.

their desolate graves.[1] These survivors were in process of being disbanded. Large desertions were reported—shrewdly suspected to be a device of the officers to get rid of their men without paying them;[2] it was sorry treatment for the heroes of those jungle battles. But a Memorial of October wound up the whole affair in the true phrasing of the Mandarin dialect. "The French, after fighting three years in Annam, have now a wholesome terror of the Imperial troops, and, in consequence, went to Tientsin to pray for peace, which was graciously accorded."[3]

Throughout the war, the British Government's policy, as elicited in Parliament, was indistinct and reticent. Tonking, it may be remarked, drew vastly greater public attention than any other Far Eastern topic of these years (except opium), and marked the first awakening of modern interest.

The earliest Parliamentary reference was in the spring of 1883, when Lord Harris drew attention to French operations in Indo-China and their possible effect on the Singapore-Hongkong route. Granville replied that he had "no official information on the subject". Lord Salisbury was much astonished that we had no agent at the Court of Annam.[4] (Why had he not sent one himself?) In succeeding months, answers to questions were so monotonous and so uninformative that Mr Onslow asked if the Government was *trying* to get information; to which the Under-Secretary replied that it had no means.[5] Gladstone, asked if our good offices were to be used, gave it to be understood that peace was ever the deepest concern of his Cabinet, and that the tried specific, "careful consideration", was being employed without stint.[6] In summer, 1883, Ashmead-Bartlett—the Io's gadfly of the Liberal Ministry in foreign affairs—kept dragging Annam in, but without extracting anything from the Treasury Bench worth hearing. The House

[1] Copy with O'Conor 494, 26.12.85, 17. 986.
[2] O'Conor 292, 15.6.85, 17. 982.
[3] Copy with O'Conor 413, 1.10.85, 17. 984.
[4] Hansard, 3rd Series, 278. 414. De Lanessan's book (*Expansion Coloniale de la France*, 1886) dwells on the value to France of colonies in Indo-China in case of war with England, for cutting British communications (p. 588).
[5] Hansard, 3rd Series, 278. 1416.   [6] Hansard, 3rd Series, 279. 1487.

did not meet again until February 1884, when the question was put whether it was true that Her Majesty's Government had been in "confidential correspondence" with Paris. The Under-Secretary thought it necessary to amend the phrase to "confidential communication", and said that what had passed could not be laid before the House.[1] In the autumn the Formosa blockade aroused great indignation. The Government declined to be drawn.

On 23 February (1885)—it was the nearest approach to a debate—the Earl of Dunraven said that England was being widely condemned for letting the French make use of Hong-kong in their barbarous activities. "No reasonable man could be expected to believe...that H.M.G. had any distinct comprehension of its duties, or distinct determination to carry them out." Was France at war? If not, what right had she to blockade? The practice of carrying on warlike operations without declaring war was spreading mischievously. The Foreign Secretary replied: We refused to recognise a pacific blockade, but recognised a belligerent one. Salisbury found the answer unsatisfactory.[2] When the French declared rice contraband of war, resentment was intensified. It was an action which, a contemporary wrote, "electrified the civilised world".[3] On 26 February, asked if they meant to acquiesce, Ministers for once replied audibly that they did not.[4]

Questions multiplied. Members thought the contraband problem a grave one for a food-importing country like England. By this time, it is clear from the tone of discussion, the idea was gaining ground that the Franco-Chinese war might very easily grow into an Anglo-French one. Lord Sidmouth maintained on 27 March that our squadron in the Far East ought to be strengthened. Viscount Bury, in an alarmist speech, said: "It is well known that this country was in a position in which it might at any moment be involved in war."[5] All that the Government explained in Parliament of its

[1] *Ibid.* 287. 756.   [2] *Ibid.* 294. 1107.
[3] Mrs Gordon Cumming, *Wanderings in China*, ch. XXVII.
[4] Hansard, 3rd Series, 294. 1418.   [5] *Ibid.* 295. 815 ff.

policy towards the war, has been given.[1] It amounted to very little; grudging half-answers to a long series of questions. The Opposition, again, put forward no definite rival policy, but left the task of harassing Ministers to its skirmishers. The impression created is one of surprising complacency towards France, a surprising readiness to avoid seeing opportunities for complaint. Contemporaries had taken it almost as axiomatic, beforehand, that a Franco-Chinese war meant an Anglo-French war. Gordon said that "humanly speaking, China going to war with France, must entail our following suit".[2] Colquhoun, the explorer and war-correspondent, agreed that our greatest efforts could not keep us out of a Franco-Chinese war.[2] Another English writer in 1884 said that before the war ended England, as mediator or ally, *must* intervene.[3] Sir Charles Dilke wrote later that in a real, unambiguous war between France and China we could scarcely keep out.[4] Yet a long campaign was fought and England remained inactive. China received a foretaste of her disappointments with England of 1896 and 1937.

The British attitude was governed partly by the great complexity of our imperial interests in the Far East, partly by an irresolute lack of policy. It was in general our wish to save China from being attacked and broken up. On the other hand we shared the common anticipation that from any earthquake in the Far East circumstances more favourable to commerce might evolve. Bowen saw a good deal of the French naval officers, and said they confessed to a fear "that English and not French commerce...will really profit by French conquests in the Indo-Chinese peninsula".[5] Intervention against France might make things worse, by provoking a general scramble

[1] The remaining references are—On mediation: 287. 756, 289. 1759, 292. 635, 296. 818 and 1300; On the Formosa blockade: 293. 346 and 528, 295. 47 and 1057, 296. 230 and 372; Calls for information: 279. 913, 283. 1735, 293. 538 and 1096, 294. 635, 296. 818 and 1300; On French brutality: 280. 1128, 294. 1170: On the danger of trade losses: 287. 454, 288. 675, 1294 and 1770, 290. 677; On the rice issue: 278. 913, 294. 1418, and nearly twenty references in 296.   [2] Colquhoun, *Truth about Tonking*, Letter 4.
[3] Norman, *Tonking*, VI.   [4] *Problems of Modern Politics*, 104.
[5] *Letters, etc. of Bowen*, ed. Lane Poole, II, 277.

for "compensation"—as it was wittily called—all round. It was plain from the start that France would not enjoy a military promenade, and some believed with Bowen that if she attacked Peking she would find another Moscow.[1] We could watch and wait, finding sources of a modest satisfaction. France was wasting her forces gratifyingly. Dilke was among those who thought France was acting very foolishly.[2] Inevitably, we were suspected of *fomenting* the war. Parkes' position at Peking was difficult (apart from the tremendous pressure of work which made him declare "No convict could be at harder labour");[3] his conduct was jealously scrutinised; there were "suggestions that England and Germany were not sorry at heart to see France engaged in a costly struggle".[4] In a Tonking debate in November 1884 Clemenceau declared it was Bismarck—more dangerous as friend than as foe—who was pushing France into Indo-China; and that England also had too many causes of rivalry with France to be an honest mediator.[5] Challemel-Lacour once referred in a speech to "a certain Great Power" which was egging China on to resist, and a British spokesman's remark in Parliament that Her Majesty's Government "did not believe the statement in question could possibly be intended to affect them in any way" was disingenuous.[6] So far as the British documents go, we did *not* in any way egg China on to fight. Documentary records never go the whole way; but in fact we had no need to do anything positive. The intellectual indolence of the Foreign Office found an easy groove to run in. And one can see why Salisbury was so sparing in his attacks on the Administration. To watch a rival Power bleeding itself in a severe fight was for him no hardship. It is probable that had he been in office he would have managed the affair very much as Granville did.

[1] *Letters, etc. of Bowen*, II, 287.   [2] *Problems of Modern Politics*, 49.
[3] *Life of Parkes*, II, 220. When he took up his post in 1883 he expected Tonking to prove "a most unpleasant baptism". (*Ibid.* 365.) It killed him.
[4] Article from *Shanghai Courier* with O'Conor 146, 4.4.85, 17. 979.
[5] Lyons 671, 28.11.85, 27. 2718.
[6] Hansard, 3rd Series, 279. 1911, 280. 225.

What is to be said as regards the masterliness of this inactivity? It might seem as though the inconclusive end to the campaign fulfilled our wishes to a nicety. China was not shaken to pieces, yet she had had a fright that might make her more amenable to foreign influence. "France is doing good work in the East", wrote a Hongkong journalist, "if it is only in giving the Chinamen a lesson."[1] France had won something of unascertained value, and while she was fighting the British annexation of Burma was insensibly being prepared, and the British occupation of Egypt being consolidated. Moreover, as the *Economist* had written in 1882, France had been certain to attack either Tonking or Siam—"and the British Government could not allow the latter Power to be seriously molested".[2]

But in two ways the war had effects the reverse of what England could desire.

A traveller, a year or two later, found the Peking rabble grown most insolent since the war.[3] The Chinese, wrote another, Kipling, had been taught "a great many things which, perhaps, it were better for us that they had left alone".[4] This misgiving was in the minds of all foreigners in the Far East. For the first time soldiers of a yellow race had fought hand to hand with Europeans, and not been disgraced. A momentous national spirit, hitherto unknown, wrote Bowen early in 1885, was revealing itself: in 1860 we could get as many coolies as we wanted in our war, but in 1884 not a Chinese in Hongkong would work for the French ships: many believed the war would prove "the turning-point in the modern history of China".[5] It was feared that the Chinese would put on a new "arrogance"

---

[1] Article with C.O. to F.O., 4.4.84, 27. 2708.

[2] 25.11.83. The article ably states the dilemma in which a decisive win by either side would have placed us.

[3] De Windt, *Peking to Calais by Land*, 1889, 57. Even in the remote West Rockhill, a few years later, found the prestige of all foreigners at a low ebb since the "miserably managed" Tonking war. (*Land of the Lamas*, 1891, 274.)

[4] Kipling, *From Sea to Sea*, ch. x.

[5] Bowen 89, 23.2.85, 27. 2772; published in his *Letters, etc.* II, 346 ff. Cp. p. 374: "It is certain that the late war has materially strengthened the Chinese Empire."

now they had met a Great Power in the field and held their own; that one day the recapture of Langson might be magnified into the expulsion of all Occidentals from the Far East. This sense of common racial interest did much to tie the hands of British diplomacy during the war: that the West was eternally invincible was a belief one dare not carelessly undermine. It is said that peasants in Annam planted the Japanese lotus in their fields to salute the battle of Tsushima as a victory of the Orient. They might have done so after the battles in Tonking and Formosa, even though these ended in their own subjection.

During the course of the war, British commercial reactions changed greatly. In the early stages Grosvenor wrote that the world would not be the worse if France annexed Tonking: trade would improve for everyone with a Western state in control of the Red River.[1] Just two years later O'Conor wrote warningly that the capital of Yunnan was 630 miles away from our traders at Canton, and only 330 miles from the Tonking coast.[2] "And in addition it can hardly be doubted that the principle of protection will be applied by the French officials to the exclusion of British manufactures. Taking a low estimate, there is reason to apprehend an immediate decrease of British imports to the value of perhaps half a million sterling."[3] This ought, it is true, to have been foreseen in official quarters. It was foreseen by such a man as Colquhoun; but he found Tonking a *terra incognita*: "Ignorance grows as England is left and culminates at Hongkong." Hongkong traders—"practical business men who cannot afford to look to the future"— rejoiced in the war orders created, and hoped for the best.[4] They had long refused to believe that China meant to fight; partly no doubt because they had in general "a distinct abhorrence for the Chinese", whom they talked of "as if they were beasts".[5]

[1] Grosvenor to Currie, 4.5.83, 17. 923.
[2] Lanessan (*Expansion Coloniale de la France*, 457) argued that China, ot Europe, must be the market for the products of French Indo-China. It ᴡas natural that entry into S. China should bulk very large in French plans.
[3] O'Conor 242 conf., 25.5.85, 17. 981.
[4] Colquhoun, *Truth about Tonking*.
[5] H. W. Lucy, *East and West*, II, 115.

There is an amusing record of the exploits of one Englishman who hailed the war as an escape from the "dead and rotten" condition of the market. He got a shipload of ponies from Singapore to Haiphong, and sold them to the French at fabulous prices. He even sold the French Army a miscellaneous consignment including hairpins and jew's harps, and was offered a decoration for his services. Such men naturally criticised the putting in force of the Foreign Enlistment Act.[1]

The Foreign Office was not indifferent to the question of trade, as its close scrutiny of the peace terms shows, but it seems to have devoted little thought to that aspect of the matter earlier and to have cultivated an easy optimism. At this date it, like our merchants, was only just grasping the fact that whereas England annexed areas where she had interests to protect, France annexed areas where she *wished* to have interests to protect, and so had to shut out competition from the start. Yet our consul at Saigon, before ever the French entered Tonking, was made aware of the obstacles that French political control offered to British enterprise.[2] Such warnings were fully borne out after the annexation.[3]

[1] J. D. Ross, *Sixty Years in the Far East*, ii, ch. lvii.
[2] Acting Consul at Saigon 6 Political, 22.9.83, 27. 2705. In May 1884 Lyons sent the Foreign Office an article by Leroy Beaulieu according to which France would not be so foolish as to let other nations enjoy the S. China trade on equal terms with herself. (With Lyons 289, 19.5.84, 27. 2708.) Cp. a strong Imperialist article in the *Économiste Français*, vol. ii of 1885, 166, and an editorial by Leroy Beaulieu, *ibid.* 657. Lyons was expressing regret that France showed no signs of meaning to admit any trade but her own into Annam. (*Life*, by Lord Newton, ii, 328.)
[3] See e.g. H. Norman, *Peoples and Politics of the Far East*, 102 ff. Bureaucratic rigidity and jobbery made things difficult even for French capital.

CHAPTER THIRTEEN

The Anglo-Russian Crisis, 1885

A young poet wrote fifteen sonnets for *The National Review* in the spring of 1885, which he called "Ver Tenebrosum". He bewailed in tones of patriotic dejection—his poor spirits only equalled by his poor versification—the buffets Britannia was suffering in Asia and Africa.[1] It was on 9 February that news of the death of Gordon reached London, and the Government all but fell. The French Ambassadress went out into the Row and heard "a tall man on a handsome chestnut talking to Admiral C. most energetically, 'I am a moderate man myself, but I would willingly lend a hand to hang Gladstone to that tree'".[2] The Tories were far from thirsting to turn their rivals out. It would be taking office under ill-omened skies. Salisbury wrote to Lord Cairns on 3 March: "Matters are gloomy—I never saw them gloomier."[3] It was left to the worn-out Liberal Ministry to face the Russian crisis, the theme of our young poetaster's most turgid declamation:

> But most it angers me, to think how vile
> Art thou, how base, from whom the insult came,
> Unwieldy laggard, many an age behind
> Thy sister Powers, in brain and conscience both....

An extraordinarily complicated situation arose in the Far East in the last year of our troubled lustrum. The dispute between China and Japan over Corea entangled itself with the Franco-Chinese hostilities, and with a further crisis which almost brought England and Russia into conflict throughout all Asia. The crisis that arose in Afghanistan had repercussions in

[1] William Watson, in *National Review*, June 1885.
[2] Mary Waddington, *Letters*, 9.2.85.
[3] Lady G. Cecil, *Life of Lord Salisbury*, III, 129.

the Far East fully as significant as the happenings at Herat—
a fact neglected by its chroniclers. The earliest reaction made
itself felt a little before the middle of March, when Vice-Admiral
Dowell found himself compelled to collect his ships from the
Ports "in consequence of complications with Russia". Parkes
at once interviewed the Yamen and the German and American
Ministers, and engaged them to protect British interests in case
of war.[1] When a Chinese Minister asked the cause of the tension,
Parkes made the orthodox reply that it was all due to Russia's
expansionist bent.[2]

It must be borne in mind that China was at war with France,
and threatened with war with Japan. Of these two the former,
and perhaps the latter, was a friend of Russia; therefore an
explosion between Russia and England might well put them
against England, making England automatically China's ally.
It might well be that war between Russia and China was sooner
or later inevitable. At this moment rumours were coming in
of a new insurrection in Kashgar, "well known to, if not
abetted by, the Russian Authorities".[3] It looked as though the
fear of Russia attacking in the north while China's strength was
locked up in the south, was about to be realised. It had also been
hoped at Peking from the beginning of the Tonking war that
England would come to China's rescue. If she were now forced
by circumstances to do so, China might hope to regain what
she had lost to Russia in 1881 and earlier. In short there were
good reasons on the Chinese side for taking part with England
in the quarrel that had blown across the Indian Ocean.

Parkes' interview with the Yamen was almost the last scene
of his fabulous career in the East. But Chinese interest in the
crisis soon displayed itself more actively. Brenan, a new Acting-
Consul at Tientsin, called on Li to pay his respects. The Viceroy

[1] Parkes 107 conf., 18.3.85, 17. 979.
[2] Parkes 113 conf., 20.3.85, 17. 979.
[3] O'Conor 140, 31.3.85, 17. 979. The *Shanghai Courier* wrote on 23 March
that "to Russia was almost certainly due the rising in Kashgaria". (Article
with O'Conor 146, 4.4.85, 17.979.) The Governor of one region in Mongolia
was reporting that there also the tribes were out of hand. (O'Conor 171,
17.4.85, 17. 980.) Perhaps Russia was insuring herself against war with China.

brought up the question of Afghanistan, asking what allies Britain would find if she went to war. Then, in his blunt way, he made the startling proposal of an Anglo-Chinese alliance. He dwelt on the advantage to England of a diversion by Chinese armies in Turkestan, and "finished up with some bitter remarks on Russian aggressive policy". Shortly afterwards Li returned the call and again brought up the subject. He stated that the British Government had approached Tseng and proposed a secret treaty; that, as the Yamen "could not understand these delicate foreign questions", the point would be referred to him, and he would support it.[1] About the same time, a telegraph agent named Dunn who was in touch with Li discussed an English alliance with him; Li said he would welcome it, but thought British policy vacillating. Dunn passed this on to two *Times* correspondents. One, Michie, sounded Count Ito during his visit to China, and Ito said that Japan would join England and China against Russia, though not against France. The other, Colquhoun, sent two telegrams to the Viceroy of India by way of the Straits Government, warmly advocating alliance with China.[2]

The problem now emerged which was to be the focus of the crisis in the Far East—that of Port Hamilton. Port Hamilton was a pair of Corean islets, embracing like two arms a roadstead that had long fed speculation in naval circles. They were ruled, a visitor found in 1875, simply by their own elders, grave men, of whom one visited the ship, asked to hear the band, and began incongruously to dance.[3] In September 1884 Tseng, and in December Parkes, had wind of Russian designs on the islands,[4] and in the latter month it was decided to send a ship from time to time to the harbour "with orders to report any movement there".[5] Early in April the British Government made up its mind to occupy Port Hamilton as a naval base for the approaching war. Warships were sent there in the first week.

[1] O'Conor 178 Secret, 20.4.85, 17. 980.
[2] Dunn to F.O., 8.5.85, and Straits Govt. to C.O., 13.4.85 Most conf., 17. 1002.   [3] Bridge, "A Glimpse of the Korea", *Fortnightly*, Feb. 1875.
[4] Memo. by Currie, 11.9.84, 27. 2712; Parkes 320, 13.12.84, 27. 2719.
[5] F.O. to Parkes 308 Very conf., 31.12.84, 17. 947.

The Times applauded the decision, but ludicrously confused Port Hamilton with Quelpart, and Hertslet wrote: "It is to be hoped the Admiralty have not hoisted the British Flag on the wrong Island."[1] The flag was not in fact hoisted until the second week of May, when a Russian ship visited the harbour.

A group of memoranda, just before the decision was taken, betrays a good deal of confusion in official counsels. The Admiralty thought highly of Port Hamilton.[2] Our act, which might have provoked the rupture it was meant to guard against, we were to justify by saying that if we had not taken the harbour "someone else" would; a plea later dismissed by a naval expert as "absurd"—only the Power which controlled the seas could hold Port Hamilton in time of war.[3] But the stroke was part of an *aggressive*, not a defensive, strategy. Port Hamilton was to be our base of attack on Russia's Far Eastern possessions. On 10 April someone in Downing Street with illegible initials complains that the matter has been put before the Cabinet in an ill-digested form: a new naval station is no trifle—think of Ascension Island. Could not the Admiralty have furnished practical estimate of costs? Northbrook, the First Lord, rejoins: "I am of opinion that an arrangement should be made with China that we should occupy Port Hamilton in the event of war with Russia. It will be necessary as a base for any operations agst. Vladivostock." Pauncefote writes from Paris on the 12th that the occupation has been "fully considered by the Royal Commission on National Defences. . . .The question of Chinese suzerainty over Corea is a burning one. We have refused to recognise the claim of China, though I apprehend that it is well founded." Now that attention has been called to the place, Russia may "make a dash" at it; so we ought to hoist our flag quickly.[4]

[1] Minute 6.4.85, 17. 1001.

[2] Admiralty to F.O. conf., 4.4.85, 17. 1001; cp. Conf. Report of Admiralty Foreign Intelligence Committee, April 1884, and extract from Report of Commission on Defence of British Possessions, in 17. 1002. Both these recommend Port Hamilton. We had also thought of Port Lazarev as a coaling-station: F.O. to Admiralty conf., 20.3.84, 17. 969.

[3] Admiral Willes, 7.1.86; *B.F.S.P.* LXXVI.   [4] Memo. in 17. 1000.

On 8 April Tseng made an enquiry about our intentions, and was put off.[1] On the 16th the Foreign Office informed him that we meant to occupy Port Hamilton temporarily "in view of the probable occupation of these islands by another Power", but that we had no wish to injure Chinese prestige, and desired an agreement with Peking.[2] Tseng's answer, while emphasising China's suzerainty over Corea, welcomed the British assurances and asked what accommodation was proposed.[3] The Foreign Office furnished him with a draft binding England to pay rent to Corea, with a deduction for China of whatever might normally go to her as tribute.[4] So far, all was going smoothly. Li assured O'Conor that a temporary occupation would not be objected to, because if taken by Russia the islands would be lost for good.[5] Meanwhile, the international crisis deepened: on the 17th a young politician wrote to Wolseley: "Public attention is wholly engrossed in the prospects of war with Russia....We are not in a position to fight".[6] Three days later Granville told the German representative that negotiations were going very badly.[7] The seizure of Port Hamilton leapt at once into prominence in the Press, and on the Continent.[8]

On 6 May the President of the Corean Foreign Office, asking Carles about the Russian trouble, did not mention the presence of the British squadron at Port Hamilton.[9] But on the same day Macartney came to the Foreign Office to say that Tseng had learned by cable of an obstacle: the Russian Minister at Peking had threatened to occupy another part of Corea if China acquiesced in the British action; and therefore the proffered draft could not be signed.[10] The same happened to O'Conor when he heard that Port Hamilton had been taken, and called at the Yamen to see which way the wind was blowing there. They did not, the Ministers said, doubt England's *bona*

[1] F.O. to O'Conor 75A, 8.4.85, 17. 975.   [2] B.F.S.P. LXXVIII, 143.
[3] Ibid. LXXVIII, 145.   [4] Ibid.
[5] O'Conor 180 conf., 21.4.85, 17. 980.
[6] Lord Esher, Letters and Journals, I, 113.
[7] F.O. to Berlin 212, 20.4.85, 64. 1074.
[8] Grundry, China and Her Neighbours, 275.
[9] Carles to O'Conor conf., 7.5.85, 17. 996.   [10] B.F.S.P. LXXVIII, 147.

fides; but the Russian and Japanese envoys had called to urge China to protest, and hinted broadly that certain Governments might find they owed it to themselves to take other naval bases as an offset. Was England prepared to guarantee Corean integrity? If so, no protest would be made. O'Conor said he could not answer so large a question. But Port Hamilton was a trivial place—we had taken it merely as a coaling station—our taking it prevented others doing so—in short, he wound up with charming impudence, "both the Chinese and the Corean Governments should appreciate the service which the force of circumstances had thus rendered them". This was really killing China with kindness. The Ministers did not turn hostile, and he had the impression that they were only making a show of protesting, to throw dust in Russian eyes. He also had a feeling that they were privy to Li's ideas of alliance, and did not disapprove them.[1] If their protests *should* go beyond formalities, O'Conor was ready to take a high hand. When he heard that Admiral Ting had sailed from Taku to convey a remonstrance to our Admiral, he prepared to use the butt end of the pistol— to say that England would call in question China's suzerainty over Corea altogether.[2]

At Seoul it was denied that Russia was being offered any group of islands she liked in return for a guarantee of Corea.[3] Still, when we tried to get permission to lay a cable to Saddle Island near Port Hamilton, the Yamen laid down awkward conditions. O'Conor remonstrated, only to learn—what was to be expected—that the Russians had been making trouble. Prince Ch'ing begged him to lay the cable via Nagasaki, so that China should not seem to be abetting England's conduct. In the end a temporary permission was given. "Although China dislikes our occupation of Port Hamilton," wrote O'Conor, "she dislikes still more the idea of that island being taken possession of, as she fears may happen, by Russia."[4]

[1] O'Conor 218 Very conf., 9.5.85, 17. 980.
[2] O'Conor 221 conf., 10.5.85, 17. 980.
[3] Carles to Plunkett, 18.5.85, conf., 17. 996.
[4] O'Conor 227 conf., 15.5.85, 17. 981.

Admiral Ting had gone to Corea, where he had a secret audience with the King[1] and picked up two Corean representatives whom he carried to Nagasaki to lodge a protest with Admiral Dowell.[2] O'Conor attributed this show of spirit to the German Möllendorf, who was one of the two representatives, and whom he denounced unsparingly in his despatches. Möllendorf had been a German consular interpreter, an officer of the Maritime Customs, and one of Li's secretaries. It was through Li that he obtained his Corean post, at 300 taels a month and quarters. He was on bad terms with Hart—he had "personal grudges"[3]—but also with Brandt.[4] He treated his Corean colleagues arrogantly, the English said.[5] It is fair to say that one can find much more favourable accounts of him. His biography, letters, and photographs, show a well-meaning German scholar in spectacles rather than a spider of intrigue. Clearly he viewed Japan as Corea's great enemy, and Russia as her only possible defender.[6] His confidence in Russia was shortsighted, but may have been honest, and his case could be made to look much more plausible than it did through English eyes. He complained bitterly of Anglo-German intrigues against him, and denunciations in the Press of the Far East.[7] Nothing, however, was too bad for O'Conor to write about him. He was an unscrupulous agent in any matter in which he can serve his own private aims. Some short time ago I heard that he had suggested to the Russian Government to buy Port Hamilton from Corea, and he offered to act as intermediary in the purchase. It may well be that the occupation of the island by Her Majesty's Government has deprived him of a promising business and induced him to exert his influence in inducing the Corean Government to its present action. I fear however that it is impossible to acquit the Chinese Government of participation in the decision of that of Corea.[8]

[1] Carles to F.O., 16, 19.5.85, 17. 996.
[2] For Dowell's detailed report see *B.F.S.P.* LXXVIII, 149–52.
[3] Aston, 19.5.85 Very conf., with O'Conor 265 conf., 4.6.85, 17. 981.
[4] Grosvenor 140 Most conf., 25.11.82, 17. 900.
[5] Carles 58 conf., with O'Conor 314, 26.6.85, 17. 982.
[6] See a letter of his of 2.3.85, in his *Life* (by R. von Möllendorf), 78 ff.
[7] *Ibid.* 83, etc.   [8] O'Conor 314.

O'Conor went to the Yamen and taxed the Ministers with Ting's conduct. They denied complicity in the Corean protest. He complained of Seoul's having proceeded without notifying our consul. Lord Granville, he continued, warming to his work, had "shown much friendliness" by informing them "at an early stage" of our intentions. What did they think would happen if we left Port Hamilton? The Prince replied humbly that he did not find fault with England's course, and would advise Seoul accordingly.[1] It was a trying thing for the Yamen to have its authority over Corea dragged up just now, when it was already being contested by Japan. Russia's and England's wishes were contradictory, and either if unsatisfied might dispute China's right or her ability to influence Corea at all. Corea herself might take the bit between her teeth. The Nagasaki protest had contained a threat of appeal to the Treaty Powers. O'Conor directed Aston and Carles in Corea to lay themselves out to avert this.[2] But Corea repeated her protest in a more formal shape. O'Conor concluded that it would be easier to exert pressure at Peking than at Seoul.[3] Our policy was to recognise Chinese suzerainty, or not, according to our convenience of the moment. The Coreans added to their misconduct by sending round to the foreign representatives copies of our correspondence with them about Port Hamilton, though Carles had warned them to treat it as confidential. He found this out because a letter meant for the German, Zembsch, was sent to him by mistake.[4] He remonstrated with H.E. Kim Yun-sik, describing England's friendly feelings towards Corea, only to be told that she could best show them by leaving Port Hamilton.[5] Zembsch maintained that Corea was right: we were giving Russia an excuse to attack her, without promising her protection: that sort of thing would prejudice her against the West in general. He admitted having said as much to the

---

[1] O'Conor 236 Very conf., 23.5.85, 17. 981.
[2] B.F.S.P. LXXVIII, 148.
[3] O'Conor 251 Very conf., 26.5.85, 17. 981.
[4] Carles to F.O. 19, 21.5.85, 17. 996.
[5] Carles to O'Conor 54, 23.5.85, 17. 996.

Coreans.[1] Lieutenant Foulk, U.S. Chargé d'Affaires, was behaving better; he was on close terms with the Coreans, and argued the British case to them.[2]

As regards Afghanistan, danger of war with Russia may be said to have receded in May. The hot-headed youth of the Foreign Office was wild with Granville for letting the Tsar, the Arch-fiend of its universe, go off without a drubbing, but it had to resign itself and go back to copying more or less peaceful despatches.[3] But there was still Port Hamilton to dispose of; and this factor helped to prolong the Anglo-Russian crisis in its Far Eastern theatre. At Hongkong £200,000 was being spent on forts and batteries. Lord Northbrook observed that Willes and Dowell did not think Port Hamilton very useful, and that politically he himself was not sure; it would be awkward if Russia raised the question with us.[4] The Board of Trade thought the islands not worth keeping for commercial purposes.[5]

At the beginning of June O'Conor had another interview with the Yamen to recount. He renewed his complaint about the proceedings of Admiral Ting, adding something else he had heard in the interval, that Möllendorf was deep in intrigues with an aide-de-camp of the Governor of Eastern Siberia. The Ministers professed themselves quite neutral. It was too much, they said, to ask them to put pressure on Seoul. They would be compromised with other Powers if they did so, and would be inviting Russia to follow the English lead. O'Conor asked why, seeing that the Coreans had consulted several foreign agents, they had not consulted the Chinese representative. To be frank, answered the Ministers, Lord Granville had asked Tseng the same question in London; Tseng had cabled it to them; they had submitted it to the Throne; the Empress had forbidden them to interfere in the matter; they had no choice. It was an instructive answer, whether true or not, and it is quite possible that they left it to Tzu Hsi to decide the point, to be

[1] Memo. of conversation, with above.
[2] Carles to F.O. 21 conf., 23.5.85, 17. 996.
[3] Lord Howard, *Theatre of Life*, 51.   [4] Memo. 20.5.85, 17. 1002.
[5] Board of Trade to F.O. Immed. and Very conf., 9.7.85, 17. 1002.

rid of the responsibility. O'Conor found them less cordial than before, from fear of a series of annexations being provoked by England's action. He wrote to Li, who, if with misgivings, wrote to the King of Corea advising him to suffer in silence.[1]

Suspicions as to the ambiguous Möllendorf thickened. Plunkett at Tokio scented an agreement between him and the Russian Minister there. The *aide* of the Governor of Siberia— he bore the suitably histrionic name of the Duke of Dadesh- koliani—was on the scene. With proofs, O'Conor hoped they might get Möllendorf dismissed;[2] the Duke had stayed with him at Seoul early in April.[3] He was out of favour, naturally, with his erstwhile patron Li.

Aston wrote canvassing a different plan. The Corean Government was so hard up that it found itself unable to meet a debt of 8000 taels to a British firm. Indigence might force it to cede or rent Port Hamilton for the sake of hard cash.[4] It had been decided to make no reply to the Nagasaki protest, but O'Conor had been authorised to let it be known that we were ready to strike a bargain.[5] In the first week of June a money offer was again held out. Li said that no trouble need be en- countered so long as formal consent from Seoul was not required. So Dowell was commissioned to make a rent agree- ment with the local authorities at Port Hamilton. After a careful search, he reported that there were no local authorities.[6]

On June 7 word reached Peking of what China had feared all along. Russia was demanding permission to occupy Port Lazarev.[7] Although the Afghan pot had gone off the boil, Russian designs on Corea had not, and it was only to be expected that our action would be answered.

O'Conor heard another piece of news, which he passed on to Li to keep that dignitary's ideas running the right way:

[1] O'Conor 259 conf., 2.6.85, 17. 981.
[2] O'Conor 260 conf., 3.6.85, 17. 981.
[3] Carles 12 conf., 6.5.85, 17. 996, reporting a talk with the Japanese Chargé.
[4] Aston 19.5.85 Very conf., with O'Conor 265 conf., 4.6.85, 17. 981.
[5] B.F.S.P. LXXVIII, 147–8.   [6] O'Conor 268, 6.6.85, 17. 981.
[7] O'Conor 269 (ext. tel. 46), 7.6.85, 17. 981.

namely that in the previous September a Russian Admiral, weighing anchor from Chefu for Japan, had had aboard with him a snug 25,000 dollars, and that he had been seen to halt at Port Hamilton—intending, presumably, to bring off a deal with the non-existent local authorities. O'Conor also communicated this titbit to Plunkett, "who will no doubt make capital out of it with the Japanese Government".[1]

England was in a position not altogether dignified for a nation of moralists. Her *coup* had been Copenhagen over again; in a wicked world, England has not infrequently had to do such things. We seized Macao in the Napoleonic wars— in case France should seize it. But England was so accustomed to feeling herself incapable of the duplicity of less enlightened races, that when she committed a robbery she was pained to find that some onlookers could find no better name for it than—robbery. England is always above her own suspicion; unluckily, not always above that of others.

Perplexities had not been exorcised from the Government's mind. Three sheets of Foreign Office notepaper hereabouts contain flickers—scarcely lightning-flashes—of ministerial wisdom on the question. They are headed "Cabinet June 5", though some of the notes have earlier dates. Granville remarks to Currie that a rent will be best, and asks how much will do. Northbrook contributes: "It is difficult to name a sum but we clearly should not niggle about this.... The island is worth nothing new—say £5000 a year?" (28 May.) Someone scribbles vilely in brown ink: "Has the Chr. of the Exc. agreed? Can it be done without the Cabinet? I very much doubt whether the *Vote* will always be an easy affair in H. of C. Remember there has never been any free (consultation?) of the (?) by the Cabinet—it was hustled through as a military necessity of the moment. May 31." A few days further on we turn up other fragments. On 9 June, when rumours of Russia's demand for Port Lazarev reached London, Northbrook tried to look on the best side: in case of war it would really be convenient if there were some enemy outpost nearer than Vladivostok for

[1] O'Conor 276 conf. (ext. tel. 48), 10.6.85, 17.981; and see *B.F.S.P.* LXXVIII, 144.

us to attack. The difficulty with Russia was always where to hit her. The King of Spain's beard might be singed, but the Tsar was a giant, his beard was out of reach. Dilke discussed more than once in his books how Russia might best be attacked, and he pointed to the Far East.[1] A cable arrived now from O'Conor asking if Her Majesty's Government would offer a lump sum for Port Hamilton instead of rent. Northbrook minuted that he would offer £10,000, even £20,000. But the Ministry was out. "If we had not resigned I would buy, but...." "This is a change in substance, not in form. It seems to me a (?) for us in *our* position to acquire territory, and I don't think this could be brought under vote of credit."[2] It is evident that the Cabinet had thrashed out no real line. "Defence experts" had apparently taken policy out of the hands of politicians; though all our officers in the East deplored the seizure, as adding to our weakness and not our strength. Bowen informed Gladstone as well as the Colonial Office of this.[3]

The new Parliamentary Under Secretary for Foreign Affairs, Lord G. Hamilton, at once consulted the permanent officials about Port Hamilton, "which he understood was a pressing matter", and they explained that the choice lay between renting and buying.[4] O'Conor was asked what lump sum might reasonably be offered instead of rent. He replied that a preliminary few thousands, judiciously laid out at Seoul in presents to the Royal Family, would have an excellent effect. He was writing under the influence of advice from Li—"we might get all we wanted, if we wished to spend some money at Seoul".[5] The righteous British Government had set its feet in devious paths indeed.

There were indications that Germany was meddling in her usual way, though Brandt assured O'Conor that Zembsch's language was unauthorised. A telegram of the 14th said that Russia had taken an island near Port Hamilton; though the report proved untrue.[6] Carles was still impressing on the

[1] E.g. *Imperial Defence*, ch. III.   [2] Minutes in 17. 987.   [3] *Letters, etc.* II, 361.
[4] Memo. in 17. 987.   [5] O'Conor 284 conf., 12.6.85, 17. 982.
[6] O'Conor 298 Secret, 17.6.85, 17. 982.

President of the Corean Foreign Office (a caricature of the Tsungli Yamen, itself a caricature) that we had occupied Port Hamilton simply and solely to forestall Russia. The argument did not satisfy His Excellency's digestion: he persisted tediously that we had no right there and ought to haul down our flag. Aston also was given to understand that a rent agreement would be repugnant to opinion both in Corea and abroad.[1] He said discreetly little on this occasion; there were too many people listening, and it was clear that a bargain was only to be arrived at, so to say, morganatically. Meanwhile at Peking the Russian Minister was angrily berating the Tsungli Yamen. The Yamen shuffled, and said that the harbour belonged to Corea, not to China.[2] China was being pushed into a tight corner by these Western quarrels.

All the same, the hints on China's part of a movement towards alliance with us did not vanish. Peace with France had been reached, but to return to peace was for China's unwieldy organism as hard as to mobilise for war. What should be done with the year's great levies of troops? Very likely, masses of them would be moved up to the Manchurian frontier, a course easier than disbanding them. "The advantages of an alliance with a strong naval Power against Russia had not escaped the serious consideration of the Chinese Government."[3] It may be conjectured that China's game was to let war begin, and then, if England made a good start, join in and try to recoup herself in the north for what she had just lost in the south.

Near the end of June came "an exposure of Russian intrigues", as O'Conor complacently termed it, which promised to improve our standing. It transpired that Möllendorf, that father of evil, had promised during his mission to Japan to get Russians employed as drill-instructors to the Corean army. The Corean Government repudiated the promise. Speyer, a Russian Secretary of Legation despatched to Seoul to arrange the matter,

[1] O'Conor 321, 27.6.85 (ext. tel. 57), 17. 982 (B.F.S.P. LXXVIII, 149); Aston 70, 19.6.85, with O'Conor 342, 7.7.85, 17. 982.
[2] O'Conor 320, 26.6.85, 17. 982.
[3] O'Conor 304 conf., 17.6.85, 17. 982.

resorted to threats; the result was to irritate the Coreans and bring about Möllendorf's disgrace.[1] "I am told", wrote Aston, "that M. de Speyer then insisted in strong and indeed violent language on the engagement to employ Russian Drill Instructors being carried out, threatening the Corean Government that, if it were not, a Russian force would occupy Quelpart."[2] Speyer's language (of course, it would lose nothing in the telling by Englishmen) shows what expectations, in the way of political influence, Westerners built on getting their officers accepted to train native armies. According to a fuller account, Speyer had an audience with the King and demanded an answer on the spot, "in a menacing and peremptory tone" which gave great offence. At an interview with Kim of the Foreign Board Speyer said: "My Government never yield to any Power in any point however insignificant, and will not on any account put up with any slight or rudeness; your Government must simply accept Russian drill instructors, and you will not be allowed to dispense with their services even though you may wish to do it." On 24 June another interview took place. Speyer began conventionally about the weather, but came to business quickly enough to please his hosts. But it was found that the Russian, for all his braggadocio, possessed no credentials, and Kim refused to go on talking to him. Undeterred, Speyer was back at the Foreign Office on 2 July, demanding an answer. He met with a refusal, and went off growling ferociously— "There will, of course, be another way of settling the matter."[3]

O'Conor reapplied himself to his task much refreshed by the collapse of Möllendorf. His problem was "to come to an understanding free from pledges in regard to the integrity of Corea, such as I feel sure would not be acceptable to Her Majesty's Government".[4] The Russian danger still weighed on the Chinese

[1] Möllendorf's version of the story was that he was dismissed through English pressure at Peking, to the chagrin of the King and Queen. (*Life*, 82–3.) Such pressure *may* have been used, but it does not appear in the documents.

[2] Aston 72 conf., 22.6.85, with O'Conor 345, 8.7.85, 17. 983.

[3] Aston 76 conf., 26.6.85, with O'Conor 347, 8.7.85, 17. 983. Another version in Plunkett (Tokio) 187 Secret, 20.7.85, 46. 332.

[4] O'Conor 327, 30.6.85, 17. 982.

mind. Li was ordering troops into a disputed strip along the Russo-Corean frontier. The Yamen assured O'Conor that any protest they might make about Port Hamilton would be simply "for the eye", and might be accompanied by a secret exchange of views between the two Governments. They wanted this to begin with an English guarantee of Corea. O'Conor wanted to steer clear of promises. He dwelt feelingly on the idea that friendships begin with small favours, and one of these China could now have the happiness of doing us. The Chinese were not inclined to discuss one-sided favours, they desired a bargain. They went further than ever before in hinting at an Anglo-Chinese entente.

The remarks were probably thrown out as feelers of considerable political importance which were meant to show that the Chinese Government is watching the course of the negotiations between Russia and England with keen interest, and that they were waiting on the upshot of these negotiations before taking any more definite line. I was to-day strengthened in the impression already reported in an earlier despatch, that should hostilities unhappily break out between Great Britain and Russia, it would not be difficult to bring China into a strong practical alliance with Her Majesty's Government.[1]

O'Conor, it should be said, wrote with a confidence he somewhat qualified a week later, when he received from London copies of Colquhoun's telegrams to the Indian Government. These seemed to him to distort China's policy. She was *not* making precise offers of alliance. The idea of an alliance was really Li's, and the Viceroy was "wild and extravagant at times in his proposals and ideas, often no doubt with a set purpose and in order to draw out his interlocutor". The Government's attitude was in fact "extremely cautious, and the most that could be said was that there were symptoms that if war broke out between Great Britain and Russia the Chinese Government might seriously consider the advantages of an alliance with England against Russia". O'Conor heard, incidentally, that

[1] O'Conor 331, 1.7.85, 17. 982.

Colquhoun had advised Li to protest over Port Hamilton, because "England was always ready to accept substantial assistance, but when other countries were in trouble all she had to give in return was sympathy and fine phrases".[1] It seems doubtful that the explorer should have said this, in view of his highly patriotic style, but it is likely that the Yamen was not without misgivings of the sort.

At home, the Foreign Office was most anxious to batten down Corean protests. Tories could not enjoy themselves by rubbing the theft into its loudly virtuous Liberal authors, because they had to defend it against foreign criticism. "The delight of flaying Gladstone alive", as one ardent Tory called it, had to be foregone.[2] Numerous telegrams followed one another to Peking. O'Conor was to insinuate to the Yamen that Corea was slighting her Chinese masters; and that after the communications that had been passing between Lord Granville and Tseng (a draft treaty even is mentioned)[3] it would be unfriendly of China not to help us.[4] Some of our tactics were suggested by Macartney—for instance, a hint conveyed to Peking that Russia meant to resume an old quarrel about the Sungari river as soon as she had finished her British quarrel.[5]

But pressure from London was more than counterbalanced by pressure from Petersburg. The Yamen was "decidedly apologetic", but with the Muscovite cudgel suspended over its head could not afford to be obliging. The British Minister was watching Japan also with a suspicious eye. He believed that Admiral Enomotto was fanning the opposition to us over Port Hamilton. Li said the Admiral was pressing him to advise Corea to appeal to the Treaty Powers; but that he (Li) replied by saying that of those Powers Russia was no use, the United States would not interfere, and "Germany had been so active in appropriating territory of late that she would find

[1] O'Conor 357 conf., 18.7.85, 17. 983.
[2] "A Seat in the House", in National Review, June 1885.
[3] O'Conor 349 conf., 8.7.85, 17. 983.
[4] F.O. to O'Conor 170, 10.7.85, 17. 976.
[5] F.O. to O'Conor tel. 40, 13.7.85, 17. 987.

it difficult to raise her voice".[1] Li even said that Enomotto called on him at Tientsin and proposed, under orders from Tokio, joint Sino-Japanese action in case Russia encroached on Corea or England did not give up Port Hamilton. Li, faithful to his Anglophil policy, had answered that Russia would be "forcibly resisted", but that China would not pick a quarrel about Port Hamilton.[2] We hear more of this conversation, because our Peking and Tokio Legations differed as to who was really putting spokes in our wheel. Each was convinced that it had its own charges well in hand, and all the trouble came from the other's territory. Plunkett cabled that the Japanese Government denied having instructed Enomotto to hold language hostile to England. Li asserted that Enomotto actually read out to him his Government's orders to clear the British out of Port Hamilton. Li, to continue his own account, asked if Japan could not be content with a promise from London that Port Hamilton would never be used as a base against her. "To this Admiral Enomotto had replied that such a promise would be as easily broken as the wine-glass which he then held in his hand."[3] The Viceroy, of course, had his own reasons for painting Japan's enmity to us in high colours. But there is no doubt that the Japanese were seriously alarmed at the hoisting of an imperialist flag in waters so near their coasts.

Aston was unable to prevent the Coreans from circulating their protest to the Foreign Representatives; he was able, however, to secure its withdrawal.[4] Ch'ing assured O'Conor that it was only a formality designed to placate Russia. O'Conor pointed out to his own Government what a convenient dilemma the Chinese were in. Möllendorf's conspiring with the Russians "would afford a plausible reason for not abandoning Port Hamilton, should Her Majesty's Government wish to retain possession. China as well as Corea believes Russia as a limitrophe Power is a serious menace to Corean integrity, and only waits a

[1] O'Conor 339, 5.7.85, 17. 982.
[2] O'Conor 351 conf., 15.7.85, 17. 983.
[3] O'Conor 359, 20.7.85, 17. 983.
[4] O'Conor 352 conf., 15.7.85, 17. 983.

fair pretext to seize upon a part of her territory." China felt, none the less, that we were asking her to run a grave risk, and on our part offering nothing. O'Conor went as far as his orders allowed, but in vain. The Yamen wanted its price in solid metal. As our Chargé wrote:

The Chinese Government is just now in a very delicate and difficult position.... The Chinese Government are prepared to resist any act of aggression by Russia on China Proper. They hesitate whether to do so on behalf of their vassal. Were Corea to come to an arrangement with Her Majesty's Government in respect to Port Hamilton and Russia execute her threats, a decision would be forced upon the Chinese Government.[1]

Things remained in this posture for some time. In August it was learned that Waeber, another Russian agent, was being sent to Seoul. O'Conor pressed Li to eliminate Möllendorf at once and fill his post before Waeber's arrival; for he believed that Möllendorf had not merely "grossly mismanaged" the Customs but had gone so far in his intrigues as practically to invite a Russian protectorate over Corea.[2] Waeber reached Seoul on 6 October and was welcomed with a great show of cordiality. He was understood to deprecate the tone Speyer had used.[3] Within a month he had completed his business—ratification of the Russo-Corean treaty of 1884.[4]

Despite this return of the velvet glove, anxieties in Seoul and in Peking were not erased. On 13 October O'Conor called on Li and found him again shaking his head over Port Hamilton. He told his visitor positively that if Corea agreed to accept rent from us, a demand for a similar concession "would be presented from another quarter within ten days". He suggested that it would serve our purpose equally well if we withdrew from the islands and kept a warship at Chemulpo ready to reoccupy

[1] O'Conor 360, 22.7.85, 17. 983.
[2] O'Conor 382 Very conf., 25.8.85, 17. 983.
[3] O'Conor, Corea 23, 22.10.85, 17. 985.
[4] O'Conor, Corea 24, 26.11.85, 17. 985. Waeber was to continue active on the Corean stage for many years. He figures in particular in some shady dealings of the year 1896. (Rosen, *Forty Years of Diplomacy*, I, 126.)

them at need. O'Conor fancied that China was disappointed at the peaceful solution of the Afghan crisis.[1]

Corean impecuniosity was a factor we continued to make play with. Aston threw out a hint at Seoul that it would be very useful to Corea to be able to put her hand on some ready cash. There was an interval while the Foreign Board digested this. Then the President asked if England would lend Corea 500,000 dollars. Aston, not beating about the bush, said: I suppose you mean, will we buy Port Hamilton for that much. He cabled home that the Coreans might accept such a sum, paid them ostensibly as a loan; "secrecy indispensable".[2] The Admiralty did not like the plan, preferring rent to purchase.[3]

Probably on account of Waeber, in November Corea again requested an answer to her protests. Currie minuted cavalierly that there was no need to send any reply.[4] But Li was anxious to have the matter on some regular footing. He now suggested that we should lend Corea a million taels and treat Port Hamilton as the security.[5] During November a report reached Peking that Waeber was "offering" to concentrate Russian warships at Chemulpo as a "protection" to the King of Corea, and that the latter did not frown on the plan.[6] Li instructed his new Agent at Seoul, the afterwards famous Yüan Shih-kai, to remind Waeber that Corea was under Chinese protection. Li hoped England would post a squadron to keep watch on the Russians. O'Conor remarked that this would be rash.[7]

At the end of the year the Yamen referred once more to Port Hamilton. O'Conor suspected that some foreign Minister had been jogging its memory, and found that he was right. The offender was Russia's Honest Iago, Brandt.[8] O'Conor

[1] O'Conor 429 conf., 14.10.85, 17. 985.
[2] Aston Separate and secret 30.9.85, with O'Conor 430 Secret, 14.10.85, 17. 985.   [3] F.O. to O'Conor 270 Secret, ext. tel. 49, 13.10.85, 17. 976.
[4] O'Conor 451, 8.11.85, and minute, 17. 985.
[5] O'Conor 457, 17.11.85, 17. 986.
[6] O'Conor thought it a pity that China went out of her way to injure the poor King's susceptibilities. (Corea 25 conf., 8.11.85, 17. 985.)
[7] O'Conor 463 conf., 20.11.85, 17. 986.
[8] O'Conor 479 conf., 5.12.85, 17. 986.

countered by asking whether, if England left Port Hamilton, China would guarantee that no one else should take it. The Chinese hesitated, and said it was *Corean* territory, not for *them* to guarantee.[1] This was the answer we had played for; it was a piece of strategy of Currie's invention.[2]

Everything thus remained unsettled. Nothing is clearer than that the Anglo-Russian crisis was not "solved" in May, but transferred itself to the Far East, partly because of England's hasty coup. The moral pre-eminence of the English statesman consisted in the fact that, while foreigners simply did not understand honesty, *he* understood it perfectly; of course, with things as they were, he could not always *practise* it. But it turned out that in this case he had burdened his conscience for nothing. Early in 1886, Her Majesty's Government asked itself what Port Hamilton was worth after all; and our naval commanders said, as Dowell had said before, that unless fortified at prohibitive expense, it was not worth anything.[3]

This was indeed awkward, with Russia renewing her threats to "compensate" herself.[4] A group of Foreign Office minutes dated March 1886 breathe the strongest suspicion of Russia, particularly, now, on the Kashgar frontier. "Macartney thinks that the Russians are preparing a great 'coup' in that direction." In November the Japanese Government was terrified by a threat of Russia's compensating herself by seizing Tsushima.[5] It was essential for us to devise a dignified exit. We first proposed to China that she should get Russia "to enter into an international arrangement guaranteeing the integrity of Corea"[6]—a sweeping proposal to which Russian assent was most unlikely. But before the end of the year we did secure from St Petersburg the astonishing promise "that if the British would evacuate Port Hamilton, the Russian Government would not occupy Corean territory under any circumstances whatever".[7]

On 27 February 1887 the British flag was hauled down.

[1] O'Conor 479 conf., 5.12.85, 17. 986.
[2] Memo. by Currie in 17. 985.   [3] B.F.S.P. lxxviii, 156.
[4] Ibid. 17. 986.   [5] Takekoshi, *Prince Saionji*, 113.
[6] B.F.S.P. lxxviii, 160.   [7] Ibid. 164. 6.

CHAPTER FOURTEEN

China's Army and Navy

TWO thousand years ago, Roman legions on the Parthian frontier came in sight of the Dragon banners of the Han Generals. There is something that appeals to the imagination in the rediscovery of an Empire whose standards the remote forefathers of our Europe saw, distant on the horizon, so long before us.

But the Dragon banners under which countless armies, almost through human history, lived, marched, fought—more armies than have followed all our parvenu lilies or lions, covered themselves thereafter with few glories, though they were fluttered by the winds of centuries in which the Legions had long ceased to march. If the country of poets had kept a Laureate at Peking to celebrate its arms, he would have needed more than a butt of Canary to fertilise his invention. In the seventeenth century, when the armies of far-away Europe beyond the borders of civilisation were still only the mercenary regiments of Europe's petty kings, a barbarian could boast with only too much truth that "30,000 German or English foot, and 10,000 French horse, would fairly beat all the forces of China".[1]

Europe's boasts a little outstripped her real confidence. Even when we come into the nineteenth century we see the foreigners surrounding the Dragon in his lair with misgivings, with gusts of trepidation. They, with the military habits of mind that had spread into their art, religion, science, could scarcely grasp the existence of an unwarlike nation, content with dull peace. "There is a kind of fear of attacking China", wrote one of them in 1880, "as of attacking an unknown

[1] Defoe, *Robinson Crusoe*.

quantity."[1] A Frenchman, criticising in 1883 his Government's Tonking policy, prophesied: "We shall find ourselves at war with the most powerful and irreducible nation in the world."[2] Were there battalions concealed in the Middle Kingdom, waiting to spring into life at the stamp of some General's foot?

Military weakness was an integral part, not an accident, of the old Chinese polity. The army was originally a foreign garrison, its function soon outlived. The atmosphere of China was entirely unwarlike. A perfunctory War-God somnolently reclined in the Pantheon, where a celebrated commander of classical days sat level with him. But as Disraeli's Ixion found in Heaven, "These moustachio'd gentry are by no means the rage". It was more honourable to bear the hoe than the shield. A ninth-century poet wrote China's opinion of glory:

> Do not let me hear you talking together
> About titles and promotions;
> For a single general's reputation
> Is made out of ten thousand corpses.[3]

To think of the soldiers guarding China's one real military position, the Great Wall, shut up in some solitary fortress "amid a thousand mountains", hearing "the Tartar flute wailing over a frost-bound land",[4] inspired no ardour, only commiseration. Most of those who made the War-God their patron were pirates or brigands. We must beware of putting effect before cause, of fancying the contempt for "military virtues" to lie in something unelucidated in the racial character. The sentiment had its causes in historical circumstances and political interest. China had no true feudal period. She had her patriotic wars of defence, but they were not the continuous crises that have coloured so deeply the mind of modern Europe. The butchery

---

[1] Report by the British Military Attaché at St Petersburg, with Dufferin 335, 12.8.80, 65. 1081. Cp. articles on Chinese military power in the *United Services Journal*, vol. II of 1883, p. 417 and vol. I of 1884, p. 293; there were similar articles occasionally in *The Times*.

[2] Simon, "China."

[3] *Ts'ao Sung* (translated by Waley).

[4] *Fan Chung-yen* (translated by Ch'u Ta-kao).

which accompanied periodic upheavals gave her an aversion from bloodshed. We must allow for the secular inculcation of peaceful modes of thought by an administration in fear of revolts; the ennobling of patience under injury into a virtue. Confucius, the more he is studied, emerges as neither seer nor philosopher, but above all things a *Counsellor of State*. Sentiments once created could react on the circumstances out of which they had arisen; they could quicken the "demobilisation", so to say, of invaders like the Manchus; they could make it more difficult for China to modernise her army when the attempt was made.

The ragamuffins on whose unworthy shoulders rested the warlike fame of the Empire were organised in the well-known "Banners".[1] If it were not that in our period they came to be (except for the foreign-drilled "Peking Field Force" of some 20,000 men) the only bulwarks between China and half a dozen military nations, the whole spectacle would be one of "innocent merriment". Provincial units were inspected from time to time by emissaries from Peking. The units in question hardly existed, but the inspection presented no terrors to the experienced officers in charge. A number of coolies would be scoured up for the occasion, until the muster-rolls were filled; these unpretending citizens assembled, for a consideration, on the drill-ground and executed a travesty of a parade. The visiting mandarin was so warmed by tokens he received of the commanding officer's esteem for him, that his eyes played him tricks, and he believed himself to be watching a well-found, well-trained body of troops. The illusion persisted in his mind until after he had sent in his report. A further step in refinement of the procedure might have been taken, by dispensing with the coolies and calling up in the inspector's mind a vivid but purely imaginary picture of an army at drill. There was, however, a form in these things, and the mandarin's sense of the *convenances* was strict.

Clearly, as a British Intelligence report observed, an officer's

[1] See an unflattering memorandum on China's military strength sent by the Legation in 1883. (With Parkes 12 conf., 13.9.83, 17. 924.)

life was "not conducive to an elevated military tone".[1] Government allowed the comedy to go on, not merely because corruption extended to the highest regions, but because it was no part of the Court's wishes to see strong armies at the disposal of provincial authorities. In that enormous, mountain-hindered country, it was the fear of every Dynasty that its distant servants might turn against it. Japan was a small country, and could come to grips with a Satsuma Rebellion and crush it. By comparison with Europe or Turkey or Rome it seems strange that Proconsuls were not perpetually marching their armies on Peking. The administration was carefully designed to check this. The Central Government had not the means of making itself strong. It could only see to it that its local organs were kept weak. In effect, the Government did not pay generals to keep up an army, it paid them *not* to keep up an army, much as we pay farmers for not raising hogs. Thinking of the war-lords of the years after 1918—men just being born in our period, here and there through the Eighteen Provinces—one readily concludes that the paper armies were preferable to the real ones.

The same reasons were an insurmountable obstacle to the formation of an army of modern type, now that China, as one of her Viceroys said, must arm herself like a traveller among tiger-infested hills.[2] At first sight it would seem that there were many factors in her favour. There was a prodigious supply of man-power. No system of unpopular levying would be necessary to come at it; in fact a modernised army would enable the Government to provide for those classes—boatmen, carriers, craftsmen—who were displaced by introduction of foreign technique. As to pay, the state was already paying for an army without having one. But all the old handicaps would weigh on the undertaking. A Manchu Government could hardly appropriate the Manchu dole—for reasons of appearance, and in part perhaps because there must have been pickings for strong vested interests out of its distribution. An army could

[1] "Notes on the Chinese Army", in 17. 943.
[2] Chang Chih-tung, *China's Only Hope.*

not be kept up until mandarins had other pay than plunder. The peculiar character of the dominant class, so different from the ruffling clansmen of Japan, made the task the more impossible. The Samurai, a military ruling class, were ready to take charge of an up-to-date army. The spectacled graduates of the Han-lin Academy could not step into Western redoubts and gun-pits, engine-rooms and staff-rooms. The army would have to be placed under other elements: that meant, since the landed gentry were closely allied in temper and composition to the literati, under new, progressive, middle-class elements, slowly being set free by the chemical reaction of Western contact in the Chinese body politic. But these were, by historical necessity, potential enemies of the régime.

In short, a modern army could not be created by an archaic Government. That was one of the reasons why the Dynasty had to be brought down by a party of "progress".

The Government was readier to adopt foreign weapons for use against rebels than against invaders. The Taiping and Panthay rebellions caused sporadic experiments in rearmament before 1880: the Lay Flotilla scheme being the salient one. And as, at the other end of Asia, a long struggle among foreigners for the control of Turkish armaments ended in a division just before the war between British Admirals and German Generals, British and German arms-manufacturers, a similar struggle was carried on in China. The protagonists were the same, with the addition of America. It is in our period that their intrigues began to assume importance.

The attitude towards Chinese military reform taken up by different Powers varied according to their political and economic designs in the Far East. Russia, to begin in the north, could not watch complacently the development by an independent China of her gigantic "war-potential". Without great effort Russia could only concentrate a few thousand troops on the frontier, and succeeded only so long as one Russian soldier was worth ten or twenty Chinese. No war was as yet likely wherein Russia and China would be allies. Above all, Russia was not a country with munitions to export—Chinese arsenals were not customers for *her*. She had only drill-sergeants to send; and tried energetically to send them into that microcosm of Far Eastern politics, Corea.

Germany, as a Power whose Far Eastern policy was not such as to exclude the chance of a war with China, could not wish to anticipate strong resistance. On the other hand, Krupp and his energetic fellow-workers were anxious to leave no market untried. Then, German policy had, twice within the short space of our six years, reason for using China to exhaust the strength of Bismarck's European rivals. China could not serve this purpose without an army. Germany had, therefore, urgent need to win influence with the heads of China's military and naval organisation, and to push officers of her own into important places there.

Japan was an importer, not an exporter, of arms; and she could not compete for the drilling of the Chinese army when her own was still listening to the parade-ground orders of Western instructors. Unless she adopted the improbable policy of alliance with China for defence of the Yellow Race, Chinese armaments could in no circumstances favour her ambitions. France also was at present a negative force. During three years of our period she was on such terms with China as to deprive her of any influence over Chinese policy. American views were not methodically developed. Still, several American officers figured prominently in the scuffle for employment, and their Government probably hugged the idea that their teachings would assist China to ward off the sinister machinations of Europe.

England's attitude was the most complex of all. Like all foreigners we knew the hatred of the Chinese, and had to fear expulsion from a militarily strong China. As Gordon wrote to the Governor of Hongkong in 1880: "A strong armed China would be certain to be extremely independent towards every foreign nation; she might denounce the opium trade."[1] We

[1] Gordon to Hennessey 4.7.80, with Hennessey to C.O. Secret and conf., 5.7.80, 17. 847. Cp. Brandt's observation some years later: "It must not be forgotten that the completion of much desired internal reforms would raise China from a passive to an active state; in this case, the country would then exercise an influence difficult to estimate." (In Helmholtz' *History of the World*, II, 114.)

were eager to sell guns and ships, but, again, there were terrible risks to us in the efforts our enemies would certainly make to get control of China's General Staff. But for China to buy guns would give her a taste for other foreign amenities, and our exports might go up accordingly. If China armed, she could resist the depredations of France and Russia, and since it was our policy, fumblingly, to support Chinese integrity, it was our interest to see China equipped with the weapons without which her life would not be thought a safe risk by an insurance company. It was essential to England to influence the direction of China's strength, and more especially of her fleet.

Well-meaning friends, it may be noted, were apt to tell China that she needed weapons simply for keeping order; or, if she needed more than that, it was only for protecting herself against *other* foreigners. Admiral Lord Charles Beresford, touring in 1899 (when there were Indian Army officers in China on leave, learning Chinese in the expectation of a British-officered force being raised),[1] warned the Yamen that Westerners were not satisfied with the protection they received, and might go in for partition unless things improved. He deprecated construction of artillery.[2] Small arms would be enough to deal with rioters. Curzon naïvely criticised China for spending money on gunboats and coast defences, "unaware that her sole genuine danger lies upon her land frontiers".[3]

As to China's potential energy, there were scarcely two opinions. A British traveller wrote: We have trained fellaheen into soldiers, and "the Chinaman is twenty times the man that the fellah ever was"; if we handled China as we handled Egypt, "we could raise in twenty years an army that would hold the world at bay".[4] It is not too much to say that one of the chief inducements to a partition of China was her most copious raw material, man-power. Had partition begun in

[1] Reid, *Peking to Petersburg*, ch. II.
[2] Beresford, *Break-Up of China*, ch. I.
[3] Curzon, *Far Eastern Problems*, ch. X.
[4] Reid, *Peking to Petersburg*, ch. X.

earnest, China would have been made the Illyria of the modern world. The time when she was most in danger of conquest was also the moment in military history when man-power attained its maximum importance. Even in an epoch of conscription there was something awe-inspiring in the possible size of China's armies. The Grand Armies of the West paled by comparison into insignificance. By the 'eighties France had regiments of Annamite tirailleurs, and was enrolling similar ones in Tonking while the campaign there was still in progress.[1] And Russia and England would have obtained vast assets in this way for their mutual struggle. With a few years' possession of a few Chinese provinces, either might throw a million soldiers against the Indian or the Siberian frontiers. The possibility has not realised itself in fact—though Japan is now trying to realise it—but the historian studies tendencies by drawing them out to conclusions in the same way as the geometrician produces lines in a theorem.

At the very beginning of our period, in February 1880, we hear of Chinese youths serving in the British navy, and leave was being asked for five Chinese who had studied at the Cherbourg École de Construction Navale to visit Woolwich.[2] Hart had recently seen Li Hung-chang, and been empowered by him to engage British officers for the fleet; Hart recommended that the same should be done for the army.[3] International jealousies at once revealed themselves. Wade reported that a relative of General Grant was being mentioned. "This of course is the work of the American Legation." There was also talk of a brother-in law of Brandt. A uniformed relative of Herr von Brandt is, political prejudice apart, a forbidding notion. One German *had* been engaged. "Americans, if capable men, would very likely upset the country." Military reorganisation, Wade continued, mus be in the hands of one Power alone, and if *we* were not that Power it would be "prejudicial to our interests in an extreme degree".[4] He had,

[1] War Office Report on operations in Tonking, 30.9.84, p. 30; 27. 2769.
[2] Tseng to F.O., 5.2.80, 17. 844.
[3] Wade 4, 5.1.80, 17. 829.   [4] Wade 14, 27.1.80, 17. 829.

incidentally, a favourite hobby-horse of his own, which he was always getting on at the Yamen: the idea that a Chinese force should be sent to India, drilled and trained there with the Indian Army, and constantly renewed in personnel, so as to give China a large number of reserves.[1] Admiral Ting was in England about this time, to take back some gunboats built by Armstrong's for the Customs Service, and he was given every facility in the way of inspecting dockyards. Several arsenals were at work in China, with varying levels of efficiency.

When Grant was in China in 1879 the Government fawned on him, wanting his good offices in the Lewchew dispute, and an honorarium was probably offered in the shape of employment for American officers. Wade had some information early in 1882 from Dunn the telegraph agent, who was seeing much at his hotel of Schufeldt—"a friend, I might say a protégé, of General Grant". Schufeldt had been virtually offered command of the Navy, but before his arrival two Frenchmen were installed, with high rank and salary and no work. A German agent besides was working hard to get a monopoly of posts for his countrymen. Mortified at finding nothing to do, Schufeldt abated his enthusiastic Chinese sympathies, denounced Tientsin as a labyrinth of intrigue, and said China was incapable of becoming a warlike nation.[2] A Foreign Office minute on this enquired how the reconquest of Kashgar could be accounted for. The West had not yet made up its mind as to the sharpness of the Dragon's claws. The plurality of officers being engaged shows, perhaps, that the Chinese felt it necessary to balance one set against another. Schufeldt addressed a letter to the local Press in which his personal animus appeared under a disguise. He declared that foreigners ought to bear in mind what China might do if her immense strength were once really set free; that it was the true interest of the West to *discourage* her from arming[3]—now that Commodore Schufeldt was not to tread the quarter-deck. It was only a few philosophical observers who protested: "Is the

[1] Wade 7, 14.1.80, 17. 829.   [2] Wade 1 Very conf., 16.1.82, 17. 895.
[3] Copy with Wade 18 conf., 12.5.82, 17. 895.

all but dormant military spirit of four hundred millions to be aroused in order that dealers may find markets for rifles and guns?"[1]

In May of the same year Wade wrote that Li was desirous of hiring British naval officers. A Chinese agent was off to Germany, where two ironclads were being built for his Government. Wade suspected that the German Government was secretly bearing part of the cost of these vessels, telling China that its object was to stimulate heavy industry, but in reality also with the aim of promoting its political influence in the Far East. "The Minister Li Feng-pao is greatly petted at Berlin."[2]

Sir Thomas took deeply to heart the lessons of the prolonged Kashgar crisis. "I believe", he wrote, "that, with some years of peace, China has a great future." Had she gone to war with the Tsar, nothing could have saved her except foreign aid. Germany would have lent any number of soldiers, and it still disturbed the English Minister to think what a footing in China this would have given her. He confessed that our Ambassador at Berlin did not agree with him in the full extent of his convictions on Germany's Far Eastern ambitions. But he remained positive that Germany was trying to elbow a way into Chinese administration; Detring, Li's German adviser, had an unusual measure of his master's confidence; unless our Service Regulations were altered the Chinese would naturally prefer engaging officers who could continue with their units in wartime.[3]

The London Office of the Chinese Customs informed the Foreign Office that Hart had got an offer of the chief post under Admiral Ting for a Captain Lang, and requested that Lang might be allowed to count this service as time spent in the Royal Navy. Mr J. D. Campbell, head of the Office, supported the request with a confidential paper addressed to Pauncefote and to Admiral Sir Cooper Key. Li, he said, much admired Lang; but other Powers were making great efforts, and Germany in particular was "working hard to secure for Germans the

[1] Sir Robert Hart, *These from the Land of Sinim*, 103.
[2] Wade 25 conf., 25.5.82, 17. 895.   [3] Wade 30, 29.5.82, 17. 895.

supply to China of Guns, Railroads, Telegraphs, etc." Hart
had therefore sent a most urgent cable.[1] The Foreign Office
at once begged the Admiralty to fall in with the request, in
order to induce Lang to take the post. "Perhaps you would
make your draft a little less enthusiastic", wrote back the First
Lord, to whom the issue did not seem quite such a burning
one—partly because he considered that "It is a matter open to
question whether it will be an advantage or a disadvantage to
us that the Chinese should have a strong navy."[2] Captain
Lang was given three years leave on half-pay, and Prince Kung
was informed that his agents would be welcomed in England
in their search for other officers.

Recruitment of foreign officers proceeded. In the summer
of 1884 Li was asking for instructors for his naval college at
Tientsin.[3] Hart was impatient at the Foreign Office's lack of
ardour. He had struggled for twenty-five years, he wrote, to
give England control of the Chinese navy, and, had he been
a Frenchman or a German, could have got "startling results".
He held the best cards, "but my partner—British officialdom—
forgets what cards are out and where others are, revokes, will
not return trumps, etc."[4] Trouble in Tonking created complications. Lang, who found himself "virtually at the head of
the Chinese Army", had to resign when fighting broke out.
The Chinese would not care, wrote Parkes; they had never
taken any notice of him.[5] He was replaced by a German,
Sebelin, not much of a success according to his English critics.

The Tonking campaign assisted the modernising party in
China. In May 1885 O'Conor noticed "a very strong belief
amongst well-informed persons that a strong military impulse
has been given to China by the prosecution of the war with
France and strenuous efforts will be made to reorganise the
Chinese Army on a European system". He met the Russian

[1] 17. 912.
[2] F.O. to Admiralty, 17.4.82, Immediate, 17. 912; memo. by Lord Northbrook 21.4.82, 17. 912.   [3] Parkes 112, 10.7.84, 17. 951.
[4] Hart to Campbell, with Campbell to Currie, 12.6.84, 17. 970.
[5] Parkes 120, 17.7.84, 27. 2709.

Military Attaché, Colonel Schnéour, at dinner at the German Legation, and the Colonel poured loud contempt on the Chinese army; but O'Conor thought his real opinions questionable. A hundred German officers had entered service, and it looked as if German methods would supersede the existing English model; this would entail purchase of guns from Germany instead of from England, and O'Conor considered that we could do with a Military Attaché.[1] A rumour went round that a fiery secret Decree had ordered certain provincial authorities to raise thirty or forty million taels for ironclads, coast defences, and communications.[2]

The chief concrete plan that emerged from the war was that of Li for the creation of an effective Admiralty Department. He wanted Lang back, Admiral Ting being ready to resign in the latter's favour, and he instructed Tseng to place an order with Armstrong's for two further ironclads. German technique, however, was very much in vogue in Chinese army and navy circles, as a Mr Pethick, U.S. Vice-consul at Tientsin and also in Li's employ, wrote to his old friend Macartney;[3] and the Germans were prompt in offers of assistance, whereas the more lethargic British Admiralty declined to give Tseng some information he wanted. O'Conor wrote in alarm that we must stop being so careless: "no efforts are spared either here or in Berlin to gain the patronage and good-will of His Excellency"[4] (Li). The Foreign Office at once sent someone round to the Admiralty to jog its wits;[5] the Admiralty declared that the refusal of information to Tseng had been merely a subordinate's blunder.[6]

In October an important Decree announced the formation of a Naval Board. The Chief Controller was to be no less a

[1] O'Conor 253 conf., 29.5.85, 17.981. Parkes questioned the German Minister about the batches of German officers who were arriving, and he denied that Germany had anything official to do with the matter. (Parkes, 307, 3.12.84, 27. 2718.)

[2] O'Conor 324 conf., 29.6.85, 17.982.   [3] *Life of Macartney*, 426–7.

[4] O'Conor 395 (ext. tel. 59), 15.9.85, 17. 984.

[5] Currie to Cockerell, 16.9.85, 17. 987.

[6] F.O. to Tseng, 25.11.85, 17. 1000.

person than the Seventh Prince, Ch'un; his coadjutors were to be Prince Ch'ing and Li Hung-chang.[1] Li took Ch'un on a trip to Port Arthur, to rouse the old reactionary's interest in implements for killing foreigners.[2] Lang was offered the Chief Instructorship; Hart pressed that he should be encouraged to accept, and before the end of the year he had made up his mind to return to China.[3]

Of the many reverses suffered by the great Viceroy, few were more complete than that which awaited his defence plans. Navy funds were plundered on a colossal scale, above all for the building of the Summer Palace. There were too many "Footais, Tootais, and birds of that feather" (as an Englishman called them)[4] perched in the riggings of the Chinese navy. When war with Japan broke out, Chinese harbours sent out a fleet of heavier tonnage than the enemy's; but like all fleets that have encountered Japan's, Li's was soon at the bottom of the sea. The Army fared even worse. The ghosts of long-perished armies straggling the frontiers they had once protected against Mongol raiders, were not more powerless to defend China now.[5]

The Chinese standards seemed to be under a spell.

[1] O'Conor 426, 12.10.85, 17. 985.   [2] Mrs Little, *Li Hung-chang*, 152.
[3] Correspondence in 17. 1003, 17. 1004.
[4] Quoted by Allen, *Gordon in China*, 124.
[5] See memo. on Li's own troops with Parkes 267 conf., 12.11.84, 27. 2717.

CHAPTER FIFTEEN

The Structure of China

THE last word in Chinese counsels lay with Tzu Hsi, in 1880 titularly Empress of the Western Palace, and after the death of the Senior Empress Tzu An in 1883 sole Regent. The screen from behind which she listened to the reports of her Ministers is symbolic of the obscurity that enshrouds her. Foreigners in Peking were impressed by the accounts of her that filtered through to them. When Parkes came back in 1883 he imagined her a "noble woman" misled by that "most unscrupulous intriguer in all China", Li Hung-chang.[1] As a psychological study, she is of unique interest. As ruler of China, probably we should not seek in her character even for that degree of influence on events that *can* be ascribed to individuals. During her inordinately long tenure of power, her strange life unrolled itself in something of studied aloofness from the eddies of politics. When her rule was threatened from within the Imperial Clan, or when foreign guns shook China, her will, even in old age, was able suddenly to project itself from her citadel of illusions, to cross centuries, and emerge in the outside daylight and overcome whatever threatened to penetrate her retreat. At other times her energies seemed content to absorb themselves in the profligacy, the arts, the intrigues of an Oriental court.[2] She painted on silk, studied and composed poetry, amused herself with eunuchs, suspended a Boxer attack on the Legations to prevent interference with a view she was sketching. She lived in arrogant inability to believe that her power, her palaces, could ever be thrown down,

[1] Lane Poole, *Sir Harry Parkes in China*, IX. For the most favourable opinion on Tzu Hsi, see Headland, *Court Life in China*; for the opposite, R. F. Johnston, *Twilight in the Forbidden City*.

[2] On the Imperial Household and its bottomless corruption, see Johnston, *Twilight in the Forbidden City*.

careless of what came after her. The tact, the sure touch of affairs, the dominant authority, that had lifted her from being one of many playthings among the Imperial Concubines of the Third Rank, she preferred to leave dormant in the unreal world from which she rarely emerged. Perhaps her political insight enabled her to realise even this, that to reorganise Old China was impossible; that to push too strongly at the walls of her omnipotence would show it to be a mirage, a castle of shadows. She chose not to learn by experience restraints on her sovereign will. Transforming into the substance of her life the necessity of history which shut up her activity within doors, she could create for herself illusions of uncontrolled power as perfect as the vistas of the Iho Park and its Hill of Ten Thousand Ages, in the midst of an external world admitting no such glorious absolutes; a region held poised, by the exercise of her other, realist, *waking* faculties, by her bribes and her spies, amid the pressure of intractable forces. She was intent on clinging, by devious ways, to a realm where the laws of the outside were suspended—an Atlantis preserved under the waves of time. Cruel, luxurious, gracious, endlessly complex, she was as far from the tailored foreigners of the Legation Quarter as though she had been the tyrant Empress of eight centuries ago whose spirit might indeed have come to earth again in her. What philosophy she distilled from the passions, intoxications, languors, of her existence, what thoughts passed through that mind as she sat immobile on the Throne between the lengthening tablets covered by her titles, we cannot try to discover. They were not the thoughts and sensations that were making and being made by the tides of Far Eastern history.

China's was an essentially archaic Government. It struck onlookers as primitive. "The Chinese are schoolboys who never grow up", wrote Winwood Reade in 1872 in his sombre masterpiece. "The patriarchal system of the steppes has been transferred to the imperial plains." And for him it was tyrannical as well as primitive. Asia and its peoples will never advance "until they enjoy the rights of man, and these they will never obtain except by means of European conquest....

Asia is governed by a few kings and by their soldiers; the masses of the people are invariably slaves."[1] He was repelled by a vision he conjured up of the whole power of a vast state concentrated in one hand. Such a *plenitudo potestatis* was, as regards China, a fantastic deception. Intense state force did not exist there. The state was an extremely exiguous outgrowth from the social organism, untempered either by external struggle or by continuous social conflict. It was an imposing regalia, not a force controlling national life. An Emperor in the tranquil maturity of a Dynasty knew scarcely more of the great country and its myriad life than did the most obtuse foreigner. He lived in isolation almost as complete as that of the indifferent gods of Lucretius. Tzu Hsi, driven from Peking by foreign invasion, found consolation in at last seeing China *alive* instead of in the cramped phrases of official Memorials.[2] The Dragon Throne reposed not on force but on custom. There was government (or lack of government) "by consent", to a degree only attainable in a static community.

The historiographers who set down the daily words and acts of an Emperor placed their records in a sealed room not to be opened until after his death, and were charged to blame as well as to praise. There can be found in our period more solid indications that the supposedly absolute Government had to take account of the feelings of those it ruled. Consul Sinclair doubted the Fukien Viceroy's having taken a step attributed to him, on the ground that it would irritate the local gentry and "be certain to lead to disastrous results to himself".[3] The Censorate acted to some degree as a "constitutional check". In April 1884, when several Censors criticised as irregular an important Decree concerning the Grand Council, the Empress issued another Decree modifying it.[4] In February 1885 Parkes

---

[1] *Martyrdom of Man*, ch. IV.
[2] Bland and Blackhouse, *China under the Empress Dowager*, ch. XX.
[3] Sinclair to Wade, 7.4.79, 17. 854. Cp. Douglas, *Society in China* (1894), 122: "Probably there is no potentate on the earth who can say as truly as the Emperor of China can, 'L'empire c'est moi'."
[4] Parkes 83, 19.4.84, 17. 950.

observed that the carefulness with which the Court expounded its purposes in a Decree of that month showed how far China was from being an autocracy, "though little is known in the outside world of the political machinery of this Government".[1] A letter of instruction addressed by the Tsungli Yamen in 1875 to the Inspector-General of Customs contained the striking sentence: "If the Chinese public again discuss the question of transit duty and the general levies on ships, pulse, etc., the withdrawal of prohibitions must be capable of satisfactory explanation, and the Yamen must not find itself without effective arguments against objections."[2]

To see in China an oppressed nation appealing to them for enfranchisement was a flattering unction to Western souls. A parallel misconception was to see a people held down by rulers of alien race. If Chinese could be ruled by Manchus, why not by Europeans? Sir Edmund Hornby talked of a Dynasty "for which the majority have neither reverence nor affection, and of which the minority have lost all hope". Hart, a more sober observer, warned his countrymen not to dream of curing the Boxer disorder by dethroning Kuang Hsü or Tzu Hsi, and wrote: "The Manchoo dynasty has been part and parcel of the nation for three hundred years, and the Emperor is no more hated by Chinese than the Queen by British."[3] China might expel a descendant of Aisin Gioro, but she would not let Europe do so. It is true there was always hunger in China, therefore always the spirit of mutiny, which often assumed fanciful names. Most of the Secret Societies that were the terror of officialdom in the South were anti-Manchu. The haughty phrase, worthy of a tragic drama—"Alive, we do not submit to the Ch'ing: dead, we do not submit to the Ch'ing"— survived during all the Manchu centuries. The cry of "Down with the Manchus" came in as an eloquent touch to heighten agrarian discontent. Famished crowds found in Manchu rule a symbol of their suffering, and looked back to an imaginary Golden Age in

[1] Parkes 65, 13.2.85, 17. 978.
[2] Printed in Hart, *These from the Land of Sinim*, 190.
[3] *Ibid.* 97.

Ming days. It was the more natural because the populace—rightly or wrongly—blamed the Westerners for its troubles, and then in a steadily swelling chorus blamed its Government for failing to get rid of them. This brought to mind that the Ch'ing House had once been "foreign", and nursed suspicion that they were selling China to foreign hucksters. Newly emerging classes, which were one day to constitute the Kuomintang Party, found it convenient to use the anti-Manchu watchword for appealing to the people; convenient also after 1911 to declare: The Manchus are expelled, the Revolution is finished. In a not dissimilar way, theorists of the French middle class in the eighteenth century raked up against the aristocracy its supposed "Frankish"—un-Gallic, foreign—origin.

Normally, the Manchus with their dole were an economic burden only; not a crushing one to the nation, though it might lie heavy on the fisc. The bulk of them were, as Hosie described them, "a slipshod, down-at-heel, lazy-looking people". Officials were not Manchu, for the most part.[1] In the crisis of 1898 racial division appeared, merged however in the economic and cultural cleavage between North and South. There is a histrionic sound in an outburst of Prince Ch'un in Council after the Tonking campaign: "It would be better to hand over the Empire to the foreign devils, than to surrender it at the dictation of these Chinese rebels."[2] Prince Ch'un had a diehard Tory's reputation to keep up; though it is true that the Imperial Princes, mostly cut off from useful activity and sinking into "low, vicious pursuits and cringing imbecility of character",[3] may have felt more and more isolated from the vigorous national life around them. In our years a policy was taking shape that revealed the dwindling reality of Manchu-Chinese separation. Hitherto the homeland of the conquering race had been kept shut against Chinese entry. "Between 1880 and 1890

[1] Sun Yat-sen laments that Ch'ien Lung knew how to destroy national sentiment among the Chinese literati by wiping out distinctions between Manchu and native officials. (*The Three People's Principles*, Part I, Lecture 3.)
[2] Bland and Blackhouse, *China under the Empress Dowager*, ch. XI.
[3] Wells Williams, *The Middle Kingdom*, I, 405.

the Government began actually to promote colonisation", in Manchuria and in Mongolia.[1]

The bureaucracy of China had for ages received and absorbed, by an education as arduous as that of Plato's Guardians, the finest talents of the Empire. Those who emerged from its long series of tests, the *Cursus honorum* of China, were men changed for life, transformed into pale and spectacled pedants. The reverence in which they were held by a whole, mainly illiterate population, would be incredible, were it not that the scholar in China had no rivalry to fear from the soldier, the artist, or the priest. He himself was all three. It cannot be supposed that, any more than in the Occident, love of learning was always the impulse that carried the student up his steep path,[2] and the highest post did not go to the purest scholar, any more than the Deanery to the saint; in fact pure scholarship and examination studies were distinct fields, between which an early choice had to be made.[3] Verses were often read because they came from the pen of a Governor with patronage to bestow; as elsewhere, poetry unaided stuffed no purses. None the less, the fusion of political with literary emulation helped to deepen and spread the culture of the Middle Kingdom into an all-pervading influence. At the same time it promoted stability, by grinding all politicians into the same chastened shape. There were no local magnates, no erratic demagogues, jostling their way aboard the sober Junk of State; a vessel in any case so barnacled with vested interests that it could do nothing but stand still.

The entire bureaucratic structure rose with a graceful, ornate, pagoda-like symmetry, from the district Magistrate to the metropolitan Boards. Its whole constitution was an equilibrium, designed by checks and balances not to interfere with the myriad shuttles that wove from age to age the same

[1] Lattimore, *Mongols in Manchuria*, 97. In 1876 the southern province of Manchuria was reorganised on the lines of an ordinary Chinese province. (Mayers, *Chinese Government*, 48.)

[2] "Candidates for magistracy sitting and awaiting their chances in Peking know by heart and conversation which district is 'fat' and which district is 'thin'." Lin Yu-tang, *My Country and My People*, 186.   [3] *Ibid.* 217.

patterns in the complex texture of China's life. It seemed to have solved the problem of perpetual motion—the ticking of an invariable pendulum. Precautions against irregularity were strong. The laborious education of the officials instilled into them a sense of membership in an eternal, divinely constituted hierarchy, whose head was sacrosanct. To subvert it would enfeeble the popular respect they themselves reposed on. Before any ambitious Governor's schemes could get under way he could be deposed and finished by a Decree—for the Emperor's power, within strict limits, functioned with a perfection that produced illusions of strength, from which foreigners were slow in clearing their eyes.[1] Magistrates were not feudal magnates with local loyalties to call on, but strangers from another province, without influence except as deputies of the Son of Heaven. Being civil servants and not territorial nobles, they rose to high position gradually and were as a rule old by the time they "arrived". They did not have full control of the provincial armies—such as these were. The Government subsisted by the weakness, not by the strength, of its administration. Wade, remarking in 1880 that Governors were by no means independent satraps, added: "Still, in the present condition of the empire they are gently handled by the Central Government."[2]

Such was the presumptive virtue of a Chinese official, that he would not merely report the stumblings of an erring colleague, but would report his own and supplicate punishment with equal alacrity. Aloof in ripe impartiality stood the Censors, and above, animating all in paths of rectitude, was the Son of Heaven. How well did facts, those churlish creatures, agree with the ideal picture? Surly foreigners detected none of the more refined arts and graces of Chinese administration; they saw only a throng of useless, grasping, and ill-washed mandarins.

[1] Lord Macartney wrote in his Diary: "Indeed, the machinery and authority of the Chinese Government are so organised and so powerful as... to produce every effect that human strength can accomplish." (R. Hall, *Eminent Authorities on China.*)

[2] Wade 15, 28.1.80, 17. 829.

We never know when we are well off; we may now see one
of these same foreigners so carried away by dislike of the post-
war student-politician of China as to recall with a sigh the
dignified reticence of the mandarin, who at least did not make
speeches.[1] There were, indeed, human features in the bureaucracy
which bore out criticism. Officials were usually ready to bate
something of their lofty carriage when there was a scent of
money in the wind. A magistrate, had he got nothing but his
regular pay, would have had to support himself by begging
gratuities from the prisoners before him in the dock. Naturally,
he did not confine himself to his regular pay. He lived off the
country very much as did the pilfering ragamuffins of soldiers.
The heroine's father in "The Western Chamber" is mentioned
as having occupied his high office with such probity as to have
left nothing to his family; but he is mentioned with surprise,
and not with any great admiration.[2] A story in the amusing
though spurious memoirs of Li Hung-chang (composed in
gaol in Honolulu by a Yankee who felt that America could
supply the Chinese with all their requirements better than they
could themselves, including their autobiographies) relates how
Li, to test the integrity of his staff, came up to his own door in
disguise, and could not get past so much as the porter without
bribing him. The system extended to the Throne itself: the
Chief Eunuch Li Lien-ying, who succeeded An Te-hai in the
Imperial favour after the latter's abrupt demise, and retained
his influence to the end of an evil life, developed corruption
on a heroic scale, sharing the proceeds with his Mistress.[3] This,
however, was a fleecing of well-fed sheep, not a direct shearing
of the needy masses. As to sale of office, that was forbidden in
1879, but to the regret of intelligent Chinese it had to be re-
introduced to raise funds during the Tonking campaign.[4] It
may have had the effect of invigorating officialdom by an

[1] J. O. P. Bland, China: the Pity of It, ch. VI.
[2] Part I, Act 2 (translated by Hsiang).
[3] It would be interesting to know how many foreign diplomats and con-
cessionaires were among Li Lien-ying's customers.
[4] Parkes 26, 24.1.85, 17. 977.

infusion of commercial, "progressive", elements; though it seems that the selling was chiefly of *titles*, not of posts.[1]

Notable cases of venality are touched on from time to time in our documents. A passage in a trade report of 1880 proved with figures that the Hoppo or Customs Receiver at Canton was making, in respect of Pakhoi alone, £13,000 a year over and above expenses plus disgorgements to Peking. The Foreign Office decided to suppress this from publication, as calculated to wound the Hoppo's feelings.[2] In April 1885 O'Conor sent home a Memorial according to which members of the Customs Administration in Anhui were raking in no less than ten times as much as they were remitting to the Board of Revenues.[3] Their post was essentially what Sidney Smith would have called "a snug thing"; though apparently this was making oneself a little *too* snug. Even Censors were not above suspicion; they were suspected of taking bribes to advise the Tai Wen Kun's return to Corea.[4] In 1887 the central revenue was 75½ million taels,[5] and it was estimated that four times as much revenue was absorbed locally. If we allow local administration to cost as much as central, then three times 75½ million taels will represent the takings of the provincial bureaucracy; a solid enough weight of bullion to keep it loyally anchored in the lagoon of Confucian principle.

If all government is robbery, the mandarins were the most genteel robbers imaginable. They were not sharks, not tigers, but—caterpillars, a glossy band quietly cropping the Chinese garden. Wells Williams points out that, jostling and elbowing one another for promotion, they rarely lost all sense of character;

[1] But accounts differ on this point. Mayers (*Chinese Government*) said not merely that honorary degrees and distinctions were "indiscriminately obtainable by purchase" (18, 29), but that sale of offices had definitely brought new classes into the bureaucracy (117). Similarly J. H. Gray, *China*, I, 84.

[2] Report with Wade 43, 18.3.80, 17. 830.

[3] O'Conor 197, 28.4.85, 17. 980.

[4] O'Conor 252 conf., 27.5.85, 17. 981.

[5] S. K. Chen, *Taxation under the Ch'ing Dynasty*, 42. A more popular writer, calculating in a rough manner, says that Central Revenue was "less than one-ninth of what was undoubtedly collected". (Krausse, *China in Decay*, 78.)

they did not use poison, like their compeers of Turkey or old Rome.[1] He considers also that it was usually the magistrate who deserved well of his people, who won promotion.[2] Officials were at any rate not loungers: their positions forced them to be "intensely laborious" and to shun the unbuttoned amusements of the ordinary citizen.[3] There were signs in our period that men of integrity were coming to the top, backed by a public feeling that the times were critical.[4] The public enjoyed great license of criticising its rulers, in placards, pavement scrawlings, and a luxuriant literature of the street. True, one could not always say that governors and governed were in tune like voice and echo, as an old sage enjoined. An official's hangers-on were known as his "claws", for the mandarin was essentially prehensile. On the other hand, while to give way to litigious passions was to court ruin, those who stayed outside his Yamen were usually beyond his reach.[5] If he attempted extortion beyond his own court-house, it was, so to speak, a private speculation. A vicious official had practically no force to bring into an argument, and would not make himself liked by his superiors if he had to ask for soldiers. As a result, he used cruelty to crush discontent at the outset, but the moment discontent assumed serious proportions he was powerless. In the summer of 1883 there was unrest at points along the Yangtze, due to crop failures. A riot took place, and a magistrate turned up with 300 men to arrest the ringleaders. Peasants mustered in force, and he had to beat a retreat.[6] Events at Hankow in May of that year are an even better illustration. Rumours got about of a forthcoming insurrection. The authorities were gripped by panic. They pounced on some fool who was boasting in a brothel of being a rebel leader, and "by a free application of the bamboo" got out of him details of an imaginary plot. Mass arrests were made, and forty suspects were summarily put out of the way of ever doing mischief. There was further uneasiness

---

[1] *The Middle Kingdom*, I, 451–2.   [2] *Ibid.* I, 461.
[3] Colquhoun, *China in Transformation*, 187.
[4] Memo. by Carles, with Grosvenor 158, 18.12.82, 17. 900.
[5] Ross, *The Manchus*, 647.   [6] Intelligence Reports, Kiukiang, 233. 13.

because some disbanded Braves insisted on being put ashore at Hankow, though the officials wanted them to go on up-river—"another instance of the utter weakness of the Authorities here".[1] We are told of one magistrate who had his ear bitten off because he obstinately went against the sense of his parish.[2]

In a Decree defending the examinations Tzu Hsi said: "If the candidate is really a man of ability, the fact that he has been made to compose verses in accordance with the time-honoured methods... will never prevent him from making his way in the world."[3] This sounds like damning the system with faint praise. She herself once complained that her orders were passed down from one functionary to another and "eventually pigeon-holed as so much waste paper".[4] But we must remember that ministers who proved weak, even treasonable, in the exigencies of contact with aggressive modern states, were not therefore inadequate to their traditional functions. Administration was limited by popular democracy, not by over-mighty subjects. China's structure was such that no intense compulsion was needed to sustain it. All testimony confirms that in normal times China was orderly and peaceful. Sun Yat-sen, interviewed by travellers in 1924, said: "The Chinese are a civilised race. They do not need government, really, save to formulate a foreign policy...."[5] He remarks in one of his lectures that the ordinary people had "almost no relations with the officials".[6] The real administration was that of the groups of family elders who managed village affairs under the lead of their hereditary headman, the *ti-pao*.

Chinese economy stood or fell with artificial water-control; drainage and irrigation. For want of water, very much land

---

[1] Consul Alabaster 7 to 16, May 1883, 17.934.
[2] Douglas, *Society in China*, 145; for a similar but lighter story see Simon, *China*, 15–16.
[3] Bland and Blackhouse, *China under the Empress Dowager*, ch. xv.
[4] *Ibid.*
[5] Hutchinson, *Far Corners around the World*.
[6] Sun Yat-sen, *The Three People's Principles*, Part II, Lecture I.

always remained uncultivated, and watered land was much more valuable than unwatered.[1] We even hear of farmers damming roads into impromptu reservoirs. China might almost be said, like Holland, to have created herself.[2] And water-control was the work of bureaucracy; the work which formed and developed it, if it did not call it into existence. Among the Eighteen Provinces there is still only one where *private* water-works are important.[3] In this sphere, the Government had a vital function, and a weight in the economic life of the country which is not equalled by the Western State except at a highly advanced stage. Waterworks "were used by successive dynasties as an important political lever and a powerful weapon in social and political struggles". Each dynasty manipulated them in favour of the provinces it particularly depended on.[4] But they were also a heavy responsibility, and a Government which failed in efficiency in this respect was likely to incur trouble. It may be that the cyclical phases of Chinese history—attributed by the Court Chronicles to degeneration of ruling houses in the drugged secrecy of the Forbidden City—were caused by growth of population, demanding extended cultivation and irrigation. Such a demand would be difficult for a rigidly formal bureaucracy to satisfy; the result would be economic decline, social anarchy, a sweeping off of surplus population, and a fresh start under a new Dynasty. It is an all-important question for us, whether the Manchus, towards the end, were failing in mastery of their economic function.

[1] K. A. Wittfogel, *Wirtschaft und Gesellschaft Chinas*, 55, 195. Cp. 83–4: "Das Hauptgebiet der chinesischen Agrikultur, die Grosse Ebene, weist Niederschlagsziffern auf, die nur im Suden und auch dort um ein sehr geringes jene Grenze überschreiten, innerhalb deren ein lohnender Ackerbau ohne künstliche Bewasserung 'sehr beschränkt und unsicher ist'....In Mittelchina ist nicht einmal eine Reisernte ohne künstliche Bewasserung möglich." Cp. also Cressey, *China's Geographical Foundations*.

[2] "It is wellnigh impossible, by word or map, to convey an adequate idea of the magnitude of the system of canalisation." (King, *Farmers of Forty Centuries*, 97.)

[3] Ch'ao Ting Chi, *Key Economic Areas in Chinese History*, 44.

[4] *Ibid.* II, 43.

This must remain a matter of surmise. Statistics are at present imperfect and discordant.[1] None the less it is worth suggesting that when Peking found new sources of income—Customs-duties, loans, etc.—and was not so dependent as formerly on land-tax and rice-tribute, it would pay less attention to water-control. The fact that its mind was distracted by foreign affairs would have the same consequence; at a time when growth of population—despite the Taiping War—required that more, not merely the same, money and energy should be spent on irrigation. It is true that even in the early nineteenth century it was military expenditure that swallowed up the biggest part of the budget, but water-control had a good share of the rest. It is also true that up to 1895 China was solvent; but the proportional importance of land to the Treasury— not of course to the people—was dwindling. After 1895 the decrepit finances which foreign pressure helped to produce may well have pinched supplies for canals and dykes; and it may not be fanciful to see a correspondence between the stronger radicalism of the South and the South's greater need of waterworks. The foreign responsibility implied would be the greatest, though not the most obvious, of all the injuries done by the West to the old polity. Apologists of the West, whose aim is to palm off on the Manchu Government a certificate of natural death, have naturally not investigated the question.

In all other respects, the bureaucracy reflected a decentralised economic and social life. The three great sections of the people—

[1] Wittfogel (443) compiles from figures of Parker, Navarro and Morse a table that would bear out our argument astonishingly:

Time	Total Expenditure	Expenditure on Water-works	Percentage
Before 1850	Tls. 31,522,800	3,800,000	12·0
Before 1900	Tls. 52,500,000	1,500,000	3·0
1905	Tls. 102,454,000	1,389,000	1·38

However, the figures given by Chen Shao-kwan (*Taxation under the Ch'ing Dynasty*, 33) for the regular Treasury appropriations of the nineteenth-century, his budget survey for 1911 (p. 43), and Jernigan's figures for 1904 (*China's Business Methods and Policy*, 57) do not altogether agree.

gentry, peasants, traders—were alike scattered over the country. None of them had any wish to create and use a strong state power; none needed strong authority to keep them in order; none, in old times, was evolving in any direction. Society functioned automatically.

In the innumerable villages of the Great Plain and the mountain valleys there was, despite the absence of a feudal nobility, a clear distinction between the farmers who waded in the flooded rice-fields and the gentry who sat by windows opened to the summer airs, drank tea, and scratched their back with an ivory toy hand. It was the latter who were the ruling, the possessing, class of China. From it the bureaucracy was largely recruited; with it the provincial officers worked in harmony; on it the administration rested.[1] A local official stood in much the same relation to a landowner as a parson in old days to his squire. It was not a feudal landownership of large estates worked by serfs or employees. The gentry lived in idyllic idleness, protected in normal times by the same atmosphere of custom, prescription, tradition, as preserved the mandarinate. They were not a "ruling class" in the sense of operating the machine of government, for the machine scarcely existed. There was an equilibrium, the relations of class with class being of only latent hostility. From time to time agrarian distress caused an upheaval, and then the gentry were swept away in a tide of ruin.

Two consequences flowed from the character of this class. First, it was not oppressive enough to need an effective army and police to maintain it. Second, it was irredeemably opposed to Westernisation: hence the fundamental reason why the Chinese polity could not reorganise itself to meet modern conditions. Japan, in the clansmen, had an element intimate with public affairs, and predisposed towards change by the onset of a money-economy. China was large, and the bulk of the landowning class lay far inland, out of sound of the sea and of the ideas blowing across it.

[1] "Trotz aller gesellschaftlichen Verwandschaft, ja teilweise: Identität mit den Grosslandbesitzern sah sich die Regierung...genötigt." (Wittfogel, *Wirtschaft etc.*, 386). Cp. Gray, *China*, I, 182.

There was a sort of intermediate layer through which gentry and bureaucracy melted into one another—the body of literati, who integrated the two castes and seemed to Westerners to unite the vices of both. "Not one in a score of graduates ever obtains an office, not one in a hundred of competitors ever gets a degree; but they all belong to the literary class, and share in its influence, dignity, and privileges....They make the public opinion of the country."[1] These men hung about the law-courts for odd jobs, or got pickings out of the numerous petty local tax farms. They diffused through the country the habit of mind, and the current opinion, of the capital.

It is a very difficult task to estimate the position of the peasantry in old China; and instinctive, and contradictory, impressions are often given instead of argument. Are we to think the population so teeming because so many of the souls awaiting in the Underworld their entry into the sunlight desired to be sent to the Flowery Kingdom? Or are we to think of their lives as a burrowing of countless insects in the black soil, inhuman, swarming, ignorant, wretched?

For a very long time, the dominant type of Chinese agriculture had been intensive working of small plots by the labour of large families: the basis of China's philoprogenitive sentiment and all that went with it. The work was skilled, especially in rice-culture, although conservative—for few could afford the risk of experimenting—and produced an intelligent peasant stock with a complex technical experience. In a way it was a life of leisure; farm work in China only absorbs ninety-five days out of the year on an average.[2] There were no vast estates. An occasional one that emerged was soon divided among heirs. Land was an article of commerce, and even the estates around Peking originally granted to the Manchu leaders had long ago slipped back into Chinese hands; but land purchase was a matter of stable investment, not of speculation. There was no cultivating of demesnes by serf or hired labour. There were small landowners who hired out their fields, and cultivators who either owned or rented land.

[1] Wells Williams, *The Middle Kingdom*, I, 562.
[2] Buck, *Chinese Farm Economy*, 53, 231.

For the peasant, Government at least was a cheap luxury. Land-tax, made up of four distinct elements, was vexatiously complicated,[1] but it brought in only 31,000,000 taels a year, a minute sum per head of population; 18,000,000 being paid in silver and 13,000,000 in kind.[2] Like our seventeenth-century "subsidies", it rested on an obsolete assessment, to disturb which would have been very difficult for the Government.[3] Officials added surcharges for their own benefit only up to a point where the public would unite to resist. As to the Central Government, Wade observed in one of his Opium Reports that when it was hard up it stiffened imposts on traders rather than on farmers. "Voluntary" subscriptions, reminiscent of Tudor Benevolences, were a common device. For the peasant, the landlord's claims were more serious. A landowner need not possess half a million acres to be extortionate; in fact slender means may invigorate his greed. There was not enough money in China for rents in cash to become general, though other economic prerequisites of money rent were present. Speaking of the present day, Tawney puts rents at 50 per cent of the crop in parts of Hupeh, 55 per cent in Kiangsi; and landlords' rates of profit at 8 to 11 per cent.[4] Buck, examining 2866 farms, found tenants handing to their landlord between 24·6 per cent of their crop and 66·6 per cent (the latter in Shansi, under the cropping system); the landlord making 8·5 per cent on his investment.[5] It could easily be argued, however, on several grounds, that rent-levels were less oppressive fifty years ago than they are now.

As to the proportion of tenants to non-tenants, it is given for 1917 thus—Peasant proprietors, 24,587,589 families; Tenants, 13,825,446 families; Part-tenants, 10,494,722 families.[6] Buck's figures are more favourable, showing one-sixth of his

---

[1] Huang Han-liang, Land Tax in China, 108.

[2] Wells Williams, The Middle Kingdom, I, 289, quoting estimates of the Imperial Maritime Customs.

[3] Chen, Taxation under the Ch'ing Dynasty, 68.

[4] Land and Labour in China, 64.

[5] Chinese Farm Economy, 149, 159. An observer in our period thought that landlords in N. China were making 10 per cent profit. (Ross, The Manchus, 661.)   [6] Quoted by Wittfogel, Wirtschaft etc., 389.

farmers part owners, one-fifth tenants, and nearly two-thirds full owners.[1] Probably flood and famine—natural substitutes for the cyclical crises of the West—assisted social differentiation, by forcing the poorest to abandon their land. The surviving proportion of independent owners is remarkable.

The determining factor in the peasant's situation was that the forces which impoverished him were not so much direct as indirect; not so much the demands of Government or landlord, as the suffocating network of relations inside which he lived. In the first place, growth of population made pressure on the land so great that he could not own, or afford to rent, sufficient ground. In 1887, 924,000,000 *mou* were reported under cultivation; in 1661 there had only been 549,000,000. In the interim most of the public domain had been given up to the farmer.[2] By now, subdivision has gone so far that the average Chinese farm is well under five acres;[3] and it seems clear that the smallest units are economically inferior, not superior, to the larger ones.[4] In the second place, the peasant was chronically placed by weather and other accidents at the mercy of the village money-lender—the real "Asiatic tyrant". "Money-lending in China is a world in itself, which cries out for investigation."[5] Charges were so exorbitant that once enmeshed it was hard to get free. Thirdly, the craft-work or silk-culture that filled up the peasant's vacant hours did not put much money in his pocket, since he was dependent on a middleman who bought up what he produced. He knew nothing of what his fellow-craftsmen, scattered over the province, were doing, and the merchant could beat him down by refusing his goods. Here usurer and trader played into each other's hands. The

---

[1] *Chinese Farm Economy*, 145.

[2] Chen, *Taxation under the Ch'ing Dynasty*, 49. Smith (*Village Life in China*, 310) emphasises the intense overcrowding of China's land.

[3] Buck, *Chinese Farm Economy*, 43. Wittfogel gives the following distribution: Landowners, 2·8 millions; big farmers 5; middle farmers 10; small ones 13; poor ones 17 (*Wirtschaft etc.*, 380).

[4] "There is no argument in favour of the small farm." (Buck, *Chinese Farm Economy*, 116; cp. 107, 110, 122. Wittfogel argues on the same lines; *Wirtschaft etc.*, 361–2).   [5] Tawney, *Land and Labour in China*, 64.

peasant had to borrow because he was ill-paid, and he had to accept any price because he was in debt. The poorer the peasant, the better he could be exploited.[1] Lastly, the Chinese village was never—historically—self-sufficient. "If the regions so far investigated are typical, rather more than a quarter of the goods consumed by agricultural families are purchased."[2] Here again the poorer peasant could not bargain effectively with the trader who transported his grain to the big provincial markets and sold him in return tools, shoes, salt, at very inflated prices. Salt was perhaps the most profit-weighted article of all. Syndicates owned the sources and worked them with exploited labour; smuggling laws discriminated against the poor; "the producers and the consumers have been entirely at the mercy of the monopolists."[3]

In sum, the agricultural masses had to bear a society largely parasitical, without the oppression being obvious or vulnerable enough to require a highly organised state support. It is significant that the standards of living of tenants and owner-farmers do not show a very wide difference.[4] Tangible mulcts did not weigh very heavily on the Chinese farmer. And, apart from the consolations of Confucius, he could take comfort in the career open to talents that his sons might enjoy. Hung Niang in the play remarks: "You say the poor always remain poor; instead of that Prime Ministers and Generals are produced from the homes of the poor." This may sound like the spreading in our days of illusions about every apprentice being able to make his million, but the biographies of many Chinese states-men bear out the claim.[5] A China resident has left from our

---

[1] Cp. Wittfogel, *Wirtschaft etc.*, 705: "Nicht aus dem *Reichtum* des bauer-licher Produzenten also zieht der chinesischen Aufkaufer seinen Haupt-gewinn, sondern aus dessen *Armut*."

[2] Tawney, *Land and Labour in China*, 55. Cp. Buck, *Chinese Farm Economy*, 196–7; he speaks of a "fairly commercialised agriculture".

[3] Chen, *Taxation under the Ch'ing Dynasty*, 73–90.

[4] Buck, *Chinese Farm Economy*, 418.

[5] There is a story that an Emperor once called on his Grand Secretaries to describe the details of agriculture. All but one had begun as farmers' sons, and were able to answer. (Bland and Blackhouse, *Annals and Memoirs of the Court of Peking*, 30.)

period a detailed account of a family in Fukien, with which he was on intimate terms. It is a picture of a small but highly productive farm, and of comfortable and humane living.[1] The majority were certainly less prosperous. "The Chinese state", it has been said, "was frankly based upon the theory of class rule, and class rule meant the concentration of surplus resources, very often including a large proportion of the necessities of life squeezed from the people."[2] Yet this cannot stand alone as a definition of the average of life in Chinese history. There was enough diffusion of modest comfort to warrant the statement that the peasantry were "the most contented and loyal subjects of the Empire".[3]

China was an agricultural country. But she was really a complex of many countries; and if we look for the real force binding these together, we shall find it not in the stilted ornamentation of the Government but in the busily circulating stream of commerce. "No matter where you stop to listen to two Chinamen in conversation", wrote a missionary of our period, "the topic will invariably be money and the prices of various commodities."[4] Foreigners who grumbled at the meagreness of China's foreign trade were at the same time struck by the large volume of her internal trade. They saw forests of junk-masts on the rivers, porters everywhere on the villainous roads. Evidently, this commerce implied the presence of commercial classes, outside the framework of agrarian society. Clearly also these classes were not insignificant. Here and there in Chinese history we come on men who, we learn, have made large fortunes in trade; and we find intriguing references to the part played by the guilds. It was the guilds of Peking which, anxious for order, led the way in submitting to the Manchu conquerors.[5]

[1] Simon, China, Part V. Cp. Coltman, The Chinese (1891): "A middle-class farmer is, perhaps, the most independent man in the empire" (p. 107).

[2] Ch'ao Ting-chi, Key Economic Areas in Chinese History, 122.

[3] Jernigan, China's Business Methods and Policy, 28.

[4] Coltman, The Chinese, 105.

[5] See Morse, Gilds of China; for a contemporary account see article by Macgowan in Journal of the China Branch of the R.A.S. XXI (1886), 137–92.

Capital in China was essentially *merchant* capital. The man with money to invest bought up goods (or lent someone else the means of doing so) from their producers, and sold them elsewhere. Craftsmen in the towns, peasant workers in the villages, equally put money in his pocket, having little defence against him. An entrepreneur class came into existence early, and became very prosperous. Industrial capital on the contrary was rudimentary, for various reasons—mainly the cheapness of labour. The chief offshoot of trading capital was banking capital. The scarcity of money entitled capital to high rates of interest.[1]

How comfortable for the trading classes was the China of tradition? It gave them an enormous and orderly market, unhampered by internal feudal divisions. Western writers often made out that the officials, from Peking outwards, were as bad as bandits in plundering trade. It is true that Provincial Governments depended for their revenues, and individual mandarins for their incomes, largely on commerce; but this was a reason for not killing the goose, even if screwing up of tolls was not rare. It was the habit of traders to defeat exactions by suspending operations. The likin system—internal duties—was inaugurated at the instance of the merchant guilds themselves, to provide funds for the overthrow of the Taipings. The fact that it was prolonged beyond original purposes was due, in part at least, to the increase in Government need for revenue caused by Western pressure. Local officials kept on good terms with the guilds, to which even the Central Government did not turn a deaf ear, and these organisations, with their salaried officers drawn from the lettered class, knew how to protect their members.

The absence of a feudal environment freed the merchant from any galling aristocratic contempt, even though he did not stand very high in Confucian categories. Chang Chih-tung makes a special point in his book of commerce being an accepted institution—if in bookish language: "There is a clemency

[1] For a description of the famous Shansi banks see Jernigan, *China's Business Methods and Policy*, 76 ff.

shown to the merchant class that was unknown to the earlier Dynasties, who forced these men to sell at 'mandarin' prices, below the market value."[1] Trade was a fundamental of the Empire, not a luxury. In reality the bureaucracy had little less contact with the commercial world than with the gentry.[2] It was a favourite investment for moneyed men to finance an official just starting in a new post, until he had made enough out of it to pay them back with interest. It would be gratifying to discover that some of the literati who launched Memorials against Chung Hou in 1880 were in debt to merchants who sold tea in Kulja, or belonged to families owning banks which financed tea and silk caravans along the routes of Kashgaria. An individual might belong to all four sections of China's dominant class—he might be landowner, official, trader and financier (or pawnshop-owner).

We have then in old China a nicely harmonised group of sophisticated classes, transferring to themselves part of the producer's output by methods unobtrusive and not intolerably extortionate. All these appropriating groups were comfortable —on condition that they did not try to overstep conventional routine. Their wealth did not solidify into blocks of fixed capital in the hands of a definite caste, as it tends to do in an industrial society. "The beauty of our democracy", says a Chinese writer, "is that the money thus robbed or stolen always seeps back to the people. . .through all the people who depend upon the official and serve him, down to the house servant."[3]

But now external forces were acting upon and polarising the molecular structure of China. It is worth seeing how the leading mandarins of our period reacted. "For three decades from 1860 there were two great parties in China", the conservatives and the progressives.[4]

---

[1] *China's Only Hope*, 38.

[2] "Enquiry will show that (great fortunes) have invariably been made possible by the more or less direct connection of the 'merchant' with the bureaucratic world." (Morse, *Gilds of China*, 2nd ed., 4.)

[3] Lin Yu-tang, *My Country and My People*, 174.

[4] Morse, *Trade and Administration of China*, 48.

Chang Chih-tung was the Han-lin graduate *par excellence*, who could not think except in classical tropes, and whose library was his world. When our period opened he was exercising himself on a scheme for catching invaders, as they landed, in huge locust-traps.[1] The crisis of 1880 brought him into prominence. Later, surprisingly, he turned into a moderate, a very moderate, Westerniser. At present he was important because his pen was the delight of what we may call Peking's Clubland. His bent was for erudite research. His official character was pure. His influence, in 1880 and 1884, was for war.

Tso Tsung-tang was an ogre rather than a man; no great scholar—the energies of his humble origin had not been starved out of him. Cruel, ascetic, ambitious, he came back from Kashgar in triumph, offended the Court by his arrogance, and went off to the Viceroyalty of the Two Kiang, where he tolerated no rival. We have a description of a meeting between him and Count Szechenyi, a Hungarian traveller, by someone who was with them for a few days. The narrator represents Tso as intolerant, dreaded, honest, frugal, a misogynist, with an executioner always in attendance who earned his living by hard work—during the stay seven persons, including three mandarins, lost their heads, Tso watching the executions and sipping tea.[2] His watchword in fact was that of the Duchess—"Off with his head!" He was savagely anti-foreign; especially anti-French, and, because of opium, anti-English. On that account he was in foreign circles perhaps the best-hated of all Chinese. They looked forward to his demise, and were inclined to count their corpse before it was coffined. A despatch of November 1882 records with satisfaction that Tso is ill, and has taken three months leave; he cannot last much longer.[3] In March 1884 complacent note is taken that Tso has again had to go off on leave.[4] He died at last in September 1885.

[1] From a character-sketch by Mrs Little, in *Li Hung-chang*, 110 ff.
[2] Article from *Shanghai Mercury* with Wade 28, 15.6.81, 17. 858.
[3] Grosvenor 139, 25.11.82, 17. 900.
[4] Parkes 47, 3.3.84, 17. 849. There is an essay (of 1883) on Tso in Boulger's *Central Asian Questions*.

It is always as difficult to distinguish the man from the myth as the features of a Victorian portrait under the swathes of whisker. Especially so with Li Hung-chang. Li's was a life spent on the frontier of two worlds; repudiated by one, not accepted by the other. All his faults were set in a notebook, learned, and conned by rote. He was by early education an initiate of the old aristocratic culture; born it would seem to rise steadily in office, enjoy the esteem of his district, celebrate the recurrent festivals, and exchange verses with his friends. The Taiping war which brought him in youth fame and the friendship of Tseng Kuo-fan, swept him for ever from these tranquil moorings. Like soldiers of many wars and countries, he could not return home to the lotus-eating of scholarship. Henceforth Li elaborated the convictions that were to guide his public life—the necessity for China to resist the Westerners on their own ground, with their own weapons. There was no question of an infatuation with Western ideas. Of European culture he knew and cared nothing. His model was Bismarck, to visit whom at Friedrichsruh gratified years of curiosity. In the schoolroom in Anhui Li had hated the foreigners, and when he came to know the Outlanders he did not love them—"these avaricious tradesmen and blustering officials with their bad manners and want of culture".[1] In fact, denunciation of them was a staple of his talk. He wanted only their telegraphs, their medicines, their steam; above all, their cannon.

> Thou hast taught me language, and my profit on't
> Is, I know how to curse.

In the eyes of the conservatives of Peking, Li was touching pitch: to have *any* dealings with the enemy must mean treason. In integrity he was far behind his leading rivals. He chose his

[1] Prof. O. Franke, "Li Hung-chang" (in *Meister der Politik*, ed. Marcks and Muller). And: "Natürlich war Li ein viel zu wohlgeschulter Literat, als das ihm auch nur der Gedanke hatte kommen können, dieses Neue etwa auf geistigem oder gar ethischem Gebiete suchen zu sollen; es konnte sich nur um ein Werkzeug, vielleicht um eine technische Fertigkeit handeln, die man in China vernachlässigt hatte und schleunigst ersetzen musste."

creatures from among discredited politicians who would be soul and body dependent on him.[1] Yet—growing it may be too overbearing and proud—he dominated the scene by pure ability. The twilight of the Empire would have been meaner without him.

As a steersman in the troubled current of history, to use the modest description of statesmanship given by his hero Bismarck, Li failed. His unformulated "theory" was that the régime might adapt itself to modern forms of life and self-protection. He could not be expected to discover by ratiocination that the theory would not work. The historical experiment was bound to be made. It was no unpredictable reversal that, at the end, Li was ranged with the reactionaries against Kuang Hsü's reformers, and the enemy was inside China's gates. His career closed as it had begun, the country ablaze with insurrection. He lived and died a Mandarin of the Empire. We must beware of seeing in him an over-enlightened *pater patriae*. The admiration of foreigners for him as a "leader of progress" is enough to put us on our guard. Li was plunging into enterprises and innovations with too little care for whether they might not betray China. He pooh-poohed the notion that railways and so on could do China harm, and foreigners applauded. But it was true, and the less gifted Tso Tsung-tang knew it by instinct. Unconsciously, Li's policy contradicted itself, and led in the direction of a China dominated by foreign capital. Those who talked of him as "China's strong man" intended him to be another Porfirio Diaz, holding the country under repression whilst *they* made profits in it. Let us not believe that, had he seen such a destiny before him, he would have accepted it. He could have allowed foreign bayonets to set him on the Throne as a puppet—had he wished.

Li's policy harmonised with his character. It would be a mistake to think of him in tragic terms. The Empire was dying,

---

[1] Li "seems to have gathered all the most hopelessly corrupt men in China about him". (Mrs Little, *Li Hung-chang*, 159.) "The Viceregal Yamen at Tientsin became in the 'nineties a gathering place for greedy place-seekers and sordid schemes." (Bland, *Li Hung-chang*, 73; cp. pp. 22, 121, 124.)

the barbarians were gathering, but he never lost interest in life: the strong nerves, that allowed him to sentence a criminal to the death of a thousand cuts and *watch* its infliction,[1] never gave way. He paid himself for his services. He overlooked the arguments against railways and factories partly because *he* was going to make something out of them. Had it been the incorruptible Tso whose navy went to the bottom because eunuchs had sucked its funds, we should have had to pity him indeed; but it is too much to be feared that Li *shared* in the plundering of the fleet. Unluckily, his policy was distrusted even when it was right. Those who scorned bribes could see no good in him.[2] Chinese officials who had the virtue of honesty rarely had any other—their vitality exhausted itself in that effort.

Li's most individual trait was his zest in the business of living; it made him indisposed to take things tragically. He saw his armies, his fleets, his civilisation, following one another into the dusty oblivion of history; but he found, like Voltaire, that after all it was a passable world.

It is the greatest of philosophies, the only one which cannot be refuted.

As has been seen, the Chinese official mind did not browse exclusively on the Sung poets and the chances of place. It was not, then, so paradoxical as might seem, that the leading "Westernisers" as regards forms of industrial enterprise were high officials. Mandarins, whose departed spirits we may fancy, by the Yellow Springs, still discussing notable banking fortunes and rates of exchange, were not likely to ignore altogether the lure of new money. In contemporary Japan the example was being set by Government subsidies, Government monopolies, Government inspiration, over the whole economic field. It would be advantageous to the régime to establish similar official contact with new forms of enterprise in China. Li may have felt that one of his services to the state was his engrossing of steamships and mines into his own politically reliable hands.

[1] Douglas, *Li Hung-chang*, 126.
[2] The passage in Witte's *Memoirs* where his offer of a bribe to Li is mentioned need not imply that Li accepted; but see *Life of Macartney*, 462.

When however, one remembers the character of the mandarinate, one sees that it would be illogical to expect any large
number to follow Li's example. The prejudices which saturated
them expressed a sound conviction that to open the gates to
foreign ways would be, in the long run, to undermine their
interest as a class. A Han-lin graduate, unless a very exceptional
one, was not qualified to compete in business with a comprador
of the Ports allied with a foreigner. He might understand well
enough the elementary operations of the good old days, lending
and borrowing, collecting jewels, farming taxes, the sweet
simplicity of ten per cent. To buy machinery and make it pay
was a different proposition, calling for a new type of man.
Those high officials who ventured into the new realms had very
qualified success—not excluding Li himself.

Hornby met a Taotai at Shanghai named Ting, who represented a hybrid section in the general body of the mandarinate,
brought into being by Western contact. He was not a scholar,
as scholarship went—very likely he came from the commercial
class, for he had been appointed to Shanghai because long
intercourse with foreigners had rubbed away his prejudices
against them. Ting deplored the obstinacy which set itself
against telegraphs and railways.[1] Another Taotai with whom
Hornby talked had been comprador in a foreign *hong*, and had
visited America. He criticised his comrades of the mandarinate
as uncharitably as any foreigner, dismissing them as addle-pated
to a man, and saying that when China had learned more from
the West "We shall insist on our rulers being as intelligent as
ourselves...they will at least cease to be pig-headed ignorami.
The literati know all this notwithstanding their stupidity."[2]
It was inevitable that the sort of man who graduated from an
English hong and set up business in Shanghai should labour
under no overpowering respect for the man who had been
thumbing night and day, as Horace ordains, the versification of
the ancients. Conversely, officials who had won their places
by years of the most artificial toil would not often be prepared

[1] Hornby, *Autobiography*, 212.
[2] *Ibid*. 273.

to sacrifice those years and adopt new ways and new sciences which would subvert their traditional prestige. The mandarin and the steam-engine could not coexist in the same country.

How the steam-engine began to rumble in the mandarin's ears is touched on in the next chapter. At present it may be noted how sounds less corporeal could equally disturb his serenity.

"By the accumulated wisdom of six successive sovereigns", said Tzu Hsi, "our dynasty has succeeded in establishing a system of government, based on absolute justice and benevolence, which approaches very nearly to perfection."[1] It *did* answer almost to perfection the wishes of those who benefited by it, even if these were not the entire people. At any rate, compared with whatever other systems have been devised, it was surely a Government that deserved the philosophic defence of a Burke; that merited his "lenient arts to extend a parent's breath"—not solely by its antiquity, its reassuring continuance through the mists of time like a mountain "familiar with for-gotten years". But the tranquil immobility of a vast population, the suspension one is tempted to say of natural law, needed the drug-laden atmosphere of its own world of ideas to preserve it. Custom and inherited belief had to do the work that in our intellectually disintegrated Europe is done by the truncheon. Intricate, all-pervading formalism kept society moving calmly, like action on a stage, where only rehearsed words and gestures occur. Much of the detail was meaningless convention; but in political as in moral philosophy, the conservatory usefulness of an idea is not measured by its "truth". And custom had to be harmonised by the deeper tones of religion. The mind had to be enclosed within walls and courts extending far beyond the plot of time on which it existed. China's was the most consummate achievement that has been reached in the art of attuning human society to its inanimate environment. We think of her people as an unreligious race because of the suave ease of their diplo-matic relations with Nature and with Heaven. Religion has come to have for Europe a *Thibetan* meaning; anguish, un-

[1] Bland and Blackhouse, *China under the Empress Dowager*, ch. xv.

certainty, immolation. But just as the Chinese painter allowed his thoughts to enter into the wild scenery of his pictures with no sense of hostility or alienness in it, so around the humdrum business of Chinese life the metaphysical world stretched placidly away. Not merely was concord broken by no jangling of Church and State: the State administered three religions, of each of which the Emperor was head, in assured agreement. Clerics were arranged in gradations of rank in the same way as officials.[1] Divinities were treated "much as if they were highly respectable functionaries of a superior order, promoted to some kind of upper house".[2] The Peking Gazette commended the services of a river-god or weather-god as familiarly as it might those of a magistrate on circuit. Canonisation, elsewhere in Asia performed by prelates, was here in the hands of the bureaucracy, which interfered peremptorily to settle disputed lamaic incarnations in favour of the politically soundest candidate. (One has heard of a cautious though aspiring Hindu consulting the local Deputy Commissioner before coming out as a new prophet.) Undesirable persons were prohibited by Imperial order from returning to life. The bureaucracy was at the same time an urbane priesthood. In April 1885 the Viceroy of Shensi and Kansu reported an earthquake, occasioned by disturbance of the dual elements animating Nature, whose nice balance could only be maintained by upright behaviour on the part of all officials.[3] It was the bureaucracy, beginning with the Emperor himself at the appointed festivals, who invoked and placated the forces of the Universe, and secured prosperity to the Flowery Kingdom.

The problem of what spells thus converted the stormy sea of religious emotion into an unrippled, serviceable lake, loses itself in speculation. But in that society, the novel ideas impatiently recommended by foreigners were certain to have a destructive effect. The science and religion of Europe, mortal

---

[1] Mayers, Chinese Government, 77.
[2] See a brilliant essay in Lyall's Asiatic Studies (1884); cp. an amusing page in The Golden Bough (abridged ed. 103).
[3] Report with O'Conor 168, 17.4.85, 17. 980.

enemies at home, were allies against the simple ritualism of China. Every chapter in the corpus of Chinese wisdom communicated with every other. Admiration of scholarship preserved obedience to the magistrate. The magistrate's scholarship was composed of classical rhetoric, with fanciful medicine, meteorology, and so on. If the former were to be derided as useless, and the latter as absurd, where would be his authority? Missionary propaganda, above all, laid an axe to the root of order and prescription. It was not from heathen vice that China's rulers hated the missionaries: they recognised in them a dangerous menace. In China one could not attack the Church without attacking the State. The Emperors who in seemingly endless succession announced to Heaven and Earth their ascent of the Dragon Throne would be reciting to deaf ears if the old ideas were swept away. Along the southern coasts the corrosive influence could be felt at work. By its nature, the Government was bound to oppose to missionaries and to all other bearers of new thoughts an inveterate hostility.

Moribus antiquis stat res Romana virisque.

CHAPTER SIXTEEN

British Enterprise and China

CHINA was the El Dorado of the age, over which hard-headed business men and politicians allowed themselves their dreams. The disparity between vision and fulfilment was acutely felt. "Our trade with China has been miserably small hitherto", said a speaker in an Opium Debate in Parliament in 1883—Belgium was taking more of our goods than all China. "On the Manchester Stock Exchange, there is nothing that excites so much astonishment as the little elasticity of our trade with China. At the present time the outlets for British capital seem almost choked up. There is nothing that the country needs so much as a large field for the investment of its capital. What field in the world would equal China?"[1]

One trouble was the monetary problem that came so much in those days between economists and their sleep. Gold production was not keeping pace with commercial expansion, which helped to make prices droop. Simultaneously silver was being thrown on the market in vast quantities, from the mines of Nevada and the demonetised stocks of Germany; while the Indian absorption of silver was slumping. Silver, therefore, depreciated seriously against gold (and, in China, against copper). All transactions involving silver countries became risky, more because of uneven fluctuations in the fall than because of the fall itself.[2] Trade that up to about 1875 had been financed with bills on London, now had to buy bills from the Eastern banks, who to cover themselves against loss charged very high rates.[3] In 1885 Goschen said: "I fear that the un-

---

[1] Hansard, 3rd Series, 277. 1333 ff. The *Economist* was pointing to China as an immense market (3.9.81, 29.7.82).

[2] Remer, *Foreign Trade of China*, 78.

[3] See evidence of A. D. Provand, exporter to China, before the Gold and Silver Commission of 1887. He complained that India merchants were better

certainty in the trade with the silver-using countries will become even more acute." [1]

There were more fundamental difficulties in the way of trade with China. The "complexes" and "inhibitions" of the Chinese Government, which so irritated foreigners, had their origin in the nature of China's economy. All the interminable talking and day-dreaming about how to "get hold of the trade of China" was based on a miscomprehension. There was a huge internal trade in China, but it moved in an equilibrium evolved over many centuries; it could not be grafted on to foreign commerce without a radical alteration of the national economic life, which could not but bring sweeping political changes with it. Foreigners demanded at once political stability and economic revolution—an impossibility. "Chinese", wrote Hart, "have the best food in the world, rice; the best drink, tea; and the best clothing, cotton, silk, and fur. Possessing these staples, and their innumerable native adjuncts, they do not need to buy a penny's worth elsewhere." [2] More serious still: "The whole power of trade in China rests on combination and monopoly. This has been weakened by foreign influence, but every attempt at developing new branches of trade leads to an attempt to return to the old principles, by seeking Government protection against competition." [3] It was not a mere bureaucracy, it was the entire organism, that resisted the Open Sesame of the West. Such a country *could not* abruptly begin to buy large quantities of goods from abroad. Lancashire manufacturers, especially, could not grasp this. They had been lulled in their cradles by the Higgling of the Market; and they had India in their minds, not seeing that only a disintegrated

off, because Council Bills kept their money market fairly stable; also that the fall of silver favoured Bombay exporters of yarn to China as against Lancashire.

[1] Speech to the Manchester Chamber of Commerce.

[2] *These from the Land of Sinim.* Cp. Sargent, *Anglo-Chinese Trade and Diplomacy*, 245: "The economic self-sufficiency of China was perhaps the most formidable barrier which we have as yet encountered in our career of industrial and commercial expansion."

[3] Consular Report, quoted by Krausse, *China in Decay*, 240.

economy brought about by conquest had made India a market
for them. There was one grand exception. China could not
manufacture cannon and warships, and by their pressure the
Westerners made this peculiar variety of consumption goods
necessary to her.

Trade figures of our years point to two main conclusions: a
solid British lead, and a lack of elasticity.

The period opened hopefully. There had been recovery since
the huge famine of 1878, and 1879 showed an increase of trade
in spite of a 10 per cent fall in the tael. The British Empire had
77½ per cent of the total: the runner-up was America with
7½ per cent. In coastal traffic the British flag covered 50 per cent
of shipping, the Chinese 42 per cent, the German 5 per cent.
Five years later Britain had 299 firms engaged in the Treaty
Ports, with 2070 nationals. America had 31 firms with 469
nationals; Germany 64 with 364; France 20 and 228; Russia
16 and 170; Japan 2 and 61. The totals are 451 and 3995, giving
England a percentage of 66 in firms and 52 in residents.[1]

O'Conor in 1885 compiled an interesting survey of the ups
and downs of trade between 1875 and 1885. 1880 was a year
of gradual increase. 1881 showed higher imports chiefly in
opium and cotton. 1882 fluctuated: oil imports trebled, silk
prices suffered through speculation. 1883 was marked by a grave
financial crisis, because of heavy speculation, Yellow River
floods, and the French menace. In 1884 trade decreased on
account of the war.

From his tables of figures from 1871 to 1883, one finds six
years with an increase, six with a decrease; and at the end the
total was one twentieth higher than at the beginning. China
still kept up a slight excess of exports, though this was about
to be reversed, and she was exporting gold because of the
European demand[2] but her silver imports—about 80,000,000
Haekwan Taels between 1871 and 1884—more than balanced

---

[1] In 1897 there were 595 foreign firms with a personnel of 9363; of these
England had 374 and 4929, percentages of 62.5 and 52.6. (Krausse, *China
in Decay*, 258.)

[2] See Giffen before the Gold and Silver Commission of 1887.

both these amounts. "It is obvious", Remer points out, "that there must have been, since 1880 especially, a large and increasing remittance of funds to China by the Chinese in foreign countries."[1] So early as 1889 a Chinese diplomat showed himself aware of the fact.[2] Chinese emigration, constantly sending back both funds and ideas to the home country, was to prove one of the main forces tending to revolutionise China both economically and politically. With this to bolster the international balance of payments, and as a result of commercial pressure exerted in our period, trade was destined to show from 1885 a marked expansion.

But for British merchants in the early 'eighties the position was not exhilarating. If we divide the number of firms into the total turnover, which did not all pass through their hands, and calculate an average commission at 5 per cent, it is evident that a normal firm's returns could not be high. The result, it must be confessed, was to make the trading community a little inclined to be cantankerous; especially the Shanghai merchants, surrounded by the ugly wastes of mud brought down by their river, and "keeping themselves alive" by paper-chases two or three times a week.[3] Four thousand Lilliputians, strung out round the sleeping Chinese Gulliver! By the end of the century foreign pressure on China made the British traders nervous, as it seemed to portend Spheres of Influence; but in our period they welcomed almost any sort of pressure as likely to jog China out of her slumbers. Gordon formed the impression during his 1880 visit that "any war would be popular with them; so they will egg on any power to make it".[4] China seemed to them, as the world to Pistol, an oyster to be opened with a sword.

A merchant of the 'twenties or 'thirties, revisiting the Treaty

---

[1] Remer, *Foreign Trade of China*, 213–19. Morse pointed to the same fact in 1908; *Trade and Administration of China*, 327–9.

[2] Edkins, *Chinese Currency*, 53.

[3] Mrs Gordon Cumming, *Wanderings in China*, ch. I. Other visitors, it should be said, painted a more attractive Shanghai, and expatiated on its theatre, its cricket matches, and its dozens of clubs. (Percival, *Land of the Dragon*, 3 ff.)   [4] Boulger, *Life of Gordon*, 321.

Ports in 1880, would have found them a transformed world. The "halcyon days when China firms made large fortunes, lived in palaces", and amused themselves with race-horses[1]— the days of the genial commercial society painted by Hunter— were a regretted memory. Competition, and currency difficulties, had let many a chill draught in through many a chink in the walls of the merchant palaces. Telegraph communication and the Suez Canal had worked a vast change; markets could now easily be glutted, and there had been brought to life a crop of struggling small firms, without much capital or ability to "hold on and wait", who were "degenerating", as stern critics put it, into commission agents;[2] while big firms had somehow to enlarge their business, to offset falling profits.[3] Michie's book describes the pre-commission form of trade, with some of the professional gloom of the Old China Hand, who partly to discourage fresh competition wore the air of a mourner assisting at the last rites of China trade—as having fallen into a perpetual cycle of losses. One sold goods in China to buy tea to lay down in England to buy goods to sell in China. At every stage one was losing money, but losses were concealed by the revolving circle.[4] Changing times were symbolised by the dying out of the grand tea-ship races to Europe. After the clippers' races from Fuchow came, with the Suez Canal, steam races from Hankow. The last great one was fought out between the "Gleneagle" and the "Stirling Castle" in 1883.[5] But China tea was, to the detriment of European culture as well as of the Treaty Ports, giving way to the vulgar product of Ceylon. The "transcendentally aloof foreign

[1] Hornby, *Autobiography*, 263.

[2] A commercial traveller in S. America nowadays finds customers *requesting* to be bribed with presents, and specifying what they would like. It was towards such base uses that the China merchants were slipping. But my friend Mr Greenberg, who is working on the Jardine Matheson archives (now at Cambridge), tells me that in the early part of the century the biggest houses worked mainly on commission. There seem to have been *four* phases.

[3] Sargent, *Anglo-Chinese Trade and Diplomacy*, 201–2.

[4] Michie, *Englishman in China*, 173–5.

[5] *Ibid.* 244.

merchant",[1] who had inhaled some whiffs of his own opium and left sordid details to his comprador, now had to take a very lively interest in business. *Some* must have continued to do well. China merchants whom Kipling met in 1889 were redolent of prosperity, indulged in frequent trips to England, and talked of the country as "only waiting to be opened up to pay a hundredfold". One of them remarked: "God knows I hate the Chinaman, but you can do business with him."[2]

"The Chinaman", however, was sometimes too keen a competitor. The 1884 Trade Report mentioned that all articles except opium and lead were now brought into Fuchow by *native* firms. This, of course, was not what we wanted when we exhorted the Chinese to "waken up" (but what did we want?). An attempt of the China Merchants Company in 1881 to run ships to London failed because, an Old China Hand commented naïvely, "it naturally met with uncompromising opposition from British merchants and shippers".[3] A Chinese firm which gained a footing in London complained to the Chinese Minister in 1883 that its ships were prevented from finding return cargoes by a ring of jealous English merchants.[4] Growth of Anglo-Chinese trade was hindered by British as well as Chinese sectional vested interests.

The traders' grand whipping-post in these years was Likin. For the benefit of foreign goods in the interior, the transit-pass system had been devised; but according to our merchants' jobations it was easier for a camel to pass through the eye of a needle than for a bale of cloth to penetrate the choking network of barriers. Levying tolls was the ideal exercise of the mandarin —the quintessence of Chinese politics. Chinese writers, it may be noted, say that likin told against *native* goods, which had no

[1] Gowen and Hall, *Outline History of China*. There was a good deal of leeway to make up as regards technical competence. When it was complained that Russian brick-tea dealers were getting on better than ours, Wade commented "The Russians, I do not doubt, speak the language". (Wade, 28.5.79, 17.855.)

[2] Kipling, *From Sea to Sea*, ch. xv.   [3] Eitel, *Europe in China*, 558.

[4] It added that foreigners were supplying inferior war material at high commission, and advised that the Government should buy through Chinese houses abroad. (Canton Intelligence Reports, 12.7.83, 233. 13.)

transit-passes;[1] and Tso, who believed in calling a spade a damned spade, once described the transit system as "the abomination of all the authorities of the inland provinces".[2] It harassed them with endless vexations, and lessened their revenues; and as Peking had to encroach on their funds to meet needs imposed by foreign contact, they in turn had to stiffen imposts on native trade. Hence, perhaps, a major grievance against the Dynasty.

Likin was perpetually, from Chefu onwards, under discussion. While in 1878 the author of *Treasure Island* was beating his donkey over the Cevennes, Wade was cudgelling the equally obstinate Yamen over stony paths of debate. Next November likin formed one main subject of a joint Note sent in by the Diplomatic Body. To a list of twenty complaints about likin Kung retorted that he might, if he chose, make a much longer list of charges against foreigners.[3] Wade forwarded the reply to London with a learned excursus on the word "wu", in which he detected something impertinent. Controversy dragged on interminably. In 1883 Sinclair reported from Fuchow that vexatious likin charges had strangled all but two hardy importing firms at that port. Beresford was told at Amoy in 1898 that no goods could get more than twenty miles inland.[4]

A great many quarrels arose to add to diplomatic friction. A typical suit arose thus. In May 1881, Messrs Herton of Pakhoi received an order from a Hongkong firm for 2500 piculs of Cassia Lignea. The agent conveying the merchandise was laid by the heels by likin men, and it could not be delivered. The Hongkong firm had to buy at Canton, and the price meanwhile having risen, they came on Messrs Herton for the difference, 4520 dollars. The aggrieved party lodged a claim on the Chinese Government for 12,858·16 dollars, alleging losses to that amount through obstruction of their transit business in the foregoing and other cases. Grosvenor examined their claims

[1] T'ang Leang-li, *Inner History of the Chinese Revolution*, 38; cp. Hart, *These from the Land of Sinim*, 176.   [2] Notes of Opium Conferences, in 17. 922.
[3] Wade 19, 31.1.80, and enclosures.
[4] *Break-Up of China*; section on Amoy.

and knocked off a third, but told the Foreign Office that they deserved something, and, unless a very strong line were taken, would not see a penny.[1] A great number of papers were produced. Spence drew up a memorandum for Wade—they were in London together. One at least of the items was found "preposterous".[2] Such claims would rarely be made up in a niggardly spirit, and there was a danger that Ministers might take them up without discrimination, to display their zeal. Most of the seventeen disputes which the Legation had in hand when Wade left were commercial cases of this sort.[3]

"I congratulate you", said Governor Bowen to his Legislative Council in 1884, "on the probable prospect of, ere very long, seeing China thrown open, through the extension of railways and telegraphs, to the influence of European commerce and civilisation." What indications were there that China *wanted* to give up conservatism and adopt foreign ways? There were enough to keep foreigners in two minds, and prevent their seeing the final truth that the old Chinese régime at least could not modernise itself.

In small ways we notice more *savoir-faire*. The Chinese were learning to be citizens of the world. In 1880 high officials contributed to the Lord Mayor's Fund,[4] which really should entitle them to be classed as civilised. Li also gave two hundred dollars in that year to the Irish Famine Fund,[5] which may or may not have been a hint that he was cognisant of ill-governed spots in other Empires than his own. In 1883 China agreed to take part in the international Fisheries Exhibition presided over by the Prince of Wales.[6] In the same year the Court of Peking instituted an Order of the Double Dragon, and informed the Court of St James of the designs for its decorations—also of the sashes to be worn, an important point of which Tseng had to remind his Government.[7] Wade was offered the first Division of the Second Class, but had to decline. So, more reluctantly,

[1] Grosvenor 150, 8.12.82, 17. 900. [2] Wade to F.O., 7.5.83, 17. 923.
[3] Grosvenor 7, 21.1.83, 17. 921. [4] F.O. 112, 17. 828.
[5] Wade 72, 26.5.80, 17. 831. [6] Correspondence in 17. 932.
[7] See 17. 932.

had a certain Rajah Surindas Mohun Tagore of Calcutta, who presented his works on Asiatic music to the Emperor, and after getting Tseng to jog the Emperor's memory, was offered a gift and a decoration.[1] There were more serious advances. The Press had made more than a beginning. Hosie found in 1882 that the Governor of Kweichow could discuss intelligently, from a Press article, plans for a new type of light vessel for the Upper Yangtze, and he remarked: "The vernacular Press seems to be doing good work throughout the whole of China."[2] It was in telegraph building that the new spirit most clearly expressed itself. Acting-consul Wilkinson of Ningpo, in an exhaustive account of the native telegraph management in 1884, speaks of polite young operators, fluent in English and well trained at the Imperial Telegraph College at Tientsin; and gives a general impression of a system very well developed.[3] In a further report (the Postmaster-General asked for more information) Wilkinson observes: "Since the date of my last report events, favourably unfavourable, have excited a wide activity of telegraph extension in China....Stations continue to be opened from week to week, so rapidly that any report professing to give their full number may be incomplete and out of date, before it reaches the hands of the reader....Nobody in all the world knows how many lines there exist, every viceroy and mandarin builds after his own head...."[4] O'Conor wrote that opposition had been surprisingly shortlived, and that telegraphs "already appear as a very important factor towards the centralisation of Power".[5] It is likely that there had been more hostility in Japan a few decades since to foreign innovations, more riots and protests, than could be found in China at

[1] See 17. 869.
[2] The first native journal, the *Shen Pao*, was started in 1870, by an Englishman.   [3] In 17. 1010.   [4] In 17. 1011.
[5] *Ibid.* It was an indication of Peking's real authority over at least its officials that telegraphs were so readily accepted. When we read that the Provinces raised difficulties about their quota payments, we might suspect that it was because they did not want orders to reach them too often or too quickly. But apparently a good deal of the capital was subscribed by the Provincial Governments. They were jealous of their profits, not of their power.

our date. The Aborigines Protection Society still included China in its purview; but it was generally felt that the Chinese were better than ordinary aborigines.

With all this in view there was a natural tendency to think that China could go ahead fast enough were it not for the private wrong-headedness of the mandarins. At the close of the Tonking war great hopes were indulged, and Li was deluged under applications for concessions.[1] Especially now that foreign enterprise was forming new ambitions, alongside the old simple interests, it was exasperating to see an official like Chung Hou regard with "the most listless indifference" the marvels that met his eyes in Europe. "The Chinese mandarin", said Curzon dogmatically, "is China's worst enemy." What he meant, was that the bureaucracy was hostile to enterprise. What was true, was that the bureaucracy would not allow enterprise to expand into new forms which foreign capital wished to introduce. We are not confronted by a repetition of the old "commerce against feudalism" struggle of Europe. It was a struggle of *new forms* of commerce to penetrate an old commercial-political framework. China's polity had hindered industrial capital from growing up spontaneously, and would now hinder it from being imported.[2] An allusion to Corea throws the state of affairs into relief, for commerce in Corea was more backward than in China. In June 1884 Parkes was discussing Corea with Li. Hitherto Corean internal trade had been dominated by Government brokers, who raised or depressed prices at will. This system was now being ended. None the less, Li criticised the treaty Parkes had made at Seoul on the ground that it would increase friction between nobles and people, because by allowing direct trade between the latter and foreigners it would "emancipate them from the thraldom to which they had hitherto been subject in even the smallest mercantile

[1] Douglas, *Li Hung-chang*, 219.
[2] Ch'ao Ting-chi writes (*op. cit.* 70): "In China, the growth of merchant capital has been repeatedly nipped in the bud by the ruling landlord bureaucracy." Had he written "industrial capital" he would have been more correct. The bureaucracy was almost *identifiable* with merchant capital.

transactions", and enable them to strike out fresh activities free from official inspection.[1]

In our years the issue took shape in China in four fields—manufacture, mining, railway-building, banking.

It was towards the end of 1882 that the idea of turning out foreign goods inside China came into prominence. Only a start had hitherto been made; still, we have a list of fifteen foreign establishments in Shanghai, producing matches, paper, gas, and so on. Eleven were British, two American, one German, one French—proportions reflecting British ascendancy. In half a dozen of these enterprises the capital was of mixed nationality, and in several of them shares were held by Chinese.[2] The latter fact seems at first sight one that would smooth over animosity between Chinese and foreigners by creating common interests. But it could not be palatable to the Chinese Government to see some of its subjects seduced into sympathy with the Westerners, and in circumstances moreover that would increase the insidious encroachments of the foreigners at the Ports.

Foreigners considered that a right to develop industries in Treaty Ports was secured to all of them by Article 7 of the French Treaty of 1850, by Article 6 of the German Treaty of 1861, and by Article 11 of the German Treaty of 1865. On finding themselves obstructed by local officials, they in November 1882 addressed a joint Note to the Yamen enforcing their views.

The Note, a very long one,[3] regretted that instead of fostering industry by giving it free play, the Chinese Government was crushing its every growth by taxation, and was giving monopolies to "a few officials or speculators". The taxation referred to was partly a mark of official disfavour, partly the untutored rapacity of mandarins who saw new prey in sight. Factories of modern type were protected neither by guilds nor by the ability of the older, looser forms of enterprise to take refuge in a suspended animation until the official shark swam away elsewhere.

---

[1] Parkes, Corea 19 conf., 20.6.84, 17. 951.
[2] The list, which includes dock companies, is in 17. 919.
[3] Copy with Grosvenor 15, 27.1.83, 17. 921.

Prince Kung replied, at equal length, that the claim was a novelty, and if granted would ruin many thousands of Chinese undertakings. He found fault with the meaning "industry" attached to the word "kung" in the Treaties; according to him it signified "handicrafts"—as if businessmen wanted to go from Europe to Shanghai in order to turn a spinningwheel. Foreigners ought to be content with what they made out of trade. He concluded by saying that a ten years' monopoly had been given to a group of native cloth producers at Shanghai, who had been first in the field, "lest dishonourable merchants, seeing that others had successfully commenced something, should try to wrest their lawful profits from them by competition".[1] The phrase must have fallen strangely on the ears of foreign Ministers, brought up to revere Competition as the divine spirit "that moves through all things". The representatives of these opposite economic systems were entirely at cross purposes. "The principles of political economy", commented Grosvenor, mystified, "have a long way to travel before they find their way into the brains of Chinese statesmen." These "principles" had done yeoman service in defence of certain features of the Industrial Revolution in England; why should they not set to work again in China? Grosvenor wrote to his Government: "The right of foreigners to manufacture in the Treaty Ports of China has of late assumed considerable importance, owing to the desire of foreigners to start manufactories with the assistance of Chinese capital." (This has a double significance: it proves that foreigners believed China to be possessed of enough liquid capital to start industries and that it was *as yet* a question of private businessmen anxious to employ technical knowledge, rather than of the pressure of European capital eager for outlet.) Grosvenor added that he had entrusted to Brandt negotiations for permission to bring materials from inside China to the Ports under transit-pass, not for export but to be worked up by machinery.[2]

Correspondence was also being conducted at Shanghai, between Consul Hughes and Shao Taotai. The latter was induced to withdraw his objection to an Electric Light Company,

[1] Copy with Grosvenor 15, 27.1.83, 17. 921.   [2] Grosvenor 15.

but natives associated with foreign undertakings were being victimised. Hughes heard that a cotton factory was being set up under the patronage of Li; who later tried to keep a monopoly in Shanghai for his company. "China does not improve upon acquaintance": the Yamen was now saying it could not interfere with the line taken by Provincial Governments. Grosvenor gave a sigh for the old days when, if an Englishman was injured, armed force was at once sent to set the matter right. But his phrase, "The burning question of the day amongst merchants is that of their rights under Treaty to manufacture at the Ports", is interesting.

An incident in January showed what friction might result. Three hundred iron pans belonging to a Chinese subject of Britain were seized by likin men. The pans were released, but the native foreman was kept under arrest, and a great deal of correspondence accumulated. The Germans had a similar case pending, and Brandt threatened to send a warship to recover *his* pans by force. The threat was actually carried out, though on a protest by the Chinese Minister at Berlin the German Government disowned Brandt's action.[1] The action tallied with the inclination of the foreign community, which was always to obtain satisfaction "without tarrying for the magistrate".

The iron pans continued to clang discordantly under the beating of their powers. Granville minuted on the statement of the compensation they wanted: "The claim seems preposterously high."[2] Kung maintained an obstinate refusal to change his ground.[3] The Foreign Office took counsel with the Germans, French, and Italians. Tseng tried to enlist Wade's sympathy for the Chinese argument, though personally the Chinese Minister was strongly of opinion that entry of foreign capital ought to be *invited*. No doubt he had in mind Japan; but he was not allowing for the problem of whether China was strong enough to control foreign capital, or whether it would control *her*. Sir Thomas, in his comprehensive manner, sat down to run his eye over the whole question. There emerged

[1] Grosvenor 15.   [2] Minute on Grosvenor 70, 31.5.83, 17. 923.
[3] Grosvenor 85, 14.6.83, 17. 923.

from his cogitations one point, obvious enough, which had hitherto escaped notice. Why should we be so eager to precipitate Chinese competition with our own manufactures? China would be certain to enter on competition with Lancashire soon enough. It might not be our best policy to join with Brandt too wholeheartedly.[1] Germany stood to gain by setting up works in Shanghai: unlike us she had no great textile exports to the Far East, and would not be cutting her own throat. She would then be able to undersell British trade by cheap production with native labour. Even so, *all* nations had reason to think twice before creating Chinese industrial competition—which might well produce, Leroy-Beaulieu was writing, "one of the most immense revolutions in the history of humanity".[2]

The first cotton mill was not put up in Shanghai until 1890; its capital was mainly official, provided by Li. One or two small ones were built each year from then up to the Japanese war.[3] England for one reason or another did not much enforce her rights until after the Treaty of Shimonoseki. Possibly Wade's argument went home.

It is clear how the Chinese governmental mind was working. If the foreign claim were admitted, two new and restless elements would be generated inside the body politic: an industrial employing class and a wage-earning class. The Government detested seeing masses of men brought together, except on public works where they were indispensable. On the same grounds, Lord Burleigh advised Queen Elizabeth to discountenance the weaving industry. Secondly, when foreigners maintained that an undertaking like the Kuang Ping Filature, employing 141,000 taels and 347 women and children, was doing China good service in providing work for surplus hands, Prince Kung took the opposite view: that it would tend rather to ruin native firms and so diminish employment; which would mean trouble for a Government which had no force capable

[1] Wade conf., 3.7.83, 17. 923.
[2] Quoted in *Economist*, 5.9.85. Cp. *Bankers' Magazine* of N.Y., XL, 436.
[3] A. S. Pearse, *Cotton Industry of Japan and China*, 153. He says that native and foreign mills alike made little profit before 1906.

of quelling disorder. Finally, with Chinese working for Europeans, friction and disturbances would be inevitable.

China's minerals had never been more than scratched, a fact important for the evolution of money forms.[1] Marco Polo found coal being used. The nineteenth century found it being used in much the same primitive way. Without industries or means of heavy transport there was no point in producing much coal in any one spot. Mines were numerous but small, and technique stationary. Hosie found a hundred little mines around one city in Szechuan, but the price of coal was doubled by carriage of five miles or so. In Kweichow he came across a silver mine, whose owner lamented that proceeds barely met costs. "It is the same story everywhere."[2]

The first idea of a mining concession is said to date from 1868.[3] By 1880 a good deal of interest had been aroused, and greatly exaggerated estimates of China's resources were current.[4] In 1880 we hear of a rich anthracite bed near Ichang being worked.[5] Brandt showed Wade a German consular report on the Kaiping mines then being developed by a Chinese company under the auspices of the ubiquitous Li. Progress was being retarded there both by workmen who saw their livelihood, wretched as it was, threatened by the use of machinery, and by conservative gentry whose peacefully succeeding seasons were disturbed by any unfamiliar sound in the hum of life about them. None the less, the enterprise seemed sound.[6] In 1881 a state mine at Kelung, with foreign machinery worked by natives, raised 54,000 tons of coal.[7] In 1884 Parkes called for a report on the export of coal from Shanghai, which was not being hindered by officialdom.[8] In 1885 the Board of Trade was interesting itself in the coal output of Saghalien.[9]

---

[1] See e.g. Wen Pin-wei, *Currency Problem in China*, 39.

[2] *Journey in Western China*.   [3] *Life of Macartney*, 168.

[4] E.g. *Journal of the Iron and Steel Institute*, vol. I of 1885, p. 261.

[5] *Ibid*. vol. I of 1880, p. 329.   [6] Wade 53, 2.4.80, 17. 830.

[7] *Journal of the Iron and Steel Institute*, vol. II of 1882, p. 806. The management, however, was wrongheaded, according to the 1883 Tamsui and Kelung Trade Report.   [8] Report with Parkes 242, 29.10.84, 17. 952.

[9] Parkes 90, 3.3.85, 17. 978.

During 1881 there occurred an instance of the Government refusing (to its own people) permission for mines to be worked; gold mines in Darbagatai.[1] Publicly, its attitude was that greed was demoralising, and therefore that to explore inside the earth was not the part of a good citizen. Actually it was in fear, as always, of the disorders that might arise from the bringing together of masses of workmen. The Yunnan miners had taken years of fighting, not long since, to subdue. There was a case on record of officials, on a visit to some mines, being fired at with cannon.[2] The dislike of seeing masses of people together sounds odd when the teeming urban populations are thought of; but it was dislike of masses capable of being organised by common interest into common action. China's old labouring class was not a *constant* element, forming collective traditions, outlook, solidarity. A medical resident, for instance, spoke of the coolies as too exhausted at the end of their day's work to think of women, and rarely marrying.[3] They were the wastage and overflow in each generation of the farming class. At moments of anxiety, indeed, any kind of crowd was suspect. In 1880 a disturbance arose at Wenchow from the authorities trying to suppress a lottery because of the crowds it collected. "Nothing", remarked Sir Thomas in the Johnsonian diction he sometimes affected, "so alarms this government as the conglomeration of multitudes, be it for work or play."[4]

The distaste might be overborne either by the participation of officials like Li in mining, or by the desire of penurious Provinces for new revenues. Thus in 1885 Fukien asked permission to solicit investments and develop lead mining.[5] In 1883 high officials at Canton were in favour of developing the Yunnan mines; a subsidy was to be given and machinery bought.[6] Tong King-sing, manager of the China Merchants

---

[1] Edkins, *Chinese Currency*, 75.   [2] *Ibid.* 55.
[3] Coltman, *The Chinese*, 110.
[4] Wade 50, 27.3.80. Cp. O'Conor 438 conf., 24.10.85, 17.985: "Nothing is more dreaded by the governing powers than popular disturbances."
[5] Memorial with O'Conor 407, 28.9.85, 17.984.
[6] Canton Intelligence Reports, 233.13.

Company, visited England on mining business in 1882.[1] China had to think now of securing metal for guns and ammunition. Even for her primitive wars in old days, metal supplies had been a difficulty. Some officials were also thinking about securing bullion for coinage. In 1887 Viceroy Chang started a provincial mint at Canton. But when the régime fell it was still arguing about how to give the country a national currency. Here again, perhaps, is one cause of its fall. Old Chinese enterprise could get on with the currency chaos of former days; the new Chinese enterprise could not.

By 1885 railways were very much in the air. "Great syndicates had been formed in Europe in anticipation of a China boom after the French war."[2] It was in 1885 that the unclean word first sullied the Peking Gazette, when a Censor, Hsu Chih-hiang, was pulled up for a violent Memorial against railway-building—"which", wrote Parkes, "there is no doubt is at present under the serious consideration of the Court".[3] British heavy industry badly needed such a fillip. Goschen pointed out in his speech to the Manchester Chamber of Commerce that America's huge railway construction had given rise to intense activity in Britain, "with a desperate and terrible reaction afterwards". The situation was reflected in the formation in 1883 of the Rail Syndicate, the first international combine. Construction of railways was an industry that had to export itself once the home lines were finished. Now, China was being thought of as a field where railways could be built on a scale so vast as to "revive the whole iron trade of Britain".[4] Dunn of the Telegraph Company wrote excitedly in 1883 that there was a prospect of 3000 miles of track being laid.[5] His Chairman, Mr John Pender, M.P., wrote to the Foreign Office next year that he felt certain China was about to go in for railways, which would be "of the greatest importance to England—

---

[1] Kent, Railway Enterprise in China, 22.   [2] Ibid. 30.
[3] Parkes 65, 13.2.85, 17.978. A British merchant was buying land at Tientsin in the expectation of a railway being built. (Letter in the Jardine Matheson Archives, Cambridge.)
[4] Mrs Gordon Cumming, Wanderings in China, ch. xxx.   [5] 17. 1010.

I mean in giving employment to our languishing iron industries and to our mechanised industries now hard pressed by foreign competition"; he was therefore sending out an engineer from India, and asked for support—which Parkes was instructed to give.[1] In 1886 Chamberlain pressed on the Foreign Secretary a memorandum on development of Chinese railways by British capital.[2]

It was against railways (and river steamboats) that the frog-chorus of Chinese "prejudices" was most noisily raised. There *was* something to criticise: the Woosung railway fiasco of 1876 had foreshadowed the reckless competition of 1897–1900—its unauthorised construction had been "a deliberate violation of international law".[3] Foreigners expounded the principles of classical economics. "Railways and telegraphs", exclaimed one consul, "and the vigorous national life that accompanies them, are the true antidotes to the excesses of the opium pipe."[4] After all, they perhaps reflected, the same classes that opposed railways in China had once done so in England—the stage-coach drivers, the gentry of Leicestershire, and the literati of Cambridge. They rejected with doctrinaire contempt the idea that railways would diminish employment. Mobile as Chinese labour was, however, in some ways, it would not be able to adapt itself to such a change except fumblingly and painfully. Old occupations, organised almost on caste lines, would have to be thrown over for entirely different work, distant perhaps, problematical certainly.

Thus river steamers projected at Suchow in 1882 fell through because of opposition from local boatmen. It made no difference to the authorities whether the Ministers' hackneyed quotations from Smith and Ricardo were correct or not. Quotations would not assuage a turbulent crowd of men out of work. Sun Yat-sen observes that formerly one porter carried one picul in ten days from Canton to Hankow, and when

---

[1] Pender to Currie 10.4.84, 17. 969; F.O. to Parkes priv., 16.7.84, 17. 947.
[2] Garvin, *Life of Chamberlain*, II, ch. 6.
[3] Documents in pamphlet *England and China*, by "Justum".
[4] Chinkiang Trade Report, 1883.

trains began to run they carried 10,000 piculs in eight hours with the help of ten men.[1] Steamboats were worse than railways, they did not even afford work on construction. When the Port of Tientsin was opened to trade the Grand Canal fell off in importance, since steam transport along the coast competed with the Canal junks. A report in the *Gazette* showed that it had fallen into disrepair; yet the Government still transported part of the tribute rice along it, for fear of offending two classes with vested interests, a swarm of officials and a set of hardy boatmen who enjoyed a hereditary monopoly of the work.[2] The ruin or depression of much junk business along the coasts, through foreign shipping, must account for a great deal of the Westerners' unpopularity in the Ports.

As usual, a few officials headed by Li approved of railway building.[3] It was only imminent foreign danger that put even the modernists in a mood to want railways; they only wanted *strategic* railways. Two long Memorials of 1881, by Li and a certain Liu, are worth summarising. They present the case as seen by such patriots as were willing to learn from the West in order to keep out the West—and show that there *was* patriotism in China.

Japan, wrote Li (with misgivings, for opposition was violent), "is a petty little country that has laid down railways everywhere. She considers that the adoption of the higher arts and appliances that she has learned under foreign teaching (give her a right) to look upon China with contempt." China must have railways for her armies to operate along on the Russian frontier, and to give Peking organic connection with the provinces.—Liu couches his arguments in more dramatic form. His talents are "worthless as a common weed", but yet he can take thought for his country. "Constantly has he risen at dead of night and cast fierce glances around him, while tears have rolled down

---

[1] *The Three People's Principles*, Part III, Lecture 1.
[2] Parkes 105, 18.3.85, 17. 979.
[3] Kinder, the English manager of the Kaiping mines, built a locomotive in 1881 to use on a short stretch of line belonging to the mines. In 1882 two locomotives were brought out from England.

his cheeks with rage because of his inability to do what even a faithful dog or horse might do in repayment, however slight, of the debt of gratitude he owes to his sovereign." China "has thrown open the doors of the Empire...and never throughout all her past history have the dangers from foreign countries been so many or so formidable as they have been since that time". "The mainspring of an independent policy, is prompt construction of railways."[1]

"The characteristic condition of profitable financing of foreign trade by the international banks arises where trade springs up between a comparatively poor and undeveloped country, with great undeveloped resources in raw material, and a rich settled manufacturing country with a large surplus to invest."[2] It might be a description of nineteenth-century China; and trade banks had not been slow in going there. By the early 'eighties the Oriental Bank had "probably a more comprehensive branch system than any commercial bank has ever operated, before or since".[3] There were risks as well as profits: this bank failed in 1884. Home banks were not yet very much interested in China. The first six volumes of the *Journal of the Institute of Bankers* (1879–1880) have hardly anything to say about China. But branches of British overseas banks in China numbered 17 in 1870, 19 in 1880, 30 in 1890; their united capital in 1880 was £16,810,000.[4] The Hongkong and Shanghai Banking Corporation, founded in 1864, in 1880 definitely won for itself "a commanding position in the China Trade".[5] Most of the British trading-houses were interested in it. Like all overseas banks, it was accused of manipulating trade in the interests of its nationals, but the main criticism against it was that it had the privilege of holding the Customs receipts and sometimes used them for its own purposes; a factor that has created "the overwhelming financial strength of that institution, which is a strong prop of the Bank of England".[6]

[1] Copies with Wade 36, 22.6.81, 17. 858.
[2] A. J. Baxter, *International Banks*, 5.   [3] *Ibid.*
[4] *Ibid.* 167, and Appendix.   [5] Eitel, *Europe in China*, 550.
[6] Gowen and Hall, *Outline History of China*.

In our period it was the only Eastern bank making much profit, because it was capitalised locally, in silver; and so was not hurt by the silver fall; whereas the others had to write down their capital, in spite of charging 10 or 12 per cent for their bills.[1]

But the most sought-for, most lucrative business of the banks was to issue Government loans. It was said abroad that China could not raise loans internally because her commercial classes distrusted their Government[2]—a partial statement, though coming nearer and nearer to being true. But sober opinion was right in feeling that foreign loans, at exorbitant interest, would do China far more harm than good.[3] A European bank, standing persuasively at the door of an Oriental Court, was a danger to the whole people. It was so that Egypt lost first her money and then her independence. Why the Court of Peking— the insatiable Tzu Hsi and her eunuchs—did not clutch eagerly at the proffered millions, is one of the mysteries of China. Anti-foreign prejudice may have helped, and the eunuchs may not have comprehended these exotic modes of wealth. Anyway, China accumulated only small debts until placed under the compulsion of war. Loans were used sparingly and successfully.

"Until the Chinese-Japanese war of 1894 China had had practically no foreign debt."[4] This, which is repeated by most writers, is only true as regards large sums. About 1884–5 there was a stream of loans that might easily have swelled into a flood. (There had been a few small loans previously, mostly repaid in 1885.) These transactions began through Provincial Governments accepting loans on their own account, an insidious procedure more dangerous than central loans. One great objection to loans was that they might carry territorial guarantees.

[1] Provand, before Gold and Silver Commission of 1887. He was asked: In the Far East "the whole banking business is a speculation in the exchange?" —and agreed. See also evidence of McLean, Manager of the Hongkong and Shanghai Bank.

[2] E.g. *Economist*, 25.11.82.

[3] E.g. *Economist*, 25.1.79, which argues that China has really been paying heavier interest than appears in the contracts.

[4] Willoughby, *Foreign Rights and Interests in China*, 488.

Also, the strain of debt service might tell more seriously on Canton or Fukien than on Peking. Governors would be reluctant to apply to the irascible Board of Revenues for help, and might give away valuable concessions. They might be tempted to contract loans in order to pocket a share of the commission.

In March 1884 the Yamen sanctioned a loan of 2,000,000 taels at 9 per cent placed by the Hongkong and Shanghai Bank with the Canton Government.[1] Before the end of the year the same province contracted a loan from the same bank of 1,000,000 taels plus 200,000 dollars. The March loan was for maritime defences; the 200,000 dollars were for the Canton Riots indemnity. At the same time the Legation, concerned in these affairs in a purely ancillary way, heard that Jardine Matheson were to lend a larger sum, £1,500,000, to the Peking Field Force. This Department was under the Seventh Prince, who wanted an experimental railway to serve an Arsenal he had built near Peking. The loan was a complicated and tendencious affair. The text of the agreement shows that the Customs were to be hypothecated. £60,000 was to be paid over at once to China, and £90,000 to the Chinese Minister in London for purchase of rail materials. The rest was to be paid over only as the Company disposed of bonds, to be issued by them at interest fixed by themselves. Profits were likely to be very large.[2]

The million taels loan of the Hongkong and Shanghai Bank fell through, ostensibly because the bank lacked funds at hand, perhaps really because it feared a Chinese financial collapse on account of the Tonking war, and the attitude of the British Government was not friendly enough to make its help in securing repayment certain. Another bank was willing to

[1] Parkes 61, 31.3.84, 17. 849. There were earlier loans in our period—e.g. one, from the same bank, raised by the Viceroy of Shensi and Kansu on local security to give him the means of paying his troops. (Shanghai Trade Report, 1881.) But with these the Legation had no connection. When it began to be drawn into assisting loan-mongers, opinion in the Foreign Office and the Cabinet was sharply divided. [2] Parkes 310, 5.12.84, 17. 953.

speculate. The Yamen informed the Legation in February 1885 that Canton had taken a million taels from the Chartered Mercantile Bank, at 10·2 per cent. Simultaneously two fresh Canton loans were heard of. One was a sum of £505,000, lent by Mr John Pender, M.P., and secured on the Customs. The second, of the same amount at the same interest, was from the Hongkong and Shanghai Bank—10 per cent finding it either funds or courage.[1]

Parkes reckoned in February 1885 that China would owe 8,740,000 taels in all to British capitalists, besides 2,740,000 taels left outstanding from earlier loans.

O'Conor's trade-survey of 1885 gives a list of all Chinese debts hitherto. The first loan had been brought into the London market in 1875.

1875	£627,615	8 per cent
1875	£250,000	8 ,,
1877	£1,604,276	8 ,,
1879	£487,280	8 ,,

(The above four by now paid in full.)

1881	£1,096,000	8 per cent
1883	£500,000	9 ,,
1884	£285,000	9 ,,
1884	£1,500,000	10 ,,
1885	£500,000	10 ,,
1885	£250,000	10 ,,
1885	£750,000	9 ,,
1885	Tls. 4,000,000	9 ,,

The total was only £5,470,000; but this was not small for a Government with a revenue of £15,000,000. O'Conor had to say: "The Chinese Government has shown remarkable punctuality in the payment of both the interest and capital of all its foreign loans." But China's good behaviour would make foreigners all the more eager to lend, and the chronic imminence of war would make opportunities for them. A financier told

[1] Parkes 54, 7.2.85, 17. 978.

the Governor of Hongkong in 1884 that China would find no difficulty in borrowing as much as £6,000,000 to pay a French indemnity.[1] It is noticeable in the above list how the usurious interest rises with the Tonking campaign. We close our documents in 1885 with rumours that China is about to borrow a really large sum—£10,000,000—from a British house, for military and naval defence. There was every symptom of a period of heavy loans setting in. A state bank, one of Li's projects, was under consideration, though the jealousy of the Board of Revenues threatened to scotch it.[2]

The firmly held belief that the foreigner and the ordinary Chinaman had a common enemy in the mandarin, was at least too simple. Its expounders should have suspected their views if only from their being repudiated by the vast majority of the people, whose feelings might be expressed in the Biblical question—"Why do the heathen so furiously rage together, and imagine a vain thing?" It would be very hard to trace all the ways in which foreign contact has benefited China, and the reverse. Certainly, the Chinese masses were in old days poor enough.[2] But it is to be feared that too often the result of foreign competition was to force the native producer to lower his living standards still further in order to undercut it.[3] In the 'eighties this must already have been in progress near the Ports, and have helped to inflame popular feeling against the foreigner. It was probably the outcries of impoverished craftsmen that made officials like Tso, with their ignorance of classical economics, believe that "wealth was being drained out of the country".

[1] Bowen 115, 7.4.84, 27. 2708.
[2] Gamble (*Peking, a Social Survey*, 170) says that workpeople protected their standard of living by strikes, and employers were fined for lowering wages. But the profit-sharing that some Western writers refer to was not common, and the "industrial proletariat", so far as it existed, was miserably off.
[3] Wittfogel, *Wirtschaft etc.*, 670: "Was der kleinbauerliche Betrieb in der Sphäre der Agrikultur tat, das wiederholt in der industriellen der hausindustrielle Zwergbetrieb; er unterhungert den Grossbetrieb." Other old Chinese forms have displayed, at the same cost, the same surprising tenacity of life.

CHAPTER SEVENTEEN

The Other Powers

THE thought of another American Perry voyaging the perilous seas of the Far East, ready to open doors with a broadside, would in 1885 have seemed preposterous. In the spring of 1906, word was passed round in the Ports that America meant to send 40,000 troops to China in case of disorders.[1] A decade more, and an American clergyman said in his pulpit: "The God of Israel has anointed us to champion the cause of the poor, the weak, and the downtrodden. We also shall struggle for world power."[2]

In qualification of the U.S.A.'s stay-at-home habits in our period, a curious similarity might be pointed out between Russia's advance across Asia and the U.S.A.'s advance across America. Each was hurrying towards the Pacific, each, with scientific weapons, was crushing thin and backward nations, each had frontier trouble with a neighbour, in each case that neighbour was the British Empire. It was because we were less anxious over Canada than over India that we saw the two processes with such different eyes. But the Civil War broke down the Slave States' plans of expanding into Latin America, and the discovery of enormous resources at home made the United States content to occupy themselves with a colossal, if jagged and uneven, industrial progress. During the Civil War they lost most of their interest and trade in China. It was not until the end of the century that manufacturers began to talk seriously of a need for Asiatic markets.[3] In our years such thoughts occurred only spasmodically. Economic progress

[1] Putnam Weale, *Truce in the Far East*, 414.
[2] Bedborough, *Arms and the Clergy*, 106.
[3] Yakhontoff, *Russia and the Soviet Union in the Far East*, introd. Dennett (*Americans in Eastern Asia*, 461) refers to Washington's somewhat casual interest in its Corean Treaty.

suffered huge crises in 1879, 1884, 1893. At these crises thoughts turned to foreign markets. There were a few, including General Grant, who were anxious to draw the country's attention to vast neglected markets in Asia.[1]

The *Bankers' Magazine* of New York may be taken as reflecting the degree of interest felt in China. Most of its references between 1879 and 1886 are perfunctory; but during their course a certain change is noticeable. In 1883 it was announced that China was at last going in for railways. "American enterprise will certainly not permit the enormous field which China is destined to afford to be monopolised by our English brethren."[2] Next year Japan was mentioned as a customer for railway material.[3] In 1885 there was a discussion of whether industrial machinery ought or ought not to be sold to China. The writer concludes that British capitalists will decide to sacrifice their Chinese cloth market for the sake of selling machinery. "And especially do they gloat over the supposed fact that nowhere except in England can the Chinese obtain the capital required by the railroad system which they are believed to contemplate, and must therefore submit to the terms which British bankers may choose to impose." But Peking will be on its guard against usury, and London and Paris no longer monopolise loan capital. America must carefully watch the Far East, the last region left unpartitioned by the Europeans.[4] In the same year it was remarked that financiers were crowding to lend their money to China.[5]

On the whole, the chief object of jealousy of the New York bankers seems to have been their "English brethren". When they were ready, their Government was to respond to their wishes more quickly, or at any rate more palpably, than could happen in mature, refined, ornamented, secretive, *Venetian* polities. It was in the 'seventies and 'eighties that wholesale buying up of Legislatures by Corporations was developing into a science.[6]

[1] See Young, *Around the World with General Grant*, passim.
[2] XXXVII, 378.   [3] XXXVIII, 917.   [4] XL, 436.   [5] XL, 220.
[6] See Ostrogorski, *Democracy and the Organisation of Political Parties*, II.

America's absorption in home affairs appeared in the peculiar
—not to say extraordinary—character of her Diplomatic
Service. Elsewhere, diplomats were born and not made. (The
better among them were born with a title.) They were astonished to see the Yankees turning scribblers and attorneys
into diplomats; it was putting ploughmen into livery, like
Goldsmith, and calculated to lower the dignity of the profession.
There were vices more real than lack of dignity. Lincoln sent
a politician named Cameron away to a Legation because his
corruption had grown unbearable at Washington[1]—a very
Chinese mode of selection. Besides money-grubbers there were
rich idlers who joined for social purposes and succumbed without a struggle to European wiles. About the end of the century
a beginning was made experimentally of "career diplomacy",
and some youngsters were picked up for training in South
America and the Far East.[2] In our period it was not thought
necessary. The State Secretary in the 'seventies was paid a
beggarly 8000 dollars, and his staff was as slender as his stipend.[3]
There were actually suggestions of abolishing formal diplomacy
and appointing men *ad hoc* for particular negotiations.[4] Even
at the end of the century the U.S. Consul-General at Shanghai
complained that there had *never* been an American consul who
could speak Chinese; that consular buildings were mean; and
that the entire diplomatic and consular staff drew less than
double the salary of the British Minister.[5]

The system had some virtues as well. The Service was more
unbuttoned, had less affectation, than elsewhere; men wrote to
their Chief and stated their views frankly, without the self-
effacing obsequiousness of English despatches. An Envoy who
was a man of character could help to mould policies himself.[6]
Another virtue possessed by American diplomacy, when it was
not corrupt, was a slightly naïve idealism. There was a tendency

[1] Ostrogorski, *Democracy etc.*, II, 114.
[2] See W. F. Sands, *Undiplomatic Memories*.
[3] J. W. Foster, *A Century of American Diplomacy*, 131.
[4] Beard, *Readings in American Government and Politics*, 292.
[5] Jernigan, *China's Business Methods and Policy*, 242–50.
[6] Later, American like other envoys fell to the status of errand-boys.
(E.g. Child, *An American Diplomat Looks at Europe*, ch. 1.)

for ideas of a passing epoch to find in the Service an old age retreat. There were still men who nourished enthusiasm for the simple Republican qualities which steel, beef and oil millions (and their wives) were rendering *démodées* at home. America was still in repute a revolutionary state, not quite respectable, of different stuff from the European "despotisms". She felt that in trade they were all against her. Bingham, Minister at Tokio in our years, "was convinced that all Europe had been organised in opposition to the expansion of the trade of the United States in Asia except Russia and Italy".[1] The rest on their side felt that America was exploiting her "disinterested-ness". Honesty was the best policy for America, because it stood out in relief from the policies of her rivals. In 1877 Bingham welcomed the setting up of mutual representation between Yedo and Peking, as portending Sino-Japanese self-protection against European encroachment.[2] Our Minister Plunkett on the contrary did not want to see China and Japan too friendly. It was for less interested motives than England's that the State Department tried to dissuade Japan from entering the Franco-Chinese war.[3]

America's attitude was well known. But for ill-feeling over immigration into the States it might have led to close diplomatic intimacy between Washington and Peking. When General and Mrs Grant landed at Canton in 1879 the whole town turned out in a "stupendous demonstration"; as soon as they got to Peking they were waited on by the highest functionaries, and for the first time the Temple of Heaven was opened to a foreigner.[4] In Japan, the same; Grant was taken at once to see the Mikado, who shook hands with him and later—more incredible still—visited him in person.[5] England looked askance at American highmindedness and popularity.[6]

[1] Treat, *Diplomatic Relations between the U.S. and Japan*, 26.
[2] *Ibid.* 47.   [3] *Ibid.* 180.
[4] Young, *Around the World with General Grant*, II, 368, 401.
[5] Kennedy (Chargé, Yedo) 15.10.79, Tenterden Papers, 363. 1.
[6] Augell's mission to China in 1880 to negotiate an immigration and commercial treaty was closely watched by England. (Wade 168, 10.12.80; 172, 16.12.80, and tel. 24.12.80, 17. 833; 1, 6.1.81, 17. 857; Thornton (Washington) 172, 7.6.80, 5. 1722.)

A document of 1882, of much human interest, illustrates the idealism of these early days, and the manner in which it might wilt.

As narrated above, Commodore Schufeldt had returned to China expecting to be bowed deferentially into the post of Celestial First Sea Lord and First Lord of the Admiralty, and, as such, Liberator of the Orient. He was grievously disappointed, and in the glum idleness of his hotel he put together a scathing paper of advice to his Government. This he showed in confidence to the telegraph man Dunn, and Dunn (who wanted the Legation's help over telegraph business) felt it his "plain duty" as a British citizen to transmit to Wade as much as he could decipher of Schufeldt's cacography. Dunn, Wade remarked, had precisely the qualities of a successful newspaper reporter.[1]

He landed in China, said Schufeldt, a citizen of a free country, "a friend of humanity who always felt for the underdog", with a fixed belief that foreign—"and especially English"—policy in China was grasping and oppressive. "His blood boiled when he saw force applied to coerce an unwise, ignorant, obstinate, but absolutely helpless people." The United States, he held, must stand up for human rights. But now, he had come to perceive the corruption of the Chinese Government. He had felt upon him the "cold, cruel eye" of Li Hung-chang. Worst of all, he realised that the Empress was "an immoral woman". Our honest Yankee must have been shocked by Tzu Hsi's striking unlikeness to a White House hostess. He recanted all his opinions. He now found American policy in the Far East contemptibly weak. China must be handled with "justice untainted by sentimentality". A Confucian nation would never learn to fight. America would one day have enormous Pacific interests, and ought to lay the foundations at once.[2]

French activity in our period took place against a background of economic change and depression, both producing restlessness.

---

[1] Wade 1 Very conf., 16.1.82, 17. 895. The sympathy with downtrodden China lingered till at least the end of the century; see e.g. Mrs Conger's *Letters from China*. But Jernigan's book, in 1904, marks a change; it is quite free from "sentimentality" as regards China.

[2] With Wade 1.

Railways and America had brought competition in grain into the French home market. Industrial progress was discouraged by the loss of Alsace-Lorraine. Prices were sagging, and manufacturers calling for protection, but the expiry of commercial treaties had to be awaited, and the great Méline tariff did not come until 1891. Colonising was a welcome supplement.

It was a distinguishing feature of French economy that after the fall of the Empire industry progressed only along certain lines, at least up to the end of the century, while energy poured into finance. The concentration of French banking was in progress in our period. The Press was notoriously under financial control, and links between finance and politics were remarkably close. It was under essentially financial inspiration that France acted in the Far East. The less trade a country had there, the less reason it had for not starting a war.[1]

Political conditions added to the restlessness of overseas policy. There was, for instance, Boulanger. Ministries were transient and embarrassed, and their members often trivial. "Some of the Foreign Ministers of France in recent years", wrote Dilke, "have been of the calibre of chairmen of the Metropolitan Board."[2] Ferry, according to Granville, "arrived at the Quai d'Orsay quite ignorant of foreign affairs".[3] When the Freycinet Government was formed, reshuffling of personnel extended even to the Foreign Office. Bourée went to China as a result of it.[4] The splintering of parties made it easy for a few votes in the Chamber to exercise influence;[5] at the same time public ferment made a striking foreign policy desirable, and this could not be had inside Bismarck's Europe.

[1] See H. D. White, *French International Accounts*, and C. Southworth, *French Colonial Venture*. Both tend to show that France's empire—like part, but only part, of our own—represented from first to last a swindling of the nation by high finance; a species of capital levy on behalf of the Banks.

[2] *Present Position of European Politics*, 92.

[3] Lord E. Fitzmaurice, *Life of Lord Granville*, II, 434.

[4] Hanotaux, *Contemporary France*, IV, 516 (Eng. ed.).

[5] The system of Grand Committees lent itself especially to the shuffling of financial cards. (See R. K. Gooch, *French Parliamentary Committee System*.)

A French writer sums up thus the position reached:

Arrivé au pouvoir dans les années 1880, le cabinet Jules Ferry, jouet de l'oligarchie financière, entreprit une politique d'expansion coloniale intense, organisa une série de guerres coloniales (Tunisie, expédition au Tonkin, etc.). Cette politique déçut totalement la petite bourgeoisie dont les suffrages avaient porté les opportunistes au pouvoir.

Une explosion de mécontentement aigu suivit dans le pays la croissance du capitalisme, l'évincement de la petite industrie et du petit commerce, la crise économique, la crise de l'agriculture....[1]

It was not long since an English traveller in Germany, puffing a sixpenny cigar, was gaped at as a millionaire.[2] Berlin could still strike a visitor as an unpretentious sort of capital.[3] But Treitschke was lecturing on the British Empire, and Nietzsche was waging more brilliant and less successful warfare against the *Bildungsphilisterei* of modern Teutonism.

Germany in the 'eighties was not a leading Power in China, but she already wished to be one, and nothing that an un-scrupulous diplomacy could achieve was neglected. The German Satan was landing on Mount Niphates and viewing what lay around. He saw in the Far East "a boundless field of action".[4] Von Brandt was credited with a wish to start a Sino-Japanese conflict.[5] The Japanese Foreign Minister remarked in 1880 "that he had of late observed signs of renewed activity on the part of German representatives in the East"—the German at Yedo said he regretted that Germany in the past had not annexed part of Formosa.[6] (There had been suggestions of such a move in the 'sixties.[7]) As a weak naval Power, Germany was at a disadvantage; one reason for working with Russia. In 1880 she proposed the neutralisation of the China Seas,[8] a

---

[1] Vidal, *Mouvement Ouvrier Français*. "Les élections de 1885 ont rassemblé à un plebiscite anticolonial; le mot 'Tonkinois' est devenu une injure." (Deschamps, *Histoire de la Question Coloniale en France*, XIII.)
[2] S. Whitman, *German Memories*, 25.   [3] Rennell Rodd, *Memoirs*, ch. II.
[4] Bülow, *Imperial Germany*, ch. VIII.   [5] Kennedy 12, 24.1.80, 46. 256.
[6] Kennedy 13, 24.1.80, 46. 256.   [7] Keltie, *Partition of Africa*, 170.
[8] F.O. to Wade, 17, 2.2.80, 17. 827.

rather devious outcome of this factor. Berlin was very keen on having a German nominated as successor to Hart at the head of the Customs Service, a pretension England was determined to resist.[1] According to one diplomat, the seizure of Kiaochow was no new thought: "In his time Prince Bismarck had dreamt of extensive operations in China, and had actually fixed in 1868 upon Kiao Tchao as the necessary 'jumping off' place."[2] In 1886 a syndicate inclusive of Krupp had an agent in China, and was said to be trying, with Bismarck's resolute assistance, to get railway and other concessions worth at least £30,000,000. The Times raised an alarm.[3]

Foreign trade was already fundamental to Germany, and she was organising herself for scientific competition. Political pressure, diplomatic intrigue, price-cutting, all aimed at monopolising markets. It was a strategy not remotely akin to colonising. Concentration of industry and fusion of industrial with banking capital, which became the most striking feature of Germany's economy, were already in progress. It was the concentration undergone in the 'seventies by coal, metallurgy and chemicals, that enabled these industries to join effectively in agitating for tariffs when depression set in at the end of the decade.[4] Tariffs in turn further stimulated the process. Seventy Cartels were formed between 1879 and 1885. The diminishing number of magnates in control of these industrial complexes were also getting hold of the strings that made the German Eagle flap his wings.

These features in Germany's economy combined with the ambitions of Hamburg exporters to produce an agitation for colonies to which the Government in 1884 abruptly gave way. Bismarck was as unwilling to enter the colonial gambling-house as Lord Granville, who was succumbing at the same time in England. He was not at all given to analysing the economics of international struggle. He discussed politics always in terms

[1] F.O. to Wade 102 conf., 27.7.80, 17. 894.
[2] Schelking, Game of Diplomacy, ch. III.
[3] The Times, 2.2.86; see also Economist, 9.6.86.
[4] Clapham, Economic Development of France and Germany, 310.

of national units. But it was a favourite saying of his: "You cannot regulate a current, much less attempt to go against it; at most you may succeed in steering carefully with it." He wanted armaments to defend his unified empire, and there must be money for them. There must also be money for insurance schemes to counteract socialism. The "Exceptional Law" was passed in 1878, and in 1880 the Socialist Party voted the achievement of socialism "by any means". It is really accident that Bismarck did not find the colonies he needed in the Far East.[1] Had there been war in 1880, or had the Tonking war gone heavily against China, a German Shantung would have been seen twenty years earlier.

For Englishmen of that time Russia was an entity constituted of pure evil; *negotium perambulans in tenebris*—the thing that walked in darkness.

To penetrate old Russia is as difficult for the historian's pen as for the invader's sword. Russia was a mist-clouded, malevolent, above all an expanding thing. Why expanding, hardly anyone gave a thought to. What was it that was bringing into the Far East the tall, bullying Russian of Japan's popular imagination, with his long beard and huge nose?[2] Writers will speak of Russia being lured into Asia by the "mysterious ties of an ancient kinship"[3]—apparently the Russian spirit was Slav in Europe and Mongol in Asia. "Russia wanted the Straits...." "Russia had a vital interest in Corea...." But the Bronze Horseman of Pushkin stared from beside the dark Neva across millions of peasant insects as ignorant of Corea as of Atlantis. "Our noble, mighty Russia, our holy mother!..."[4] Impulses of foreign policy arose from that welter of peoples and oppressions as "ideas" come from the intestines and the glands.

[1] In 1871 Hamburg wanted Cochin China annexed. (M. E. Townsend, *Rise and Fall of Germany's Colonial Empire*, 63.)

[2] Granville wrote in 1872: "I can understand the Russians pining for Constantinople, but why they should push on to the extreme East I cannot understand." (*Life*, II, 410.) For the popular Japanese idea of the Russians see cartoons in *Japan Monthly*, a propaganda magazine in English of 1904.

[3] A phrase used, assuredly with irony, by Li at Moscow.

[4] Dostoievsky, Letter to Maikov, 18.1.56.

Russian self-enlargement at the expense of China had something peculiarly unaccountable about it. Old China and Old
Russia seem to share a common undifferentiated backwardness.
Bureaucracy, corruption, famine, poverty, agriculture—one
description seems to serve for both. Religion in both consisted
of a naïve animism, though China's anti-missionary riots were
no parallel to the pogroms or the May Laws of 1882.

Skoboleff, it is said, viewed his Central Asian campaign simply
as a diversion to keep Britain's mind off the inevitable war for
the Bosphorus.[1] It is notorious also that the expansion in
Central Asia was often the work of irresponsible agents—
officers whose promotion could come only by active service,
who attacked the next tribe because they wanted medals, or
merely because Turkestan was a dull place. Pursuit, ambush,
massacre, went on in the retreating gloom on the border of
civilisation, despairing fights of savage figures against the Russian
vanguards in the flickering light of burning tents. It was all at
a vast distance. There was no one to stop it. Russia came to
resemble a snake, unable to cease swallowing. One suspects
that had Russia annexed the five continents, outlying officials
would have started annexing one another, from pure force of
habit. In 1886 the Naval Department wanted to annex Hawaii.[2]

But not soldiers only were interested in Turkestan. When the
Russians began to penetrate Central Asia it was thought to
be a rich country—"regarded almost as a promised land".[3]
The most solid enticement was cotton, raised in value by the
American Civil War. After the conquest, indeed, officialdom
was slow in fostering cotton cultivation. It was precisely about
1880 that firms began buying land to plant cotton, and introducing the right grades.[4] Witte points out how the Samarkand
Railway built in 1881–4 at once stimulated cotton-growing in

[1] Marvin, *Railway Race to Herat* (pamphlet of 1885).
[2] Rosen, *Forty Years of Diplomacy*, I, 82. Count Baranoff, a hard-drinking
Governor of Alaska in the early nineteenth century, had the idea of colonising
Hawaii: there was a Russian flag hoisted at Honolulu and fighting at Waimea,
where relics of a Russian fort survive. (Papers of the Hawaian Historical
Society, 1892–1908, no. 6.)
[3] Schuyler, *Turkestan*, II, 212.
[4] Woeikoff, *Le Turkestan Russe*, 255.

Bokhara.[1] From then, the acreage sown rose by leaps and bounds. Equal success could be hoped for in a Chinese colony; and better success in other respects, for in Turkestan it was found that crops could only be grown without irrigation above 400 metres altitude.[2]

The interest in cotton is an illustration of how confusing is the habit of describing Tsarist Russia as "feudal". In a purely feudal state there would not even be professional soldiers to hang about and make trouble on the frontiers. Russia had undergone modifications since feudal days, in the same way as the Western countries, though more slowly. In sixteenth-century Russia the old feudal classes were splitting into groups and an urban class was growing up to challenge them; and about 1800—the Romanoffs had always had intimate connections with trade—the talk of the Court was of "business, potash, hemp, flax, and the like".[3] Merchant capital played a strong part in the nineteenth century. It is easy to see how the early seventeenth-century adventurers who fought with Chinese soldiers by the Amur were in search of furs and such articles: merchants in those days were a sturdy race, and did their fighting for themselves. Later, trading interests were concealed under the more ostentatious activity of the military. The weightiest of them was the tea trade. Large fortunes were made out of the painful caravan route across Mongolia, and tea merchants were among the influential citizens of Moscow. Kiachta, the caravan depot, was very prosperous; in the 'forties its annual commerce was estimated—liberally—at 100,000,000 roubles.[4] "Russia draws great advantage from the China trade", said a Russian pamphleteer.[5] The trade frequently desired protection against Chinese officials, or it wanted lower duties. Since camel transport of 35,000,000 lb. of tea annually across Mongolia was expensive, the trade would stand to benefit from a Kiachta-Peking railway or telegraph; also, like

[1] *Memoirs*, 341.   [2] Woeikoff, *Le Turkestan Russe*, 3.
[3] Pokrovsky, *Brief History of Russia*, I, 84.
[4] Wells Williams, *The Middle Kingdom*, I, 207.
[5] Muller and Pallas, *Conquest of Siberia*.

Russian shipping interests, it could do with a warm water Pacific port—exactly as in former years merchants had inspired Russia's struggle for an ice-free Baltic port.

Industrial capital existed in the nineteenth century side by side with its forerunner, though their interests were not always at one. It was only after the reforms of 1861 that industry gained a real chance. On the one hand, the ranks of the— partially servile—labour previously employed by it needed to be swelled by peasants free to leave the land. At the same time, the backwardness of the old agricultural community had to be broken down before a large home market could come into existence. The latter process was far advanced in the 'eighties, when there was an enormous export of grain and import of machinery for large-scale farming. Enclosures had once per- formed the same function in England. There were 706,000 industrial workers in 1865, 1,433,000 in 1890. "By the begin- ning of the twentieth century, Russia was definitely and un- questionably a country of developed industrial capitalism."[1]

But the home market thus being created could not keep pace with productive power. Customers were many but poor. Foreign markets had to be sought. English traders and officials did not understand this need, for absolutely, compared with theirs, Russian output was negligible. Russian traders were importunate because they were weak. The Russian tariff must accompany Russian goods like a tutor. Central Asia was seized. Admirable in size, it was less so as a market, because it turned out that, especially after Kaufmann and Skoboleff had covered themselves with glory, there were hardly any people in it.[2] Thoughts sped on to China. In China there were at least plenty of people. China had the most unobtrusive of tariff protection, and even that could be beaten down on the land frontier. But China suffered from foreign competition, which Russian industry was not strong enough to cope with.

[1] Lenin, *Development of Capitalism in Russia*.
[2] As Byron wrote of the Russians:
"Achilles' self was not more grim and gory
Than thousands of this new and polished nation...." (*Don Juan*, 7. 14.)

Hence the perpetual craving for extension, in one shape or another, of political control over North China. The Russo-Chinese crisis of our period bears strong traces of economic motive. The treaty which ended it dealt largely with commercial points, and Russia stood firm on these while giving way on the territorial issue. And, while it may be true that the influence at work was still that of mercantile capital rather than industrial, and that Russia wanted to sell other goods besides her own in the East, it seems clear that Russian *goods* were being thought of as well as Russian *merchants*. In May 1880, while the quarrel was at its height, the Society of the Volunteer Fleet held its Business Meeting, in the Ainitchin Palace, and its President, the great Pobedonostsef himself, observed that attention in Russia was now concentrating itself on the Far East. He deplored the competition felt by Russian goods in Russia's own east-Asiatic possessions, and announced that the Society's committee had arranged with Moscow tea merchants to carry freight for them, and with the Ministry of Marine "for the yearly transport of prisoners and stores to the Island of Sakhalin".[1]

A complication of the economic position bears on our special period. The 'eighties were years of depression. All countries were producing more of everything; naturally, they all found themselves so much the poorer—this did not begin in 1931. Russian wheat was by now geared not only to a market but to an international market, and with American and other competition the price fell from 8.87 roubles in 1871 to 4.51 in 1896.[2] Cargo capacity of shipping at Russian ports fell by a third between 1878 and 1881.[3] 1878–82 was a stagnant time in railway construction—hence Russia badly wanted to have the building of Bulgaria's railways. The results of the depression looked in several ways to the Far East. Low food prices would enable the manufacturers to produce more goods. Capital would flow from agriculture into industry. The power of the home

[1] Report with Dufferin 235, 26.5.80, 65. 1080.
[2] Pokrovsky, *Brief History of Russia*, I, 202.
[3] Lenin, *Development of Capitalism in Russia*, 341.

market to absorb goods would weaken. The Far Eastern market was the more urgently required. Bureaucrats, it is true, were notably vague about the uses to which they would put China once she was conquered. By a confusion of ideas they dreamed of enriching themselves there in the same way as the British had done in India. When news of the Boxer outbreak reached St Petersburg, Kuropatkin the War Minister hurried to Witte "beaming with joy" at the thought that now Manchuria could be annexed. "I was curious", Witte remarks, "to know what my visitor intended to do with Manchuria once it was occupied."[1]

How did economic forces in Russia translate themselves into political terms?

Formally, the Tsar was of all rulers the most inaccessible to influence. The dull-witted Alexander III, chopping his trees and filling his stupid diary, decided everything over a sixth of the world's land surface. The absurdity of the fiction is sufficient to hint that private influence really had great scope. To begin with the Autocrat of all the Russias himself, he was head of a family with colossal financial interests of every sort. "It is known that on one occasion in the 'eighties Alexander III transferred the sum of 300 million roubles from one foreign bank to another."[2] This family, moreover, had an excessively growing number of mouths to fill. Then, industry was nourished upon capital borrowed and distributed by the Government, and fattened largely upon Government orders. Its Far Eastern visions would not find Ministers indifferent. The Government itself was always hard up, and always in hopes of loot from fresh colonies. Central Asia was won very cheaply, which probably encouraged ideas that a conquest of North China would be equally lenient on the Budget.

Yet there was not any regular, exact correspondence between commercial wishes and official actions. Bureaucratic corruption was useful here and there, but it was altogether too wholesale—when the state might fall at any moment into clutches of a

[1] *Memoirs*, 107.
[2] Pokrovsky, *Brief History of Russia*, I.

Bezobrazov or a Rasputin.[1] When the three rockets went up into the dark from the Golden Hill at Port Arthur in 1904 and announced the declaration of war, the fortress became a confusion of soldiers trying to find unmapped posts, the streets swarmed with spies, officers were sunk in orgies.[2] It was all symbolic of Russian administration. Officialdom did not faithfully interpret the interests of any one section of the people. At the last gasp of Tsarism it dwindled away to what in theory it had always been—the Tsar himself; even bureaucrats wanted reform and a constitution.

Russian policy emerged—spasmodically—out of the uneasy creakings of a very ramshackle machine. There was no Cabinet; each Minister paddled his own Department. A British Intelligence agent, in St Petersburg during the war, found that "every department seemed to have a Secret Service and nobody exercised any central control"; while the Office of the General Staff stopped work on every public holiday.[3] Alexander III was perfectly ignorant of finance. Obviously a man with all *his* work to do—to say nothing of his *Mujik-verstand*, as Herbert Bismarck called it—could not give any thought to Far Eastern intricacies; if he gave orders, they were hasty plunges, or else routine. Russia never possessed anything that could be dignified with the name of a Policy; which was why opponents stood in awe of her supposedly profound strategy. "Russian policy is the incarnation of the Russian mind", and has "almost

---

[1] Cp. De Schelking's description (*Game of Diplomacy*, ch. v) of the salon of an ex-mistress of Nicholas II. "Grand Dukes rubbed shoulders with a crowd of interlopers and ne'er do wells. . . .Orders for war material, railway concessions and many other matters of like character were there talked over and contracted for." Witte writes contemptuously of the aristocrats who besieged him for concessions—"It was then that I found out of what inferior stuff all these people with ancient names were made." (*Memoirs*, 52.) Leroy Beaulieu (*Empire of the Tsars*, Eng. ed. Part II, 101) points out what an extension was given to official corruption by the development of a Stock Exchange.

[2] E. K. Nojine, *Truth about Port Arthur*, 3. An Admiral at Vladivostok was discovered in 1885 to be in Chinese pay. (O'Conor 366, 28.7.85, 17. 983.)

[3] Sir S. Hoare, *The Fourth Seal*, 52.

invariable success "....The crowning example of this incarnation was when Goremikin, President of the Council of Ministers, *slept* through the discussion on the Austrian Ultimatum of 1914.[1] The point is not, of course, that it made any difference whether Goremikin was asleep or awake.

What is to be said of the Foreign Office itself? It was enveloped in mystery. Each and all of its documents were marked *Secret*. Its strategy came upon the other capitals out of a dark room. By some, it was credited accordingly with prodigious subtlety and concentration.[2] There are a good many indications of a different sort. Rosen speaks of "the usual delay with which communications were answered".[3] The Office had to put up with intermeddling in its policies by the Department of War.[4] It had also to manage the Tsar, sometimes by devious routes. Mouraviev kept in with his master by amusing the Empress with feeble jokes.[5] The diplomatic service did not always answer to the helm. For the highest post, there was a paucity of talent. Lobanov had to be succeeded by the Minister at Copenhagen. Probably most Foreign Ministers, like their colleagues in London, knew next to nothing about the Far East. "In those years", Witte writes, "very few statesmen in Russia had a clear notion about Korea, Japan, and, especially, China and their mutual relations. Prince Lobanov-Rostovsky, Foreign Minister, knew no more about the Far East than the average schoolboy."[6] Rosen says that Mouraviev's knowledge had "almost incredible deficiencies".[7] Alexander III liked to order his Ministers about like clerks, and Giers was ready to "stand to attention, hand to cap, saying 'Yes, Sire; Yes, Sire'." Giers said, and perhaps believed, that Russia had done enough

[1] Schelking, *Game of Diplomacy*, ch. x.
[2] E.g. Diósy, *The New Far East*, 3: "The imperturbable statesmen, unhampered by Parliament or Press, who steadfastly direct the unchanging policies of the Russian Empire, were, as usual, prepared for any emergency."
[3] *Forty Years of Diplomacy*, I, 158.
[4] Rosen (I, 153) says that the scheme of drilling the Corean army was a favourite hobby-horse of the War Office.
[5] Witte, *Memoirs*, 115.   [6] *Ibid.* 82.
[7] *Forty Years of Diplomacy*, I, 175.

annexing, but he could not stop the process.[1] According to Schelking, in the Afghan crisis of 1885 "M. de Giers was in a desperate mental condition of excitement and worry", and was quite unable to make the Tsar see reason.[2]

Yet it is clear that a great deal of thought was expended by *someone* on the Far Eastern problem. The Office was divided into the "Ministerial Chancellery", where European affairs were dawdled over by bureaucratic heads and gentlemanly scribes, and the famous "Asiatic Department", with its somewhat sinister repute. It observed an especial secrecy.[3] Its social standing was lower than that of the Chancellery; there was less reluctance to employ—barely baptised—Jews, it being felt that more than the brains of a noble cadet were needed. One dimly distinguishes a group of men whose whole minds were engrossed in the intricacies of policy—diplomatic chess-masters like Holstein, men without other interests. When Russia thought, it was with their brains. How she acted, might be a different matter. Dilke met Vlangali (who of course had served at Peking) and Jomini in Russia, and noted in his Diary that with them and "their marvellous subordinates, Hamburger the hunchback Jew, and his head of the Asiatic Department, Westmann, I do not wonder that two stupid men, Gortschakoff and the drill-sergeant Giers, were able successively to pretend to rule the Foreign Office without the policy of the country suffering".[4]

English critics of their own Diplomatic Service were much given to admiring that of Russia. But from Schelking, who entered it in 1883, we hear of farcical examinations, entrance by influence, fossilised seniors, young men sent to remote posts without the slightest information about them. In Rosen's pages we find nepotism, indiscipline, "incredible levity".[5]

[1] See his circular to Russian agents on the accession of Alexander III. (Lowe, *Alexander III*, 78.)   [2] Schelking, *Game of Diplomacy*, ch. 1.
[3] "The energies of the Asiatic Department are always directed towards the suppression of news relating to developments in the direction of the frontier." (Krausse, *Russia in Asia*, 145.)   [4] *Life of Dilke*, I, 117.
[5] Rosen, *Forty Years of Diplomacy*, I, 65, 107, 129.

Some of these qualities might make Russian diplomacy more, not less, disquieting to other countries. A memorandum by the German Foreign Office in 1884, for instance, complained of the "activity of members of a Russian embassy in stirring up agitation".[1] Some of the methods employed could not easily be countered by staid British diplomats; someone narrates having seen a row of assassins sitting outside the Russian Legation at Bucharest, waiting for jobs.[2] As regards the Far East, an exception seems to have been made to the lounging tone of the Service; there was promotion by merit, and admission of Jews.[3]

The political landscape of the 'eighties was moulded by economic depression and social disintegration; reactionary agrarian policy, discontent, fear. The terrorist "Executive Committee" came into being in 1877. Its Resolution of August 1879 declared war on the Tsar in person. Next year there was an abortive attempt, and General Gourko informed the troops in an Order of the Day: "En sauvant Son Élu la Providence a de nouveau manifesté Sa grace infinie." But Providence was to become impatient of the too many calls upon it, and its grace proved less than infinite. A year later the doomed monarch met his end. The Nihilist Manifesto which in vain called on his son to institute reform was followed by a series of desperate attempts against his life, followed by the public, Pokrovsky remarks, with the keenest interest, like a hunt.[4] The Autocrat had to shut himself up under as close a guard as his Siberian prisoners. Mme Waddington's letters in 1883—her husband represented France at the Coronation—embody the tension then prevailing. "I really am nervous", she wrote on learning that she was to go—"...Russian Nihilists and dynamiters are terrible elements to contend with." It spoiled her sleep, and when she got to Moscow she and her fellow-*ambassadrices* were divided between fears of being blown up in the Opera, the Kremlin, anywhere, and "hideous tales" of ladies becoming

---

[1] *Grosse Politik*, III, 365.
[2] Diösy, *The New Far East*, 343.
[3] *Ibid*. 342.   [4] *Brief History of Russia*, 197.

entangled in their train while backing away from the Tsar.[1] The Government was reduced to pitiable straits when it had to organise a counter-terrorist "Holy Brotherhood", and the sober Witte found himself in Paris with a colleague commissioned to assassinate Hartmann.[2] More serious still—for Nihilism was a dying force after the triumph of 1881—was the industrial discontent. With the depression, factories and mills were turning off half their workers. Between 1881 and 1886 there were forty-eight large-scale strikes, affecting 80,000 workmen.[3] The Morozov strike of 1885 is a landmark. "With regard to Russia", Bismarck had said, "no one knows what eruption of revolutionary elements may suddenly break out in the interior of the huge Empire."[4] The authorities were frightened into granting a pretence of factory legislation, and the industrial crisis was allayed by tariffs, but, as in Germany, the need to secure a degree of prosperity to the country and keep the people quiet was a factor to encourage expansionist ideas.[5]

It was a period of morbid psychology. The upper classes were infected with the scepticism, the "world-weariness", so often portrayed by Tchekov, and which Tchaikovsky distilled into music. Nekrassov's great poem was published in 1879,[6] and the melancholy of the poet who had lived in boyhood near the Vladimirsky road and watched the prisoners driven towards Siberia, found a home in his readers' souls. As the Russian armies spread across Asia, the deep Russian pessimism,

[1] Letters of 18.3.83, 6.5.83. The Nihilist movement is very interestingly described in Leroy Beaulieu's *Empire of the Tsars*, Part II, 510 ff.

[2] Witte, *Memoirs*, 22.

[3] Pokrovsky, *Brief History of Russia*, 223.

[4] *Grosse Politik*, III, 39.

[5] Bismarck wrote to the Kaiser in 1885: "If the Russian army is unemployed, it becomes a danger to the internal security of the empire and of the dynasty." (*Grosse Politik*, IV, 124.) Probably one idea of the Government was to find areas where dispossessed peasants could be settled, instead of drifting into the towns and swelling the dangerous urban crowds. Far Eastern settlements offered a certain scope.

[6] "Who Can be Happy in Russia?"

welling from a tragically disharmonic society, crept West-
wards across Europe. The spirit of Pobedonostsef was supreme.

A good state—according to a modern Japanese publicist—
will take as its first aim the perfecting of itself by "benevolence
and sincerity". "Then, this leading nation will be tempted to
embark on a grand scheme of reconstructing the whole world
for the benefit of humanity."[1] To judge by Japan's foreign
policy, she would appear to have perfected herself very early
after beginning to modernise. It is true that, had we not been
better informed, it would have been easy to confuse Japan's
modern forays abroad with the piracy she cultivated so flourish-
ingly in the Middle Ages.

Examination of Japan's problems and policies in the early
'eighties shows that they were in all essentials the same as when,
in 1895, Japan first came into the limelight as China's newest
conqueror. Except in degree of military strength, Japan was
ready for wars of aggression ten years earlier, and almost
attempted them. It seems at first sight a freak that a country
barely out of danger of being "colonised" should think of
colonies for itself. Some have put it down to imitation of his
betters on the Mikado's part. One need not deny that foreign
example accelerated the internal tendencies at work.

All later Japanese history inherits organic features from the
Restoration. As in the case of Russia, we cannot think of the
archaic Government of former times as undilutedly "feudal".
Usury, for instance, reached in old Japan a quite sophisticated,
one might say a civilised, pitch. Most feudal lords borrowed
heavily, and the Shogunate itself was well versed in financial
subtleties. "There seems no end to the cunning doings of the
Shogunate in its currency revisions", which always yielded
profit to officials and bullion dealers;[2] there was much writing
on monetary theory. There was a considerable amount of
trading capital inside the feudal framework. The lords of

---

[1] Fujisawa, *Japanese Political Philosophy*. An almost unbelievably absurd book.
[2] Yosoburo Takekoshi, *Economic Aspects of the History of the Civilisation
of Japan*, III, 215.

Satsuma and Tsushima flourished by importing Chinese and Corean goods.[1] Society was already quite complex. A large noble class lived on the cultivators, and, with the onset of money economy, tried to meet the increasing cost of Court or city life by dabbling in trade. Their chiefs, the daimios, lived in somnolent parasitism. The Tokugawas, simply daimios who had achieved a military supremacy, were weakened by the gradual transformation of feudal society, and by their inability to protect Japan against foreign aggression. Some samurai drifted entirely into commerce; some *chonin*, moneyed men, bought land. The heads of the *Kumiai* or trade-guilds "were already partly in the position of capitalists".[2]

Modern Japanese orthodoxy explains 1868 as a triumph of pure national consciousness. One exponent of the view awakens our suspicions by assuring us that the Japanese peasants regarded taxation as "a loyal duty in which they took more or less pride".[3] The real moving forces are obscured by the fact that, formally, it was the feudal lords themselves who transferred power from the Shogun to the Mikado and then—crowning paradox— "abolished feudalism". Of course the Restoration was not a measure consciously conceived and carried out by anyone. The Tokugawas were seen to be failing for several years before 1868, and the clans that had always unwillingly submitted to them were preparing to be in at the death. At the same time the lower samurai disliked the incompetence of the effete nobles who filled the hereditary clan offices. The real revolution occurred unobtrusively inside the clans, in the taking away of control from the daimios by their lower officers and advisers. The latter were possessed by the *cupido rerum novarum*. They needed new sources of income, they wanted a stronger Government to protect the nation. The danger of foreign attack complicated and accelerated these currents. The Imperial Court at Kyoto was carrying on propaganda, because the Shogunate's decline inspired it with hope, but it had no clear programme.

---

[1] Honjo, "Transition from the Tokugawa Period", in *Kyoto Univ. Econ. Review*, 1932.   [2] Takekoshi, *Economic Aspects etc.*, 256–7.
[3] Uyehara, *Political Development of Japan*, 28.

At one stage the Shogunate was in favour of admitting foreign trade as a necessity, while Kyoto, out of touch with foreign affairs and simply in a factious spirit, opposed it. It was accident that, in a complex series of intrigues on the part of domestic parties and foreign agents, brought the Meroving ruler back from his long seclusion, as nominal autocrat in an oligarchy based on the now dominant samurai of certain clans, and their sleeping partners in the cities.

The tutelary spirit whose home was the crater of Fujiyama watched henceforward over a new country. The samurai, in place of their rice revenues, received Government posts or bonds. Only those of the leading clans could be accommodated in the new bureaucracy, swollen as this might be. The Government encouraged them to enter trade. The gilt swords of former days were bought up by dealers in curiosities. Daikoku the God of Wealth outshone all his rivals in the pantheon. Some of the translated warriors prospered, and, with such of the old commercial elements as could adapt themselves to changed times, founded Japan's economic strength. Others could not do so, and were miserably stranded.[1] Their bonds were soon capitalised at rates amounting to confiscation. The lords—stage-managed by their energetic clansmen[2]—surrendered their privileges to the Throne. Their manifesto repented anachronistically the depravity of their ancestors in laying hands on rights that should pertain to the Mikado alone. What did this new "Night of August 4" signify? Feudal administration was handed over to the bureaucracy. The lord's trading monopolies in his fief disappeared. As local governor he was pensioned off, but, freed from all duties and burdens, he was better off than before.[3]

Commercial ambition was now given its head, for economic

---

[1] See E. I. Sugimoto, *A Daughter of the Samurai*, ch. IV, for a story of a samurai who failed to adapt himself.

[2] "The daimio, it cannot be too often repeated, was a nobody...and his intellect, owing to his education, was nearly always far below par." (Satow, *Diplomat in Japan*, 38.)

[3] As Mounsey pointed out (*The Satsuma Rebellion*, 49–50).

progress was peremptorily needed if Japan was to keep herself alive. But progress was faced with barriers. On account of the foreign-imposed treaties, industry could not be fostered by tariffs. Government, to find revenue, had to monopolise various fields of profit which were thus lost to the new middle class. Most important, the "emancipation" of the agricultural masses was, as in Russia, incomplete; their status and tenure had always been intricate, and the Government was slow to define what it had become. Whatever independence may have been intended for them was soon nullified by the burdens laid on them. Tax-paying and usury quickly developed the already existing movement towards speculation and investment in land, and a fungus of small landowners spread over the country-side, mingling with what remained of the older, feudal, land-owning class. Industrial growth could not be vigorous enough to arrest this tendency by drawing capital into manufacture and away from parasitical rent-sucking. As it was, industry had to adapt itself to the state of affairs, sinking roots of its own into the agrarian system through loan-companies, speculation in rice, sale of fertilisers at monopolist prices, and through drawing a cheap labour supply from pauperised village families. All this was bound to weaken the home market so far as long-term prospects went. The Japanese manufacturer could produce goods, but to whom was he to sell them? Here lay one cause of the startlingly early demand for colonies.[1] Simultaneously, population was rising, grain had to be imported from Corea; an independent Corea could cut off these supplies in time of scarcity. The Government was directly concerned, since in the absence of tariffs it had to foster business by subsidies and super-vision.[2] In addition, political life was quite corrupt enough to

[1] Cp. Tanin and Yohan, *Militarism and Fascism in Japan*, ch. 1, and Freda Utley, *Japan's Feet of Clay*, passim.

[2] In 1885, for example, the Government ordered the amalgamation of the two big steamer companies, the Mitsubishi and the Kyodo Unyu. "A stronger case", said Plunkett warmly (for foreign enterprise suffered by these tactics), "of Government interference with the ordinary operations of commerce can not be imagined." (213, 28.9.85, 46. 334.)

allow of commercial interests exerting influence. Okuma, who founded his party in protest against the jobbing off of public property to a private company,[1] was himself accused in the 'eighties of being in close relations with the Mitsubishi.

The political situation in the early 'eighties was, then, exceedingly tense. Impoverished swordsmen and struggling salesmen clamoured for war and promotion, war and profit: there was thus both a "Right" and a "Left" Opposition pushing in the same direction, while the Government's immediate basis was only a dominant clique drawn from a few clans. It was not at all the perfect machine, the organiser of victory, that later successes made it appear. Corea, of course, was viewed as natural prey, as in the old days when the legendary but well-named Empress Jingo had set off, cheered by miraculous omens, to conquer it. Some Japanese statesmen were willing enough to plunge into action, because in the excitement of war "they saw the outlet for the seditious and turbulent portion of the population".[2] Others, less incautious, were able to discern the risks involved, and one can believe that they sometimes felt they had been modernising their people too fast, as a Japanese official remarked to an Austrian globe-trotter on board ship for Ceylon in 1886.[3]

It is not accidental, therefore, that our period was a time of repression on the part of the authorities, and of Liberal sentiment—reflecting a new order striving for power—on the part of the articulate public; which was at the same time violently critical of the Government's lack of success in the Treaty Revision negotiations which were being carried on. The *Japan Daily Herald* (a foreign-owned paper with a grudge against the Government because of a subsidy given to a rival contemporary) wrote in 1884 that to gratify the desire of the ruling clique for power "the aspirations of the nation for political freedom have been despotically and remorselessly crushed..."—and again: "The smouldering embers of dis-

[1] Vinacke, *History of the Far East in Modern Times*, 101.
[2] Parkes 115, 20.3.85, 17. 979.
[3] Baron von Hübner, *Through the British Empire*, I, 388.

content in many *ken*. . . seem to threaten to burst into the flames of insurrection."[1] It was the climax of the Westernising period. European fashions and dress were the rage, and gentlemen might be seen attending functions in evening dress with trousers thrust into top-boots.[2] Men read Western philosophy and political theory (as usual, of the *previous* age), intoxicated themselves with talk of Liberty, wrote novels about Epaminondas,[3] and dreamed of a Constitution. The Social Contract, *laissez-faire*, and all the rest of the flock, migrated from the winter that was overtaking them in Europe to the sunnier climate of Japan. In March 1880 a congress of political societies met at Osaka and demanded an elective assembly. Itagaki organised this year a sort of Liberal Party, rather Jacobin in its methods. Okuma, who while in office had disliked the excessive weight in affairs of the ruling clans,[4] formed another progressive party in 1882, the Rikken Kaishin-to. In the same year was formed a "Conservative Imperialist Party", including Fukuchi, editor of the *Nichi-nichi Shimbun*.[5] A traveller in the interior had noted in 1878: "Very wild political rumours are in the air. . . and it is not very wonderful that the peasantry lack confidence in the existing order of things."[6]

The Government countered in several ways. It promised a constitution within ten years. This promise, and its bogus fulfilment, fobbed off middle-class aspirations until it was possible to satisfy them in another way: by conquest. The whole situation resembled that in Bismarckian Germany. In 1880 a Law of Meeting and Association was promulgated; in 1882 it was stiffened. In 1883 the drastic Press Law of 1875 was tightened.[7] Meanwhile ultra-patriotic ideas were fostered, as an antidote to Liberalism. The authorities endeavoured to

[1] Extracts with Plunkett 16 conf., 16.1.85, 46. 327.

[2] Diösy, *The New Far East*, 66.

[3] One Japanese author was able to retire with a competence after writing a single popular novel on this topic. (B. H. Chamberlain, *Things Japanese*, 291.)   [4] Uyehara, *Political Development of Japan*, 85.

[5] *Ibid.* 92.   [6] Isabella Bird, *Unbeaten Tracks in Japan*, 26.

[7] It is quite wrong to suppose that the Japanese Press was without influence at this date.

conjure up "the broad and deep sympathy which enables (the Japanese) to communicate spiritually with one another".[1] In 1882 a Doctor Kato came out with a Germanising defence of absolution against "natural rights".[2] Liberalism in Japan was to be as fleeting as the embryo's recapitulation of the ancestral fish-life. In 1891 began the custom of bowing to the Mikado's picture.[3]

The prime necessity for the Government was success in foreign policy. Hence the quarrel with China on the Lewchew issue, and the persistent intriguing in Corea. But a rash venture and a defeat would mean ruin. From 1880 to 1885 Japan hesitated on the edge of war. In 1885 the conflicting pressures were intensified, and Japan's hesitations were at their most painful. It is only in this light that Japan's policy in the 'eighties can be studied.

All travellers who saw the Emperor in those days dwell on his inscrutability—the "impassive, reserved, changeless, dark, far-removed countenance".[4] The Mikado had only too much to think of, and only too much reason for not betraying his thoughts.

[1] Fujisawa, *Japanese Political Philosophy*, 76.
[2] Uyehara, *Political Development of Japan*, 115.
[3] B. H. Chamberlain, *Things Japanese*, 76.
[4] Arnold, *Seas and Lands*, ch. XXXVIII. Takekoshi, *Prince Saionji*, 92–113, describes this period of Liberal movements and political unrest.

CHAPTER EIGHTEEN

British Policy

O F Britain's two hereditary enemies, France could, if necessary, be met in a direct fight, in Africa, in Asia, or in the Mediterranean. How to conduct a vendetta with the Tsar was a different problem. His Empire stretched half across the world, hidden in northern fogs. In the centre we held India against it. In the West, we had for decades tried to turn decrepit, crumbling Turkey into a fortified bastion. At the other end of the continent there was another Sick Man. Exactly the same considerations applied there, and with perhaps greater force. If China fell, the way to India would be uncovered on another side, to say nothing of losses to our commerce. If hostility to Russia was indeed an immutable law, and not merely, as one journalist called it, a "moulting and mangy prejudice",[1] China would seem to be marked out by the Englishman's Providence as his partner in an alliance that would combine half the human race.

It was easy after 1895 to inveigh against the "fatal illusion that China was not only our natural ally, but an ally whose alliance was worth cultivating".[2] But was not that being wise after the event? It is decidedly possible to assert that, in the years we have surveyed, informed opinion *on the whole* believed the star of the Chinese Empire to be rising and not setting. This, said Bowen of Hongkong in 1883, was the conviction of all the most competent judges.[3] Ruled either by Christianity or by some Napoleon, wrote a missionary scholar, China must soon powerfully affect the destinies of the world.[4] The *Chinese Recorder* wrote: "It is evident that China has learned much from the conflict (with France), and comes out of it stronger than ever

---

[1] Stead, *Truth about Russia*, 90.　　[2] Chirol, *Far Eastern Question*, 144.
[3] 17. 1010.　　[4] J. Ross, *Corea*, VII.

before."[1] The *Shanghai Courier* wrote that China had "come to be considered as a factor not only in Asiatic but in European politics."[2] There was in England at least one public and official avowal of the same conviction. Speaking in an Opium Debate in 1883, the Parliamentary Under-Secretary said that not long since it had been an open question whether or not China was falling to pieces. "But that day was over. The Chinese Empire in the last few years had shown an extraordinary recuperative power. It...occupied a position in Asia almost equal to the most palmy days of its history." Her Majesty's Government was "fully aware of the great and transcendent importance of a good understanding with that country".[3]

Four of the greatest authorities on China then living placed on record a similar persuasion. "I believe", wrote Sir Thomas Wade in 1880, "that if it can tide through a quarter of a century without a foreign war, this country has a great future before it, and I regard its people as thoroughly deserving the independence they will be well able to maintain."[4] "Hopeful signs abound on every hand", wrote Wells Williams at the end of his monumental survey of China in 1883.[5] A year later Professor Boulger closed his *History* with the words: "We leave China stronger, wiser, and more united within herself than perhaps she has ever been since the dawn of her existence."[6] The same writer had said a little earlier: "A war with China will on the next occasion be no child's play for the best equipped and most determined of nations."[7] And Colquhoun, addressing the London Chamber of Commerce in 1885, said: "The masses of China are in much better case than the masses of Russia—less ignorant, enjoying infinitely greater freedom, and decidedly happier." "Nothing can now prevent China attaining to the position of a formidable Power in Asia." At the end of the Tonking war "people saw visions of Chinamen overrunning the world".[8] A partner in

[1] Jan. 1886.   [2] Quoted in Martin, *Hanlin Papers*, 330.
[3] Hansard, 3rd Series, 277. 1333 ff.   [4] Wade 15, 28.1.80, 17. 829.
[5] *The Middle Kingdom*, II, 738.   [6] *History of China*, III, 949.
[7] *Central Asian Questions*, 312–13.
[8] Grundry, *China and her Neighbours*, 315.

Jardine Matheson, consulted about the opium negotiations, wrote that a settlement *must* be reached, "when we consider that China will henceforth be no longer regarded as 'une quantité négligeable' in the councils of diplomacy".[1] Die-hard editors in the Ports might stick to it that ideas of China becoming strong were due to manipulation of an ignorant London Press by the Tsungli Yamen;[2] elsewhere, Tseng's famous article—"The Sleep and the Awakening"[3]—fell on ready ears.

Besides, the war of 1895 did not necessarily prove anything with regard to China's utility in an Anglo-Russian war. China left alone, to fight without stiffening and mainly by sea, was not the same thing as a China acting behind a British expeditionary force and sheltered by the British navy.

In any case it required an effort to believe that a nation of four hundred millions *could* be so weak as China sometimes seemed. Through our period there were occasional hints that a Chinese alliance with *someone* was in the air. One of Tso's Memorials from Kashgar in 1878 recommended a policy of close friendship with some one Power as a means of defence against the rest; a policy he said Tseng Kuo-fan had mooted in 1869. The plan, commented the British Chargé d'Affaires, would have the drawback that "the Power chosen, no matter where the choice of China might fall, would hardly be free, consistently with her proper engagements elsewhere, to accept a purely selfish and exclusive alliance. Nevertheless, it may be worth notice."[4] In another Memorial Tso put forward as an alternative the grouping of the Powers into a bloc directed against Russian aggression. After discussion in the Grand

---

[1] Bulkeley Johnson to Currie, 6.4.85, 17. 1001.

[2] See a group of articles from the *Shanghai Mercury* of Nov. 1885, in 17. 1004. The Editor, Mr Rivington, was in the habit of sending his best passages to the Foreign Office, which did not much relish them. The first batch were acknowledged, "and this seems to encourage him". (Minute in 17. 941.) Some Old China Hands could still dream of China being regenerated by a fresh Taiping Rebellion. (Hongkong *Daily Press*, 17.3.84.)

[3] *Asiatic Quarterly*, Jan. 1887.

[4] Fraser 105 conf., with copy of Memorial, 27.6.78, 17. 826.

Council the idea was dismissed as impracticable.[1] In 1879 the German *Army Gazette* canvassed a German-Chinese alliance[2]— which *might* have been adopted by Berlin instead of the strategy of partition; Germany would then outflank Russia just as Russia, by joining France, outflanked Germany, and German trade in China would be greatly helped. In 1880 Wade thought that the Yamen would be glad of a defensive alliance with Britain. During the Tonking war China undoubtedly hoped to be joined by Britain. In 1885 the hope was reciprocal. China, like Turkey, had not given up the design of recovering the provinces lost to Russia, and to fulfil it she needed the British fleet. It was to guard against this that Russia was planting settlements in Eastern Siberia; the Volunteer Fleet was bringing out yearly a couple of thousand Cossacks from the Dnieper, who were furnished with land, cattle and tools.[3] England on her part was in the crisis of 1885 quite isolated in Europe. Even Turkey, alienated we may surmise by Gladstone and Egypt, wanted to keep neutral,[4] and there was talk at Constantinople of whether England would force the Straits.[5] Prince Reuss at Vienna remarked truly that England had no longer a friend on the Continent.[6] It is likely that had war broken out in May Turkey would not, against the whole Continent and against her own inclination, have joined us or let our warships into the Black Sea. The war, therefore, would have had to be fought out at the other end of Asia.[7]

[1] Milbanke (Peking) 7 conf., 1.1.79, 17. 826.

[2] Treat, *Diplomatic Relations between the U.S. and Japan*, 83.

[3] Memo. by Parker with O'Conor 309, 18.6.85, 17. 982. It may be suggested that the strain of the 1885 crisis helped to bring about the decision to build the Trans-Siberian Railway.

[4] Radowitz tel. 53 Secret, 23.4.85, *Grosse Politik*, IV, 117.

[5] Radowitz 84 Very conf., 13.4.85, *ibid.* IV, 114.

[6] Reuss (Vienna) 105, 15.4.85, *ibid.* IV, 116.

[7] A German observer in 1890 notes: "Endlich ist in englischen Militär-kreisen die Ansicht verbreitet, dass diese Frage nicht öffentlich behandelt werden dürfen." (*Antagonismus der Englischen und Russischen Interessen in Asien*, von einem Reichsrathsabgeordneten, 132.) He considers Dilke's idea of attacking at Vladivostok strange (p. 137), but neglects the factor of a Chinese alliance.

It is not clear from the Foreign Office papers to what exact point discussions of an alliance went in 1885. They must have consisted mainly of verbal exchanges between Tseng and British officials. Colquhoun was probably right in saying in *The Times* that if war broke out an Anglo-Chinese alliance might be "looked upon as almost a certainty". The clearest light on what was in people's minds is thrown, perhaps, by a letter written to Gladstone in May by Dr Dudgeon, the celebratèd medical missionary of Peking. It was a massive document, on sheets of paper about two feet long. "Nothing", said Dr Dudgeon, "would advance British interests in Asia and Europe *now* and *in the future* more than an alliance offensive and defensive with China and also, if possible, with Japan." Too little heed had been taken of Russian ambitions in the Pacific. Russia meant to take Manchuria, and, if she could, all North China. We had besides to think of dealing with France in Indo-China, and of safeguarding Thibet. Only co-operation with Peking could enable us to face these tasks confidently, and prepare for the inevitable war with Russia. When that came we ought to help China to win back the Amur region, and consolidate the Asiatic khanates into a strong Moslem state under our tutelage. "China has virtually and seriously entered the comity of nations." She could supply us with "limitless material" for "the finest armies in the world". Commercially also, alliance with her would give us much.—When the Liberal Government fell Dudgeon wrote to Salisbury, arguing that a Conservative Government was the natural one to take this great step, which would rid us of the need to buy German friendship with colonial concessions.[1]

Dr Dudgeon's letters were read by several Ministers, and their comments show how seriously the question was taken. Even before reading Dudgeon, noted Lord Northbrook, he had realised how valuable Chinese (and Japanese) help would be in a Russian war, and for subserving Indian interests. "My object in writing this note is to press for serious consideration of the question."[2] When the next Ministry came in Lord

[1] Letters of 2.5.85, 8.7.85, 17. 1002.   [2] 22.5.85, 17. 1002.

G. Hamilton wrote: "The advantages of an alliance with China are so obvious, that the settlement of the opium difficulty has I hope removed the last impediment to such a combination."[1] Mr W. H. Smith agreed with Dudgeon; war with Russia was inevitable, though it ought to be postponed until we were more ready for it. "I am therefore strongly in favour of an alliance or a cordial understanding with China on the basis of a common interest."[2] There is not much trace in these minutes of a love of Splendid Isolation.

In subsequent years, many critics took it for granted that 1885 had left England and China, more or less explicitly, allies. The idea was among the "commonplaces of diplomatic conversation".[3] It grew naturally out of the intimacy forced on the two countries, in spite of their disagreements, by the events of our period. In 1882, requesting permission to place a Chinese consul in Hongkong, the Marquis Tseng said: "Never have the relations between the two countries been so cordial as they are at present."[4] In 1885 Bowen wrote to Lord Kimberley that in case of war with Russia a Chinese diversion in Central Asia would be of the utmost value to us, while with Chinese and Japanese ships to help us we could clear the Pacific and destroy Vladivostok. "Lord Dufferin agrees with me as to the vast importance of extending our intercourse and consolidating our relations with China and Japan, with a view not only to the increase of trade, but also to possible war with Russia in the future."[5] Next year Boulger wrote an article called "England's Two Allies in Asia" in which he expressed a conviction that despatches from our Peking Legation must for years have been advising close co-operation with China.[6] In 1890 a Japanese writer alluded without qualification to "the Anglo-Chinese alliance".[7] In 1896 a Russian diplomat observed that up to the previous year China was always assumed to be the country that England was nursing as her ally.[8]

[1] 25.7.85, 17. 1002.   [2] 24.7.85, 17. 1002.
[3] H. Norman, *Peoples and Politics of the Far East*, 261.
[4] Tseng 22.7.82, 17. 911.   [5] Bowen, *Letters etc.* II, 377.   [6] *Asiatic Quarterly.*
[7] Inagaki, *Japan and the Pacific*, 35.   [8] "Vladimir", *China-Japan War*, 3.

Yet, as a matter of fact, there *was* no alliance. Governments fall easily under suspicion of harbouring portentous policies. St Petersburg was supposed to be crammed with them, and Baron von Rosen tells us: "There was a total absence of any clear conception of what the aims of our Far Eastern policy should be."[1] An American diplomat remarks that he and his fellow-juniors in the Far Eastern Legations began by viewing their chiefs with awe, as repositories of stratagems profound beyond the compass of words, and adds cynically: "That is not a belief that one retains long in diplomacy."[2] While many Englishmen were persuaded that a Chinese alliance was being methodically put in shape, there were always others who thought nothing of the kind; who absolved their own Government, if no other, from all suspicion of Machiavellianism. One of them in 1885 denounced its "complete disregard and even contempt for all foreign affairs", its "ludicrous timidity", its "criminal apathy and indifference".[3] A second held it up to ridicule as a Government that did nothing but "slumber and blunder" and was invariably "grossly misled and roundly beaten".[4] A third deplored the "drifting and vacuous policy" which was making it futile to dream of arresting Britain's decay in the Far East.[5] Such words were repeated *ad nauseam* by patriotic Britons who did not always inform the Government what it *ought* to be doing, and who, curiously enough, often bore very un-English names. This language flowed with especial freedom when, as in our years, the Gladstonians were in office—the sinister villains of Tory platform rhetoric, intent upon the subversion of the Empire: "these children of revolution, these robbers of churches, these destroyers of property, these friends of the lawless."[6]

[1] *Forty Years of Diplomacy*, 34.
[2] W. F. Sands, *Undiplomatic Memories*, 28.
[3] Colquhoun, Letters to *The Times*, 1885.
[4] B. H. Chamberlain, *Things Japanese*, 495.
[5] Hamilton, *Korea*, 144.
[6] Randolph Churchill, quoted in Rosebery's essay on him, p. 93. At one Election a newspaper organised a poll in Hongkong and Singapore, and the voters treated Gladstone severely.

To accuse a Government, with decades to think in, of having no Far Eastern policy, sounds far-fetched. It would, all the same, be no unique lacuna. In general, Chancelleries were too busy ferreting out one another's plans to have time for forming any of their own. Lansdowne wrote to Balfour in 1905 that he had never detected any sign of Austria's possessing a Balkan policy.[1] If the Dual Monarchy could live from hand to mouth on that life and death question, Ministers in Downing Street would not reproach themselves for lacking specific intentions about the remote East. They were too busy to think, and would not let others think for them.[2] The immense complexity of Imperial interests made it impossible to take a step anywhere without laborious consultation. It was simpler not to take any step until circumstances pushed the Foreign Office into a particular line. Bismarck was the last great intellectualist in world politics. One might, it is true, say that he was also the first. Curzon wrote to Brodrick in 1899, when Ministers were being hard pressed in the House about their Chinese line of action: "We have never had and we have not any policy towards China. No one knows that better than you or I who have successively had to conjure up makebelieves. But of course the supreme lesson of the F.O. is that there is no predetermined policy about anything."[3] Back in Opposition, Curzon would excoriate the next Administration for "having no policy". A Foreign Policy was, indeed, in the nature of a fiction kept up between the two Front Benches for the edification, or mystification, of simple-minded followers.

Of those in the Foreign Office who were supposed to be constructing plans, Dilke had visited and liked Japan and called on a Tartar General in his Yamen at Canton.[4] Lord E. Fitzmaurice gives us a hint of how much he himself, as Parliamentary

[1] Lord Newton, *Life of Lord Lansdowne*, 305.
[2] A General on service against the Boxers wrote: "As far as one can gauge political secrets, our Minister in China is merely a figurehead, who has to implicitly carry out any instructions sent by Lord Salisbury, who appears to let things slide." (Maj.-Gen. Stewart, *My Service Days*, 275.)
[3] Lord Ronaldshay, *Life of Lord Curzon*, 282.
[4] Gwynn and Tuckwell, *Life of Dilke*, I, 194.

Under-Secretary after Dilke, thought about China, in his biography of Lord Granville, where, apart from two or three allusions to Tonking, he says absolutely nothing about the Far East in these years. This neglect has been imitated by historians: Pauncefote's biographer has no reference to the Far East between 1880 and 1885.[1] Pauncefote knew China at first hand, having spent years in practice in Hongkong, but at the Foreign Office he had no leisure for *thinking* about the subject. As for Lord Granville, he contributed nothing beyond his signature. It would be laughable to think of searching in that urbane mind for "thoughts of great moment, worthy cogitations", on the destinies of the Middle Kingdom. So far as public and Parliament were concerned, the Foreign Office, except on the opium question, was untrammelled. As Esher wrote to Balfour a good deal later: "The public generally have no notions about the Far East. They never use maps. You can do exactly what you believe to be right with impunity."[2] But the "persistent attitude of contemptuous indifference displayed by Parliament", as one of our traders called it,[3] had the effect of damping rather than giving scope to cerebration in the Foreign Office. The niceties of Peking politics could not be expected to be the nightly theme of the House, but an occasional debate ought to have been the minimum of attention bestowed. Instead, the dusty catacombs of Hansard reveal, between 1880 and 1885, exactly thirty references by Lords or Commons to the Far East apart from Tonking and opium; most of them trivial, and including not one debate.[4] The sole occasion when

[1] Mowat, *Life of Lord Pauncefote.*

[2] In 1899. Viscount Esher, *Letters and Journals,* 1; letter of 1.4.98.

[3] Curzon, *Far Eastern Problem.*

[4] Five questions on the Chefu Convention and its non-ratification (Hansard, 3rd Series, 250. 149, 252. 323, 254. 471, 272. 279, 277. 1633); four questions on the Russo-Chinese crisis (253. 1260 and 1895, 254. 635, 259. 736); six references to Hongkong, chiefly on abuses such as delation and domestic slavery (253. 398 ff., 250. 514, 251. 1254, 286. 1009 and 1711 ff., 254.1633); two questions on the Anglo-Corean Treaty of 1882 (273. 1360, 276. 584); one on whether a consulate should be opened in Kashgaria (293. 348); one on the Chinese embassy of 1882 to Siam (274. 270); six

the problem as a whole was considered from any Bench was
when Ashmead-Bartlett argued that we ought to join with
Germany and America and stop the Tonking war: we ought
to address France as Lord Palmerston would have done—in a
"friendly and determined way": we ought to sustain China as
a counterpoise to France and Russia, or they might partition
her: we ought in sum to be discussing not the Franchise but the
Navy, "which was of infinitely more importance to the nation
than 20 Franchise Bills".[1] The Government declined to be
drawn; it was in Committee of Supply, an occasion always
seized by Ashmead-Bartlett for lecturing on foreign affairs, and
he was something of a known Club Bore in the House. But he
was the only man who in six years raised in Parliament the issue
of Far Eastern policy. England had not learned the truth of
what Sir Rutherford Alcock wrote in 1876: "Our concerns with
this almost unknown Empire are of more real importance to
the British Empire than many continental disputes about a river
or a province."[2]

It was not that no decisions needed to be taken before 1895.
It is the fact that they were made negatively and through
inertia that makes the history of our activities seem incon-
spicuous. In retrospect politicians at the end of the century and
after were inclined to fancy that all had been plain sailing before
the Japanese opened Pandora's Box in 1895. Before then,
one of them wrote, England enjoyed "an almost undisputed
ascendancy in the Far East".[3] Nothing could be falser. When
Wade asked in 1880 what he was to do in face of a palpable
Chinese desire for an alliance, and the Foreign Office *ignored*

trivial references to Japan (255. 459, 261. 949, 274. 851, 284. 1731, 299. 1060,
281. 1887); one on the salary of the Peking Legation (282. 2117); four
miscellaneous questions (254. 768, 293. 1379, 296. 1304 and 1468). It may
be remarked that at this date questions in the House were not considered
negligible. When Dilke wanted to put pressure on his colleagues to have our
Far Eastern squadron reinforced during the Kashgar crisis, he got a Member
to put him a question on the subject. (*Life*, I, 357.)

[1] 21.11.84; see 294. 187.
[2] "Relations of Western Powers with the East", *Fortnightly*, Jan. 1876.
[3] Chirol, *Far Eastern Question*, 2.

the query, an important step was taken. Alliance with China would of course involve risks; she would want a territorial guarantee, which might provoke a coalition against us. The instructions given to Parkes when he went to Peking illustrate the Foreign Office's drifting habit of mind. He was told to cultivate the friendliest relations with China and with everyone else, and to foster our interests sedulously. These ideal orders—universal benevolence—involved a contradiction. Pushing British interests meant pushing China in another sense. The same contradiction had been latent in Clarendon's exchange of Notes with Burlingame, the Chinese representative, in 1866,[1] when he said that England would exert no "unfriendly pressure", but must enforce respect for her treaties. Within a few years followed the Margary case, and England enforced respect with a fleet and an ultimatum. For while the man in the street—or in the House—was as indifferent as the Foreign Office could desire, there were strong commercial vested interests, whose philosophy was crudely summed up in the dictum that "the old gunboat policy" was the best, and, "in the long run, earns the approbation of the Chinese themselves".[2] "The truth is", we were told from this quarter, "that, like all oriental peoples, the Chinese can only be impressed by the display of power. So long as we thrashed them at intervals, they accorded us their respect."[3] It was the colonies of merchants in the Ports who made most clamour, and therefore had most weight with the Foreign Office, even if the latter was inclined to view their robust convictions a little askance. By the end of the century British industry and finance were in touch directly with the Far East, and the influence of our merchants dwindled. Their interests were not of a nature to evolve any logical policy. They did not very much want to see fresh parts of China opened up; each simply wanted his own special area to be made safe and profitable for him. Colquhoun confesses on one page that "the merchant comes to China to

[1] B.F.S.P. LIX, 279–81.
[2] Little, Gleanings from Fifty Years in China, 41.
[3] Krausse, China in Decay, 166.

make money...he is quite indifferent as to the country of origin of the goods he handles"; yet on another page he declares that "the British merchant must be encouraged and supported through thick and thin".[1] Thus the British Government was confused not only by the arguments of "high politics" but also by those of what may be called "low politics"; and moreover the two were in conflict. The gunboat policy at once weakened and alienated a potential ally. Gordon wrote in 1882: "I think the only two alliances worth having are France and China", but he pointed out how our behaviour, especially over opium, was weakening and humiliating China.[2] And then, the doubt always crept in whether in the last resort we wanted to see a strong, armed, modernised China, producing with the energy of the most laborious quarter of mankind. Modern Japan sixfold—one can understand the bad dreams that sometimes visited Western politicians. "Our only wish", said Austen Chamberlain in 1927, "is for a strong, united, independent, orderly and prosperous China."[3] So it was, in theory; whenever there were slight signs of it coming into being, we were the first to take alarm. Our whole outlook on China was contradictory.

This dilemma, added to the Foreign Office's congenital distaste for thinking, explains why our policy of supporting China was so imperfectly carried out in its fifteen or twenty years of life before the Sino-Japanese war. In 1896 we dropped it altogether. The celerity with which we did so suggests that China's defeat had made us instantly instal Japan in her place as our prospective ally; but the lapse of six years before the Anglo-Japanese alliance corrects such a notion, and leads us to see the English diplomacy of 1896 as confused rather than masterful. From China's point of view, our declining to stand with the other Powers in demanding the retrocession of the Liao-tung must have seemed *perfidia plus quam Anglica*. It threw Li Hung-chang, hitherto the chief partisan of alliance with England, into the

[1] *China in Transformation*, 144, 164.
[2] Boulger, *Life of Gordon*, 324.
[3] Quoted in Soothill, *China and England*, ch. IV.

Russian camp, where, much to our discomfort, he remained. Russia's "Cassini programme" was the penalty of our inaction. So early as 1879 it had been pointed out that China would be forced one day to accept either a British or a Russian alliance, and that therefore "the apathy displayed in regard to Chinese affairs generally" was altogether as inexplicable as it was mistaken.[1] Japan was destined to serve our turn and drive Russia out of Manchuria. But we gained this at the—ultimate—cost of handing over the Far East to Japanese Imperialism.

An alternative policy was often urged: the partition of China.[2] It was an idea with long antecedents. Lord Macartney's diary mentions "the project of a territory on the Continent of China (which I have heard imputed to the late Lord Clive)", though he—Macartney—thought it "too wild to be seriously maintained".[3]

China like Africa was betrayed by her rivers to the foreigners. Africa invites comparison in other ways. Why was the one partitioned and not the other? "China...is worth a dozen Africas to our trade."[4] Africa diverted some energies away from China, but after all it was subdued with remarkable ease and with very few soldiers. There were many differences, however. African penetration was begun by parties of unofficial freebooters—as in Rhodesia. China had enough pretence at organised government to prevent this, though a start was made of it during the Taiping turmoil. The Chinese wisely kept foreigners penned up on the coast. Then, China's wealth was not in ivory, to be knocked over with an elephant gun; it was grain and minerals, and needed methodical exploitation. And Africa, compared with China, was empty.

Europe—astonishingly—succeeded in partitioning Africa without war. Could it have done so with China? Almost

[1] Giles, in *Fortnightly*, Sept. 1879.
[2] In 1885 General Sargent at Hongkong wanted to extend the colony's territory. The War Office disapproved. F.O. to O'Conor 5 Very conf., 6.6.85, 17. 975.
[3] Quoted in section on Macartney in Hall, *Eminent Authorities on China*.
[4] Little, *Gleanings from Fifty Years in China*, 100.

certainly not. In Africa vast deserts separated many of the settlements; in China encroachments could not be made in unnoticed stealth; in Africa there were no Russian diplomats; in China frontier stresses would have been the more acute because Japan and Russia would have been vulnerable in their own territories. The work of the Berlin Conference, acrimonious as it was, would have been child's play compared with that of a Conference for the partition of China. Even when the allied forces were marching on their crusade against the Boxers, their mutual jealousies almost brought them to blows.[1] The West could not even combine to lend China money without severe quarrelling. Had partition been entered upon, a Chinese Sarajevo would have been found.

Vague ideas of partition were afloat in Europe, awaiting a moment to crystallise. A Belgian Minister wrote to someone in the 'seventies that he had suggested to "you know who (Leopold II), the proposition of occupying a Chinese province with a Belgian army and Belgian colonists".[2] England's attitude was governed by the wide diffusion of her commercial stakes. Thus there was some ground for saying that she was China's best friend. Still, the policy was not axiomatic. Englishmen reflected at times that it might be better to be sure of a part of the spoils, than to risk losing all. Our trade was minute when compared with what we thought it ought to be, and the obduracy of the Chinese in not welcoming our enterprise was an incitement to thoughts of conquest. Had there not been other continents, and outlying Chinese dependencies, to employ our troops in the years (before 1880) when we had little fear of rivals and their political schemes, we should have set about conquering China. Englishmen who realised what profits we were drawing from India were dazzled by the idea of what we could do with the more serviceable Chinese. England would have had a genie like Aladdin's to wait on her and raise her

---

[1] See Stewart, *My Service Days*, 206, 341, and 220: "This curiously composed multitude of armed men look at each other with intense suspicion, if not hatred...."

[2] Lichtervelde, *Life of Leopold* II (Eng. ed.), 116.

above all rivals. "If we had control over as many Chinese as we have natives of India, we should long ago have been expelled from, or have reaped the reward of, the richest land on the face of the earth."[1] Accidents helped to hold off conquest. The Arrow War coincided with the Indian Mutiny and the Persian expedition—England was at war with all Asia. The Boxer Rising coincided with the Boer War.

Our "friendship" for China was, in short, an exceedingly ambiguous one. And from our side, it is a sad commentary on international relations that Lyall concluded: "On the whole, we can never look for a better neighbour than China has been for us—exclusive, uncommunicative, but pacific and incapable of aggression."[2]

It is not our business to patch up dead quarrels, or to prove that China was the victim of injustice. There is no right or wrong in history, except the higher or lower standard of living of the generality. "China"—the Dragon Throne—is in itself an abstraction, an illusion, like any other. It is much less our business to show that one of the Western Powers was better or worse than another. None of them had the slightest "right" to be in China, but it would be idle to leave the question there. When seventeenth-century historians dispute gravely upon the genealogical titles of contending princes, we turn over their pages; because those titles, though the private morality of the princes depended on them, do not seem to us to give anyone a right to own a country and its people. Posterity in the same way will not read our arguments on war-guilt, or on which nation had the best case in the Far East. What is of significance is the transformation of the globe by forces, fundamentally economic, and themselves altering from year to year.

"The great fact", said a Consular Report, "that the cause of the foreigner is in the main the cause of the Chinese people is the great justification for the presence of Europeans": their inventions make possible for the country a hitherto "unattain-

[1] Kipling, *From Sea to Sea*, ch. VIII.
[2] *Asiatic Studies*, II, 386.

able Utopia". It has tragically little resemblance to Utopia in
1938. The Eighteen Provinces are deluged with war; while
these words are written the capital of China is being sacked by a
barbarous soldiery, and an invader's flag floats over the tomb
on the Purple Mountain. It is for the Westerner to ask himself
what Western capitalism, not in its pernicious incidents but in
its entire energy, has meant for the Far East.

China was once beneath the waves. Whether it would have
been better for her to have remained hidden by the sea, and the
Black-haired Race, its poetry and its myriad miseries, never to
have existed, it is impossible to argue. Metaphysicians tell us
that the past cannot be proved to have taken place. There may
be a frosty consolation for the reader of history in that.

And it was a Chinese who said: "Confucius and you are
both dreams; and I who say that you are dreams—I am only a
dream myself."

BIBLIOGRAPHY

MANUSCRIPT

Foreign Office China Correspondence, 1880 to 1885, and sections of the Japan, Russia, America correspondence between these years.

PRINTED DOCUMENTS

British and Foreign State Papers.
Accounts and Papers (China and Corea Blue Books, Gold and Silver Commission of 1887, Trade Reports).
Hansard (all references to the Far East from 1880 to 1885).

PERIODICALS

Asiatic Quarterly.
Bankers' Magazine of New York.
Economist.
Économiste Français.
Fortnightly Review.
Journal of the American Oriental Society.
Journal of the China Branch of the Royal Asiatic Society.
Journal of the Institute of Bankers.
Journal of the Iron and Steel Institute.
Kyoto University Economic Review.
Quarterly Review.
Transactions of the Asiatic Society of Japan.
United Services Journal.

BOOKS (mainly confined to contemporary publications, or at least to works belonging to the last thirty years of the nineteenth century)
Allen, B. M. *Gordon in China*, 1933.
Arnold, Sir Edwin. *Seas and Lands*, 1891.
Balfour, F. H. *Leaves from my Chinese Scrapbook*, 1887.
Baster, A. S. J. *The International Banks*, 1935.
Bau, M. J. *Foreign Relations of China*, 1922.
Beresford, Lord Charles. *The Break-up of China*, 1899.
Bird, Isabella. *Unbeaten Tracks in Japan*, 1880.
Bland, J. O. P. *Li Hung-chang*, 1917.
Bland, J. O. P., and Backhouse, Sir E. T. *China under the Empress Dowager*, 1910.
—— —— *Annals and Memoirs of the Court of Peking*, 1914.
Boulger, D. C. *Life of Sir Halliday Macartney*, 1908.

Boulger, D. C. *Life of Gordon*, 1896.
—— *Central Asian Questions*, 1885.
—— *A History of China*, vol. 3, 1884.
Bredon, Juliet. *Sir Robert Hart*, 1909.
Buck, Prof. J. L. *Chinese Farm Economy*, 1930.
Bülow, Prince B. von. *Imperial Germany*, 1914.
Burnaby, General. *A Ride to Khiva*, 1876.
Carles, W. R. *Life in Corea*, 1888.
Cavendish, A. E. J. *Korea and the Sacred White Mountain*, 1894.
Cecil, Lady G. *Life of Lord Salisbury*, vol. 4, 1921.
Chamberlain, B. H. *Things Japanese*, 1890.
Chang Chih-tung. *China's Only Hope*, 1900.
Ch'ao Ting-chi. *Key Economic Areas in Chinese History*, 1936.
Chen, S. K. *Taxation under the Ch'ing Dynasty*, 1914.
Chirol, V. *The Far Eastern Question*, 1896.
—— *The Middle Eastern Question*, 1903.
Clapham, J. H. *Economic Development of France and Germany, 1815 to 1914*, 1936.
Colquhoun, A. R. *China in Transformation*, 1898.
—— *Across Chrysê*, 1883.
—— *The Truth about Tonking*, 1884.
Coltman, R. *The Chinese*, 1891.
Conger, Mrs P. *Letters from China*, 1909.
Cordier, H. *Relations de la Chine avec les Puissances Occidentales*, vol. 2, 1901.
Cressey, G. B. *China's Geographical Foundations*, 1934.
Cumming, C. F. G. (Mrs). *Wanderings in China*, 2 vols., 1886.
Cumming, J. Gordon. *Russian Travellers in Mongolia and China*, 1884.
Dennett, Tyler. *Americans in Eastern Asia*, 1922.
Dilke, Sir Charles. *The Present Position of European Politics*, 1887.
—— *Imperial Defence*, 1892.
Diösy, Arthur. *The New Far East*, 1898.
"Un Diplomate." *L'Affaire du Tonkin*, 1886.
Douglas, R. K. *Society in China*, 1894.
—— *Li Hung-chang*, 1892.
Edkins, J. *Chinese Currency*, 1901.
Eitel, E. J. *Europe in China*, 1895.
Esher, Viscount. *Journals and Letters*, vol. 1, 1934.
Fitzmaurice, Lord E. *Life of Lord Granville*, vol. 2, 1905.
Fortune, R. *Journey to China and Japan*, 1863.
Foster, J. W. *Practice of Diplomacy*, 1906.
—— *A Century of American Diplomacy*, 1900.
Fujisawa, C. *Japanese and Oriental Political Philosophy*, 1935.
Gamble, S. D. *Peking: a Social Survey*, 1921.
Gérard, A. *Ma Mission en Chine*, 1918.

Gill, W. J. *River of Golden Sand*, 1883.
Gray, J. H. *China*, 2 vols., 1878.
Griffis, W. E. *Corea, the Hermit Nation*, 1882.
Gwynn, S., and Tuckwell, G. *Life of Sir Charles Dilke*, 1917.
Hall, R. A. *Eminent Authorities on China*, 1931.
Hamilton, Angus. *Korea*, 1904.
Hart, Sir R. *These from the Land of Sinim*, 1903.
Headland, I. T. *Court Life in China*, 1910.
Holcombe, C. *The Real Chinaman*, 1895.
Hornby, Sir E. *Autobiography*, 1928.
Hosie, A. *Three Years in Western China*, 1897.
Howard of Penrith, Lord. *Theatre of Life seen from the Pit*, 1935.
Huang Han-liang. *Land Tax in China*, 1918.
Hughes, Mrs T. *Among the Sons of Han*, 1881.
Inagaki, M. *Japan and the Pacific*, 1890.
Jernigan, J. R. *China's Business Methods and Policy*, 1904.
Johnston, R. F. *Twilight in the Forbidden City*, 1934.
Joseph, P. *Foreign Diplomacy in China 1894-1900*, 1928.
Kang, Younghill. *The Grass Roof*, 1931.
Kent, P. *Railway Enterprise in China*, 1907.
King, F. H. *Farmers of Forty Centuries*, 1927.
Kipling, Rudyard. *From Sea to Sea*, Collected Works, 1913.
Krausse, A. *China in Decay*, 1898.
Ladd, G. T. *In Korea with Marquis Ito*, 1908.
Lane-Poole, S. *Life of Sir Harry Parkes*, 2 vols., 1894.
Lane-Poole, S., ed. *Thirty Years of Colonial Government. From the Despatches
    of the Rt. Hon. Sir G. F. Bowen*, 1889.
de Lanessan, J. L. *Expansion Coloniale de la France*, 1886.
Latourette, K. S. *The Chinese, their History and Culture*, 2 vols., 1934.
Lattimore, O. *The Mongols of Manchuria*, 1934.
Lee, Hoon K. *Land Utilisation and Rural Economy in Korea*, 1936.
Lenin, V. I. *The Development of Capitalism in Russia*, Selected Works,
    vol. 1, 1936.
Leroy-Beaulieu, A. *The Empire of the Tsars*, 3 vols., 1893.
Lin Yu-tang. *My Country and my People*, 1936.
Little, A. *Gleanings from Fifty Years in China*, 1910.
Little, Mrs A. *Li Hung-chang*, 1903.
Lowe, Charles. *Alexander III of Russia*, 1895.
Lucy, H. W. *East and West*, 1885.
Lyall, Sir A. C. *Asiatic Studies*, 1899.
Martin, W. A. P. *The Hanlin Papers*, 1st series, 1881; 2nd series, 1894.
Mayers, W. F. *The Chinese Government*, 1878.
Medhurst, W. H. *Foreigner in Far Cathay*, 1872.
Michie, A. *The Englishman in China*, 2 vols., 1900.

Möllendorf, R. von. *P. G. von Möllendorf: ein Lebensbild*, 1930.

Morse, H. B. *Gilds of China*, 1932.

—— *Trade and Administration of China*, 1921.

Morse, H. B., and McNair, H. F. *Far Eastern International Relations*, 1931.

Moule, A. E. *Half a Century in China*, 1911.

Mounsey, A. H. *The Satsuma Rebellion*, 1897.

Newton, Lord. *Life of Lord Lansdowne*, 1929.

—— *Life of Lord Lyons*, 2 vols., 1913.

Norman, C. B. *Tonkin*, 1884.

Norman, H. *Peoples and Politics of the Far East*, 1900.

Omura, B. *Prince Saionji*, 1938.

Overlach, T. W. *Foreign Financial Control in China*, 1919.

Parker, E. H. *China Past and Present*, 1903.

—— *John Chinaman*, 1909.

Pearse, A. S. *Cotton Industry of Japan and China*, 1929.

Percival, W. S. *The Land of the Dragon*, 1889.

Pokrovsky, M. N., trans. by D. Mirsky. *Brief History of Russia*, vol. 1, 1933.

Redesdale, Lord. *Memories*, 2 vols., 1915.

"Von einem Reichsrathsabgeordneten." *Antagonismus der Englischen und Russischen Interessen in Asien*, 1890.

Reid, A. *From Peking to Petersburg*, 1899.

Remer, C. F. *Foreign Trade of China*, 1926.

—— *Foreign Investments in China*, 1933.

Rockhill, W. W. *Land of the Lamas*, 1891.

Rodd, J. Rennell. *Social and Diplomatic Memories*, 1922.

Ronaldshay, Lord. *Life of Lord Curzon*, 1928.

Rosen, Baron R. von. *Forty Years of Diplomacy*, 2 vols., 1922.

Ross, J. *History of Corea*, 1880.

—— *The Manchus*, 1880.

Sands, W. F. *Undiplomatic Memories*, 1931.

Sargent, A. J. *Anglo-Chinese Diplomacy and Commerce*, 1907.

Satow, Sir E. *A Diplomat in Japan*, 1921.

Schelking, Baron E. de. *The Game of Diplomacy*, 1918.

Schuyler, E. *Turkistan*, 1876.

Sears, L. M. *A History of American Foreign Relations*, 1928.

Simon, G. E. *China*, 1887.

Smith, Arthur H. *Village Life in China*, 1899.

Soothill, W. E. *China and the West*, 1925.

Southworth, C. *The French Colonial Venture*, 1931.

Stead, W. T. *The Truth about Russia*, 1888.

Sugimoto, E. I. *A Daughter of the Samurai*, 1933.

Sun Yat-sen. *San Min Chu I: The Three Principles of the People* (trans. F. W. Price), 1927.

Takekoshi, Yosoburo. *Economic Aspects of the History of the Civilisation of Japan*, vol. 3, 1930.

T'and Leang-li. *Inner History of the Chinese Revolution*, 1930.

Tanin, O., and Yohan, E. *Militarism and Fascism in Japan*, 1934.

Tawney, Prof. R. H. *Land and Labour in China*, 1932.

Taylor, J. B. *Farm and Factory in China*, 1928.

Townsend, M. E. *The Rise and Fall of Germany's Colonial Empire*, 1933.

Treat, P. J. *Diplomatic Relations between the U.S. and Japan*, 1917.

Ular, A. *A Russo-Chinese Empire*, 1904.

Utley, Freda. *Japan's Feet of Clay*, 1937.

Uyehara, G. E. *Political Development of Japan, 1867–1909*, 1910.

Vinacke, H. *History of the Far East in Modern Times*, 1928.

"Vladimir." *China-Japan War*, 1896.

Waddington, Mary. *Letters of a Diplomat's Wife*, 1903.

Weale, B. L. Putnam (pseud. for Simpson, B. L.). *Indiscreet Letters from Peking*, 1907.

—— *Truce in the Far East*, 1907.

—— *Manchu and Muscovite*, 1904.

Wen Pin-wei. *Currency Problems in China*, 1891.

White, H. D. *French International Accounts*, 1933.

Williams, S. Wells. *The Middle Kingdom*, 2 vols., 1883.

Willoughby, W.W. *Foreign Rights and Interests in China*, 2 vols., 1927.

Windt, de J. *Peking to Calais by Land*, 1889.

Witte, Count S., trans. by A. Yarmolinsky. *Memoirs*, 1921.

Wittfogel, K. A. *Wirtschaft und Gesellschaft Chinas*, 1931.

Woeikoff, A. I. *Le Turkestan Russe*, 1914.

Yakhontoff, V. Y. *Russia and the Soviet Union in the Far East*, 1930.

Young, G. R. *Around the World with General Grant*, vol. 2, 1879.

INDEX